**FOURTH EDITION**

# RESEARCH METHODS FOR SOCIAL WORKERS

**Bonnie L. Yegidis**
*University of Georgia*

**Robert W. Weinbach**
*University of South Carolina*

**Allyn and Bacon**
Boston • London • Toronto • Sydney • Tokyo • Singapore

*Editor, Social Work and Family Therapy:* Patricia Quinlin
*Editor-in-Chief, Social Sciences:* Karen Hanson
*Series Editorial Assistant:* Alyssa Pratt
*Marketing Manager:* Jackie Aaron
*Composition and Prepress Buyer:* Linda Cox
*Manufacturing Buyer:* Suzanne Lareau
*Cover Administrator:* Kristina Mose-Libon
*Production Administrator:* Deborah Brown
*Editorial-Production Service:* P. M. Gordon Associates

Internet: www.ablongman.com

*Library of Congress Cataloging-in-Publication Data*

Yegidis, Bonnie L.
    Research methods for social workers / Bonnie L. Yegidis, Robert W. Weinbach. — 4th ed.
        p.  cm.
    Includes bibliographical references and index.
    ISBN 0–205–33233–1
    1. Social service—Research—Methodology.  I. Weinbach, Robert W.  II. Title.
    HV11.Y43  2001
        361.3′2′072—dc21

                                                                    2001022589

Printed in the United States of America

10  9  8  7  6  5  4  3            05  04  03  02

# CONTENTS

**Preface**    ix

**PART I**    *Knowledge Building for Social Work Practice*    1

**1**    **How Do We Get Our Knowledge?**    3

*Historical Origins of Current Attitudes*    3
   Tension between Research and Practice    4
   Efforts to Close the Gap    5
   Research and Practice—No Need for a Gap    7
*Types of Knowledge*    8
   Descriptive Knowledge    9
   Predictive Knowledge    9
   Prescriptive Knowledge    10
*Where Do We Get Our "Knowledge"?*    10
   Two Examples    12
*Characteristics of the Scientific Alternative*    14
*Quantitative and Qualitative Research*    16
   Quantitative Approaches to Knowledge Building    16
   Qualitative Approaches to Knowledge Building    17
*The Traditional Scientific Research Process*    18
*The Environment for Scientific Social Work Research*    20
*Summary*    23
*References*    23

**2**    **Ethical Issues in Social Work Research**    25

*Treatment of Research Participants*    26
   Evolution of Ethical Standards for Treatment of Participants    26
*Today's Standards for Treatment of Participants*    36
   Voluntary Informed Consent    36

No Unnecessary Pain and Suffering     39
Anonymity/Confidentiality     40
Need to Conduct the Research     41
*Other Ethical Obligations of Researchers*     42
*Summary*     43
*References*     43


**PART  II**     ***Beginning the Research Process***     **45**

**3     Research Problems and Questions     47**
*Why We Begin with Research Problems*     48
*Setting Problem Priorities*     49
*Identifying the* Real *Problem*     54
*Selecting Research Questions*     56
*Summary*     60
*References*     60

**4     Using Existing Knowledge     63**
*What Is the Review of Literature?*     63
*Purpose of the Review of Literature*     65
*Potential Sources of "Literature"*     66
Standard Reference Materials     66
Computer-Accessible Databases     67
The Internet     67
Books and Articles in Professional Journals     68
Personal Interviews with Authorities     71
Research Reports and Monographs     72
Presentations at Conferences and Symposia     72
Content of Workshops     73
Public Documents and Records of Public Gatherings     73
Newspapers     73
Radio and Television Broadcasts     74
Magazines and Periodicals     74
*Organizing the Literature Review*     76
*Writing the Report of a Review of Literature*     77
Direction and Flow     77
Use of Quotations and Citations     78
The Role of the Researcher in a Report of the Literature Review     79
*Summary*     80
*References*     80

**5     Focused Research Questions and Hypotheses     81**
*Focused Research Questions*     81
*Hypotheses*     83
Related Definitions     85
Types of Relationships Expressed in Hypotheses     89
Forms of Research Hypotheses     92

When Are Hypotheses Appropriate?     93
Wording of Hypotheses     94
The "Perfectly Worded" Hypothesis     96
Use of Subhypotheses     96
*Summary     97*
*References     98*


**PART  III**     *Research Design Issues     99*

**6     Introduction to Research Design     101**
*What Is a Research Design?     101*
*The Purpose of Research Designs     102*
*Broad Research Typologies     102*
Cross-Sectional Designs     103
Longitudinal Designs     103
*The Knowledge-Building Continuum     105*
Exploratory Designs     106
Descriptive Designs     109
Explanatory Research     112
*Internal Validity and External Validity     117*
Internal Validity     118
External Validity     122
External Validity and Cultural Issues     123
*What Is the "Best" Research Design?     124*
*Characteristics of Good Designs     125*
*Summary     127*
*References     128*

**7     Qualitative Research Methods     129**
*Interviewing in Qualitative Research     129*
Focus Groups and One-on-One Interviews     130
Purpose of Interviews     130
Relationship with Participants     131
Structure     131
Dealing with Sensitive Topics     132
*Research That Relies on Qualitative Methods     132*
Unstructured Systematic Observation     133
Ethnographic Research     135
Cross-Cultural Research     138
Case Studies     139
Grounded Theory     141
Oral Histories     142
*Criteria for Evaluating Qualitative Designs     143*
*Feminist Research     144*
Goals and Assumptions     144
Feminist Research as a Response to Traditional
Research Methods     145

Design Features    146
Examples of Feminist Research    146
*Using Qualitative Methods to Evaluate Practice Effectiveness    149*
*Summary    149*
*References    150*


**8    Quantitative Research Methods    153**

*Research That Uses Secondary Data Analysis    154*
Sources of Secondary Data    154
Different Uses of Secondary Data Analysis    155
Tasks Required in Secondary Data Analysis    156
Advantages of Secondary Data Analysis    156
Disadvantages of Secondary Data Analysis    157
Some Specialized Methods of Secondary Data Analysis    157
*Research That Collects and Analyzes Original Data    162*
Experimental and Quasi-Experimental Research    162
Structured Observation    162
In-Person Interviews    165
Telephone Interviews and E-Mail Surveys    169
Mailed Surveys    171
*Using Quantitative Methods to Evaluate Practice Effectiveness    176*
*Summary    176*
*References    177*


**9    Case Sampling    179**

*Sampling Terminology    179*
*Probability Sampling    186*
Simple Random Sampling    186
Systematic Random Sampling    187
Stratified Sampling    187
Cluster Sampling    189
*Nonprobability Sampling    190*
Convenience Sampling    190
Purposive Sampling    191
Snowball Sampling    192
Quota Sampling    192
*Selecting a Good Sample    193*
Available Resources    193
Overall Design and Purpose of the Study    193
Type of Statistical Analysis to Be Used    194
Level of Representativeness Required    195
*Summary    195*
*References    195*


**10    Measurement Concepts and Issues    197**

*Preparation for Measurement    198*
Conceptualization    198
Operationalization    199

*Levels of Measurement    200*
*Criteria for Good Measurement    202*
    Reliability    203
    Validity    206
*Cultural Issues in Measurement of Variables    211*
*Summary    212*
*References    212*

**11  Use of Data Collection Instruments    213**

*Fixed-Alternative and Open-Ended Items    214*
*Indexes and Scales    215*
    Indexes    215
    Scales    216
    Construction of Scales    221
*When Are Existing Instruments Appropriate for Use?    222*
*Use of Revised Instruments    223*
*Constructing New Instruments    224*
    Issues in Development of New Instruments    225
*Use of Self-Administered Instruments    228*
    Advantages of Self-Administered Instruments    228
    Supervised Administration of Self-Administered Instruments    229
*Summary    230*
*References    231*

**12  Analyzing Data and Disseminating Findings    233**

*The Data in Perspective    233*
*Preparing for Statistical Analysis of Data    235*
*Statistical Analysis of Research Data: An Overview    236*
    The Uses of Statistical Analysis    237
*Interpreting and Reporting the Results of Statistical Analysis    243*
*Disseminating Research Knowledge    244*
    Reports and Monographs    244
    Internal Correspondence and In-Service Training    247
    Major Conference Presentations    247
    Other Professional Gatherings    249
    Publication in Professional Journals    250
*Summary    252*
*References    252*

**PART  IV    *Evaluation Research*    255**

**13  Evaluating Programs    257**

*What Is Program Evaluation?    258*
    Planning/Evaluation Models    259
    Needs Assessment    260
    Evaluating Program Implementation    262
    Evaluating Program Outcomes    264

*What Is the Appropriate Design for a Program Evaluation?*    *266*
*Other Types of Evaluation Research*    *268*
    Cost-Benefit Analysis    268
    Program Impact Evaluations    269
    Program Structure Evaluations    270
*Who Should Conduct Evaluative Research?*    *271*
    Use of an In-House Evaluator    271
    Use of an External Evaluator    272
    Empowerment Evaluation    273
*The Political Context of Program Evaluation*    *274*
*Ethical Issues*    *276*
*Reports of Program Evaluations*    *277*
*Summary*    *279*
*References*    *280*

**14  Evaluating Individual Practice Effectiveness    281**

*Alternatives to Single-System Research*    *281*
    Supervisor Feedback    281
    Consumer Feedback    282
    Goal Attainment Scaling    283
*Single-System Research*    *285*
*Conducting Single-System Research*    *290*
*Design Alternatives*    *290*
    B    291
    AB    292
    ABA    294
    ABAB    297
    BAB    298
    ABCD    299
    Multiple Baseline    302
*Strengths and Weaknesses of Single-System Research*    *305*
*Ethical Issues*    *307*
*Summary*    *308*
*References*    *309*

**Postscript    311**

**Additional Readings in Research Methods    313**

**Index    319**

# PREFACE

Social work practice is changing in the third millennium. Research, now an integral part of practice, is changing along with it. In this edition of *Research Methods for Social Workers*, we have attempted to retain those features that faculty and students told us they liked. At the same time, we have added material to emphasize the needs of today's students and accountable practitioners.

## *What Can the Reader Expect to Find?*

Like the previous editions, this book is designed for a one-semester or one-quarter course on research methods. It is well suited to either undergraduate or foundation-level graduate social work courses. Its content is consistent with both current Council on Social Work Education (CSWE) accreditation standards and curriculum policy guidelines. This book offers a brief conceptual overview of statistical analysis, but encourages its readers to seek a more in-depth coverage of this specialized topic in other texts.

The book is written for both current and future social work practitioners who are likely to be involved in various aspects of research. It prepares the reader to become a critical consumer of research literature, to be able to begin to design and implement research, and to evaluate practice effectiveness either for personal feedback or to improve program effectiveness in a time of increased emphasis on accountability. It presents research as a logical, nonintimidating activity that parallels social work practice in many ways.

Designed to be "reader-friendly," this book contains no unnecessary research terminology or references to obscure, rarely used methods of knowledge building. Students, even those with no prior research background, will find the text interesting and easy to comprehend. It is written in a crisp, straightforward style and refers to contemporary social work practice on virtually every page. Examples are real—the kind of situations that social workers encounter every day.

We are consistently upbeat about research. Our belief that the knowledge, values, and skills of the social worker are much more of an asset than a liability in conducting research permeates the book. We do not believe that research is a "necessary evil" to be grudgingly studied and conducted. It is a logical extension of practice. Thus, the areas that are given a disproportional amount of attention (relative to other texts) reflect this orientation. For example, tasks such as problem formulation, question selection, and use of existing knowledge receive extensive coverage. Are these not also important tasks in good social work practice intervention? Research design—the rich array of alternatives available to get the job of knowledge building accomplished—is discussed in detail.

## *Changes in the Fourth Edition*

This edition is a response to reviewers, other faculty members, and students who took the time to suggest improvements. The reader will notice that there is more infusion of content in three major areas. First, qualitative research methods are discussed, and appropriate examples are offered throughout the book, not just in a single chapter. Similarly, research to evaluate practice, although still the focus of the last two chapters, is discussed alongside research for building our professional knowledge base at many points throughout the text. Third, discussion of ethical issues appears in many other places besides Chapter 2. It receives special emphasis in our discussion of program evaluations and single-system research.

Some of the specific ways in which we believe we have strengthened the book include the following:

- We have included new figures to illustrate the difference between research problems and research questions (Chapter 3) and between broad research questions and focused research questions (Chapter 5).
- We have revised the literature review section (Chapter 4) to reflect changes such as Internet searches and to discuss the different uses of the literature review in qualitative and quantitative studies.
- There is much more discussion of external validity and its relative importance in different research designs (Chapter 6).
- We now offer criteria for evaluating qualitative designs as well as those for evaluating more quantitative ones (Chapter 7).
- We added material on the characteristics of explanatory studies, with special emphasis on the importance of randomly selected case samples and why they sometimes cannot be used (Chapter 9).
- We revised most of the content on program evaluation (Chapter 13) and included new content on use of needs assessments in existing programs and on how qualitative and quantitative methods can be used together to produce more accurate data.
- While still focusing on single-system research as a method for evaluating individual practice effectiveness, we also added content on other ways in

which practitioners can assess whether their interventions are successful (Chapter 14).

There are again fourteen chapters. The chapters are self-contained, but they are designed to be read and discussed in sequence. Each can serve as a course unit.

Part I (Chapters 1 and 2) places current research within its historical context. It explains what social work research is and how it evolved. The two chapters stress the links between research and practice and how each is guided by similar ethics and values. For example, the issue of voluntary informed consent receives expanded coverage in light of power differentials that often exist between researchers and their research participants.

Part II (Chapters 3 through 5) centers on those "pre–data collection" tasks that generally occur before a research design is selected and implemented. It takes the reader through the process of formulating focused questions and/or hypotheses.

Part III (Chapters 6 through 12) looks at how questions are answered and hypotheses are tested—design implementation issues. Research design is examined from different perspectives. First, design is defined, and general categories of design are described. Then the differences between qualitative (Chapter 7) and quantitative (Chapter 8) research methods are presented and explicated. The components of design (sampling, measurement, use of data-collection instruments) and a chapter on analysis of data and knowledge dissemination conclude Part III.

Part IV examines the methods used for evaluating practice effectiveness. The general knowledge of research methods discussed in earlier chapters is applied to the important task of evaluating social programs and services.

## *Acknowledgments*

We are indebted to a number of colleagues who critiqued the first or second editions of this book and made many valuable suggestions. They are colleagues Gordon Casebolt, Felix Rivera, Murray Newman, Ram Cnann, Miriam Johnson, and James Stafford. Still others, Gail Leedy, Washburn University; Stephen M. Marson, University of North Carolina at Pembroke; and Donald S. Pierson, University of Idaho, carefully read and recommended revisions in the previous (third) edition. Students who used it and faculty who adopted it for classroom use were generous with their comments as well.

Valuable support for our efforts came from Dean Frank Raymond of the University of South Carolina, and the administrators and faculty at the University of Georgia. Judy Fifer and Alyssa Pratt at Allyn and Bacon have patiently guided us through the process of its publication. We are grateful to Tonya Westbrook, a Ph.D. student at the University of Georgia, for the careful and thorough preparation of the book's index.

We owe a special debt of gratitude to Barbara Morrison-Rodriguez of the University of South Florida. Because of the time constraints imposed by her present administrative duties, Barbara was unable to contribute to this edition and graciously declined to again be listed as a coauthor. However, her contributions to the third edition were substantive and offered an important perspective on research methods, lacking in earlier editions. Whenever possible we have retained them in their entirety in this book.

*Bonnie L. Yegidis*
*University of Georgia*

*Robert W. Weinbach*
*University of South Carolina*

# PART I

# KNOWLEDGE BUILDING FOR SOCIAL WORK PRACTICE

# 1

# HOW DO WE GET OUR KNOWLEDGE?

Social workers, like other professionals, require knowledge in order to make good decisions. They need it both to increase the likelihood that their interventions will be successful, and to determine whether or not they have been successful.

Some of the knowledge that social workers use is acquired through formal education in BSW or MSW programs, or from attending continuing education programs. Or it may come from reading articles in professional journals or textbooks. It may have come from senior-level practitioners who carefully studied a problem that they had observed. Whatever the source of social workers' knowledge, it is likely to have one characteristic in common—it may *not* have been derived from research!

The Council on Social Work Education (the organization responsible for the accreditation of bachelor's and master's programs in social work) recognizes the importance of research content in social work curricula. In its 1992 curriculum policy statements (effective June 1995), it spelled out what social workers need to learn. It mandated that the research curriculum must provide an understanding and appreciation of a scientific, analytic approach to building knowledge for practice and for evaluating service delivery in all areas of practice.[1] The statement goes on to describe the specific content that all professional social workers should receive. This content forms the basis for what we have chosen to include in this book.

## Historical Origins of Current Attitudes

Historically, social workers have not always emphasized the importance of research knowledge for decision making as much as have other professionals. In

1979 one writer shared his perceptions of social work practitioners and their relationship with research. Simpson noted that practitioners tend to shun abstract knowledge and to rely instead on (1) humanitarian impulse, (2) occupational folklore, and (3) common sense. He also observed that most of the knowledge that is used for practice decision making is drawn from the work of researchers in other fields. He went on to describe social work literature as permeated with faddism and lacking an empirical base.[2]

Simpson's indictment of social workers is less accurate now than when he wrote it. But the problem—an antiresearch bias among many social work practitioners and students, and even among some professors—does not seem to have totally disappeared. As recently as 1992, two professors conducted a lively debate on the question: Should undergraduate and graduate social work students be taught to conduct empirically based practice?[3] Would we expect to see such a debate in a major professional journal published within other helping professions, such as medicine or psychology? Would the importance of research knowledge and skills even be debatable? Not likely!

Social workers have always recognized the need for knowledge in their decision making. The problem seems to have been the sources that they have been inclined to use. They have tended to seek advice from supervisors and administrators and even their peers when "stuck" with a particularly difficult problem or decision. However, until fairly recently, they have been less likely to use knowledge derived from empirical research in their decision making. Often, they have turned to other sources for help, sources that are likely to contain biases and distortions. Such sources have limited utility and can even be misleading.

## *Tension between Research and Practice*

Over the past few decades, leaders in our profession have expressed concern over practitioners' reluctance to rely on scientific research knowledge for practice decision making. During the late 1970s, both the Council on Social Work Education (CSWE) and the National Association of Social Workers (NASW) devoted considerable effort and expense to examining the problem of research utilization. They convened groups of leading practitioners and researchers to study it. They tried to determine, for example, why social work practitioners rarely read reports of research or sought knowledge in their professional literature, and why they tended to ignore those research findings that reflected unfavorably on their current practice methods. They concluded that responsibility for the gap between practice and research must be shared by both practitioners and researchers.

Practitioners in the NASW and CSWE meetings described their distrust of researchers and of much of the knowledge that they generated. They viewed researchers, most of whom historically have been academicians, as people who did not really understand the realities of social work practice. Researchers were perceived as more interested in conducting esoteric research to enhance their careers than in producing knowledge that might inform practice. Consequently, they tended to present their research findings in a form that few practitioners could understand and apply to their work.

In response, the researchers described their frustration with many practitioners' lack of research knowledge and general lack of interest in research. They cited a tendency of practitioners to reject those research findings that did not agree with what they "knew" to be true and to falsely assume that research knowledge was too abstract to be of value to them.

## Efforts to Close the Gap

In an effort to resolve some of the tension between practice and research and to increase research utilization, Kirk[4] proposed four objectives for research in social work. They were:

1. *Research findings should be practice relevant.* Clearly, this still is not always the case.
2. *Specific applications to practice should be contained in research reports.* In the past, many researchers neglected this condition, allowing findings to speak for themselves. But the reality is that research findings often speak less than eloquently, if at all, to social work practitioners if the practitioners lack skill in interpreting the findings. Researchers may need to describe their findings in simple, straightforward terms.
3. *Research findings should be disseminated effectively.* A practitioner cannot use information that he or she has never seen or heard about. Although professional journals continue to be a primary vehicle for knowledge dissemination, they are certainly not the only one. Other ways to share research findings include seminars and workshops, staff newsletters, audio- and videotapes or CD-ROMs of research presentations, and the Internet.
4. *Practitioners should possess both the skill and the incentive to assess and to change their practice behaviors based on research knowledge.* In order to achieve this, social workers must possess a knowledge of scientific concepts and procedures that will allow them to critically evaluate the research methods and findings of others. This implies a capacity to read between the lines in order to determine whether research findings were obtained using those proper methods that give the researcher's conclusions credibility. Social workers should be able to recognize the difference between sound, ethical research and that which contains findings and recommendations that are suspect because they are methodologically flawed.

Of course, the incentive to change our practice based on emerging research knowledge must evolve from several sources. First, practitioners must have the knowledge and understanding of scientific methods required to gain an appreciation of them. If they learn to appreciate the rigor that is built into well-designed research, practitioners are more likely to believe in and to value the findings that are produced. They also will be more likely to trust the conclusions and recommendations of the researcher.

In addition, practitioners will rely more heavily on research only if there is an expectation of reward for this behavior. Practitioners must be able to anticipate that it will reflect positively on their annual or semiannual performance evaluation or that they will receive other recognition for it. They are likely to ask a series of questions about the value placed on research in their practice settings. For example, is there more reward for empirically based practice or for doing things the way they have always been done? Will we receive support for conscientiously evaluating our practice effectiveness, or will it be viewed by our supervisors as time that could be better spent in client services? Will we be encouraged to attend professional conferences where research knowledge is disseminated or to read and discuss professional journal articles with colleagues, or will this be viewed as more time wasted? The incentive to become practitioners who use research findings for decision making requires support at all levels of human service organizations.

The need to bring social work practice and research closer together has produced a wide variety of conceptual models. One such model was proposed by Briar some years back. It has been referred to as the clinical scientist. If the model were widely practiced, the work of social workers would have many similarities to that of professionals in some other disciplines—most notably, physicians. At the same time, the model reflects a realistic understanding that social workers are far less likely to have at their disposal the amount of cause–effect knowledge that may be available to those whose work more closely approximates the hard sciences. Clinical scientists, as conceptualized by Briar, offer both direct and indirect forms of practice intervention. But they also

- Use with clients the practice methods and techniques that are known empirically to be most effective.
- Continuously and rigorously evaluate their own practice.
- Participate in the discovery, testing, and reporting of more effective ways of helping.
- Use untested, unvalidated practice methods and techniques cautiously and only with adequate control, evaluation, and attention to client rights.
- Communicate the results of evaluations of practice to others.[5]

Another author conceptualized the practitioner's relationship with research in a different way. Garvin conceptualized three overlapping research roles that the social work practitioner can play. The roles are (1) consumer of research, (2) creator and disseminator of knowledge, and (3) contributing partner.[6] In performing the first role, the practitioner has a professional obligation to seek, to evaluate, and to use, when appropriate, the research knowledge that is generated by others. The second role implies an obligation to be directly involved in doing research and to share the results of one's own research with others. This role is a recognition that there is a wealth of untapped knowledge that exists within the practice milieu which can be systematically collected, organized, and shared for the benefit of other practitioners. The third role, contributing partner, recognizes that not all social workers may have the knowledge or interest necessary to undertake large-scale research projects. But this does not preclude their making contributions to the research efforts of others. Specifically, they can participate in some of the necessary tasks of the research process such as identifying researchable problems or providing data for evaluation of social programs.

Social workers now are also expected to learn about and use research methods to systematically evaluate their own practice. Specific methods have been developed (and, in some cases, rediscovered) that inform a practitioner whether a program or an intervention with an individual client or other social system has been effective.

Unfortunately, studies have revealed that professional journals rarely publish the results of evaluations of practice effectiveness.[7] Perhaps because the findings of this type of research often lack generalizability (as we shall discuss in later chapters), practitioners are reluctant to submit their findings for publication or review. Or, perhaps for the same reason, there is a built-in bias against publishing the reports of practice evaluations among those who make publication decisions. In 1991 it was noted that the greatest percentage of published reports of research describe findings from more traditional survey designs.[8]

For many years, our professional literature has been blamed for some of the problems related to research utilization. Writers of letters to the editors of professional journals have regularly complained that articles selected for publication have had little practical value to the practitioner. (Earlier research revealed that a large percentage of the reviewers who help decide whether a paper submitted for publication will be published themselves have little or no record of research and publication.[9]) The arrival in the 1990s of two new professional journals (*Social Work Research* and *Research on Social Work Practice*) may have helped to reverse this pattern. The creation of the Society for Social Work Research is another indication that the gap between practice and research may be narrowing.

## *Research and Practice—No Need for a Gap*

As we have taken a closer look at the activities and needs of both researchers and practitioners during the past few decades, we have come to an interesting realization. The methods of practitioners and researchers are really quite similar. Their approaches to their work are far more similar than dissimilar. There is no reason not to value and benefit from one another's contributions. What's more, in the purest sense, researchers are practitioners, and practitioners are researchers. There is no reason for antagonistic we-they feelings, because we *are* they!

Still another model for research utilization, the practitioner/researcher, was described by Grinnell and Siegel.[10] It bears many similarities to the clinical scientist model but stresses the many ways in which research methods and the

FIGURE  1.1   **Research and Practice as Problem-Solving Methods:**
              **Related Activities**

| Research Tasks | Related Practice Tasks |
| --- | --- |
| 1. Identify needed knowledge. | 1. Identify broad problem. |
| 2. Identify focus of the study. | 2. Partialize the problem. |
| 3. Specify question(s) for study. | 3. Specify problem(s) for intervention. |
| 4. Develop research design. | 4. Develop action plan. |
| 5. Collect data. | 5. Implement action plan. |
| 6. Organize, analyze, interpret data. | 6. Evaluate, summarize. |
| 7. Disseminate knowledge, identify areas for more research. | 7. Terminate intervention, identify other client needs. |

social work problem-solving process are alike. The authors note that, in its ideal form, practice problem solving follows a sequence of activities that is virtually identical to the traditional research process. Even the same kind of problems—for example, biased assessment in practice and faulty measurement in research—are likely to be present.

Some authors have drawn an even closer parallel between practice and research, going so far as to equate each step in the research process with one in human service practice. We think that might be pushing the analogy just a little too much. But Figure 1.1 illustrates some of the parallels that can be drawn when one conceptualizes both research and practice intervention as problem-solving processes.

The various models for research utilization (including several more that we have not mentioned) all share common characteristics. All of them suggest that research should not be an activity that is foreign to social work practice or that necessarily draws precious resources away from it. On the contrary, social workers who wish to provide the best possible services to their clients can hardly afford not to be actively involved in knowledge building. The models underline the fact that a research-oriented and research-involved practitioner is likely to be a better informed and a more effective and efficient practitioner. In turn, a practice-oriented and practice-informed researcher is likely to produce research findings that will have value and be of benefit to those who deliver services to clients.

## Types of Knowledge

In the past, debate among researchers has often centered on the relative merits of different research methods. However, we need more knowledge of many kinds. A wide array of methods is required for us to obtain it.

What types of knowledge are needed most by the social work practitioner? What can we realistically hope to acquire through the use of scientific research methodologies? Scientifically based knowledge can take several forms. All are valuable to the social work practitioner.

## Descriptive Knowledge

Descriptive knowledge is knowledge to help us understand. It simply gives us a reasonably accurate picture of the way things are, or to be more precise, of how they were at the time that the research took place. It does not allow us to go much beyond having a better and more accurate perception of a problem or situation at some point in time, or even what certain individuals perceived to be the situation at the time. Descriptive knowledge is limited, but this is not meant to imply that it is inferior to other types of knowledge. It is not any less valuable or (acquired correctly) any easier to achieve. In fact, descriptive knowledge often requires many months or even years of work and ingenious research methods. For example, research that accurately chronicles the grief reactions of partners of people diagnosed as having HIV infection or what it was like to grow up gay in a conservative community is painstaking work. But it makes a valuable addition to our professional literature. Learning how people experience an event or situation can be of great assistance to social workers who work with people in similar circumstances.

Descriptive knowledge, as we shall discuss in the context of research design in later chapters, may be exactly what the individual social work practitioner needs. It also frequently forms the basis for desirable changes within our society. The accurate description of a problem—for example, the statistical documenta-tion of discriminatory employment practices or identification of the amount of sexual harassment in the workplace—has been the basis both for bringing these problems into public awareness and for subsequent social change. As social workers who advocate for change, we are especially aware of the value of this kind of knowledge.

## Predictive Knowledge

Predictive knowledge is knowledge to help us anticipate. It allows us to go a step beyond describing what is or was. It allows us to project into the future and to predict with reasonable accuracy what will be. Predictive knowledge evolves following an accumulation of descriptive knowledge. It is based on the observa-tion that consistent patterns of behaviors or events exist. They tend to recur within our world. We can increase the likelihood of success in predicting the future when we observe what tended to happen when similar conditions existed in the past.

Predictive knowledge can tell a social worker what is likely to occur unless intervention occurs. For example, it can tell a social worker that an untreated abusive partner is likely or unlikely to become violent again, or that a certain psychiatric patient may become disruptive in group treatment. It can help to predict who is "at risk" of experiencing a certain problem and thus who might require careful monitoring and/or intervention. But it stops short of telling a social worker exactly how to intervene to prevent a problem from occurring or to treat one that already exists.

## *Prescriptive Knowledge*

Prescriptive knowledge is knowledge to more effectively intervene. It is what we often wish we had, but rarely do. It is based partly on the accumulation of a wealth of descriptive and predictive knowledge, and partly on the findings of carefully designed research studies in which the researcher had considerable control over the ways in which the research was conducted.

When prescriptive knowledge exists, we not only know what is and what probably will be, but we also know what needs to be done to avoid something undesirable or to cause something desirable to occur. In a social science such as sociology, descriptive knowledge and, to a lesser degree, predictive knowledge are the usual end products of scientific research efforts. In social work practice, our goal is informed intervention with a high likelihood of success. Thus, we strive to produce prescriptive research knowledge; that is, knowledge that provides guidance for successful intervention. For example, the knowledge that a client with a particular psychiatric diagnosis will benefit from a particular combination of counseling and medication has valuable implications for a social work practitioner. In terms of its value for decision making, it may be even more valuable than the knowledge that her problem occurs in approximately 2 percent of women (descriptive knowledge) or that it will probably result in problems in maintaining employment (predictive knowledge).

Purely prescriptive knowledge is relatively rare in social work. But virtually all research findings that generate any of the three kinds of knowledge tend to have some prescriptive potential. With thought, predictive and even descriptive knowledge can help to inform our practice decision making and thus increase the likelihood of successful intervention.

## Where Do We Get Our "Knowledge"?

What are some of the ways that we acquire assistance when we lack the knowledge for decision making? Many are available, but most of them are pretty unreliable. Often, we depend on the fact that some things are self-evident and logical. Unfortunately, logic can lead to beliefs that are just plain wrong in some circumstances. For example, joining a white separatist group is generally a good indication of the presence of racist or anti-Semitic attitudes. But this logical assumption may break down in the case of an FBI infiltrator. Similarly, we cannot depend on the self-evident truth that an individual who attends graduate school values an education, even if most graduate students probably do. He or she may have enrolled to appease a parent, to avoid having to work in the family business, or even to pursue a future partner.

Overreliance on logic has led to some costly errors among helping professionals. In the 1980s, a program called "Scared Straight" was promoted as a logical approach to reducing crime. It involved taking young people who had committed minor crimes, such as shoplifting, on a tour of prisons to see what might happen to them if they did not abide by the law. They experienced the booking procedure firsthand and talked with inmates who were serving long sentences. Logically, the experience should have turned the youths into model citizens. But it didn't. Subsequent research found that often those who had participated in the program had a higher crime rate than their counterparts who had not been through it!

Similarly, logic (along with the media) would suggest that a child who is abused today will become a child abuser someday. It makes sense, right? Abuse is humiliating and should leave one angry and wanting to strike back. Besides, if violence is the only parenting behavior one has experienced, why wouldn't an individual treat his or her own children in the same way? This cause-effect scenario is logical, but is it really accurate? In fact, research has shown that not all abused children, not even most, become perpetrators of abuse. To date, much more research has been conducted on perpetrators of abuse (and their childhood experiences) than on parents who do not abuse their children. Scientific research eventually may tell us what percentage of people who were abused as children fall into the first category and what percentage fall into the second. Then we can know if an abused child is even any more likely to become an abuser than one who was not abused. Until such knowledge becomes available, all we can really know about this issue is that conclusions based solely on logic cannot be trusted.

Another dubious source of knowledge is traditional beliefs. We may believe something to be true simply because it has never really been challenged, at least within our culture. This kind of knowledge is particularly dangerous. As social workers, we may confront it on a daily basis. It can take the form of relatively innocuous misconceptions (for example, that all former military people are good bureaucrats). But it is more likely to result in destructive, negative stereotyping. Traditional beliefs may promote the continued oppression of members of our society. The persistence of erroneous stereotypes, such as that gay men and lesbians choose their sexual orientation and wish to convert others to it, that all elders suffer from intellectual deterioration, or that all single-parent families are dysfunctional, have all helped to foster discrimination against members of these groups.

People have a tendency to hold tenaciously to traditional beliefs, sometimes even in the face of scientific evidence to the contrary. Human beings seem to have a need for some knowledge that represents a universal truth. We crave some areas of certainty in our lives, perhaps because so much of life is uncertain. Unfortunately, once we are convinced that something is correct, occasional selective observations are all that we seem to require to confirm its correctness. This is problematic enough for us in our social transactions, but in our professional roles, tenacious reliance on traditional beliefs can seriously affect our ability to provide competent services. The social work practitioner cannot afford to make practice decisions and to undertake intervention on the basis of traditional beliefs.

Still another way we sometimes get our "knowledge" is through deference to authority. We sometimes mistakenly conclude that "If she said it, it must be true," or "He ought to know, or he wouldn't be where he is today." Unfortunately, people in authority (perhaps our supervisors), just like all of us, are subject to bias, limited experience, and perhaps the need to confuse reality with wishful thinking. Or they may simply be relying on logic or traditional beliefs!

## Two Examples

Knowledge that has its basis in logic, traditional beliefs, or authority is very common in all societies. It often crops up quickly and spontaneously when we lack understanding of a situation. But what happens when we mistakenly rely on traditional ways of knowing? Where does this reliance lead us? Let us see how it can mislead us about two groups of people with whom social workers are likely to work: welfare recipients and Vietnam-era veterans.

**Who Was an AFDC Recipient?** There never has been any shortage of "knowledge" about welfare recipients in our society. We rarely encounter people who admit that they really do not understand their situation or do not have a solution (often, a punitive one) for it. Historically, families receiving AFDC (the program formerly known as Aid to Families of Dependent Children) benefits were especially subject to erroneous beliefs. The mother in such families was often described as a "welfare queen." According to this stereotype, she had eight or ten children. She lived well on her benefits and had no intention of finding work. When she needed or wanted more money, she just had another baby.

How accurate was this "knowledge" of AFDC mothers that served as much of the impetus for welfare reform in the 1990s? There may have been a few women who received AFDC benefits and who may have looked and acted like the stereotypical welfare queen. Unfortunately, they made good copy for newspapers and television, especially when they were caught attempting to defraud authorities. But they were by far the exceptions, not the rule. In 1994 a social work professor published the results of an eight-year study of 3,000 welfare recipients. Among his findings, the researcher noted the following:

- Most welfare recipients had no more than two children.
- During the previous twenty years, the value of welfare benefit levels had sharply declined when adjusted for inflation.
- States with the highest out-of-wedlock birthrates tended to have the lowest welfare benefit levels.
- Benefits to teenage mothers were lower in the United States than in European nations.[11]

These findings clearly argued against the widespread perceived presence of welfare queens. They also pointed out that AFDC was hardly a good deal in the United States. It would have been totally illogical for an AFDC mother to become pregnant just to receive a small increase in benefits.

**Who Is a Vietnam-Era Veteran?**  Many people in our society (and, unfortunately, some helping professionals) feel equally comfortable with their "knowledge" of Vietnam era veterans. What do they think they know about them? They are men who were drafted to fight reluctantly, under brutal and emotionally traumatic conditions. They "know" that casualties were suffered disproportionately by low-ranking men, who were most likely to be the poor and the ethnic minorities of American society. Those who survived the war are troubled. They tend to be lost and alienated, bitter, unemployed, human "time bombs" who have had difficulty adjusting to civilian life. They are dropouts from mainstream society, prone to violent outbursts, crime, substance abuse, and other antisocial behaviors. As with the stereotype of the welfare queen, newspaper and television accounts of violent acts tend to confirm what they "know." Whenever a violent, troubled person is found to be a Vietnam era veteran, this fact is reported. (Interestingly, this same fact is rarely reported when a veteran performs a heroic act.)

Of course, the emotional and psychiatric problems encountered by *some* American Vietnam veterans are real. Social work practitioners encounter difficulties like posttraumatic stress disorder (PTSD) among Vietnam veterans (as well as among victims of rape, sexual abuse, and other traumatic life experiences). But what do we really know about Vietnam era veterans as a group? Are the above perceptions really accurate? Data from the U.S. Defense Department and from other sources compiled by a concerned veteran reveal that common beliefs are often wrong. For example,

- Seventy-five percent of those who served in Vietnam either enlisted or volunteered for Vietnam.
- Ten thousand women served there.
- Less than half of all Vietnam-era veterans actually served in Vietnam.
- Casualties were proportionally distributed among all ethnic groups.
- A slightly disproportionately large number of casualties were suffered by officers, including twelve generals who were killed there.
- Today, Vietnam-era veterans are more likely than their contemporaries (who did not serve) to have a college education, to own a home, and to have an above-average income. They are less likely to be unemployed, to have a drug problem, or to have served in prison than those who never served.[12]

We have offered just two examples of the wide disparity between what was generally believed to be true and what research has revealed. Reliance on knowledge from dubious sources can create problems for the social worker. For example, social workers or other helping professionals who make diagnostic or treatment decisions based on false preconceptions about people who are financially dependent on government assistance or about Vietnam-era veterans would be likely to assume that certain attitudes and problems exist among their clients when those attitudes really are unlikely to be present. They might be misled into misdiagnosis of a problem, bad treatment planning, and/or ineffective intervention methods. This is exactly the opposite of what knowledge is supposed to do. It should inform our practice, not mislead it.

It is important to note here, however, that even research findings, unless they are presented completely and in an unbiased way, can sometimes be misleading. For example, the Vietnam-era veteran who offered the previously cited information to newspapers probably was seeking to present veterans in the best possible light as a way of compensating for the usual media portrayal. Did he perhaps neglect to mention a few facts that might give us a more complete understanding of what he offered? For example, would it be helpful to know that a high percentage of all casualties were suffered by pilots, who happened to be disproportionately both white and officers? Or that large numbers of Vietnam-era veterans (including one of the authors of this text) "volunteered" for service because they knew that they would be drafted anyway and were hoping for a better assignment. Or that the high percentage of veterans who are college graduates may have had a college education made possible by benefits from the GI Bill? Our message to the reader is this: Even facts derived from research can be used to present a biased picture. That is where research ethics (Chapter 2) enter.

## Characteristics of the Scientific Alternative

Social work practitioners need many types of knowledge. Given the shortcomings of the other ways of acquiring knowledge we have just discussed, isn't the scientific method still the best alternative? It is. Knowledge derived from the scientific method, although certainly imperfect and still subject to unethical distortion, is the knowledge most likely to help us do our jobs as social workers effectively.

The *scientific method* (alternately referred to as "scientific thinking" or simply "science") is a particular way of acquiring knowledge. It is a way of thinking about and investigating assumptions about the world.[13] It differs from *scientific knowledge*, which is really only a collection of facts that were acquired through use of the scientific method. We could theoretically use scientific knowledge even if we did not know how to practice the scientific method. But such a practice would be dangerous. Unless we engage in scientific thinking and understand and use the scientific method, we might have blind faith in scientific knowledge. That would be almost as bad as uncritically depending on logic, traditional beliefs, or authority because, as has been suggested, scientific knowledge also can be misleading. To correctly use the products of the scientific method (scientific knowledge), we must understand it. That is why we study it.

Certain characteristics of the scientific method set it apart from other ways of acquiring knowledge and, we believe, make it more likely to yield knowledge on which the social worker can depend.

- *Science is empirical. Empirical* is a word that is widely used but not always understood. It means that knowledge derived from scientific methods is based on direct observations of the real world, not on someone's beliefs or theories. Scientific knowledge has undergone a rigorous evaluation and verification process to determine whether what was assumed to be true or what was believed to be true really is true. Because science is empirical, it is not appropriate for validating some phenomenon that cannot be directly observed, such as the existence of God. However, many phenomena that on the surface would seem inappropriate for study through science (for example, how people experienced some event from their perspective) can nevertheless be studied by the imaginative researcher using the scientific method.
- *Science strives for objectivity.* No conscientious and ethical scientist would deliberately introduce biases into research findings. Scientists take deliberate actions to avoid the potential for their own preferences or beliefs to influence the results of research. At the same time, there is recognition that total objectivity may be impossible and that a certain amount of subjectivity is inevitable, and these factors influence findings in all research to a greater or lesser degree. But the scientist attempts to assess how much subjectivity may have played a role and to evaluate its effects in order to get to the truth.
- *Science produces provisional knowledge.* With science, the possibility that the researcher's conclusions may be wrong is always present. Science says, in effect, based on what we know right now, this is what we think to be the case. It leaves open the possibility that subsequent scientific inquiry may lead to modified or even to totally contradictory conclusions. In this way, scientific knowledge is always regarded as tentative. Even the conclusions drawn from statistical analyses are based on a premise of reasonable certainty, usually 95 percent.
- *Science employs a public way of knowing.* In science, it is not enough for a researcher to share findings with other scientists and with the public. It also is expected that the methods used to produce the findings will be made available for critique so that other researchers can try to achieve similar results (called *replication* in research). In this way, a researcher's findings can be checked, and, once verified, they tend to have greater credibility.
- *Science employs certain rules, procedures, and techniques.* Whereas innovation is also characteristic of science, there are definitely acceptable and unacceptable ways to conduct scientific research. There are also correct and incorrect sequences in which to perform research tasks. Even research that ventures

into problem areas where we have very little knowledge attempts to be as rigorous as possible in doing so.

## Quantitative and Qualitative Research

Two terms are commonly used to describe the broad characteristics of research. Research studies are described as either quantitative or qualitative based on their predominant characteristics. During the 1980s and 1990s, much heated debate ensued regarding the relative merits of the more traditional quantitative research and the more recently advocated qualitative research. We take the position, as we have in discussing other design typologies, that neither is inherently superior. They frequently are complementary—both can generate valuable, needed knowledge for the practitioner. What's more, many research studies are hybrids—they have elements of both quantitiative and qualitative research. Both types of research can be conducted in rigorous, scientific ways; of course, both also can produce results that are of little value if rules and procedures are not followed. We will present here a brief overview of quantitative and qualitative methods, emphasizing key differences (see Figure 1.2). We will be returning to them within various other contexts throughout this book.

### *Quantitative Approaches to Knowledge Building*

Quantitative research often has been thought of (erroneously) as being synonymous with the scientific method. (It is sometimes even called "empirical research.") It emphasizes the building of knowledge through what is referred to as "logical positivism." It stresses the use of deductive (linear) logic to arrive at conclusions. Knowledge is derived through an emphasis on objectivity (detachment) and the absence of the researcher's values (bias) in drawing conclusions. Careful, standardized measurement of variables, controlled situations, and complex statistical analysis are often components of quantitative designs.

For many years, quantitative methods were considered the best (if not the only) way to conduct research. They are still described as such in many high school science classes and in research courses in many other disciplines. Indeed, the principles of quantitative research are very helpful in guiding the researcher's quest for new knowledge. However, quantitative methods have their limitations. For example, we cannot always separate knowledge and values; they are hopelessly intertwined in human thought. Some people would also argue that an objective interview or even an objective questionnaire is a contradiction in terms. Doesn't the presence of an interviewer or any data collection method influence the findings of research to some degree? Critics of quantitative research argue that objectivity is an unattainable goal.

In addition to challenges to the appropriateness of quantitative research methods, writers have increasingly questioned in recent years whether there are not other, more effective ways of learning the answers to certain important questions. For example, are there not better ways to learn the subjective meanings of people's experiences or to learn how they experience a trauma or loss? These, along with the evolution of feminist research (discussed later), have taught us the importance of other approaches to knowledge building.

## Qualitative Approaches to Knowledge Building

Qualitative research designs seek to understand human experiences from the perspective of those who experience them. (More quantitative methods would emphasize determining how things actually are.) They employ words like *subjective, relative,* or *contextual*—words that might have a connotation of failure within quantitative studies. Qualitative research also relies on inductive logic instead of deduction. Often, vast amounts of data are collected, then sorted, and then interpreted.

Data collection often occurs through in-depth interviewing, participant observation, and/or content analysis of documents. Interviews (an important component of most qualitative studies) generally tend to be less structured and standardized in qualitative research than in quantitative research. Often, what the researcher learns in conducting one interview results in adaptations for the next. Hypotheses generally are not formulated beforehand; they may evolve as data collection occurs. Sample representativeness often is not a major concern.

In qualitative research, the researcher is really the primary instrument for data collection and analysis. The data are processed as they are received. There is no pretense that the researcher can collect data in an objective, value-free manner. In fact, when interviews are used, the relationships between the researcher and those being interviewed may be openly supportive and even therapeutic at times. A lack of detachment on the part of the researcher is believed to facilitate understanding.

When using more qualitative approaches to knowledge building, many of the same activities take place. However, they often receive greater or lesser emphasis than in more quantitative studies, or may occur in a different sequence. There are two important differences that are especially common. First, hypotheses are unlikely to be present prior to data collection, and thus are not tested. Instead, they may be a product of the research process. They may appear late in the report of a qualitative study as tentative conclusions drawn from the research findings. Second, in qualitative studies, an extensive review of the literature may not occur prior to data collection. Instead, vast amounts of data may be collected, and then the professional literature may be examined in depth to either confirm or question the initial findings of the current research.

### FIGURE 1.2  Qualitative and Quantitative Research

| Qualitative Research | Quantitative Research |
|---|---|
| • Is admittedly subjective. | • Seeks to be objective. |
| • Seeks to understand. | • Seeks to explain, predict. |
| • Uses inductive logic. | • Uses deductive logic. |
| • Produces hypotheses. | • Tests hypotheses. |
| • Data often processed as received. | • Data analyzed after collected. |
| • Researcher *is* the instrument. | • Reliance on standardized instruments to measure. |

## The Traditional Scientific Research Process

The following steps remain well suited to the more traditional quantitative methods. They are a time-proven sequence of activities that often can yield accurate knowledge that will inform the social work practitioner.

1. *Problem identification.* The problem—that is, the condition or phenomenon that is unsatisfactory—must be clearly understood to the point that it can be specified precisely, along with its magnitude and consequences.
2. *Research question formulation.* After developing a number of broad questions, the answer to any one of which would have potential to partially alleviate the problem (or at least to understand it better), the researcher selects one or more of these questions that will constitute the focus of inquiry for the research.
3. *Literature review.* The state of existing knowledge is assessed and assembled into a logical order to determine what is already known concerning answers to the research questions or at least to enable the researcher to specify the questions more precisely. The literature review is also used to formulate an appropriate research methodology for the current research.
4. *Construction of hypotheses and/or refinement of research questions.* Based on the literature review and the type of knowledge sought, the researcher formulates hypotheses and/or specific research questions that will provide the focus for research activities that follow.
5. *Design and planning.* A series of decisions are made as to how the research hypotheses are to be tested and/or answers to questions are to be sought. Tasks involved in this activity include the following:

   a. Selecting or formulating operational definitions of key terms.
   b. Specification of what people or objects will be studied.
   c. Development of a method for sampling (if the entire population of people or objects is not to be studied).
   d. Identification and definition of variables to be measured (conceptualization).

e. Specification of how variables will be measured (operationalization).

f. Identification and/or development of instruments for measurement (including their pretesting).

g. Specification and pretesting of methods for data collection.

h. Specification of methods for analysis of data.

6. *Data collection.* Data are collected according to predetermined methods.

7. *Sorting and analysis of data.* The data are examined, summarized, and analyzed using appropriate statistical methods. If hypotheses have been formulated, tests of statistical significance are used to determine if support for them can be claimed.

8. *Specification of research findings.* Results of data analysis are displayed in tables, graphs, or other standard formats.

9. *Interpretation of research findings.* Results of data analysis are examined in order to draw conclusions relative to the research hypotheses and/or questions. The findings are examined in relation to other knowledge.

10. *Dissemination of research findings.* The researcher uses one or more vehicles to report the methods and findings of the research.

11. *Use of findings by the social worker.* Practitioners who have access to the research report critically evaluate both the findings and the methods that produced them. Based on their assessment of them, they may adapt their practice methods accordingly.

This traditional sequence of events for performing scientific research is described in most research methods texts. However, steps 1 and 11 are not universally included. By including them, we have emphasized our concern for the importance of research utilization and the need for integration of social work practice and research.

By listing problem identification as the first step, we are emphasizing our belief that the limited resources available for research in our profession must be expended wisely and in the most productive ways. We rarely can afford the luxury of conducting research for its own sake; that is, just to satisfy our intellectual curiosity. We believe that priority should be given to research that promises to contribute knowledge for the alleviation of practice-related problems or to improve the quality of our services to clients. If a service-related research problem cannot be readily identified and stated, research efforts may not be justified.

We do not mean to imply that only a narrow range of research activities is of value to the social worker. Help for practitioners and, ultimately, for their clients can come in many forms. It can be in the form of knowledge for decision making, as a result of the highly structured measurement of a condition or phenomenon. It can be a heightened understanding of how a client subjectively experiences a life event. It can be the findings of research that compares the effectiveness of two different approaches to treatment. It can be the results of an evaluation that measures how well a social program is achieving its objectives. It can also be the product of practitioners' systematic ongoing evaluation of their own practice effectiveness with individual clients or client systems.

Our inclusion of step 11, practice utilization for decision making, stresses our belief that no matter how scientific and practice-relevant research findings are, and no matter how well they are disseminated, they may not improve practice effectiveness. Unless consumed by practitioners who are sufficiently knowledgeable about the scientific method to critically evaluate the findings and to know when and when not to make changes in their practice behaviors based on them, knowledge will not fulfill its purpose. All the time and effort reflected in the first ten steps in the research process will have been wasted.

## The Environment for Scientific Social Work Research

The environment in which social workers must function contains both obstacles to knowledge building through the scientific method and to research opportunities. Certain factors exert a major influence on research conducted by and for the social work practitioner.

For one thing, a high percentage of the research that is conducted by social workers occurs within either public or private human service organizations. Common and excellent sources of research data are interviews with clients or organization staff, case records, other organization data that are routinely collected, and observations of client and staff behavior within the organization setting. These data can provide valuable feedback that may be highly sought by administrators and other staff. But even if evaluation of programs and services is not actually the objective of research that uses these data, analysis of them may uncover areas where individuals and programs have not met their responsibilities or have failed to achieve their goals and objectives. This can be threatening. A question that invariably arises is: Who will have access to any information that the researcher seeks to use, and what if it falls into the wrong hands?

In recent years reduced funding for human services and an emphasis on accountability under such programs as managed care has left many administrators and boards of directors a little wary of "unnecessary" research (that is, research not required by some funding organization). The social worker attempting to conduct such scientific research within certain organizations usually can anticipate some resistance on the part of those people who must grant approval to conduct it. Even assurances that evaluation is not the purpose of the research are usually futile. Most administrators are keenly aware of the evaluative potential of any type of research, should the results of the research become public. They also usually know that the scientific method emphasizes the dissemination of findings and the methods used to arrive at them. They may recognize that many human service organizations in which social workers are employed operate in a task environment that is nonsupportive at best, and sometimes downright hostile. The community (or even another organization competing for funding) might love to secure unfavorable information about them.

Is it any wonder that administrators and board members are fearful of research? It would seem that they may have more to lose than to gain from it. Still another concern often relates to the protection of client and staff rights. Fears about the possibility of litigation (a major concern of administrators in the 1990s) are likely to surface when a researcher asks to collect data from records, staff, or clients themselves. Because of these and other concerns that exist within human service organizations, the social work researcher must be an extremely good politician in order to participate in research. Sometimes, permission to conduct research requires a series of compromises and accommodations that result in research methods that the social worker knows are less than ideal or by the book. This is an unfortunate reality. But, if done thoughtfully, these adjustments can be made in a way that will maintain the integrity of the research and its findings. As we shall discuss, no research design is ever perfect, but there are ways to make less-than-perfect research acceptable if one understands the principles of scientific inquiry.

The professionalization of social work over the past few decades also has influenced the ways in which we are able to conduct research. Through its credentialing efforts the NASW has sought to ensure high-quality services to clients and to acquire greater public recognition for the contributions that social workers make to society. Professionalization also has been enhanced by the passing of state licensing bills that protect both social workers and their clients. Professionalization has been accompanied by the codification of certain values, standards, and traditions. Overall, these undoubtedly have produced better services and served to protect clients from unqualified or incompetent individuals.

Generally, as we shall see in Chapter 2, professional values are highly consistent with research ethics. On occasion, however, a researcher will (and should) be constrained from using methods and designs that represent sound research but that are unacceptable to social workers and the values that guide their behavior. For example, professional values are likely to argue against such practices as random assignment of clients to different types of treatment, direct observation of treatment, denial of services in order to see if no treatment has negative consequences, or breaches of client confidentiality. If allowed to occur, these practices might produce research findings that are more definitive and possess greater credibility. But of course, research should serve practice; it should never be the other way around. Professional values and ethics must be adhered to, even if the quality of research suffers a little.

Professional values, such as a client's right to services and to confidentiality and the sanctity of a treatment relationship, will and should continue to present impediments to conducting scientific research. The welfare of individual clients cannot be sacrificed to the interest of knowledge building, sometimes even that which has the potential to produce better future services to clients. However, the knowledgeable researcher knows that many apparent conflicts that pit professional values against research imperatives really result from misunderstandings. Those that are real can often be resolved through compromise and trade-off. Frequently, an almost-as-good alternative exists and can be employed. On rare occasions, individual clients may even be asked to waive their rights for the greater benefit of future clients. But when this occurs, their relinquishment of rights should be voluntary. The influence of professional values may make research in the social work practice milieu a little more difficult, or it may require special creativity on the part of the researcher. But fortunately, it rarely precludes conducting good research altogether.

Some of the distrust of and resistance to scientific research that social workers have been observed to possess is attributable to their lack of a clear understanding of research. They may be unaware of the ways that it can be conducted so as not to conflict with professional values and ethics. But some of it has a basis in experience. Some of the unethical ways in which research has been conducted and its findings disseminated in the past have contributed to a climate of skepticism. We will describe a few of the more glaring examples of this in Chapter 2.

Most social workers chose their profession because they wanted to be of service to others. As a group, social workers tend to be (and should be!) people oriented. They may have difficulty believing the idea that any activity that does not directly and immediately result in better services is worthwhile. Research cannot always meet this requirement, although, as we have indicated, it could have been met more often than it has. Social workers' preoccupation with the delivery of services can be a real asset to the researcher. Convinced that a given research study can improve practice, social workers often become quite supportive and helpful.

Despite some of the obstacles and concerns that we have mentioned, the environment for social work research has never been better than it is in the twenty-first century. Social workers are becoming more aware that well-designed, credible research studies are essential if social workers are to provide the best possible services to their clients. They are also more aware that sound research is a necessity if we are to demonstrate that our efforts are worth their cost to governments and employers who must make decisions about which services will be supported and who should offer them.[14] Without good research evidence of this, the profession faces the threats of financial cuts and elimination of valuable and needed programs. Other disciplines and professions, which have a longer history of conducting research that demonstrates their effectiveness, could move in to fill roles that social workers historically have filled. Whether out of choice or out of necessity, the market for social work research is now very favorable.

# Summary

In this chapter we attempted to put the relationship between scientific research and social work practice into historical perspective. We tried to understand why practitioners often have resisted becoming researchers and why they often have been reticent to use research findings to guide their practice. Three types of knowledge that research can produce were described—descriptive, predictive, and prescriptive. We looked at some very unreliable ways that people attempt to acquire knowledge, and proposed and described a superior alternative: the scientific method. Its principal features were described. We introduced the two broad categories of research: quantitative and qualitative. We described the traditional sequence of activities that usually characterize quantitative research and suggested ways in which qualitative research may differ, differences that will be explored in more detail elsewhere in this book. Finally, we identified some factors often present in the social work environment and how they may influence the work of the researcher.

# References

1. Council on Social Work Education. (1992). *Curriculum policy statement for baccalaureate degree programs in social work education,* 8; and Council on Social Work Education. (1992). *Curriculum policy statement for master's degree programs in social work education,* 9.
2. Simpson, R. (1979). Understanding the utilization of research in social work and other applied professions. *Sourcebook on research utilization.* New York: Council on Social Work Education, 16–28.
3. Blythe, B., & Witkin, S. (1992). Should undergraduate and graduate social work students be taught to conduct empirically based practice? *Journal of Social Work Education, 28,* 260–269.
4. Kirk, S. (1979). Understanding research utilization in social work. *Sourcebook on research utilization.* New York: Council on Social Work Education, 12.
5. Briar, S. (1979). Incorporating research into education for clinical practice: Toward a clinical science in social work. *Sourcebook on research utilization.* New York: Council on Social Work Education, 132–133.
6. Garvin, C. (1981). Research-related roles for social workers. In R. M. Grinnell, Jr. (Ed.), *Social work research and evaluation.* Itasca, IL: F. E. Peacock, 547–552.
7. Fraser, M., Taylor, M. J., Jackson, R., & O'Jack, J. (1991). Social work and science: Many ways of knowing. *Social Work Research and Abstracts, 27,* 5–15.
8. Ibid.
9. Lindsay, D. (1978). The operation of professional journals in social work. *Journal of Social Work and Sociology, 5,* 273–298.

10. Grinnell, R. M., Jr., & Siegel, D. (1988). The place of research in social work. In R. M. Grinnell, Jr. (Ed.), *Social work research and evaluation.* Itasca, IL: F. E. Peacock, 18–21.

11. The researcher was Mark Robert Rank. The findings mentioned in this chapter were reported in the July 1994 issue of *NASW News* (a publication of the National Association of Social Workers), 6.

12. The veteran was B. G. Burkett, as reported in an article by Jim Wright of the *Dallas Morning News* and subsequently published in *The State,* Columbia, SC, September, 15, 1986, 32.

13. Gambrill, E. (1992). Social work research: Priorities and obstacles. Keynote address, Group for the Advancement of Doctoral Education Conference, University of Pittsburgh, October 1, 1992, 24.

14. O'Neill, J. (2000). Practice-Research Sync 'Crucial for Survival.' *NASW News, 45.* Washington, DC: National Association of Social Workers, 3.

# 2

# ETHICAL ISSUES IN SOCIAL WORK RESEARCH

In the previous chapter, we discussed how the context of social work practice can influence the scientific research process. There is another group of influences—ethical constraints—that tends to shape the ways in which research is conducted and the ways in which the knowledge derived from it is disseminated.

The field of medical ethics faces new ethical dilemmas almost daily, in part because medical technology is increasing at such a rapid pace. But medical practitioners and researchers are not the only ones who face these issues. All social work practitioner-researchers must wrestle with ethical questions. Ethical constraints must be considered when we plan for and conduct research.

The term *ethics*, derived from the Greek word *ethos* (which comes closest to the English word *character*), refers to principles within a society that reflect what the society views as right or wrong behavior. In the context of research, ethical issues generally revolve around two related questions: (1) Who should benefit or suffer from the actions of the researcher? and (2) Whose rights should take priority over those of others? In the ideal world, all individuals and groups should benefit from the development of new knowledge. Beneficiaries might include the researcher, those who provide research data, the institution sponsoring the research, the community, and other researchers whose efforts can build on the researcher's findings. But we know that, in the real world, the needs of one group sometimes are met at the expense of another. For example, the methods used by researchers to acquire knowledge can be harmful to those who provide the data that are needed to acquire it.

We will examine ways to ensure that those individuals who allow us to collect research data from them are protected. We also will look at the researcher's ethical obligations to others, such as the sponsors of research, other researchers, colleagues, and the general public. In some instances, research ethical issues have been clearly delineated. But often there is a lack of clear-cut guidelines to assist our decision making. But, as in our social work practice, ethical dilemmas and constraints are always with us. And that is good, because they cause us to question whether what we are doing is both justifiable and fair to others.

# Treatment of Research Participants

Most social work research depends on our fellow human beings—people who often give much more than they will ever receive when they provide data for our knowledge-building efforts. We have an ethical obligation to safeguard their health and well-being.

People who provide data for research purposes are referred to by various terms within the professional literature. Three of the most common are *research subjects, research partners,* and *research participants.* All three refer to the same individuals, but the terms have different connotations. Some people use the most traditional term, *subjects,* because it is universally understood within research circles. Others contend that the term is condescending or dehumanizing and that it is not consistent with the way those who provide data relate to the researcher within certain types of research. They also suggest that it implies that these individuals are somehow susceptible to exploitation by the researcher. For a combination of these reasons, this term is being used less frequently than it once was.

Those researchers who conduct certain types of qualitative research prefer the term *research partner.* It suggests a different perception of the respective roles of research participants and researcher. They contend that the word *partner* most accurately reflects the importance of volunteers to their research. They point out that those who agree to provide data (often, quite personal) to assist the researcher in building knowledge are equally as important as the researcher in this endeavor and that the relationship is thus one of equality.

We have chosen to use the third term, *participant,* throughout this book. This choice is not simply a compromise. Participant seems to recognize the importance of those who provide data for research purposes, while also recognizing that their objectives and degree of involvement generally differ from those of the researcher. The term is consistent with both the inductive and the deductive methods of acquiring knowledge in social work research. It also suggests an awareness that these individuals are entitled to both respect and attention to their rights.

## *Evolution of Ethical Standards for Treatment of Participants*

The ethical researcher has an obligation to ensure that research participants are protected from harm. This obligation is a relatively new phenomenon. Many of the ethical issues that must be addressed by today's researchers simply were not issues for researchers in the nineteenth and early twentieth centuries. The history of humanity is replete with examples of research that valued knowledge building more than the rights of research participants. It reflects a lack of concern for how research might negatively affect the physical and emotional health of those who provide data for scientific analysis. Research participants often were individuals who were either powerless and defenseless (for example, the poor, minorities, children, the mentally ill). Others, it was believed, had essentially abdicated their right to protection under the law or under principles of common decency because of their behavior (for example, those incarcerated for a serious crime).

The belated emergence of guidelines for conducting research with human participants occurred during the second half of the twentieth century. It came about because of a gradual recognition that, in a quest for scientific knowledge, the end cannot always justify the means. Our society has come to acknowledge that in some research studies the cost to research participants was not justifiable, no matter how much knowledge was generated.

A few widely publicized research studies are better known for their contribution to an increased concern for the protection of research participants than for the scientific knowledge that they produced. They employed methods that ranged from those that are now universally condemned to those that still continue to be defended by some people within the scientific community. Many examples of the unethical abuse of human participants could be given. We have chosen a few of the better known ones which served as an impetus for standards that are used to protect research participants today.

### The Nazi and Japanese Medical Experiments

Following World War II, it was revealed that concentration camps in Europe and prisoner-of-war compounds in Asia had been the scenes of heinous and repugnant medical experiments conducted in the name of science.[1] During the Nuremberg war crime trials in 1945 and 1946, many shocking stories were recounted that detailed how Jews, Gypsies, and other "undesirables" detained in German concentration camps were deliberately exposed to life-threatening diseases in order to study the course of the diseases and were subjected to unnecessary surgery. Others were exposed to severe cold, were deliberately wounded to study the effects of new antibiotic treatments, or were placed in decompression chambers to study their tolerance for lack of oxygen and other effects of high altitude. Of course, viewed in retrospect, these experiments were little more than atrocities committed in the name of science.

Prior to the Nuremberg trials, little attention had been paid to the rights of prisoners and other vulnerable groups. All too often, they were regarded as convenient targets for experimentation. The notion of voluntary consent was not applied to them. The shocking revelations that emerged at Nuremberg set about a process of questioning. People debated the issue of whether incarceration for any reason, even for conviction for illegal activity, can ever justify the nonvoluntary participation of prisoners in medical and other research. A consensus emerged that it cannot. Research participation must be voluntary.

Interestingly, one ethical issue related to the medical experiments conducted on American prisoners in Japanese prison camps did not surface until the 1980s. Access to previously classified documents revealed that American authorities had apparently suppressed information about the experiments after the War, in exchange for access to the medical knowledge acquired through them. As the news of the research became widely disseminated, current medical researchers sought access to data obtained in the prisoner-of-war camps. Newer and broader ethical questions were debated. Should research findings obtained through unethical methods be publicized or made available to other researchers for their use? Can suppression of valuable knowledge that has the potential to save lives be justified on the basis that the researchers' methods cannot be condoned? Should the survivors of the experiments (who did not participate voluntarily) or the relatives of those who did not survive have the right to decide whether data from the experiments can be released or under what conditions it can be used? Like most research ethical issues, these are difficult questions with no easy answers.

**What *Is* a Volunteer?**   In many research situations, the presence of large numbers of research volunteers is not in itself sufficient evidence that the rights of participants have been adequately protected.

Even if people volunteer to be research participants, there may still be ethical issues to consider. What is voluntary participation among people with little to lose or for those living in an environment where opportunities for rewards are few? This is not an issue that can be resolved easily. It is one that must always be wrestled with when social work researchers wish to conduct research. For example, can we ever assume that prisoners within correctional settings are *really* volunteer participants? Would they agree to be research participants if they were not incarcerated? Can we be absolutely certain that they are not being coerced by something or someone, or influenced by some implied promise of reward, such as privileges or time off their sentences? How can we know that they are agreeing to do something that they would not do under other circumstances?

When cultural differences between researchers and participants exist, people who volunteer to participate in research may also not be doing so voluntarily. A perception of a power differential or an emphasis on deference to people with more social status or educational credentials within the participants' culture may have led participants to believe that they had little choice but to volunteer. Or they may simply not have understood the subtleties of the wording in a consent form that they were asked to sign.

What about use of our own clients or former clients as research participants? Or a colleague's clients, where the colleague serves as what researchers refer to as a *broker*? What about using other people who share a problem or condition with us who we may have met through a support group or in a social situation? Can either group be considered volunteers in the purest sense of the word? We might ask: Would they agree to serve as research participants if a relationship between us and them did not already exist? Can we be certain that obligation, gratitude, or even fear of antagonizing us is not influencing their decision?

**Dual-Role Relationships.**   The problem of what researchers refer to as *dual-role relationships* is especially difficult for researchers seeking to do what is ethical. When researchers have a preexisting relationship with potential participants, it is sometimes very difficult to know if their agreement to provide research data was coerced in some way, through either threat or promise of reward.

Some very good and useful research has been conducted in situations where access to data would not have been possible had there not been a preexisting relationship with the participants. Anyone else attempting the same research would have had much greater difficulty in establishing trust and may not have been able to get potential participants even to agree to be interviewed. For example, one social work researcher interviewed the parents of adults who had died of AIDS who were her former patients.[2] Another interviewed children whose parent had suffered a massive traumatic head injury. She had experienced the problem in her own family and was able to locate her participants because she was a member of an organization that consisted of persons in similar circumstances.[3] Did these researchers simply take advantage of an opportunity for knowledge building that they alone possessed? Or did they simply exploit others who were unlikely to refuse to be interviewed because of their previous relationships? Were their research participants truly granting voluntary informed consent?

Despite concern that the research participants in these two studies were probably not "voluntary" in the purest sense, the research was approved. It was concluded that, although the interviews conducted with them probably were stressful, no one was likely to be harmed. In fact, it was probably psychologically beneficial to the participants to express some of their feelings about their losses to a caring professional. The fact that the potential benefits of the research for others in similar situations probably outweighed any discomfort to participants was probably also a factor in the decision to approve the studies.

When dual-role relationships exist, certain special precautions are required to protect research participants. Special effort must be made to assure potential participants that they will suffer no loss or disadvantage (including the respect of the researcher) if they decide not to participate. The preexisting relationship should not be damaged in any way. A third, neutral person (not the researcher) should be provided to offer counseling, if needed, and to help at any time in deciding whether or not it is in the potential participant's best interest to continue participation. Finally, if feasible, participation should be anonymous, so the researcher cannot know who participated and who did not.[4] Of course, in studies where researchers gather data using in-person interviews with participants whom they already know in another relationship (such as the two examples previously described), anonymous participation is impossible.

### *The Tuskegee Public Health Studies*

A second group of research studies that addressed some of the same issues took place in the United States. In 1932 the American Public Health Service began its studies of the long-term effects of syphilis on men in the Tuskegee, Alabama, area.[5] Ethical questions relate to whether these men were truly voluntary participants because of their vulnerability (health status, socioeconomic class, ethnicity). But the studies also were influential in the development of today's ethical principle known as "no unnecessary pain and suffering."

The research was conducted on 625 African American males. Most (425) had been diagnosed as having syphilis; the others were merely followed for comparison purposes. In 1937 penicillin was discovered. It soon was shown to be an effective cure for syphilis and became available to the general public several years later. Yet, for purposes of research, participants in the Tuskegee experiment, who were mostly poor and illiterate, were not told about penicillin, and it was not given to them unless they somehow learned about it and requested it. They continued to be given painful regular medical examinations (including spinal taps) to chart the course of their disease. They received only a placebo, an inert substance that had no potential to cure their disease or to alleviate their pain and suffering. In the interim, they experienced the long-term effects of syphilis, including skin disorders, insanity, heart disease, and even death. The study continued until 1957, at which time it was halted following public outcry.

Unlike many of the experiments conducted within Nazi concentration camps during World War II, the Tuskegee experiments probably were not the product of depraved minds. They were methodologically sound from a purely research standpoint. They were designed to gather data that would be accurate and would have the potential to benefit humanity. But perhaps in a more subtle way, those who conducted them now appear no less insensitive in their lack of regard for the protection of research participants than the medical "researchers" of Dachau or Auschwitz. Prior to the availability of penicillin, there may have been a legitimate reason to study syphilis to learn more about the course of an essentially incurable disease. But when the drug became available, there was no logical justification to continue the research, and there was a very good ethical reason to discontinue it immediately. Later, some of the researchers rationalized that the participants were fortunate in that they were given free regular medical examinations and did not have to pay for their burial expenses. Not until 1997 did the U.S. government offer a public apology for treatment of the research participants and award financial compensation for their suffering.

**Research on New or Experimental Drugs.**  Ethical issues relating to research involving new or experimental drugs are not always as clearly a matter of right and wrong as they were in the case of the Tuskegee experiments. For example, efforts to find a cure for or to delay the course of AIDS have resulted in the experimental use of many unproven drugs. Many of these experimental treatments have painful and even potentially lethal side effects. Having what they perceive as little to lose, people who are HIV positive have willingly agreed to become research participants in medical research designed to test the efficacy of various medications and treatment regimens. Their willing participation, perhaps as a result of desperation or an inability to afford more proven medication, has caused us to ask a number of questions. Would they undergo the risks and discomfort if they had any alternative? Are researchers who conduct the research taking unfair advantage of their unfortunate situations? Or are they merely trying to make something good happen?

Another old ethical dilemma has once again been discussed in relation to AIDS research. It relates to whether it is ever ethical to deny some research participants access to an intervention method that may be helpful. For example, what is the best way to examine the effectiveness of one of the many experimental drugs being developed for the treatment of persons who are diagnosed as HIV positive? Traditionally, good research on treatment drugs has used a control group (Chapter 6), a group of people that is identified as having the diagnosis but is merely followed and not given the medication. Members of the control group might instead be given a placebo (such as a sugar pill), but they would not know whether they were receiving the experimental drug. The use of a control group may be methodologically sound, but is it ethically defensible? Either method might generate more precise and more definitive findings than another research design that would simply provide the drug to all participants and then monitor the course of their illness. But what about the people in the control groups? What if the drug is subsequently found to be effective in delaying or even preventing the development of AIDS? Their lives might have been saved if they had received the drug rather than the placebo.

The notorious Tuskegee experiments are sometimes still mentioned in criticisms of other research on AIDS. Research in Third World countries has attempted to determine if infected mothers in a control group who were given a placebo or low dosages of the drug AZT (which often is very expensive) had a comparable or higher rate of passing the disease on to their babies than those given the full dosage of the drug. Critics have questioned whether such research, like the Tuskegee experiments, is unethical and exploitive of participants, in part because it would not be permitted among less vulnerable people.[6]

The pressure to find a way to prevent transmission of the HIV virus or to find a cure for it has spotlighted other common research ethical issues. For example, what about society's responsibility to others likely to die of AIDS who are denied access to experimental drugs that might save their lives or at least extend them because they have not yet been cleared for use in the United States by the Food and Drug Administration? Some very useful ones may remain in a warehouse awaiting further research into their possible negative side effects. Should the usual seven- to ten-year testing process be waived based on the urgency of the situation? These issues are not easily resolved.

Of course, people who are HIV positive are only one group of people who are vulnerable to being harmed by research. There are many other groups that are vunerable to unnecessary pain and suffering and must therefore be protected. Sieber[7] has listed different categories of people who are vulnerable. In some instances, as we noted earlier, their vulnerability might also make it difficult to determine whether their participation is truly voluntary or coerced. They include

- People who lack resources or autonomy.
- People who are stigmatized by society.
- People who are in a weakened position, perhaps in an institutional setting.
- People who cannot speak for themselves and their best interests.
- People whose illegal activities might become known to law enforcement authorities.
- People associated with research participants who may be damaged by data revealed by the participants.

### The Milgram Studies of Obedience to Authority

During the 1960s, Stanley Milgram conducted a series of ingeniously designed studies that sought to learn more about the phenomenon of human obedience to authority figures.[8] His research evolved in part from the defenses of Nazi war criminals who contended that they were just following orders and therefore could not be held responsible for their actions. (Similar defenses were subsequently used by American soldiers in Vietnam and by many others in military conflicts in Bosnia where atrocities were committed.) Milgram hoped to learn what ordinary, civilized people are likely to do when ordered by a more powerful individual to do something that they would otherwise never do. He hoped to learn how far they would go in their obedience to authority figures.

The research used adult males as its participants. They were told that they were to participate in research on learning and they would be assigned a partner for the research. (In fact, the partner was working with the researcher; he was not another research participant.) Through the use of a rigged drawing, the true participants always drew the role of the person assigned to reinforce learning through the administration of what they believed to be painful electric shocks to their research partner. Sitting in a room where they could hear but not see the other individual (the alleged learner) who was supposed to be wired to receive the electrical shocks, participants read off pairs of words and asked their partner to match them. When the learner made a mistake, the participant was told to throw a switch placed in front of him to shock the errant learner. The switches were labeled with phrases such as "Extreme-intensity shock" and "Danger— severe shock." As more mistakes were made, the participant was told to throw switches suggesting increasingly severe electrical shocks. As the higher and higher voltage switches were thrown, the learner began to beg for the experiment to end. When the switches continued to be thrown, he began to kick the wall and to scream. Finally, as the highest voltage switches were thrown, the learner became silent, indicating that he might have lapsed into unconsciousness or perhaps died.

Many participants became very emotionally upset by what they were doing and asked, even begged, to be allowed to stop. However, most did not stop when ordered to continue. Only a small number of the participants refused to complete the experiment; nearly two-thirds continued to throw the switches as ordered, despite the fact that they had reason to believe that they might be administering disabling, if not fatal, shocks to other human beings.

Of course, as was later explained to the research participants, they only *thought* that they were causing pain to the other individual; no electrical shock was ever administered. They were told that the reactions of their partners to their throwing the switches was all an act. So why did some researchers and even the general public (subsequent to the showing of a made-for-TV movie on the research) object so strenuously to Milgram's methods? How did the Milgram studies come to be almost synonymous with unethical treatment of research participants? For one thing, people questioned whether the physical discomfort and anguish experienced by the research participants could be justified in light of the knowledge acquired through the research (unnecessary pain and suffering). They experienced a great amount of stress. Critics asked if another method could not have been used to get the same results without causing so much duress for the participants. But this question had already been asked about earlier research; for example, the Tuskegee studies.

A second ethical issue raised by the Milgram research was a relatively new one. As a result of it, people began to ask if some research should not take place because its effects on participants could not be undone. Had permanent harm been done to the research participants in the Milgram research? Apparently so. As a result of participating in the research, many of the men tended to view themselves in a different way than they had before. They now knew that, under the right circumstances, they were capable of doing severe physical harm to another person who represented no threat whatsoever to them. As we might anticipate, this was a disturbing revelation. No amount of debriefing to assure them that they had harmed no one while following orders could undo its effects.

The Milgram research helped us to formulate an ethical question: Does the researcher ever have a right to leave research participants in worse physical or emotional condition than that in which they were found? A consensus emerged that such a consequence was probably not justified if the researcher should have been able to anticipate the results of the research. Certainly this had been the case in the Milgram research.

The social work researcher is perhaps less likely than researchers in some other disciplines to participate in research that will result in irreparable psychological damage to participants. We are sensitized to recognize the ways in which life experiences can negatively affect people's self-esteem or their ability to function. For example, we would not participate in or condone research that would involve telling airplane passengers that their plane was having mechanical problems in order to study their emotional responses, or lying to medical patients by telling them they had a fatal disease in order to observe what changes they might make in their lives. We might smile at first but then cringe a little at a rerun of that old *Candid Camera* sequence that administered aptitude tests to gifted and talented children and then recorded their responses of dismay when they were told that a life as a blacksmith or shepherd was most consistent with their aptitudes. We know the potentially negative consequences of any behavior designed to alter how we think of ourselves, even one conceived in good fun. Although the training in human sensitivity experienced by most social workers, combined with their professional values, will preclude most research that could negatively and permanently alter the participants in the research, we still must remain vigilant.

Designs that employ deception can be quite appealing. In some instances, deception may be necessary to study behavior or emotional responses that would be easily influenced if a complete understanding of the intent of the researcher were known. But deception also can be an unnecessary and dangerous shortcut. It often has been used when other, less potentially harmful methods such as simulations or certain ethnographic methods (Chapter 7) would have been equally effective. The researcher must be prepared to ask: Is deception absolutely the only way that I can get the knowledge that I need? And if so, what will I do to be certain that I will not leave my research participants in worse physical or emotional condition than when the research began?

### *The Laud Humphreys Studies of Homosexual Behavior*

Laud Humphreys' studies of homosexual behavior in public restrooms[9] remains one of the most controversial research efforts in the human science professional literature. It has been defended and touted by some people as a classic, as well as being denounced by others as simply unethical snooping.

The special focus of Humphreys' research was casual homosexual sex acts between strangers who led otherwise heterosexual lives. He conducted observations of homosexual encounters between men in parks. Humphreys knew that the people he wished to study would be unlikely to agree to let him observe their behavior for research purposes. Even if they did, the data thus obtained would be of questionable value. So he engaged in a series of deceptions. He first gained the confidence of his intended research participants. He frequented the public restrooms and implied through his regular presence that he shared in their activities. He began to assume the role of watch queen, which entailed being a lookout for the police or other potentially threatening people. The payoff for being a watch queen was the opportunity to watch sexual acts being performed—exactly what he needed for his research. But the deception did not end there.

Because he believed that he needed to know more about his research participants, especially about their public lives, Humphreys conducted follow-up interviews. When possible, he recorded the license plate numbers of his participants and obtained their addresses through access to police records. Disguising himself so that he would not be recognized as their watch queen, he interviewed them under the pretense of conducting a survey and obtained additional descriptive data.

Many ethical questions were raised by the Humphreys study. Some of them continue to be debated. Had he violated the participants' right to privacy? Had they been voluntary research participants because they had knowingly granted permission to him to watch? Was there really any other way that he could have obtained the same knowledge without his elaborate deception? Should he have been more honest about his real purpose for being in the public restrooms? If he had, would he have been able to acquire accurate knowledge? How much would he have had to tell them about his research in order for them to be able to give voluntary informed consent to serve as participants? Wasn't his deceit really harmless? After all, he conscientiously concealed the identities of his participants.

The way in which Humphreys learned the identities of his participants and conducted his follow-up interviews was especially infuriating to some of his critics. They charged that the men's permission to be interviewed in their homes was not valid because he had been dishonest about the real reasons why he wished to interview them. He misrepresented both the real focus and the scope of his research. He also risked someone making a connection between his survey in their homes and the activities that went on in the park restrooms. Although highly unlikely, a research participant's secret behavior could have come to light as a result of his pursuing them for a follow-up interview at home.

The issues raised over the Humphreys research have special implications for social workers. Because of the nature of their work and the trust often placed in them by clients, they may have access to very sensitive or private data not readily available to outside researchers. Clients often tend to become quite candid in what they say and do around social workers because they trust that the social worker is concerned primarily with helping them to solve their problems. Yet the same observations made in the process of helping others also can become valuable data for the researcher.

A frequent ethical issue for the social worker is whether data gathered and sometimes recorded for the purpose of helpful intervention (often available in the form of case records) can legitimately be used for another purpose for which it never was intended. Do social work clients really give voluntary informed consent to be research participants? Sometimes, but not usually. In some settings, such as teaching hospitals, patients agree from the outset that data collected relative to their treatment can be used for research and teaching purposes. Even in other settings, recorded data sometimes are still used for research. This is done in a way that some might consider ethically questionable. The organization grants its professional staff access to case records and other treatment data for research purposes, but only with careful assurances that client confidentiality cannot in any way be compromised. Whenever possible, research findings are reported in composite form and/or individual clients are otherwise deidentified when research reports are written. Some potentially valuable data must be omitted from the report so that a reader will not be able to identify a particular client. This is but one of many compromises that social work researchers sometimes must make in order to attempt to comply with both professional and research ethical standards.

# Today's Standards for Treatment of Participants

Fortunately, the social work researcher need not operate in a vacuum in wrestling with ethical issues. As a result of public responses to abuse of research participants in earlier research studies, there now exists a list of generally agreed-on standards that govern the conduct of research.

In research that uses human beings as research participants, ethical standards have been developed. Many organizations now require review and approval by a team of researchers and other concerned individuals. They are labeled an Institutional Review Board (IRB), a human subjects review team, ethics committee, or some similar title. The members carefully review proposals for research to ensure that the rights of participants will not be threatened or violated and that protection measures are in place. Until the review team is convinced that this is the case, the research is not allowed to be initiated. They apply several interrelated standards, which we have discussed throughout this chapter.

## *Voluntary Informed Consent*

Earlier, we discussed what is meant by the word *voluntary*. It refers to "by choice, not because of coercion or intimidation or because of promises of rewards." We also noted how difficult it is to determine if this condition is present.

When used in the context of research, *informed* relates to the question: Will the potential participants know what they need to know in order to determine if they wish to participate in the research? Prior to agreeing to participate in research, a person should have a fairly clear idea of what that participation will entail. This is designed to protect participants from unknowingly getting themselves into a situation that they never would have chosen had they been more fully informed from the outset. It also limits the researcher's ability to deceive research participants by grossly misrepresenting the purposes of their research or the nature and limits of the demands that will be made on research participants. If deception is to be used, it must be demonstrated that it is necessary and not potentially harmful to participants before an IRB or similar group will generally approve a research proposal.

*Consent* refers to the fact that there is a clear, generally written agreement to participate. A consent form, signed by the participant, provides a potential research participant with a description of what to expect. It also provides legal protection for the researcher, who may later need proof that participants willingly took part in the research. This principle is very consistent with the social work practice value of self-determination, which upholds an individual's right to make decisions about matters that affect his or her life and well-being. Figure 2.1 is an

FIGURE  2.1  Sample Consent Form

---

### *Informed Consent Form*

During February and March 2002, students and faculty of the Hamilton School of Social Work will be conducting research at the Jerome County Department of Social Services. Their objective is to learn more about the decisions that child protection (CPS) workers make as to whether allegations of child abuse are founded. The research will involve a review of case summaries of CPS cases and personal interviews with current CPS workers. Results will be used to better understand the decision-making process and to make recommendations for future training and staff development.

The interviews will be conducted at the Jerome County DSS office and will be approximately 30 minutes in duration. The interviewer (a graduate social work student) will not know or be known to the worker. Information collected will include demographic characteristics, parenting methods used in the worker's home of origin, and current attitudes toward employment.

Participation in the research interviews is totally voluntary; those who elect to take part may choose to discontinue participation at any time without prejudice. Information obtained will be summarized in a way that will maintain individual confidentiality. Further information regarding the research may be obtained from Dr. H. S. Nibbler at 555-3129.

If you agree voluntarily to participate in the proposed research, please sign and date two copies of this agreement and keep one copy for your records.

Signature: _____

Date: _____

example of a form that could be used to acquire the voluntary informed consent of potential research participants.

In obtaining voluntary informed consent, special care needs to be taken in obtaining consent from persons who are from groups that are linguistically or culturally different from the majority population. Consent forms should be provided in the research respondent's native language, and clarifying comments and responses to questions about participation in the research should be addressed in the language most familiar to the respondent. This may require using bilingual or native-speaking research assistants to help obtain voluntary informed consent.

Researchers also need to be sensitive to culturally determined patterns of deference to authority, which may cause respondents to feel that they cannot or do not have the right to refuse participation in the study. This may be a particular issue when the researcher is from a dominant group and the respondent is from a less powerful group where there is a shared history (for example, whites and African Americans in the southeastern United States or whites and Native Americans in some areas of the American West). In addition, special care needs to be taken when research is conducted in a setting where services are being offered and the participant is also a client (dual relationships). If a researcher is unfamiliar with the culture of the target population in a cross-cultural research situation, someone familiar with the culture should be consulted regarding issues in obtaining voluntary informed consent and protection of human participants within the specific cultural context.

The principle of voluntary informed consent also recognizes that some vulnerable people—for example, young children or people who are severely mentally disabled—may not be able to understand a description of their proposed participation in research and to make an informed decision as to whether they wish to participate. In research that proposes to use people who may be considered incapable of giving voluntary informed consent, another responsible person may serve as an advocate to protect them and to decide for them what should be permitted in the interest of scientific knowledge building. A social worker or other helping professional is a logical choice to assume the advocate role.

An example of unethical research involving participants unable to protect themselves was conducted in the 1950s and 1960s. It provides dramatic evidence of the need for knowledgeable advocates to protect those who may not be able to look after their own best interests. Newly admitted, developmentally disabled children in a state school were deliberately infected with a live hepatitis virus in order to study the course and spread of the disease. The researcher later attempted to justify his research methods by rationalizing that living conditions were so deplorable at the school that the children probably would have contracted the disease in a short time anyway.[10]

Even when advocates are used, they cannot be expected to make good decisions for others unless they have adequate descriptions of proposed research methods. Another study that was conducted by researchers from Harvard University and the Massachusetts Institute of Technology from 1946 to 1956 was referred to as the "Fernald Science Club." It was conducted at the Fernald, Massachusetts State School. Dozens of teenage boys with developmental disabilities were fed radioactive food to study its possible effects. Parents had been asked to sign consent forms for their sons to participate in the research. However, its description made no mention of radiation.[11]

## No Unnecessary Pain and Suffering

Ethical issues related to the discomfort of and even injury to research participants must address questions that cannot be easily answered. Medical research and almost all research that involves a study of human behavior have the potential to cause pain and suffering. It is impossible to know all of the potential risks to participants that proposed research poses. By definition, science always works in areas of inquiry where cause–effect knowledge is fragmentary, if not totally absent. However, the realities of science do not absolve the ethical researcher from protecting participants from *unnecessary* risk. Certain questions are appropriate. Can the knowledge be derived in a way that has less potential to cause physical or emotional harm to the participant? Have protections been built into the research design that will minimize the risk of causing pain and suffering? If the research absolutely must cause some physical or emotional discomfort, will its severity and duration be the absolute minimum that is necessary to acquire data?

One study conducted by the University of California at Los Angeles during the 1980s and 1990s illustrates the difficulty of balancing the need for knowledge and the principle of no unnecessary pain and suffering. It also shows how this principle can be related to the principle that we discussed earlier: voluntary informed consent. The researchers were attempting to learn if some people were unnecessarily taking antipsychotic drugs that may produce involuntary tremors. Fifty young patients being treated for schizophrenia had their medication abruptly discontinued. Of these fifty participants, twenty-three experienced severe relapses (including one suicide). Although their parents had signed consent forms for their children, they alleged that they were never told how severe the relapses might be or that it would be safer if the medication were continued.[12]

The UCLA research was designed with good intentions. It sought to acquire knowledge that might help to alleviate a problem experienced by schizophrenic patients—unnecessary medication and its side effects. But in attempting to address the problem, some of the patients were harmed. Many ethical questions can be raised. Did the ends justify the means? Was the pain and suffering experienced by some of the participants in the research (and their families) necessary? Wasn't there another way besides stopping their medication (perhaps by gradually reducing it) to learn if the medication was necessary, while causing the patients less pain and suffering?

An important subissue that relates to pain and suffering concerns the presence of any negative aftereffects that people might experience from their roles as research participants. (Remember, this was a major issue in the Milgram studies.)

A researcher is ethically obligated to leave research participants as they were found, or at least in no worse condition. In recognition of the fact that virtually all research involving human participants has the potential to harm or change people in some way, human subject review teams generally pay careful attention to a researcher's plans for debriefing and restoration of participants after data have been collected. They may wish to ensure that, for example, counseling or other indicated follow-up will be provided, if needed.

## Anonymity/Confidentiality

As social workers, we need not be reminded of the importance of safeguarding the privacy and identity of our clients. The ethical principles of anonymity and confidentiality exist to safeguard research participants from the harm that can come to them if their identities are intentionally or inadvertently associated with any data that are collected. The ideal condition under which participants provide data is anonymity. When it exists, even the researcher does not know the participants' names and cannot attribute to them any data that were provided. An example of anonymity might be a mailed questionnaire survey that does not use case numbers or other identification on the questionnaire or on the return envelope. The researcher cannot know who returned one and who did not or who said what in their replies. This protects the participants' anonymity, but it can have real logistical disadvantages for researchers. For example, what if researchers wish to send a follow-up questionnaire to those who did not respond or to know if those who responded differ in some way from those who did not respond?

A more realistic and generally acceptable alternative involves protection of confidentiality. Especially when data are collected by in-person interviews, researchers are likely to know and recall who revealed what about themselves. However, under principles of confidentiality, the researcher is ethically obligated not to reveal the participants' identities or to in any way let others be able to associate any of the data provided with any one participant. Upholding confidentiality may require careful editing of the data to remove any identifying information before disseminating its findings. An ethical researcher will be willing to forgo using some potentially useful data to protect the participants' rights to confidentiality.

The principle of confidentiality often governs how social workers handle data about their clients. As researchers, it seems familiar and natural to also protect participants from harm. However, people outside the academic and practicing communities may attempt to get a researcher to compromise the principle. What if, for example, a research report reveals that a participant is guilty of a crime such as fraud or has threatened the well-being of others? Does the public have the right to know the identity of that participant and to take appropriate legal action? It is a good idea to check out relevant laws and statutes when such issues arise or, better yet, before they do.

In the role of researchers, social workers may not enjoy the protection of privileged communication that most helping professionals possess. Research data can and have been subpoenaed. For this reason, some researchers have chosen to destroy the names of their research participants once the data have been coded and case numbers assigned.

It should also be remembered that, for some actions that we may learn about in the process of conducting research (such as child abuse), we may have no options. We have an ethical (and a legal) obligation which transcends the role of researcher to notify the proper authorities.

## Need to Conduct the Research

Although sometimes not mentioned specifically among the criteria by which review panels evaluate a research proposal, there is a fourth ethical concern that is always considered. Even if the proposed research represents no physical or emotional threat to them, research participants have a right to assume that whatever demands are made on them (for example, their time or other costs) are necessary for the advancement of knowledge. Ethically, research cannot be justified that merely provides a research learning experience for the researcher, that does not promise to significantly advance knowledge, or that might provide knowledge that simply is not worth knowing. Thus, IRBs may question whether some proposed research is justifiable, given the products that it promises to yield. It may represent an unnecessary imposition on its participants.

Sometimes research may not be approved because it seems designed only to advance some political or economic agenda. The issue of conducting research for purposes other than the advancement of knowledge came to the fore during the late 1980s as a result of the activities of people active in the antivivisection movement. A frequent argument against the use of animals for experimentation by the American cosmetics industry was that research on rabbits, guinea pigs, dogs, and other laboratory animals was not conducted to learn anything new. Its primary purpose was to provide legal protection for manufacturers against charges that products had not undergone sufficient testing prior to their release in the market.

Is there a danger that social work researchers might conduct unnecessary research for purposes other than the advancement of knowledge? Yes. Even ethical researchers sometimes inadvertently conduct unnecessary research. They do not conduct a thorough review of the literature to determine what knowledge is already available. They repeat the work of others and thus waste the time and energies of their research participants, as well as their own.

Research sometimes is conducted for purely educational purposes, that is, to give social workers supervised practice in conducting research. This occurs within colleges and universities and even within some social organizations. Deriving new knowledge is not a high priority—the same research questions may be studied year after year, and nothing is ever done with the data thus acquired.

Concern over the ethics of unnecessary research is a recognition that scientific inquiry involving human participants almost always represents an unequal trade. It offers less to participants in the research than it takes from them. This "bad deal" can be justified only if some greater good can come out of the research, specifically, the advancement of knowledge that can help others.

## Other Ethical Obligations of Researchers

The ethical positions adopted by the NASW provide guidelines for both professional practice and research. They limit one's behavior with clients and with research participants. In its Code of Ethics,[13] it is evident that the unethical use of human participants for knowledge building is never condoned. However, the Code of Ethics and our professional literature suggest that the researcher has ethical obligations not only to the participants but also to the sponsors of research, other researchers, colleagues, and the general public. Most obligations relate to broad issues, such as the scientific integrity of researchers, the requirement that they adhere to certain standards in conducting research, and that they honestly report and interpret findings.

What do these position statements tell us about the general characteristics of ethical researchers? For one thing, they recognize the potential of research findings to influence the work and lives of others, and they recognize the seriousness of scientific inquiry. They are aware that any research finding, no matter how unexpected or contrary to what they believe to be true, is potentially valuable and that any misrepresentation of what they learned is potentially dangerous. They place truth above personal gain through the manipulation of data to achieve desired results.

Ethical researchers function with neutrality and, to the degree possible, objectivity. They strive to keep an open mind in order to let empirical knowledge, not their own preferences, form the basis for any conclusions drawn from their research.

Ethical researchers resist outside influences, such as political or economic pressures that might influence either the results of the research or its dissemination. Although they give proper credit to funding organizations that provided support for their research, they do not allow these organizations to distort or suppress their findings.

Ethical researchers are aware of the tentative nature of scientific knowledge and remain open to reinterpretation and even contradiction of their findings. They do not claim to have more definitive answers to research questions than are justifiable. They value confrontation and debate with their fellow researchers. They take responsibility for their research methods and findings, and they welcome legitimate critique.

Ethical researchers never attempt to take credit for work that they did not perform and always share the credit for collaborative efforts. They openly acknowledge the support and contributions of others to their research. They insist that appropriate credit is given to students and/or research assistants and consultants who contributed to the research effort. They will not allow their own names to appear as coresearchers on efforts where their own contributions were only minimal.

While recognizing the importance of building knowledge to promote better client services, ethical social work researchers resist any use of research that appears to represent a breach of professional ethics. Their activities are shaped by both general research ethical practices and by their professional ethics as social workers. They are social workers first, then researchers. When using clients as research participants, they acknowledge that their clients' best interests must take precedence over knowledge building. They will not allow confidentiality to be violated without permission, even if it requires them to suppress potentially valuable findings. They discontinue any research if it begins to threaten their participants' welfare.

Ethical researchers are also concerned about the ways that research findings are disseminated and used; they want the findings of research to help rather than to degrade or harass those whom they serve as professionals. They will attempt to halt the use of their research data by others when it is taken out of context to embarrass others or to create a false public impression about them. They may insist that their findings must be presented only in their entirety. Or they may seek to discredit interpretations of their research findings that they perceive to be most self-serving or that misrepresent conditions as they really are.

## Summary

In this chapter, we examined some of the major ethical issues that social workers address when they conduct research. Past research has helped to produce current ethical codes that are designed to protect the physical and psychological well-being of human research participants. Other principles ensure that researchers relate to the sponsors of research, other researchers, colleagues, and the general public in ways that are ethical. They are designed to ensure the appropriate place of scientific inquiry in human activity.

## References

1. Katz, J. (1972). *Experimentation with human beings.* New York: Russell Sage Foundation.
2. Taylor, L. (1996). A qualitative study of families of persons with AIDS. Unpublished dissertation, Columbia, SC: University of South Carolina.

3. Pryce, N. (1995). A heuristic study using an evolutionary perspective of the experience of adolescents adapting to the head injury of a parent. Unpublished dissertation, Columbia, SC: University of South Carolina.

4. Sieber, J. E. (1992). *Planning ethically responsible research.* Newbury Park, CA: Sage Publications, 147.

5. Jones, J. H. (1982). *Bad blood: The Tuskegee syphilis experiment.* New York: Free Press.

6. Associated Press Report. (1997, September 18). Experts blast AIDS studies that endanger poor subjects. The State, A15.

7. Sieber, J. E. (1992). *Planning ethically responsible research.* Newbury Park, CA: Sage Publications, 93–94.

8. Milgram, S. (1963). Behavioral study of obedience. *Journal of Abnormal and Social Psychology, 67,* 371–378.

9. Humphreys, L. (1970). *Tearoom trade: Impersonal sex in public places.* Chicago: Aldine Press.

10. Rothman, D. J., & Rothman, S. M. (1984). *The Willowbrook wars.* New York: Harper and Row, 257–295.

11. Associated Press Report. (1993, December 17). Retarded boys given radioactive food in study. *New York Times,* B-16.

12. Health and Medicine. (1994, March 11). UCLA didn't ask schizophrenic patients' consent for experiment. *New York Times,* B-9–B-10.

13. National Association of Social Workers. (1996). Code of Ethics. Washington, DC: NASW Press, VII.

# PART II

# BEGINNING THE RESEARCH PROCESS

# 3

# RESEARCH PROBLEMS
# AND QUESTIONS

As was indicated in Chapter 1, all social work research should begin with the identification of a research problem. At least that is the way research is supposed to work. In their discussion of research problem identification, the authors of another text on research methods emphasize that "the impetus for selecting a topic should come from decisions confronting social service organizations or the information needed to solve practical problems in social welfare."[1] Other authors define a research problem as "an intellectual stimulus calling for an answer in the form of a scientific inquiry."[2] Still another author describes research problems as situations that are characterized by doubt and ignorance and that represent felt difficulties. There is something in the situation that is unknown, and there is a reason for wanting to reduce this doubtfulness.[3] All of these definitions (and those within other texts) differ slightly, but they also have a considerable amount in common.

All of the definitions suggest that a research problem ought to be stated as a declarative, descriptive statement of a condition—never as a question. What else makes all research problems similar, yet different from other kinds of problems? For example, how are social work research problems different from social problems, resource problems, or even personal problems? A social work research problem is a specific type of problem. It is an undesirable condition attributable (at least in part) to a lack of empirical knowledge. Not only is this knowledge gap felt, but there is a desire to fill it. For example, for some social work practitioners, a research problem may be a lack of knowledge needed in order to effectively influence some pending legislation. Or it may be an absence of evidence that a social program is effective. For a social work manager, it may be any knowledge gap that limits that manager's ability to plan, staff, organize, lead, or control.[4] For the social work educator or trainer, it may be a lack of knowledge that could indicate which methods are most effective for teaching the knowledge, values, or skills that students need.

Note that the preceding examples describe problems that are not deficits of individuals. The social workers whose job performance is being hampered are not merely unaware of knowledge that might help them, because they have not bothered to study it. No, the failing is not theirs—the knowledge is not there for them to find because it does not exist. It has not yet been generated.

## Why We Begin with Research Problems

One unfortunate and not uncommon research scenario involves getting ahead of ourselves. As Figure 3.1 suggests, researchers sometimes jump to later steps in the research process without first specifying the exact nature of the research problem and determining that it lends itself to scientific inquiry. Unless tasks of problem identification and specification have been carefully and thoroughly performed, all the other steps in the research process are likely to be problematic. They can be an exercise in frustration and can entail a waste of valuable and scarce resources.

The research problem that is ultimately selected and specified should set the stage for and heavily influence all later steps in the research process. It should never be the other way around, that is, all or part of a research methodology should not be developed and then a problem specified that is appropriate for it. A properly conducted project is an integrated whole from start to finish.[5] The start should always be research problem identification and specification, with all subsequent activities flowing from and clearly relating to the problem that is selected.

Identifying and then specifying research problems might seem like research tasks that can be easily and quickly accomplished. Unfortunately, this is not always the case. Often we know of research problems that we would like to study but have difficulty articulating them in a researchable form. This is true primarily because problems, by their very nature, seem to be perceived in different ways by different people. If there were perfect consensus on exactly what they are, why they exist, and what should be done about them, most problems would have ceased to exist a long time ago!

### FIGURE 3.1 Seven Common Mistakes in Beginning Research

1. Believing that all problems are research problems.
2. Beginning by "knowing" what will be found.
3. Beginning with a hypothesis.
4. Beginning with a research design.
5. Beginning with a data collection instrument.
6. Beginning with a method for statistical analysis.
7. Failing to adequately define and specify the research problem.

Because, for social workers, the identification of a problem often is a call to action, beginning the research process with a problem would seem to be a very obvious thing to do. After all, shouldn't the presence of a problem be the impetus for doing research in the first place? It should. But we must remember two things. First, not every problem, once accurately defined, is suited to research. Second, a problem is not necessarily what it initially appears to be. We will elaborate on these two important points in the discussion that follows.

## Setting Problem Priorities

Not all knowledge gaps that confront the social worker can be regarded as either equally important or equally well suited to the scientific research process. In determining whether a problem can justify the attention and limited research resources of the social worker, certain issues and related questions should be addressed.

In the ideal world of unlimited research resources, any research problem that might be hindering social workers' capacity to help others would be a problem suitable for study. But in the real world, certain problems must be regarded as higher priorities than others. In addition to other questions related to priorities, we must be prepared to ask the basic question: Among those research problems that exist and that are of current concern, which are most in need of a solution?

Identifying a problem as a higher or lower research priority can be a complicated process. In addition, it is not a task that comes naturally or comfortably to many social workers. It seems to go against some of our practice values to have to conclude that, although some problems are very real and are associated with real discomfort to people, they do not justify the expenditure of our limited research resources. It is helpful to remember that, in making this determination, we are not saying that potential research problems of lower priority are unimportant or should be ignored by social workers. We are just acknowledging that in a world of limited research resources, we must get the greatest possible benefit out of our time and efforts. We also must have reasonable assurance that our research will produce knowledge that will be of practical value. What sorts of questions can we ask to help us to objectively assess the research priority of a problem? They might include the following:

*Is the problem really an important one?* Somewhere in the research process, the social work researcher will need to demonstrate that the research problem selected for study ranked high in priority. This is an important issue if a formal proposal must be written and submitted to a potential research sponsor or for review by an IRB (Chapter 2). And after research has been conducted, researchers need to prove to potential critics, as well as to those favorable to their research, that the problems studied were important, more important than others that might have been studied.

The question of what makes one potential research problem more important than another can be complex. It relates to a wide array of factors, such as the scope of the problem, who is affected by it, how badly knowledge is needed, and the potential value of the variety of products that can evolve from the research process that it sets in motion. The question also overlaps somewhat with other priority issues we will discuss.

Sometimes, the real importance of a research problem and the research that examined it cannot be fully appreciated until years after the research has been completed. Sometimes, the fact that the findings of research are widely publicized, widely cited, or widely used seems to retroactively add importance to a research study. Sometimes, a study's importance may relate less to its findings than to some other product of the research. For example, a data collection instrument that is developed in order to better understand a problem and that gains widespread usage in other scientific inquiry may ultimately be considered a research project's greatest contribution to knowledge. It may help to legitimize the researcher's efforts, even if the findings of the original study were of limited value.

It is difficult to assess the ultimate importance of a proposed research problem. How can one envision all possible difficulties that could depreciate the value of the research? Or how can one accurately predict the final judgment of others as to whether the research effort was truly worthwhile? Fortunately, we can use certain guidelines to help us in wrestling with the issue of problem importance. We know that there are certain characteristics of research problems that seem to suggest that they are of more importance than others. For example, problems are likely to be considered significant if they reflect a widely felt and critical knowledge gap or if they relate to a difficulty that affects many people. Some potential research problems also promise to generate specific recommendations rather than highly abstract knowledge. Others are likely to produce by-products that will benefit other researchers conducting scientific inquiry on a wide variety of topics.

*Do we already have enough knowledge about the problem?* Some research problems that initially seem like good candidates for social work research, at least certain aspects of them, have been thoroughly studied. Most knowledge gaps have already been filled. For example, although poverty is indeed a problem in the Western Hemisphere, more research documenting its existence or its effects on social functioning might only confirm what we already know. Perhaps a better choice for a research problem would be one that relates to reasons for the persistence of poverty within areas where resources are adequate to eliminate it. For the social work researcher, it might be more productive to try to gain insight into either the unwillingness of a given community's leaders to acknowledge poverty's existence or the values that may contribute to a reluctance to commit the resources needed to try to alleviate it. Research on either of these problems would not only be likely to generate new knowledge, but also be likely to generate knowledge that could be of immediate use to social work practitioners seeking social change strategies that have high potential for success.

*Are persons in other disciplines as well or better suited to conduct research on the problem?* Social workers may not be the best people to conduct certain types of research. For example, medical social workers are likely to encounter patients with health problems related to the widespread use of a medication that was widely prescribed for use by pregnant women from 1947 to 1971 to prevent miscarriages (diethylstilbestrol, commonly referred to as DES). The drug was later found to be associated with an unusually high rate of certain illnesses among daughters of women who had taken it. The problem of a lack of knowledge about the long-range medical effects of the drug might be a research problem that is more appropriate for study by the biomedical researcher. But there may be other important knowledge gaps that constitute appropriate research opportunities for the social worker. For example, a social worker may well be the best person to conduct research into the apparent problem of daughters of women who took the drug but who are reluctant to take needed medication during their own pregnancies.

*What is the potential for utilization of any findings and recommendations that would be generated by the research?* Who will care, and what is the likelihood that anyone with the power to address the problem will be moved to take recommended action? A study of a research problem that is not likely to result in efforts to alleviate the problem is of relatively little value.

The lack of any positive effect from research frequently results from financial and political obstacles to research utilization. People who are in a position to take action to address the problem may lack either the necessary resources or the value commitment necessary to do what research indicates is needed. Sometimes both obstacles are present. For example, a community might have a problem of dangerous apathy among adolescents regarding the possibility of contracting HIV. The problem could be the impetus for good, worthwhile, methodologically sound research that would both identify the source of the problem and generate recommendations as to how it could be alleviated. But because of certain conditions that are present within the community, research on the problem might be a waste of time given the scarcity of resources. The research is likely to result in recommendations for improved sex education in the schools. But the probability of implementation of any such recommendations might be very small or even zero. It might already be known that a school board already operating with a deficit budget might be unable to find the money to spend to develop and teach any new courses. Or it might already be common knowledge that the powerful, fundamentalist minister who chairs the school board would be almost certain to intimidate other board members into blocking what he has already publicly described as instruction in sinning. Despite the apparent need for research to study the problem, the problem may have to be regarded as low priority because of the likelihood that research on it would generate recommendations that have little hope of implementation.

*Am I interested in studying the problem?* The development of knowledge to benefit social workers and their clients can be an exciting activity. But research is also hard work. Certain necessary tasks can become very tedious at times. Not all potential research problems are of equal interest to us. Even a general interest in a problem may not be sufficient to carry a researcher through times when necessary but less-than-exciting tasks must be performed. For example, entering research data collected from hundreds of participants into a computer, even when we are curious about the findings of our research, can be pretty boring. If we have no particular interest in what we found, it can be a truly dull job.

Is there a temptation for social workers to deliberately choose to study problems about which they have little interest? Unfortunately, yes. Various pressures from supervisors and higher-level managers sometimes make it difficult to say no. On other occasions, the lure of grant money can help to convince them that they might be more interested in problems than they really are.

Conducting research on a problem where there is no real interest is usually a big mistake. It has the potential to negatively affect the quality of the research. It also can have a negative effect on the researcher for future scientific inquiry. All other factors being equal, a problem about which a potential researcher is interested and concerned should have higher priority than one in which the researcher's interest results primarily from political or financial motives.

*What logistical obstacles are present?* Some problems may present major logistical obstacles to their study through the use of scientific methods. It is probably correct to state that any problem can be studied. However, some, by their very nature, are so problematic or would require so many variations from the accepted scientific methods for studying them that the results would lack credibility. In determining if a problem is researchable on a practical and logistical basis, the following questions can be asked.

*Is the problem just too large?* Some problems are so widespread and pervasive that they would be totally unmanageable as the focus for a single research study. It might be necessary to break off some small piece of the problem for study. For example, ageism within North American social organizations is a problem of such large scope that most social work researchers would lack the budget and other resources necessary to study it effectively. (Research almost invariably ends up costing more than anticipated.) However, social work researchers with limited resources might be able to design research to study some aspect of the problem, for example, the discriminatory methods used for advertising supervisory job openings in public organizations within their own state.

*Can the needed measurement be accomplished?* As we shall discuss in more detail a little later, good measurement is absolutely essential to sound research. But some things are more easily measured than others. For example, behaviors, generally speaking, are more easily measured than attitudes or values. Although researchers have made great progress in the development of measurement for the latter in recent years, measuring many attitudes that might be of interest to us remains an imprecise art.

Treatment success or the lack of it, something that relates to many potential research problems of interest to social workers, provides special measurement difficulties. The success or failure rate in a job training program can be fairly easily determined by counting how many graduates find and keep related jobs. However, the success or failure rate associated with a particular approach to marriage counseling can be much more difficult to ascertain. Was divorce indicative of success or failure? How are we to interpret the fact that a couple voluntarily terminated counseling? They could have stopped seeing the social worker because most of their difficulties had disappeared or because they perceived that they were getting no help! Indicators of successful or unsuccessful treatment in such instances are limited to such untrustworthy data as notations in a case record or follow-up phone calls. Thus, measurement might be little more than a judgment call.

If studying a problem would require the measurement of certain phenomena that seem to defy their measurement, the entire problem may not be regarded as researchable, and no amount of research can provide needed answers. A classic, historical example of a nonresearchable problem is the debate that preoccupied some theologians several centuries ago. The problem of not knowing how many angels can dance on the head of a pin was not a candidate for scientific research then, and it would not be now. Some contemporary social work problems—for example, a lack of understanding of why some physicians seem to undervalue the professional education of social workers—may be only slightly more researchable than medieval philosophical questions. Physicians' respect for social workers' education might be so difficult to measure that the problem, if it is indeed a real one, may not be able to be studied. Besides, it may not be a high research priority, given the other criteria that we suggested earlier.

*Do I have the necessary skills and expertise to conduct research on the problem?* Specialization is characteristic of people who conduct scientific inquiry. Some researchers are especially adept at certain specialized research tasks, such as library searches, interviewing, questionnaire construction, or statistical analysis of data, and less competent to perform other tasks. Although it is possible to learn to do what is required or to hire a consultant to do it, this can represent a very costly use of limited research resources. If a particular problem would suggest skill and expertise not currently possessed by a potential researcher—for example, the use of statistical analysis that cannot be contracted out or otherwise accessed—the problem may as well be considered unresearchable. Similarly, if the researcher's knowledge and skills lie in quantitative research methods, and the problem seems to require a more qualitative design or feminist research methods (see Chapters 7 and 8), it might be best left to someone else to study.

*Will I have access to needed data?* Some problems that would seem like excellent candidates for research by social workers may not be researchable because the information that is needed to study them is not accessible. For example, sealed court records and information about patients with certain medical diagnoses are safeguarded by law. Thus, they cannot be used for research purposes. A problem that could be studied only with access to information that is likely to be beyond reach should probably be regarded as unresearchable, at least until other ways of obtaining needed information can be found.

Inquiry into the availability of research participants and required information from records should be made prior to the selection of a problem for study. Some very promising research studies have reached a costly dead end when researchers found out too late that they would not be allowed to conduct interviews with clients or staff or to review and record data from records that were assumed to be readily available. Similarly, some social workers have just assumed that it would be acceptable to tape interviews with research participants but found out belatedly that permission was denied.

## Identifying the *Real* Problem

As we noted earlier, a careful identification and specification of a researchable problem has a way of keeping all the other steps in the research process on track. But ambiguity about the problem can haunt the researcher at many junctures in the research process and can result in a considerable amount of wasted effort. In this way, research is similar to social work intervention with individuals, families, groups, organizations, or communities. Much valuable time of social work practitioners has been wasted because they failed to obtain a clear understanding of the problem or accepted at face value the presenting complaint of a client or client group. In the role of researcher, this "barking up the wrong tree" phenomenon can be especially costly.

Several years ago, one of the authors of this text was involved in an extended discussion that attempted to specify the research problem for a proposed project.[6] The process took several hours and produced a considerable amount of frustration. But the time was well spent. The process was absolutely essential prior to the beginning of other steps in the research process. We will use this real-life example to illustrate how problem identification can be a difficult but necessary exercise.

The director of a county public welfare organization proposed that the researchers (a group of social work graduate students) might conduct research on a problem that he had identified in his organization. He had noticed that during the past year child protection workers were receiving many more reports of possible child abuse by local professionals than in previous years. A very large percentage of the cases were never opened for services because the worker assigned to investigate had determined that they were unfounded. From the director's perspective, there was a problem of inefficient use of workers' time. They were spending much of their day dealing with reports where no abuse had taken place, while not having enough time to devote to those cases where abuse was probable. Simply stated, from his perspective, the problem was too many unfounded cases.

It soon became evident that too many unfounded cases may have represented an administrative problem for the director (he was being questioned about it by his superior), but it was not a clear enough statement of the problem for the students to design and implement research based on it. Further discussion revealed that the administrator's perception of the problem, while real for him, may have indicated a misunderstanding of what really was occurring. After extended discussion with him, the students compiled a list of five other possible research problems. They included

1. Social workers might be making too many inappropriate referrals.
2. The social workers' behavior might relate to their inadequate training.
3. There might be too much missed child abuse by overworked child protection workers (erroneous unfounded conclusions).
4. There might be a tendency on the part of workers not to want to see the existence of abuse that had occurred, for fear that a determination of founded would result in more work for staff.
5. Some workers might be more likely than others to perceive that abuse had taken place.

Through continued discussion with the director, all but one of the preceding possible problem descriptions was eliminated. The great majority of the reports were apparently quite appropriate, given what the literature says about possible indicators of abuse. Their increased number was probably related in part to recent training that had been completed in various referring organizations and institutions. The training had emphasized recognition of conditions that might suggest that abuse had taken place and that suggested that a referral was in order.

Although some instances of child abuse might have been missed, the director had no evidence to believe that this was the case, at least not any more so than in previous years. He noted that, based on recent data within the professional literature, it was impossible to know whether the current rate of founded versus unfounded cases among his child protection workers was high, low, or about normal.

It also would be very difficult to measure accurately whether a case determination had been correct or incorrect, a measurement obstacle (see previous discussion) that was sufficient to preclude giving serious consideration to the third statement as the research problem. It was possible that the ratio of founded versus unfounded cases was about on target, but that the cases were being categorized incorrectly! There was simply no way to know. It also was learned that statement 4 was unlikely to be a real problem in the organization. A procedure existed whereby a case with a determination of founded was referred for follow-up services by another worker in another division of the organization. Thus, it resulted in no additional work for the worker who made the determination.

Based on the director's observations and a quick count of records, some workers seemed to have a much higher rate of unfounded determinations than others over the previous three years. Given the random assignment of cases and the large number of cases seen, such a disparity should not have existed. The director feared that the worker assigned to a referral might have more to do with the determination of founded or unfounded than the facts of the case. Consequently, statement 5 was adopted as the research problem.

To have precipitously used either the director's original statement of the problem or any of the first four problem statements proposed by the research group would have produced difficulties later on in the research. Much effort would have been wasted, only to ultimately arrive at problem statement 5 or something similar to it. The time spent in clarifying the exact nature of the research problem was a productive and necessary exercise. It improved the overall efficiency of the scientific inquiry by saving much more time than it consumed. The development of an accurate and workable problem statement provided a clear reference point that guided the rest of the research process.

## Selecting Research Questions

Having settled on a problem statement, researchers then select one or more broad research questions. Researchers generally select one or a few general research questions for study prior to immersing themselves in a review of relevant literature. The decision is not irreversible. Sometimes slight modifications are made, depending on what the literature reveals. Occasionally, a question may be dropped altogether and another one substituted. For example, reports of others' research may reveal that an answer to the original question cannot be obtained for some reason or that a reasonably definitive answer to it has already been obtained. Figure 3.2 is an example of some research problem statements and some broad related questions that might be asked. The questions are just examples. They might (or might not) be selected as the research questions that would form the focus of the research.

The broad research questions that ultimately are selected keep a researcher on track. For example, whether one is deciding what data must be collected, how to collect them, what statistical analysis to perform, or which research findings are most important to disseminate, the same question can be asked: How does that bear on the research question and contribute to its answer? Answers that can pass this test suggest an appropriate use of researchers' time.

What is the connection between a research problem statement and a research question? How do they differ? Researchers choose to focus on certain research questions because they believe that, if answers to them can be found, those answers will help to alleviate the research problem. Even if answers cannot be found, the knowledge obtained through the process of seeking them generally provides increased insight into the problem itself. Unlike a research problem statement, a research question always is followed by a question mark.

What are the characteristics of a good research question? What makes one potential research question a better choice as the focus of our research than another one? Is it better to have just one or two research questions or many different ones? Selection of research questions, like the selection of a research problem, is often a matter of priorities.

Very few research problems can be studied in their entirety in a single research effort. There are many different gaps in knowledge related to any research problem that could serve as the focus for the research. Each can produce one or more research questions. But they cannot all be studied. Obviously, some selection must occur before the research process can proceed. Researchers employ

## FIGURE 3.2 Some Research Problem Statements and Related Questions

**Problem: The parents of children who die while committing violent crimes are also victims. However, we know little about how the parents experience this tragedy.**

Q1. How do these parents perceive potential sources of support in their time of loss?
Q2. What obstacles to the grief process do they perceive?
Q3. What feelings do they have toward the families of the victims of their son's or daughter's violence?

**Problem: Homicide by children eight to twelve is increasing. Social workers working with children this age often hear them talk about wanting to kill someone. There is little available knowledge to help them decide how to respond.**

Q1. What behaviors of children immediately prior to homicidal acts might have indicated that the acts might occur?
Q2. What common experiences exist in the social histories of homicidal children?
Q3. What common experiences exist in the current life situations of homicidal children?
Q4. What have been the experiences of social workers who notified authorities when their young clients talked about homicide?

**Problem: Welfare reform has dramatically reduced the number of families receiving public financial assistance. However, we have little knowledge about the impact of welfare reform on those people who are no longer on welfare rolls.**

Q1. Have those no longer receiving welfare assistance found good jobs, or are they now relying on other institutions for financial assistance?
Q2. What has been the effect on children of former AFDC recipients who went to work after their benefits ran out?
Q3. Have day care facilities increased to adequately meet the needs of an increased number of working mothers?
Q4. How much have a strong economy and a low national unemployment rate (rather than welfare reform) contributed to the reduction in numbers of welfare recipients?

certain criteria to help identify those potential research questions that are likely to be most productive to study. Let us look at some of the criteria that are applied.

We observed in the previous two chapters that all scientific knowledge is tentative by definition. But the researcher still hopes to generate knowledge that is as definitive as possible. Therefore, as a general rule, it is better to do a good, thorough job of studying one or two research questions than it is to do a more superficial job of inquiring into the answers to many different ones.

Many of the criteria that are applied in selecting broad research questions for study are the same ones that we examined in selecting a research problem. The following questions are often helpful, both for limiting the number of questions to be studied and for producing a clearer understanding of just why the research is being conducted:

1. Which potential research questions would be most likely to contribute
   - New knowledge?
   - Knowledge for more effective practice intervention?
   - Knowledge that can be disseminated?
   - Knowledge that will make a difference?
   - Knowledge that other researchers will find useful?

2. Which potential research questions are most likely to have an answer that
   - Is attainable?
   - Would contribute the most to alleviation of the problem?

3. Which potential research questions would require
   - Measurement of phenomena that can be easily measured?
   - Access to information that is likely to be available?
   - The use of research methods that are considered ethical?
   - The knowledge and expertise possessed by the researcher?

Each of the preceding questions reflects an important issue in the selection of a research question. To see how they might come into play in the selection of a research question, let us return to the example used in our discussion of problem specification. Having settled on the exact problem that was to be the basis for their research (some child protection workers were believed to have a much higher rate of unfounded cases than others), the students began to identify possible research questions, the answers to which might help to explain and/or alleviate the problem. Some of the many possible ones that were seriously considered included the following:

1. What laws and regulations govern child protection workers' decisions about whether a case is determined to be founded? Could ambiguity contained in them be producing different reporting rates (founded versus unfounded) among workers? Could recent changes in reporting procedures somehow be affecting whether a case is regarded as founded?
2. Could different working conditions in some way help to explain the different rates?
3. Could differences in education and training of workers somehow relate to the different rates?
4. Do clients perceive that some workers are more conscientious in their investigation than others?
5. How great an influence is supervision in worker determinations regarding reports of suspected abuse?
6. Are community professionals somehow influencing the decisions of some workers more than others? If so, how is this occurring?
7. Do some workers perceive rewards for either founded or unfounded cases that other workers do not perceive?
8. How might work experience of the child protection worker affect the way that a case is perceived?

9. Does burnout somehow contribute to the different rates of founded cases among workers?
10. Are the different demographic characteristics of workers (for example, age, race, sex, or parenthood) related to their determinations?

What can we observe about the preceding questions? First, all relate to the research problem in the same way. Each, if answered, could contribute to its alleviation or at least give us a better idea as to the best way to address it. All the questions also relate to factors that may influence the decision making of child protection workers. However, each suggests a very different focus of inquiry. Note, too, that all of them are stated in a way that suggests that the cause for the different rates is unknown. This kind of noncommittal wording is very appropriate for this stage of the research process. It suggests that researchers are keeping an open mind and are not beginning the research with any preexisting biases.

All of the questions are quite broad. As we shall discuss later in this chapter, the tasks of refining broad research questions, making them more specific, and, when possible, even proposing tentative answers to them all come a little later in the process.

Because researchers hope to be able to acquire as much relevant knowledge as possible in a research study, it is desirable to select those questions that can be combined with other possible questions, whenever possible. As long as the research does not become too unmanageable or lose focus, combining questions can be an efficient use of time. It is exactly what occurred in the child abuse research that we have been describing.

Most of the original questions (including many that are not in the preceding list) were rejected for reasons related to the issues that we proposed earlier. For example, question 4 could not be examined because it was learned that the county Board of Social Services would not permit the collection of needed data from clients. Even if data collection from clients had been allowed, it was estimated that the number of clients who would be willing to be interviewed or to provide data in some other way would be small and that they probably would not be representative of cases in the organization. All the workers were found to share the same supervisor and to work under virtually identical working conditions, so questions 5 and 2 were discarded. Question 6 was summarily answered without the need for further study. It was learned that a random method of case assignment was employed.

Question 1 was concluded to be just a little too complex to study within the time available and with available resources. To study it would have required extensive interviews with the workers and the development of methods to test their job knowledge. The director stated that he could not permit workers to take enough time off from their regular duties to participate in a series of extended interviews or other similar forms of data collection. The use of question 6 also presented logistical obstacles. To answer it would have entailed collecting data from more than 100 individuals in the community who frequently make referrals, a formidable and costly endeavor. In light of the small amount of knowledge related to the problem that would be generated, the effort involved did not seem justified.

Some variation of question 10 appeared to be the best choice. The answer to it seemed obtainable. No one in the group had ever seen it discussed within current professional literature. What's more, questions 3, 7, and 9 could easily be answered along with it by adding a short personal interview designed to collect some of the needed data. The research question was restated as: Are characteristics of workers related to their determinations of whether a case is judged to be founded? The question was quite general, but it was specific enough to guide the student researchers during the next step in the research process: the review of literature.

## Summary

In this chapter, we examined the earliest tasks in the research process: problem identification and selection of broad research questions. We devoted an entire chapter to these tasks because we regard them as critical to a thoughtful, organized approach to knowledge building.

First, a distinction was made between problems in general and potential social work research problems. A research problem is a gap in knowledge that interferes with the functioning of social workers. However, not all gaps in knowledge of this kind are good candidates for research. A problem is considered to be researchable based on the priority issues that were discussed and its suitability for the application of scientific methods.

One or more research questions evolve from and are closely related to a social work research problem. If answers to them can be found, those answers will help to reduce the knowledge gap that constitutes the research problem and thus have potential to alleviate the problem. We offered guidelines to assist in selecting the best research questions to study from among those that might be studied. A continuation of an earlier example illustrated how a long list of possible research questions can be reduced to a manageable number.

## References

1.  Rubin, A., & Babbie, E. (1993). *Research methods for social work* (2nd ed.). Pacific Grove, CA: Brooks/Cole, 99.
2.  Frankfort-Nachmias, C., & Nachmias, D. (1992). *Research methods in the social sciences* (4th ed.). New York: St. Martin's Press, 51.
3.  Rothery, M. (1993). Problems, questions, and hypotheses. In R. M. Grinnell, Jr. (Ed.), *Social work research and evaluation* (4th ed.). Itasca, IL: F. E. Peacock, 17.

4. Weinbach, R. (1998). *The social worker as manager* (2nd ed.). Boston, MA: Allyn & Bacon, 8.
5. Shontz, F. (1986). *Fundamentals of research in the behavioral sciences.* Washington, DC: American Psychiatric Press, 27.
6. Bellomy, P., Berstein, H., Bickley, S., et al. (1989). Factors Affecting Child Protection Workers' Decision-Making in Sumter County. Unpublished MSW Research Project. Columbia, SC: University of South Carolina, College of Social Work.

# 4

# USING EXISTING KNOWLEDGE

Reference to existing knowledge can and frequently does occur at any point in the research process. For example, when researchers select and specify a problem or choose from among possible research questions, they generally seek out and use existing knowledge. Answering questions about how widespread a problem is or whether some phenomenon is easily measurable may require a quick trip to the library or an Internet search. Similarly, after data have been collected, they can best be interpreted and the research findings put into perspective with reference to what others have learned and published on the topic.

## What Is the Review of Literature?

A review of literature is both an activity and a product. It is an activity that occupies most of the attention of the researcher for a while, most often after broad research questions have been selected. It is the phase of the research process when researchers immerse themselves in any existing knowledge that may relate to their research questions.

Later, when a research report is written, it generally contains a separate section or chapter (usually called "Review of the Literature," "Relevant Literature," or something similar). This is a written summary of what researchers learned in their examination of the work of others and contains those findings and ideas that influenced their thinking and methods for conducting their research.

Even new problems or ones that for one reason or another have received little or no attention in the past always bear some similarity to those that already have been studied. Knowledge drawn from research on related topics can be productively brought to bear. For example, during the late 1980s and early 1990s, the problem of date rape and our lack of understanding of its causes, incidence, or impact belatedly received widespread attention. Research on the topic began. Although there initially was little or no empirically based knowledge available on the specific problem, a review of the literature on many related topic areas provided knowledge that was extremely useful for acquiring both insight into date rape and how best to design research to study the problem. Research on this newly identified problem was greatly facilitated by an examination of reports of previous studies on literally hundreds of diverse topics. Each made a valuable contribution that saved researchers countless hours of inquiry. Among the knowledge areas examined were

- Cultural dating practices.
- Male patterns of aggression.
- Spousal rape.
- Domestic violence.
- Law enforcement and judicial handling of rape accusations.
- Substance abuse and interpersonal violence.
- Historical definitions of rape.
- Intergender violence.
- Gender validation rituals of males.
- Media portrayal of males and females.
- Spouse battery.
- Incest and sexual abuse.

A new problem, our lack of understanding of unwillingness of sexually active teenagers at risk for teen pregnacy to use free contraceptive injections, was identified in the late 1990s. Because such injections (and contraceptive implants) were not even available until the mid-1990s, it would seem on the surface that a researcher wishing to study the problem would be in the dark. But there is plenty of literature on related topics that would address the problem and questions that relate to it. Related topics might include

- History of contraception.
- Success rates among various methods of contraception.
- Current attitudes about use of contraception among young women.
- Current attitudes about use of contraception among young men.
- Fear of injections among young women.
- Responsibility of males and females for contraception.
- Cultural differences in attitudes about teen pregnancy.
- Gender validation rituals of males.
- Obstacles to use of public health services.
- Societal rewards and penalties for teen pregnancy.
- Relationship between injections and future fertility.

For every research problem and for its related research questions there is a body of knowledge that would be helpful for the researchers who study them. Whenever researchers report that little is known about the problem or that no relevant literature exists on the topic, it is an indication that (1) they probably do not understand the nature and purpose of the literature review or (2) they probably did not invest sufficient energy and time in this important step in the research process. There is no research problem and no research questions for which there is no existing relevant knowledge. Although it is conceivable that no one may have previously studied the exact questions selected, there is *always* knowledge available that could help to enlighten and inform the researcher.

## Purpose of the Review of Literature

A literature review draws its focus from the broad research questions that have been selected. It has several complementary objectives. They are summarized in Figure 4.1.

In a general sense, the literature review serves to put the researcher's current efforts into perspective. It creates a foundation for them based on existing related knowledge. It also suggests the most appropriate way to further expand what is already known. A literature review is a recognition that knowledge building is a cumulative process that goes on over long periods of time, a principle to which we will return in future chapters.

### FIGURE 4.1   How a Literature Review Is Used

Before data collection, to
- Learn more about the history, origin, and scope of the research problem.
- Learn what methodologies have been applied successfully and unsuccessfully to study related research questions.
- Learn what answers already exist for general research questions.
- Identify variables that will need to be measured and learn what methods already are available to measure them.
- Decide what is the best way to acquire needed data, who or what might best provide them, and how best to analyze them.
- Refine and better specify research questions and, when indicated, propose answers to them in the form of hypotheses.
- Select the appropriate statistical analyses to be used.

After data collection, to
- Attempt to explain differences between current findings and existing knowledge.
- Identify ways in which current findings are consistent with and support existing knowledge.
- Specify how current findings advance knowledge.
- Develop theories and formulate hypotheses (in qualitative studies).

# Potential Sources of "Literature"

For researchers, the term *literature* denotes much more than just the printed word. A more descriptive term might actually be *relevant knowledge*. As we shall see, it can be found in many different places and forms.

What qualifies a source of information for inclusion in what we have called "the review of literature"? It should enlighten and inform the researcher (and the reader of a research report) about the research problem and/or question. It also should be credible. The issue of credibility is often debatable. Even the best of sources are sometimes vulnerable to political or economic influences.

The most common sources (some of them more credible than others) for a literature review include (but are not limited to) the following:

- Standard reference materials
- Computer-accessible databases
- The Internet
- Books
- Articles in professional journals
- Personal interviews with authorities
- Research reports and monographs
- Presentations at conferences and symposia
- Content of workshops
- Public documents and records of public gatherings
- Newspapers
- Radio and television broadcasts
- Magazines and periodicals

## *Standard Reference Materials*

For relevant knowledge that is available in written form, the various abstracts publications (for example, *Social Work Abstracts, Sociological Abstracts, Psychological Abstracts, Dissertation Abstracts International,* or *SAGE Urban Studies Abstracts*) are always a good place to start a literature search. Listed by topic area as well as by author, they provide a good overview of where recent publications on various topics can be found. Quotations from abstracts publications should not be used in the report of a review. They are not meant to be a substitute for the original source, just a convenient way to learn about the existence of a publication that may (or may not) prove to be helpful.

Other standard reference materials actually contain facts and thus can themselves be cited in a report of a review of literature. Generally, they tend to possess higher credibility than, for example, data obtained from the Internet (see the following sections) because they have undergone a more thorough review and verification process. However, they often tend to be fairly general and can become dated fairly quickly. They may be called almanacs, encyclopedias, atlases, statistical abstracts, directories, annuals, yearbooks, compendia, or some similar title. Two such sources commonly used by social workers to get their literature search under way are the NASW publications *Encyclopedia of Social Work*[1] and *Social Work Almanac.*[2] Such standard reference materials are a good place to begin a search of the literature, but because of the breadth of topics covered, they rarely provide the depth of coverage needed. To accomplish the objectives of a literature review, it often is necessary to venture into other areas of the literature that are more current or detailed, but also more suspect.

## Computer-Accessible Databases

Progress in technology for the storage, retrieval, and transfer of information is rapidly escalating the amount of knowledge that is accessible to researchers. It can be an excellent source, often quite reliable, and it is becoming ever more comprehensive.

Most university libraries now possess extensive databases that are electronically accessible through CD-ROMs. Although in the past they contained mostly descriptive information, such as census data, they are increasingly being expanded to contain much more, including the findings of research conducted almost anywhere on earth. CD-ROMs contain thousands of journal articles, book chapters, and dissertation abstracts within a given discipline. For example, the National Clearinghouse on Child Abuse and Neglect offers social organizations and institutions a CD-ROM database on child abuse and neglect cases within the United States. There also are CD-ROM databases for certain government documents and major newspapers. CD-ROM databases are updated on a regular basis, typically either yearly or quarterly.

CD-ROM databases are accessed electronically through computer terminals. Appropriate citations and abstracts are located through an electronic search process by specifying key words. Sources thus located are viewed on the computer screen and can be printed out in hard copy if desired. Conducting an electronic literature search is becoming a very user-friendly task. Although procedures vary somewhat by database and institution, generally once one has conducted one CD-ROM search, others are quite simple and can be highly productive. Like standard reference materials, computerized databases often are used early in the literature review process. They provide an excellent overview of what is out there.

Even various abstracts publications (see the preceding discussion on standard reference material), such as *Social Work Abstracts* (SWAB), *Sociofile,* and *PsychLIT,* are now available on CD-ROM. There also are dozens of others that address particular specializations within social work and related disciplines.

## The Internet

Increasingly, the Internet is providing a popular choice as a source of existing knowledge. Its easy accessibility and the breadth of information contained on it can greatly expedite a literature search. Unlike standard reference materials that often are out of date before they are in print, data on the Internet can be updated as frequently as is necessary. The ease with which knowledge can be put on the Internet is, at the same time, its greatest weakness. Individuals can put anything they want on it—no verification is required. Freedom of speech also permits freedom to play loosely with facts or to just plain fabricate.

If the Internet is so vulnerable to misinformation, why do we include it as a source of literature? Along with totally unreliable sources, it also contains some very useful ones for the social work researcher. Many of the other sources of literature described elsewhere in this chapter are now accessible via the Internet (for example, the *Congressional Record*); more undoubtedly will follow. Some websites are specifically dedicated to facilitating access to reliable knowledge for social workers. For example, a common place to begin searching the Web for resources related to social work practice or education is the frequently visited Social Work Access Network (SWAN). It is a popular link to many other Internet sites (also administered by dedicated social work practitioners and academicians) that are generally acknowledged to be reliable sources of knowledge. SWAN also offers a listing of websites for social work journals. The links include some with full text articles (from electronic journals) but also some links containing just abstracts or tables of contents.

Websites come and go rapidly on the Internet, and addresses are also subject to change. Thus, we will avoid the temptation to provide specific URLs. When this book was written, UnCover[3] was gaining in popularity among social work students and professors. It was free and very user-friendly. However, it will undoubtedly be replaced by other sites as they are developed and as older ones lose favor.

## Books and Articles in Professional Journals

The professional literature of a field (for example, articles within refereed social work professional journals or the books published by major commercial publishers and reviewed in journals such as *Social Work* or *Journal of Social Work Education*) usually represent a sizable and important portion of the knowledge that is brought to bear on a research question. Generally, it has undergone a peer review process that, although no guarantee of scholarliness, at least suggests that others think that it is worthy of publication. However, even these sources cannot always be trusted and must be examined carefully.

Journals in social work and related fields have proliferated in recent years. Some publications that purport to be professional journals are not refereed; that is, they do not use a blind review process that ensures that the name of the author or a prestigious affiliation will not influence publication decisions. Some of those that are refereed now receive so few submissions that they publish the majority of all that are received.

It sometimes seems as if the topic of a journal article relating to an issue that is popular or its use of a particular research method may have had more to do with its publication than its scholarliness. Sometimes the findings of research may be a major factor in the decision to publish. Undoubtedly some findings are more popular than others, especially if they are consistent with popular opinion or seem to be supportive of our profession rather than critical of it.

Similarly, just because a fact is in a book in print, it cannot necessarily be construed as trustworthy. It may not have undergone rigorous review and scrutiny. Even major textbook publishers have to focus on potential sales and other factors when they make the decision to publish (or not to publish) a book. Checks on the accuracy of the content often are delegated to a few academicians who receive only minimal compensation for their reviews and who may be less than thorough in their efforts. There are also vanity presses that will publish virtually any material in book form (including a professor's course notes and other writings) if the author is willing to pay enough to become a published author.

In certain forms of research, other considerations must be used so that the literature informs rather than misleads researchers and other readers of their reports. When a researcher is conducting a study with a different ethnic or cultural group or within a cross-cultural context, literature that helps the researcher to better understand the manifestation of the target problem or research issue within that particular cultural framework is especially useful. Additional effort may be required to locate literature written by indigenous social scientists, social work researchers, or practitioners who share an interest in the research topic.

If the literature is written in a foreign language, English translations will need to be found or undertaken if the work is considered critical to understanding the problem being investigated. Bilingual and bicultural students in the helping professions at nearby universities may be a good resource for both identifying relevant literature and for translation. International and ethnic-specific journals in the fields of social work, psychology, social welfare policy, education, health, family studies, and child welfare are excellent resources. Figure 4.2 describes some of the best of these.

## FIGURE 4.2 Scholarly Journals with Ethnic or Cross-Cultural Content

**African Americans**

*Journal of Black Psychology* Articles that promote the understanding of the experiences and behavior of black populations. This includes empirical research reports, discussion of current literature, and original theoretical analyses of data from research studies or programs in the areas of cognition, personality, social behavior, psychological functioning, child development, education, and clinical application. Sage Publications, Thousand Oaks, CA.

*Journal of Black Studies* Interdisciplinary journal of analytical discussions of issues related to persons of African descent in the United States, Africa, and the Caribbean, covering a wide range of social science questions. Sage Publications, Thousand Oaks, CA.

*Continued*

FIGURE  4.2  *Continued*

**Asian, Pacific Islanders**

*Amerasia Journal*  National interdisciplinary journal of scholarship, criticism, and literature on Asian and Pacific Americans. Asian American Studies Center, University of California, Los Angeles.

*Asian American and Pacific Islander Journal of Health*  Journal devoted to Asian/ Pacific–American health issues containing research reports written by scholars and practitioners. Asian American and Pacific Islander Health Promotion Center, Dublin, OH.

**Hispanics**

*Aztlan-International Journal of Chicano Studies Research*  Biannual, interdisciplinary refereed journal that serves as a forum for research and essays related to the Mexican population. Its focus is critical analysis, research, theory, and methodology in the study of Mexicans in the United States and Mexico. UCLA Chicano Studies Research Center, University of California, Los Angeles.

**Native Americans**

*Journal of American Indian Education*  Scholarly articles directly related to the education of North American Indians and Alaska Natives, with an emphasis on basic and applied research. Center for Indian Education, Arizona State University.

**Cross-Cultural**

*International Journal of Intercultural Relations*  Quarterly journal dedicated to advancing knowledge and understanding of theory, practice, and research in intergroup relations. The contents encompass theoretical developments, field-based evaluations of training techniques, empirical discussions of cultural similarities and differences, and critical descriptions of new training approaches. Elsevier Science, Ltd., Kidlington, Oxford, UK.

*Journal of Cross-Cultural Psychology*  Publishes papers that focus on the interrelationships between culture and psychological processes that result from either cross-cultural comparative research or results from other types of research concerning the ways in which culture (and related concepts such as ethnicity) affect the thinking and behavior of individuals, as well as how individual thought and behavior define and reflect aspects of culture. Sage Publications, Thousand Oaks, CA.

*Journal of Multicultural Social Work*  Focuses on racial and ethnicity issues within the field of social work. The latest research and theory are provided on social work issues, practice, and problems. The journal is designed to help social work practitioners understand the underlying cultural issues involved in working with diverse ethnic groups. Haworth Press, Binghamton, NY.

## Personal Interviews with Authorities

Some of the other sources in the list on page 66 should be approached with even more caution. Unless they are examined critically, researchers can be misled by assertions that are questionable, while simultaneously damaging the credibility of their own research efforts. Sometimes they should be included, and other times they should be omitted. Often the questions must be asked: Where do I draw the line? and What constitutes usable knowledge and what does not?

The reader will recall that authorities were one of the nonscientific sources of knowledge that we described as untrustworthy in Chapter 1. So why would we include them as a possible source of knowledge? Because sometimes authorities *do* know something important. The principal problem surrounding content drawn from interviews with authorities is lack of consensus regarding who is an authority. Unfortunately, in some parts of Western society, authority frequently has been assumed to reside in all individuals with certain academic credentials (or in anyone who travels a distance of more than fifty miles and carries a briefcase). For the social work researcher, an authority whose comments are worth quoting in a literature review is someone who has in-depth knowledge of some aspect of the research problem, preferably acquired through the use of scientific methods. This greatly limits the number of authorities who should be quoted in a report of a review of literature.

A researcher in colonial America might have had some justification for quoting a member of the clergy on virtually any topic, because the limited amount of available knowledge was concentrated within this profession. But today's researcher should not make any assumptions about any individual's claims to knowledge based solely on academic or other formal credentials. There are no Renaissance men or women alive today who have knowledge in virtually every area. It would be erroneous to assume that, for example, a quotation from any physician is appropriate on a medical question or that one from a lawyer will provide needed knowledge on a legal one. The physician may see primarily older patients; hence, her position on a problem related to child rearing may have no empirical basis and may even be distorted through interaction with a biased sample of patients. The lawyer may specialize in contract law and may speak more out of personal opinion than out of knowledge in discussing needed changes in child abuse reporting laws. This is not an indictment of these or other professions; it is only a recognition that the base of knowledge within most professional fields (including social work) and even their subspecialties has grown dramatically during the past century, to the point where no one can possibly know it all.

Use of a few, carefully chosen quotations from interviews with authorities in the review of literature section of a research report usually will not harm the credibility of the researcher's efforts. On the contrary, it may suggest balance and thoroughness in the final product. However, it might be wise to prevent any possible challenges to the credibility of authorities by including brief descriptions of the source of their expertise in the narrative. For example, a descriptive statement such as "one medical researcher, who has conducted National Institute of Mental Health (NIMH)–funded research on the possible relationship between the use of lithium and suicide among young men, has concluded that . . ." would help to justify why that physician was cited in the literature review section of a research report.

## Research Reports and Monographs

Research reports and monographs generally are intended to be honest communications of a researcher's methods and findings. Although the findings are only as good as the methods used to produce them, the fact that a researcher's methods are open to public critique and the possibility of replication increases the likelihood that a report or monograph will be credible. Of course, if the research was funded by some organization or interest group that may have exerted undue influence over what was found and/or reported, such sources also cannot be trusted. For example, the credibility of research findings about the health effects of cigarette smoking is generally low when the research has been conducted by researchers employed by American cigarette manufacturers.

## Presentations at Conferences and Symposia

There is a great amount of knowledge disseminated at conferences and symposia. There is also a good amount of unsubstantiated opinion and misinformation shared. A presentation may be selected using a blind review process, but this is not always the case. Often, the reputation of the presenter or the topic (if it is a popular one) is a major factor in its selection. Frequently, a conference presentation may have no empirical basis at all. It may be little more than a show-and-tell description of what the presenter has done and why he or she thinks it was good.

Most presentations at annual conferences, such as those sponsored by the NASW, the CSWE, or the Child Welfare League of America, have undergone a fairly rigorous screening procedure. Only a small percentage of proposals submitted are accepted for presentation. But the proposals usually consist of a brief abstract that is reviewed by volunteers who may have little interest in the topic and may not have the knowledge and skill to review the quality of a presentation on it. These gatherings also give program space to invited speakers whose expertise in a subject area has been recognized by one or more members of their planning committee. Personal friendships, quid pro quos, or other political concerns sometimes enter into the decision to invite these professionals.

Many other professional gatherings that call themselves national and international conferences and symposia have far less credibility. (After all, any group can describe its conference as "national" or "international" if it chooses.) Some of the most suspect of these consist of a small group of individuals who share some specialized interest. They get together annually to present to each other (sometimes on the same topic as the previous year) at geographically desirable locations. Participants take turns hosting the annual gathering and inviting each other to present their work. Although some knowledge is undoubtedly shared, there also is a liberal amount of camaraderie, rest and recreation, and sight-seeing.

Presenting at conferences does not always require access to networks. Many national and especially international conferences that sound highly prestigious will accept nearly any program proposal submitted if the person submitting it agrees to show up and pay the registration fee. After all, conference registration fees represent a major source of revenue for some organizations.

Information acquired at regional, state, and local conferences and symposia also varies widely in its credibility. Before placing too much credence in knowledge presented at them, inquiries should be made as to the selection process for presentations and the credentials of the presenters. Of course, a critical assessment of the research methods used also should be made.

## Content of Workshops

Workshop content may be based on empirical findings, or it may not. Frequently workshop leaders have been contracted (paid) to deliver content in a way consistent with the wishes of whomever is paying for it (often a social or other organization). This leaves the knowledge contained therein vulnerable to influence and distortion. The researcher may need to explore whether what was said was based on the best knowledge available or was simply reflective of what the workshop's sponsoring organization wanted its participants to hear. If it is the former, workshop content may be appropriate for inclusion in a research literature review.

## Public Documents and Records of Public Gatherings

Many good sources of information are available on request. Public documents and records of public gatherings (such as the minutes of public meetings) often are useful resources. For example, a researcher wishing to understand the values and thinking underlying current or pending legislation can learn a great deal by studying testimony of various individuals and interest groups that appears within the *Congressional Record*. Of course, because they are open to the public, these documents sometimes contain more posturing and efforts to appear politically correct than they do knowledge. Other public documents and records of public gatherings may also have undergone a certain sterilization process that leaves their credibility as a source of knowledge somewhat suspect.

## Newspapers

Perhaps the most controversial sources that we have noted are those that depend on commercial success for their continued existence. Newspaper sales may have higher priority for those who produce them than scientific accuracy. Newspapers acquire some of what they publish from such generally credible sources as reports of government-sponsored research. But they also publish findings (sometimes selectively) from research of questionable quality and from what is referred to as simply "high-placed sources." They regularly publish what is openly identified as little more than opinion in the form of editorials and minimally screened positions of individuals under the heading of "Letters to the Editor." When a topic is believed to be of widespread interest, it sometimes seems that getting the facts is less important than getting out the story.

Except when an article can be determined to possess a carefully researched origin and contains only firsthand information, it probably is best to use knowledge drawn from newspapers with extreme caution. Often, they are best used to learn about the *existence* of the knowledge-building work of others. It is then possible to seek out the original source, obtain a full report, and evaluate its merits based on the description of the researcher's methods.

## Radio and Television Broadcasts

Other media similarly offer sources of knowledge that run the gamut of scientific credibility. There is a great amount of knowledge and advice shared gratuitously by network radio and television talk show hosts and their "authority" guests. Very little of it, if any, would be likely either to enlighten the researcher or to convince others of the scholarliness of a literature review.

Some news specials and documentaries on both network and public radio and television are well researched and present excellent sources of information. However, the advent of certain types of television journalism and pseudonews specials in the 1980s and the revelation in the 1990s that some findings reported on documentaries were manipulated have cast increasing doubt on the credibility of television news broadcasts. Frequently, they now appear to be designed to entertain and to appeal to the lower interests of viewers and listeners. Special care and discretion should be used in separating knowledge from content that, if cited, would only weaken the researcher's scientific credibility.

## Magazines and Periodicals

That brings us to the bottom of our list (in many ways). Popular magazines and periodicals vary widely in how much knowledge they publish as opposed to how much pure fiction they include in order to sell subscriptions and single copies in supermarkets and other outlets. Some newsmagazines and pop-science magazines seem to walk a thin line, attempting to appear scholarly and scientific while selecting topics and presentation formats (for example, short, topical articles featuring provocative pictures) that clearly reflect an eye on sales figures rather than on the knowledge needs of their readers. They may even reflect a pragmatic mixture within a single issue; for example, a scholarly article written by a respected researcher juxtaposed with another bit of "fluff" that would be an intellectual insult to anyone with more than a superficial knowledge of the topic. The message to the social work researcher conducting a literature review on a research problem or question should be obvious—choose carefully in using such publications. You may subscribe to it, read it religiously, learn some things that are helpful to you in your work, and even display it on your coffee table without embarrassment. But that does not mean that every article in it is a potential source of knowledge that can be cited with confidence.

The popularity of a magazine or periodical is certainly no guarantee that its contents are the product of scientific inquiry or that they are worthy of citation in a literature review. In fact, we might speculate whether very high sales and financial success are not negatively correlated with the amount of scientific rigor that it employs.

Some magazines and periodicals make no pretense of scholarliness. Their readers, who may want to believe that they possess an inquiring mind, often seek nothing but recreational reading or amusing diversion. Consequently, they are less likely to purchase a periodical whose articles tend to be based on scientific research than ones that are based on the flimsiest of inquiry, if not outright fantasy. They would probably not buy (or read in the checkout line) a publication with a lead article entitled "Posttraumatic Stress Syndrome among Native Americans," but they might purchase the tabloid that promises a four-paragraph analysis of such fantasies as "Elvis Is Working as a Bartender in Cheektowaga" or "Despondent Twin Shoots Brother by Mistake."

Is there ever a place for acknowledging within a social work researcher's review of literature such unscholarly publications that occur at the extreme end of the credibility continuum? Not in the usual way. However, these publications have one thing in common: high sales. Their owners and editors maintain high sales by maintaining a good pulse of what is of interest to the general public. A social problem that is in some form the topic of virtually every magazine at the supermarket checkout stand during a certain time period (for example, spouse battering or the activities of the press) can be assumed to have reached a certain level of public consciousness. The observation that, during the week of August 8, 1998, nine of the ten most popular magazines in America carried at least one article on the increasingly chronic nature of HIV infections might be a useful contribution to a literature review, even though the sources cited might make some scholars cringe. The researcher would certainly not be saying that everything (or even anything) within the text of the articles can be construed as knowledge, only that the fact of its publication in popular magazines attests to the topic's popular interest.

We have chosen an extreme example of how far the researcher occasionally may go in seeking and using information for the review of literature. Obviously, even a single use of some of the more suspect sources of information that abound could seriously harm the researcher's credibility and others' assessment of the findings and recommendations generated by the researcher's methods. They should be used rarely, if ever, and only for the limited purposes described. If more scholarly sources would accomplish the same purposes, they should be used instead. Our tongue-in-cheek example makes an important point, however. Any source that relates to the research problem and to a research question *may* have the potential to inform the researcher in some way, even if the knowledge it contains may have no credibility whatsoever.

## Organizing the Literature Review

After a search of existing knowledge, researchers usually find themselves with a great amount of information. Typically it consists of a large stack of file cards with useful quotations on one side and the full citation (including all page numbers, volume numbers, and other necessary specifics) on the back. (A computer-assisted variation of the file card system is also popular.) A good first step in making sense out of the existing knowledge is to sort it into several broad topic areas. These may have been identified prior to embarking on the literature review, or they may simply suggest themselves during the sorting process. An example will help to illustrate how this can be done.

Suppose that a researcher has conducted a literature review on the question: What changes in the role of caregivers have been associated with the increasingly chronic nature of AIDS? The variety of relevant knowledge that was collected could be organized using an outline format like the following:

I. Historical Responses to Terminal Illness
   A. In-Hospital Services
   B. The Hospice Movement
   C. Family Roles and Responsibilities

II. History of AIDS
   A. Early Diagnostic Efforts
   B. Symptoms of the Disease
   C. Transmission
   D. Social and Political Responses
   E. Groups Most at Risk
   F. Past Treatment Approaches
   G. Efforts to Find a Cure or Vaccine
   H. Traditional Caregiver Roles

III. Recent Developments and Changes
   A. Incidence
   B. Descriptive Profile of Current Persons with AIDs
   C. Development of Life-Extending Drugs
   D. Changes in Life Quality
   E. Dependence on Caregivers

Organizing the products of a literature review into an outline containing broad topic areas can serve a number of useful purposes. Some knowledge that has been collected may not seem to fit perfectly within any of the areas. It may be concluded that it is not as relevant to the research problem or questions as had originally been assumed. Thus, it may be discarded. Or, if it seems to stand alone but clearly does enlighten some aspect of the research problem or questions, new subheadings may be added to incorporate it, and it may have to be expanded with some additional literature. It may be necessary to go back to the literature to seek out additional references.

If it appears that there is no logical sequence to the topics (note the logical progression of the preceding topics) when a broad outline is constructed, additional topics may be required to link those already identified. When all topic areas and their subtopics have been developed, they should reflect a logical flow, often from the more general to those most closely related to the current research question or questions. The topics frequently are used as headings and subheadings when the report of the literature review is written.

## Writing the Report of a Review of Literature

What are the characteristics of a good literature review section of a research report? How can the researcher's compilation of existing knowledge be organized and presented so that it will be of maximum benefit to the reader?

### *Direction and Flow*

As suggested earlier, the reader should expect to find topics (identified by subheadings) of general relevance to the research questions near its beginning. For example, in a research study seeking an answer to the broad research question: Is there a relationship between crack cocaine usage and adolescent suicide? early sections of the literature review might be devoted to a historical overview of substance abuse, a summary of what is known about adolescent drug usage, and a description of statistical trends in the incidence of adolescent suicide in North America. Knowledge that is more directly related to the research question—for example, a summary of the results of suicide autopsies conducted on recent cases of adolescent suicide or results of other studies that examined the relationship between other substance abuse and adolescent suicide—should appear later. Reports of research that studied the same questions or very similar ones should be summarized and discussed near the end of the review, so that the current research will appear to be a logical extension of previous scientific inquiries.

Good literature reviews reflect both direction and a logical progression. They demonstrate how researchers used existing knowledge to refine their thinking about their research problems and questions, and how more specific questions and/or hypotheses evolved from it. It also should be obvious just how researchers used the literature to draw conclusions about the most appropriate methods to use to study their research questions. Their thought processes should be obvious to the reader of the report. In this way, the reader can be convinced either that the researchers' conclusions are logical and justified or that they are not.

## Use of Quotations and Citations

Direct quotations should be used sparingly in a literature review. It is the *substance* of what others have to say rather than their specific words that are important to the researcher. Excessive use of quotations may mislead the reader because quotations are always taken out of context. In addition, because all writers have their own style, quotations can make the flow of the text uneven while providing more detail than the reader requires.[4]

Citations are always appropriate within a literature review. They are used to explain how and why the researcher's thinking and conclusions have occurred. But, like quotations, they should be included only if the work cited truly contributed to the researcher's thinking, not simply as evidence that the researcher found a relevant source of knowledge.

There may be a natural tendency to want to include every bit of knowledge that has been discovered. After all, finding it took a considerable amount of effort! But, if ten articles present essentially the same position, there is no reason to cite them all—that would be overkill. One or two will make the point and be less likely to disrupt the flow of the text.

How relevant should knowledge be in order to be cited? How much detail of others' work is needed or desirable? Daryl Bem has provided some useful guidelines:

> *Cite only articles pertinent to the specific issues with which you are dealing; emphasize their major conclusions, findings, or relevant methodological issues and avoid unnecessary detail. If someone else has written a review article that surveys the literature on the topic, you can simply refer your own readers to the review and present only its most pertinent points in your own report. Even when you must describe an entire study, try to condense it as much as possible without sacrificing clarity.*[5]

Are some types of citations better than others? Yes. But a good mix often is desirable. The best citations to use (all other factors being equal) may be those that refer to recent, rigorous scientific research (as opposed to those that may be a little dated or that are less empirically based). But it is perfectly acceptable to include some older citations (especially if the contribution was a major influence on subsequent thought on a topic or issue). Older citations can also be very useful for providing a historical perspective on a problem or event. They reflect the state of the art of knowledge, beliefs, and attitudes at a point in history.

It should be clear by now that the quotations and citations included in a report of a literature review are there to help explain how the researcher went from point A to point B. They are not there to impress others with how much relevant information was examined. If anything should impress the reader of a good research report, it should be the researcher's objectivity and open-mindedness.

Objectivity can be demonstrated in a number of ways. For example, it can be seen in a willingness to include the conflicting opinions and conclusions of other researchers which almost invariably exist. It is not unusual for two scholars to express beliefs and conclusions that are diametrically opposite to each other. The inclusion of references to literature that reflects both sides of an argument suggests that the researcher has been both thorough and objective in the literature review.

## The Role of the Researcher in a Report of the Literature Review

We do not mean to suggest that the researcher should always remain well behind the scenes in a literature review or express no opinions or conclusions. In fact, the opposite is true. Although biases should not be evident in a good literature review, *thought processes* should be both obvious and open to critique. The reader should be able to sense the presence of the researcher in the text. A good literature review is a carefully woven mixture of knowledge and the assimilation of it by the researcher.

It may be helpful to think of the researcher as a guide who has pulled together and organized what is of interest and value to save others' time and effort. But a guide does not *tell* others what to see or how it should be perceived or interpreted. Using the literature review, the reader is helped to navigate through existing, relevant knowledge, stopping along the way to pull together conclusions and to evaluate just where the literature seems to be leading. As a guide, the researcher tries not to exert too much influence on the reader, whenever possible letting the literature speak for itself. However, in a well-written literature review, the reader will come to the same or similar conclusions as the researcher and will agree about what the literature has to say about the research questions and how best to study them. There will be no surprises. No conclusions will seem to come out of the blue.

If we perceive the researcher's role as that of guide, neither of the two problems that frequently characterize literature reviews is likely to occur. One fairly common problem exists when the researcher's thinking dominates the literature review and appears to be invulnerable to influence by it. Scholarly development of thought is not in evidence. The reader is left with the suspicion that existing knowledge had little influence on the conclusions that were drawn. Even if a fair number of citations are present, they do not reflect balance. It appears that the researcher selectively used only that literature that would support existing biases and did not grow in an understanding of the research problem or questions. The researcher emerged from the literature review with unchanged beliefs. The reader, sensing this, is likely to doubt whether other stages of the research process were conducted in an unbiased manner.

Sometimes another problem can occur. The development of the researcher's thinking is barely evident in the literature review, but for a different reason. The literature review seems to be little more than a long series of quotations, included in the research report because they are expected to lend a scholarly appearance, but with no other apparent purpose. There is no way for the reader to evaluate the researcher's thought processes. There is not enough evidence that the knowledge assembled by the researcher was even assimilated.

In either of the above scenarios, the researcher has not made productive use of the literature accumulated. Credibility may be hopelessly damaged. But if the author assumes the role of guide, the proper mix of quotations reflecting relevant knowledge and the use of that knowledge to refine thinking about the research topic will be in evidence. The literature review will be a unified whole that seems to take the reader somewhere.

## Summary

The term *literature review* refers both to a step in the research process and to a product; namely, a section or chapter of the research report. We made the point that a body of knowledge exists for any research question. We examined how the process of reviewing existing knowledge about a research question can shape our thinking about the question and its possible answer. We discussed the other reasons why we look at what is already known relative to a question, that is, what the literature review is supposed to accomplish. The pros and cons of various sources of knowledge were discussed, with special focus on how the selection of a source can affect the credibility of the researcher and the research findings.

Practical suggestions also were given for organizing a wide array of knowledge into a logical and coherent report of what is known relative to a research topic. The role of the researcher was described as that of a guide for the reader, to help in synthesizing existing knowledge and drawing conclusions from it.

## References

1. NASW. (1995). *Encyclopedia of social work* (19th ed.). Silver Spring, MD: NASW Press.
2. Ginsberg, L. (Ed.). (1995). *Social work almanac* (2nd ed.). Silver Spring, MD: NASW Press.
3. Marson, S. M. (1999). "Uncovering UnCover." *The New Social Worker, 6(1)*, 23–24, 28.
4. Pyrczak, R., & Bruce, R. (1992). *Writing empirical research reports*. Los Angeles: Pyrczak Publishing, 41.
5. Bem, D. (1991). Writing the research report. In C. Judd, R. Eliot, & L. Kidder, (Eds.). *Research methods in social relations* (6th ed.). Fort Worth, TX: Harcourt, Brace, Jovanovich, 453.

# 5

# FOCUSED RESEARCH QUESTIONS AND HYPOTHESES

In the process of reviewing the literature that relates to a research problem, researchers acquire a clearer understanding of it. They also are helped to better specify the exact research questions that will be asked either in their research or in some subsequent research study. Depending on what is learned, they may even be in a position to predict what answers to their questions will be found. These two latter products of literature reviews, focused research questions and hypotheses, are the topics for discussion in this chapter.

## Focused Research Questions

The process of selecting broad research questions that we discussed in Chapter 3 is useful as a method for creating a study of a research problem that is of a manageable size. As we suggested, no one study could possibly do a thorough job of examining all questions that might relate to a research problem; some narrowing of focus must be done. However, one or more broad questions do not provide a specific enough focus to guide the researcher in performing such necessary tasks as identifying the most appropriate people or objects to study, determining what needs to be measured, or finding how best to measure it. Broad questions also provide little or no guidance for selecting the methods to sort and analyze data. Before these tasks can be undertaken, further refinement and specification of the research questions are required.

What is the difference between a broad research question such as those discussed in Chapter 3 (generally referred to as the general research question) and the more specific questions that are likely to be a product of the literature review? How does a review of existing knowledge help the researcher to move from the former to the latter?

To illustrate the difference between broad and focused research questions, we will return to the example used in Chapter 3[1] when we discussed which broad research questions might be most productive to examine. The reader will recall that after eliminating other options, the student researchers who were looking into the problem of large numbers of unfounded child abuse determinations settled on one broad question: Are the different demographic characteristics of workers (for example, age, race, sex, or parenthood) related to their determinations? This was a good start. The question provided a beginning focus for the study and helped the researchers to narrow their literature review to a manageable number of topics. It committed the researchers to gaining a better understanding of the decision (founded/unfounded) that child protection workers must make when they receive a referral for possible child abuse or neglect. It provided a research focus—exploration of a possible relationship between one factor (social worker characteristics) and those decisions. But the question was still too general to provide any real direction to the researchers as to exactly how they should go about seeking an answer to it.

At this point in the process, it also was not known to what degree answers already existed to the question, what methods were used to study it, or what other researchers had learned in the process of conducting research on the question or on related questions. For example, without reviewing the literature, it was not possible to know which worker characteristics would or would not be promising to examine.

Before conducting their literature review, the researchers also were left with a very impractical and vague idea of how to proceed with their research. One group member suggested facetiously that they should just find some child protection workers and ask them to write a description of themselves and how they make decisions. She and the other members knew there had to be a better way to proceed, but what was it? Until they conducted their literature review, they could not know what it was.

When they moved into the literature review stage of their research, the researchers soon confirmed what they had suspected—they were not attempting to build knowledge in a vacuum. For example, it was learned that other researchers had been studying professionals' decision making for many years; some had even used human service workers as research participants. Other literature (conflicting federal laws and procedures) confirmed their hunch that there was a lack of consistent clear federal procedural guidelines and that the definitions of what constitutes child abuse were vague. A review of state policy manuals suggested that state guidelines were no less ambiguous.

The researchers found one article that was especially helpful in suggesting how to study their research question. It described the relative merits of different research methods that were used to learn what factors seem to influence social workers' decision making in a variety of settings (but not in child protection).

As they reviewed the literature and talked more with child welfare administrators, group members began to compile a list of personal characteristics that, based on logic and past research, might be related to the decisions that they make.

Several appeared to be especially good prospects. They included level of educational achievement, discipline methods used in the workers' homes of origin, feelings about their jobs, and whether they were parents themselves. All had been found to be related to social workers' decision making in one or more other research studies. They decided to collect data on each of these and not to gather data on certain other worker characteristics (for example, age, race, or gender) that, based on past research, probably would not be related to decision making about cases referred for possible child abuse or neglect.

Some of what the researchers learned from their literature review could be described as inconclusive or even conflicting. For example, the human behavior literature suggested that parenting practices in the home of origin would be likely to have some effect on adult attitudes toward the ways that others treated their children. But organization personnel data also indicated that the child protection workers had undergone both formal education and specialized training for their jobs. Wasn't it logical to conclude that parenting practices in their home of origin might no longer influence their decision making to any great degree? Maybe, but remember (Chapter 1), logic is pretty untrustworthy as a source of knowledge.

The literature review produced focused research questions that would have been impossible to formulate prior to finding out what was already known about the problem, what related questions had been studied, and what answers had been found. Because of it, the researchers were able to take their broad research question and to reformulate it into two more focused (more specific) questions:

- Is there a relationship between disciplinary practices in child protection workers' families of origin and their decision making about cases referred for suspected child abuse or neglect?
- To what degree do workers perceive that their formal education and training in child protection services is an influence in their decision making about cases referred for suspected child abuse or neglect?

With these and other focused questions to work with, the research took on a clearer focus. As a result of conducting the literature review, it was now possible to know what data about workers and their decisions should be gathered and, by learning from the experiences of other researchers, to have a good idea about the best ways to go about gathering it.

## Hypotheses

Figure 5.1 provides additional examples of broad research questions that reflect an early narrowing of the scope of the research and a focused research question that might be produced through reviewing relevant scientific literature. In those examples where the broad research question suggests the use of more qualitative research methods (for example, questions A, B, and E), the focused research

FIGURE 5.1    **Examples of Broad Research Questions and Focused Research Questions**

| Broad Research Questions | Focused Research Questions |
|---|---|
| A. Are people with developmental disabilities unhappy working in sheltered workshops? | A. What working conditions contribute most to dissatisfaction of workers in sheltered workshops? |
| B. How do value conflicts affect client services when social workers are supervised by nurses? | B. When nurses supervise social workers, why are patients less likely to refuse painful life-extending treatment? |
| C. Have day care facilities increased to meet the needs of families denied extended benefits since welfare reform? | C. Is there a correlation between the increase in day care facilities and reports of abuse or neglect? |
| D. Why do social work students dislike courses in research and statistics? | D. Is the rate of math phobia higher among social work students than in the general population? |
| E. What obstacles to the grief process do parents of children who die while committing violent crimes perceive? | E. Why do parents of children who die while committing violent crimes often withdraw from contact with their communities? |

questions may be generated prior to data collection and may thus guide the data collection that follows. In other qualitative studies, the broad research question guides data collection. Data are then analyzed in relation to the professional literature, and focused questions for future research are generated as a product of the entire research effort. When the broad research question suggests the use of more quantitative research methods (for example, questions C and D), the review of literature is used to produce focused questions and (often) hypotheses prior to data collection. If the literature contains enough credible knowledge to suggest a possible answer to one or more focused research questions, then it may be appropriate for the researcher to predict that answer in the form of a hypothesis. However, especially when there is relatively little conclusive information that can be learned about a problem from reviewing the literature, we really do not know and cannot venture to predict what we might learn from our research. Then it is not appropriate to formulate hypotheses. How could we attempt to state or predict a relationship between variables when, in some instances, we have not even been able to identify the most relevant variables to study? When this occurs, researchers select methods that seek to produce rather than to find support for hypotheses. For example, some qualitative research entails collecting vast amounts of data and then (inductively) trying to determine what it all means. If the data suggest one or more hypotheses, they can be examined later by some other researchers.

When hypotheses are justified following a review of literature, they can be very helpful in guiding future stages of the research process. As we have suggested, a hypothesis can be thought of as a tentative answer to a research question. It should be a logical conclusion drawn from the review of literature. Another way of viewing a hypothesis is as a prediction of what the researcher thinks will be revealed about the answer to a focused research question after data are collected and analyzed. A hypothesis also is a way of stating a researcher's intention to try to demonstrate evidence of a relationship between or among certain variables.

Some authors define a hypothesis in a way that relates to its general construction. For example, it has been defined as a statement of a relationship between or among variables.[2] When researchers formulate a hypothesis, they are convinced that there is enough evidence (reflected in existing knowledge) to justify it; that is, to suggest that two or more variables may be related in some specific way. They construct a carefully worded statement (the hypothesis) saying what they think that relationship is.

Hypotheses generally are stated in either the present or the future tense. In rare instances, such as in the case of historical research (Chapter 8), the past tense is used. They also are stated in the form of declarative sentences. They are never stated as questions because, as we have noted, they are tentative answers to research questions.

## Related Definitions

To fully understand just what hypotheses are and how a literature review can be helpful in formulating them, we will first need to define certain key research terms.

**Variable.**  We have already used the term *variable* several times. It is impossible not to do so because the study of variables is essential to all research. A *variable* is an attribute or characteristic that differs in quantity or quality among different persons, objects, times, places, and so on. In our earlier example, the different parenting experiences of child protection workers within their homes of origin would be a variable. If all the workers had been parented in the same way, parenting experience would not be considered a variable; it would be a *constant*. In research, constants usually are of less interest than variables.

**Demographic Variable.**  A demographic variable is one type of variable. The term *demographic variable* really is a generic term that is used most often by researchers to refer to those commonly measured variables that give researchers (and, when reported, readers of research reports) a clearer understanding of the general characteristics of research participants. Some of the variables generally referred to as "demographic" include age, gender, income, religion, education, and marital status. Demographic variables sometimes are collectively referred to as *bio-data*.

Although certain demographic variables frequently are included in questionnaires and other research data collection instruments, there is no rule that says that they must be. Unless researchers have reason to believe that a demographic variable is related to the research question in some way (as determined through the literature review) or that the readers of their research report will require information about it (for example, to determine if their clients are similar to researchers' participants), there is really no justification to measure it. Unless one of these justifications exists, there may be some good ethical and practical reasons not to measure it. Some demographic variables (for example, age, religion, marital status, or income) may be considered sensitive and personal. Collecting data about them when the researcher has no practical use for them is an unnecessary invasion of the participants' right to privacy. Besides, requesting unnecessary data from participants who are less than eager to provide it can jeopardize the collection of other data that is really needed.

**Value Label or Value.**   The terms *value label* or *value* (as used in research) mean essentially the same thing. They are (respectively) the name or number assigned to a specific measurement of a variable.

A *value label* is a word or words used to denote a form that a variable can assume. (Some people prefer to use the term *attribute,* as in "the different attributes a variable can assume.") For example, for the variable "parenting style in home of origin," different value labels might be "autocratic," "democratic," "laissez-faire," or some other group of words that reflect the differences in parenting style that existed within child protection workers' homes of origin. Note that the differences reflect different kinds or qualities (rather than quantities) of the variable.

A *value* also reflects a specific measurement of a category, but it is expressed as a number. For the variable "number of siblings," different values would likely be 0, 1, 2, 3, 4, and so on, indicating the actual number of siblings who were present in the home.

Whether we use the term *value label* or *value* is a function of just how precisely a variable is measured (see Chapter 10). Thus, the variable "parenthood" might use value labels like "yes" or "no" to denote whether each worker is a parent. Or if measurement of parenthood was a little more precise and involved finding out exactly how many biological or adopted children under age eighteen resided with the worker, one could use the values 1, 2, 3, or 4 in a way that they would communicate a more accurate meaning.

**Frequency.**   *Frequency* refers to the number of times that a given value label or value was found to exist among the persons, objects, and the like (referred to as *cases* in a given research study) that were studied. If five workers were found to have been reared in homes that used autocratic parenting styles, we would say that the value label "autocratic" had a frequency of 5. If democratic styles existed in nine homes of workers, the value label "democratic" would have had a frequency of 9, and so forth.

**Dependent Variable and Independent Variable or Predictor Variable and Criterion Variable.**   Often, in an attempt to communicate clearly what a researcher is predicting within a hypothesis, one of two possible pairs of terms is used. The terms *dependent variable* and *independent variable* are one such pair. When they are used, the term *dependent variable* is assigned to the variable whose variation the researcher is most interested in understanding and explaining. In social work research, the different degree of treatment success that occurs among clients is a common dependent variable, but a dependent variable can be any other variable that the researcher has declared to be the one whose variations are of primary interest.

The label "dependent variable" is not applied to a variable unless at least one other variable (independent variable) has been hypothesized to be at least a contributor to its variations. The term *independent variable* is then applied to the variable or variables that the researcher believes may produce at least some of the variation that exists within the dependent variable. If, for example, the variable degree of treatment success among clients in a hypothesis is labeled the dependent variable, the independent variable might be method of treatment, degree of family involvement, or fee paid by the client. It also could be some other variable that the literature and practice experience have indicated as likely to contribute to the variations in the degree of treatment success that clients experience.

Ideally, an independent variable is introduced and/or manipulated in some way by the researcher so that its effects on the dependent variable can be monitored and recorded. Of course, this is often either ethically or logistically impossible. As long as the researcher is asserting that one variable is believed to influence the values of a second variable (and not vice versa), it is appropriate to refer to the first variable as the independent variable and to the second as the dependent variable.

The terms *dependent variable* and *independent variable* are used together or not at all. In some situations, they are not appropriate, but another pair of terms, *predictor variable* and *criterion variable*, can be substituted. These terms are used if different values of two variables exist naturally and are distributed randomly outside the control of the researcher and if no assertion about one's influencing the other can legitimately be made. The researcher may still wish to communicate which variable is of primary interest and which other variable or variables are hypothesized to be related to that variable. In such instances, "criterion variable" is substituted for "dependent variable" as a label for the variable of primary interest, and "predictor variable" is substituted for "independent variable" (the variable believed to be related to the criterion variable).

The terms *dependent variable* (or *criterion variable*) and *independent variable* (or *predictor variable*) are specific to a given piece of research. That is, they describe the focus of one researcher's investigation and the nature of a relationship between variables believed to exist within it. Another researcher is likely to have a different focus and/or to suggest a different relationship. Thus, in different research studies, different labels may be used for the same variable or variables. For example, a social worker seeking to explain different success rates among couples in marital counseling (the dependent variable) would label type of treatment used as the independent variable. Within the same organization, a social work administrator may conduct other research in which type of treatment is the variable of primary interest (criterion variable) and may label some other variable, such as the school of social work attended by counselors, as the predictor variable.

The terms *dependent variable, independent variable, criterion variable,* and *predictor variable* should be regarded simply as convenient labels. They help the reader of a research report understand the focus of the researcher's area of inquiry and better understand exactly what the researcher believes to be the nature of a relationship between or among variables. They also suggest the type of research methods used and the type of statistical analysis most likely to have been applied.

Sometimes neither pair of labels is appropriate. In some research that predicts the existence of a relationship between variables, it may not be possible or appropriate to identify one variable in a hypothesis as clearly dependent (or criterion) and another as independent (or predictor). For example, the literature may suggest that alcoholism and unemployment are related, but in a study of the relationship between the two social problems, it may not be possible to make a case for applying the label "criterion" (or "dependent") to one variable any more than to the other. The researcher may be more interested in studying their interaction than in understanding variation in rates of one or the other, or in examining to what degree (if any) one may be influencing the other. Or the research goal may be simply to learn the degree to which one problem tends to be found with the other. If either is the primary research focus, the terms *dependent* (or *criterion*) *variable* or *independent* (or *predictor*) *variable* would not be used. Then the hypothesis should be stated so that it is clear that the researcher is not communicating that one variable is of any greater interest than the other, or that it is believed that one variable is contributing to the different values of the other variable that occurs.

**Intervening Variable.** The term *intervening variable* is frequently used in a generic way to denote any variable that somehow can mislead the researcher about the true relationship between dependent and independent variables. A term that is used similarly is *extraneous variable.*

The term *intervening variable* sometimes has a more specific usage relating to the time when a variable's influence on the relationship between an independent variable and a dependent variable was believed to occur. In this more narrow usage, a variable could be considered potentially intervening only if it may have influenced the dependent variable after the independent variable occurred. For example, sexual experiences during adolescence might be considered an intervening variable if a researcher wished to study the relationship between sexual abuse as a child (independent variable) and current sexual satisfaction (dependent variable) of adults.

There is other, more specific terminology (for example, *antecedent variable, obscuring variable,* or *contingent variable*) to more precisely describe the specific way in which one or more other variables might have the potential to mislead the researcher about the true relationship between the dependent and independent variables. For example, a third (*antecedent*) variable could precede both the dependent and the independent variables and may have thus influenced both of their variations. Or another (*obscuring*) variable may interact with the dependent and independent variables in such a way as to make them appear less closely related than they really are. In an introductory book like this one, these distinctions are not important. We will use the term *intervening variable* in its generic sense to refer to any variable that has the potential to distort or misrepresent the true relationship between the dependent (or criterion) and independent (or predictor) variables, no matter how (specifically) it does or in which direction it has the potential to mislead the researcher.

Social work practitioners work with intervening variables all the time, although the label may be an unfamiliar one. In practice as in research, we would hope to control intervening variables and to minimize or eliminate their influence, but this often is not possible. For example, as practitioners, we might wish to know to what degree our treatment is influencing a client's social functioning. But we may be concerned about how the attitude or behavior of a spouse or of the client's employer (potentially intervening variables) might influence the level of success that may be achieved in our treatment. We sometimes must acknowledge that our treatment may be less a factor in the client's social functioning level than either of these other variables. Either may have a major influence on what on the surface may appear to be the relationship between our treatment and our client's social functioning. The interaction between the spouse's and the employer's behaviors and attitudes and any number of other possible intervening variables can muddy the water as we attempt to determine the relationship between our treatment and the client's level of social functioning.

Fortunately, researchers have devised ways to minimize or at least to help sort out the influence of variables believed to be intervening in the relationship between dependent and independent variables. We will discuss one way that this can be done (research design) in subsequent chapters. Statistical analysis (Chapter 12) offers another way.

## Types of Relationships Expressed in Hypotheses

A hypothesis, as we noted, states what we believe (based on existing knowledge as revealed in the literature and our experience) to be the relationship between certain variables. Its presence sends notice that we are seeking additional evidence for this presumed relationship. In addition, a hypothesis generally goes a little further. It also states the *nature* of the relationship between the variables. Certain types of relationships are commonly stated in hypotheses (see Figure 5.2). Some reflect a very subtle distinction; others are more dramatic. We will mention the three most commonly used ones.

**Causation.**   A hypothesis that states a belief in causation goes out on a limb. It states that the values or value categories of the independent variable *produce* different values or value categories of the dependent variable. It leaves little room

## FIGURE 5.2   Relationships between Variables Expressed in Hypotheses

| | |
|---|---|
| **Causation** | Values or value categories of X cause values or value categories of Y. |
| **Association** | Certain value categories of X are found with certain value categories of Y. |
| **Correlation** | Higher values of X are found with higher values of Y and vice versa; or, higher values of X are found with lower values of Y and vice versa. |

for the possibility that one or more intervening variables or any other phenomenon (such as chance or a biased sample) may have produced this apparent relationship within cases that are studied. An example of a hypothesis that states a relationship of causation between variables is: Among adolescent psychiatric patients, group treatment produces lower rates of rehospitalization than does individual treatment.

Not surprisingly, hypotheses that suggest a belief in a relationship of causation between variables (also known as cause–effect) are relatively rare in social work research. If the dependent variable is a behavior (which often is the case), we would not likely conclude that it is caused by the influence of any one other variable. That would be in direct opposition to our belief that behavior has many interrelated causes, a major tenet of systems theory. In addition, for ethical (Chapter 2) and logistical reasons it is often impossible to physically control potentially intervening variables that are likely to influence the relationship between the dependent and the independent variables. As we shall explain in later chapters, most research designs used in social work research do not presume to identify cause–effect relationships between variables.

**Association.**   A hypothesis that states a belief in an association between variables is really a pretty conservative assertion. It asserts that certain value categories of one variable (usually one that cannot be measured with much precision) tend to be found with certain value categories of another variable.

To describe a relationship between variables as an association is to acknowledge that the influence of one or more intervening variables is likely and that they probably have not been adequately controlled. It also acknowledges both the limits of measurement of the variables (see Chapter 10) and the limits of the statistical analysis (see Chapter 12) used to determine the likelihood of a true relationship between the variables. A hypothesis is likely to be stated so as to reflect only an association between variables (and nothing more) if

- The variables can be measured so that their values reflect only qualitative differences (differences of kind) and not the precise quantity of the variable present.
- Statistical analysis that produces only an indication of degree of association is all that can legitimately be used.

- The researcher was unable to introduce or manipulate the predictor variable in any way or to exert control over potentially intervening variables.

An example of a hypothesis that suggests a relationship of only association is: Among adolescent patients, those who receive group treatment are more likely to be rehospitalized than those who receive individual treatment. Note that, in this hypothesis, all three of the preceding conditions are present.

An association between variables should never be viewed as synonymous with evidence of causation. Where there is causation, there is always association. But the reverse is not necessarily true. Many variables are associated where causation is not present. These situations generally occur as a result of intervening variables.

Hypotheses that state beliefs about association between or among variables are quite common in social work research. Although an association between variables gives researchers less information about the relationship than they might like to have, knowledge of an association between variables still can be useful to the social worker. For example, if researchers were to learn that there is an association between gender and child protection decisions, this might represent very useful information, even though it would fall short of saying that being male or female alone causes one to make certain decisions.

**Correlation.** If a hypothesis states a relationship between variables as a correlation, it implies a little more about their relationship than a simple association. But a statement about correlation still falls far short of saying that the values of one variable caused the values of the other to occur, just that they covary. As in the case of association, inadequately controlled intervening variables (or some other cause) may be producing any apparent relationship between the variables. A hypothesis is likely to be stated so as to reflect a correlation between or among variables if

- The variables can be measured so that their values reflect different, precise, and measurable quantities of the variables.
- Certain statistical analysis designed to determine the strength and direction of the relationship will be used.
- The researcher was unable to introduce or manipulate the predictor variable in any way or to exert control over potentially intervening variables.

A correlation between two variables is a relationship in which one of two patterns exists. Either high values (indicating large, quantitative measurements) of one variable are found (disproportionately) with high values of the other variable, and low values of the first are found with low values of the second (described as a *positive correlation*). Or high values of one variable are found with low values of the other variable and vice versa (described as a *negative*, or *inverse*, *correlation*).

An example of a hypothesis that predicts the existence of a correlation between two variables is: Among adolescent psychiatric patients, there is a negative correlation between number of group treatment sessions attended per week and length of hospitalization. Note that the hypothesis predicts a negative correlation. It predicts that former patients who attended the most group sessions per week will have spent less time hospitalized than those who rarely attended, and vice versa. A hypothesis that predicted a positive correlation between the predictor and criterion variables would have been illogical, assuming that the group sessions were believed to be making a positive contribution to patients' recovery.

In the most common usage of the term, a correlation is just a little more precise statement of a relationship between variables (based on their measurement and the type of statistical analysis used) than an association. It is really a special form of association. Like association, it does not prove causation. Many variables are highly correlated, yet the different values of one variable do not cause the different values of the other. When hypothesizing a relationship of either association or correlation, researchers generally use the labels "predictor variable" and "criterion variable" (rather than "independent variable" and "dependent variable") to describe the variables believed to be related.

## Forms of Research Hypotheses

If a researcher predicts that variables will be found to be related (causation, association, or correlation), it is possible to express that relationship in one of two ways within a research hypothesis. Either a directional or a nondirectional hypothesis may be appropriate, depending on what was learned from the literature review.

In a *directional* (also called *one-tailed*) *hypothesis,* the researcher not only asserts that the variables will be found to be related but also predicts the direction of their relationship. In contrast, in a *nondirectional* (*two-tailed*) *hypothesis,* the researcher asserts that the variables will be found to be related, but does not wish to hazard a guess as to the direction in which they will be found to be related.[3] An example of a directional hypothesis is: Among adolescent psychiatric patients, those who received group treatment will reflect a higher rate of rehospitalization than those who received individual treatment. An example of a nondirectional hypothesis using the same two variables is: Among adolescent psychiatric patients, there will be a difference in rehospitalization rate between those who received group counseling and those who received individual counseling.

Sometimes variables are commonly believed to be related, but the researcher, based on the literature review and practice experience, has become convinced that they really are unrelated. Then a research hypothesis would be stated in such a way that it reflects the prediction that the variables will be found to be unrelated. An example of a hypothesis that predicts no relationship between variables is: Among adolescent psychiatric patients, those who received group treatment will

## FIGURE 5.3  Three Types of Research Hypotheses

| | |
|---|---|
| 1. Directional | "Males learn faster than females" or "Females learn faster than males." |
| 2. Nondirectional | "Males and females learn at different speeds." |
| 3. No relationship | "There is no difference in the speed at which males and females learn." |

be no more likely to be rehospitalized than those who received individual treatment.

Notice that, in this example, the two variables were described as having no association. If they are not even believed to be associated, they could not be correlated, or a relationship of causation could not exist. Figure 5.3 provides another example of the differences among these forms of research hypotheses.

## *When Are Hypotheses Appropriate?*

It is possible that the literature may suggest that any tentative suggestion about the answer to a research question (that is, a hypothesis) would be very presumptive on our part. There may just not be enough known about the area to justify making a statement about how certain variables might be related or even which variables are relevant to the research problem, as in the case of exploratory research and most descriptive studies. Or, if an answer is suggested, the literature, research ethics, and/or our knowledge of social work practice may reveal that it would be impossible to test that answer. If either of these is the case, a testable hypothesis might not be appropriate.

If previous efforts have been made to study the research question, if at least some tentative statement about the relationship between variables seems justified, if confirming or refuting such a relationship would be a valuable contribution to knowledge, and if it appears that a method can be devised to test that relationship, then one or more hypotheses may be in order. Whether a research hypothesis should suggest a belief in causation, correlation, an association, or no relationship between or among variables is a bit of a judgment call based on the researcher's assessment of just how much is already known about the answer to the research question and what type of measurement of variables and data analysis is believed to be possible. The same considerations would be used in deciding whether the research hypothesis should be stated in its directional or nondirectional form.

There is one additional general guideline that should be used in formulating a hypothesis. At this point, it should be obvious but probably bears mentioning anyway. When a hypothesis is tested, the results should produce a reasonable extension of existing knowledge as found in the literature. Finding support or nonsupport for it should never fail to increase our knowledge about a problem; it should do more than simply confirm what we already know. On the other extreme, it is extremely rare that the knowledge generated by hypothesis testing represents a quantum leap from what we already know. The results of most research take our understanding of a problem just a little bit further. Most good hypotheses reflect this realistic expectation.

Although we might like to demonstrate support for research hypotheses, it is not essential to the goal of advancing our understanding of a research problem. One of the beauties of research is that, if it is conducted according to scientific principles and we thus have reasonable confidence in our findings, we stand to advance knowledge by demonstrating either that variables probably are related or that they probably are not. For example, a researcher might hypothesize that one treatment method designed to reduce psychiatric depression is more effective than another method. But if it is learned that both methods are really about equally effective (nonsupport for a directional hypothesis), this knowledge can still inform practice decision making. An unsupported hypothesis is just as valuable as one for which support has been demonstrated. Among other benefits, an unsupported hypothesis can tell other researchers what hunches *not* to bother to pursue in their own research.

## *Wording of Hypotheses*

It should be obvious by now that the way a hypothesis is stated is very important. We want it to communicate exactly what we are predicting will be found, and nothing else. There are some helpful guidelines that have evolved within the scientific community,[4] based on researchers' recognition of the importance of clear communication. The following additional criteria are generally considered important.

**Consistency of Conceptualization.**  The variables within the hypothesis, usually the dependent (criterion) and independent (predictor), should be stated at approximately the same level of abstraction or concreteness. For example, the hypothesis—People who hold college degrees have a high level of self-awareness—fails to meet this criterion of a good hypothesis. The first variable, education level, is easily measured and would fall on the concrete end of the continuum of conceptualization. The other variable, self-awareness, is far more abstract and difficult to measure with precision. A restatement of the hypothesis that reflects greater consistency of conceptualization would be: People who hold college degrees will be more likely to receive a score of more than 80 on the Smith and Jones Scale of Self-Awareness than those who do not hold a college degree. Or, by moving education to a more abstract level, we could state: People with high educational achievement will have a higher level of self-awareness than those with low educational achievement.

**Relevance to the Problem.**  Good hypotheses, when tested, will generate knowledge that has the potential to contribute to the alleviation of the research problem. This criterion seems obvious. Why would a researcher ever state and test a hypothesis that is unrelated to the problem? It can happen, usually unintentionally. Sometimes, in the process of conducting the literature review, researchers can get sidetracked, losing sight of why they plunged into the literature in the first place. They emerge with some very justifiable and logical hypotheses that unfortunately have little or no relationship to the problem or its solution. This generally occurs because the broad research questions were not well formulated and did not provide enough focus for the researcher. With good, broad questions, the problem is less likely to occur. This criterion should be thought of as a reminder, a check to make sure that the researcher did not forget about the problem while immersed in the literature.

**Completeness.** A hypothesis should be stated as completely as possible. The person reading it should not wonder about the researcher's meaning or if it is missing key words. A sure indicator that a hypothesis is incomplete is the use of words that suggest comparison without the presence of a reference point. For example, the hypothesis—Women under age thirty are more assertive—lacks completeness. It leaves the reader in doubt about what exactly the researcher believes to be true about the assertiveness of women under thirty. Are they more assertive than women over thirty, than men under thirty, than all men, or than whom? A hypothesis that would be considered more complete is: Women under age thirty are more assertive than women thirty and older. Phrases like "faster," "more frequently," and so on are useless in communicating the researcher's beliefs unless a comparison group is included in the hypothesis.

**Specificity.** Specificity is closely related to completeness. Both criteria emphasize the importance of the researcher's saying exactly what is meant in a hypothesis. Specificity requires that the words chosen to describe the variables in the hypothesis and the relationship believed to exist between them should suggest only one meaning to the reader of the hypothesis. Many words and phrases in our language have more than one meaning; the researcher has the responsibility to ensure that a hypothesis is stated so that no misunderstanding can possibly result. For example, the hypothesis—Poorly timed marital counseling will reflect a low success rate—lacks specificity in at least two respects. The expression "poorly timed marital counseling" probably refers to other factors that may exist in a couple's life at the time that they seek counseling. But we cannot be sure. It may also refer to social workers' tendency to let their appointments run over the time scheduled for counseling sessions. Similarly, the word *reflect* in the hypothesis also contributes confusion regarding the researcher's meaning. It is one of those words that sometimes is used as synonymous with "result in," and other times it is used to say that factors appear to be related when they really are not. Further confusing matters, it even has a special clinical meaning to social workers—an interviewing technique designed to help clients consider the meaning of what they have said. Given the context of the word in the hypothesis, it is impossible to tell which meaning of the word is intended. The researcher's belief could be expressed with more specificity if the hypothesis were restated. For example, it could have been worded: Couples undergoing bankruptcy proceedings are less likely to judge their marital counseling as successful than those who have less severe financial problems.

**Potential for Testing.**   In order to examine a possible relationship between or among variables, it is necessary to measure those variables with reasonable precision. Different cases must be able to be sorted into different groups (assigned value labels or values) in such a way that each case clearly falls into one and only one group. Some variables seem almost to defy objective measurement and therefore are inappropriate for inclusion within hypotheses. For example, teachers and students continue to disagree on what constitutes effective teaching or on what the characteristics of good leadership are. A hypothesis that states— Good teachers exhibit leadership within the classroom—would be a difficult one to test until we can achieve better agreement on how to measure both good teaching and leadership. Like beauty or a good personality, they remain a little too subjective to be able to test the hypothesis objectively. However, another hypothesis—Teachers who post office hours are more likely to receive higher teaching evaluations than those who do not post office hours—is more testable. Here both variables are easily measurable.

## The "Perfectly Worded" Hypothesis

As we noted, the preceding five criteria for the wording of a hypothesis tend to overlap a little. Sometimes meeting the requirements of one criterion helps the researcher meet the requirements of a second one; sometimes it can have the opposite effect. The perfect hypothesis, one that meets all criteria and that does it in one or more clear, concise statements is probably an unachievable goal. The criteria should be viewed as guidelines to help the researcher improve the way a hypothesis is stated, even if perfection is not possible.

Hypothesis construction, like problem identification (Chapter 3), is one of those steps in the research process that all too often is addressed hurriedly or taken lightly. A well-worded hypothesis can facilitate decision making at all other stages of the research process that follow; a hypothesis that is vague or otherwise sloppy can cause later difficulties for the social work researcher. Time spent on hypothesis construction is rarely wasted; in the long run, it is a time saver.

## Use of Subhypotheses

One other technique sometimes can be used to help hypotheses communicate more effectively what the researcher is saying. It is a good idea not to try to say too much in a single hypothesis. If a relationship between variables is believed to exist but is a difficult one to explain in a simple declarative sentence, several different subhypotheses may be needed.

Subhypotheses often are helpful if there is an overall pattern of relationship between variables, but the pattern does not hold up for all case value labels or values or even reverses itself at some points. (Statisticians sometimes refer to this as a *nonlinear relationship* between variables.) For example, social workers working in hospice settings might be hypothesized to exhibit certain patterns of degree of involvement with patients and their caregivers at various stages in the course of the patient's terminal illness. We might predict that they generally tend to be more involved when the patient first seeks hospice care and as the patient approaches death than during the time periods in between. The relationship between their degree of involvement and the stages of illness of their patients cannot be stated simply in one brief hypothesis. Any overall pattern believed to exist could be stated first as the central hypothesis; for example: Hospice social workers exhibit different degrees of professional involvement with their patients that are related to the stages of the patient's illness. Then many different subhypotheses could be formulated to describe any other trends within the central pattern. A series of simple statements expressing what we believe to be the relationships between the variables is always preferable to a single hypothesis that is so complex that few readers could understand it.

Overall, social work researchers should strive for simple, clear communication in stating hypotheses. If they are successful in this effort, their hypotheses should be more than adequate to guide the subsequent stages of the research process.

## Summary

We examined two of the important products that may emerge from a well-conducted review of the literature. The researcher may be able to state the research question or questions more precisely, reflecting the specific focus of the research. If existing knowledge suggests a possible answer to one or more of them, it may be possible to go even further and to draw conclusions from the literature review in the form of one or more hypotheses that can then be tested using statistical analysis.

Social workers and other researchers have developed their own language (and sometimes used existing language) to communicate certain key concepts. They use it both for clarity and efficiency of communication. In this chapter we introduced many research terms and described their specific meanings for the researcher.

We defined those terms that are essential to the understanding of hypotheses. The meanings of *variable, demographic variable, value label* or *value, frequency, dependent variable, independent variable, criterion variable, predictor variable,* and *intervening variable* were clarified.

A research hypothesis was defined (among other things) as a prediction of a relationship between or among variables. It generally goes even further in predicting the way in which they will be found to be related. Terms used to describe the nature of a relationship between variables (*causation, association,* and *correlation*) were differentiated, and the forms that a research hypothesis that predicts a relationship between variables can take (*directional, nondirectional,* or *no relationship*) were explained.

The importance of wording in hypothesis construction was emphasized throughout this chapter. Criteria for evaluating the quality of the wording of a hypothesis were proposed, and the appropriate use of subhypotheses was discussed.

# References

1.  Bellomy, P., Berstein, H., Bickley, S., et al. (1989). Factors Affecting Child Protection Workers' Decision-Making in Sumter County. Unpublished MSW Research Project. Columbia, SC: University of South Carolina, College of Social Work.
2.  Weinbach, R. W., & Grinnell, R. M., Jr. (2001). *Statistics for social workers.* Needham Heights, MA: Allyn & Bacon, 83–85.
3.  Ibid., 81.
4.  See, for example, Goldstein, H. (1969). *Research standards and methods for social workers.* Northbrook, IL: Whitehall Company, 55–57.

# PART III

## RESEARCH DESIGN ISSUES

# 6

# INTRODUCTION TO
# RESEARCH DESIGN

In the previous chapter, we discussed two possible products of a literature review conducted prior to data collection: focused research questions and hypotheses. In this chapter we will begin our discussion of a third one: research design.

## What Is a Research Design?

A literature review pulls together what is already known about the research problem and the methods that have been used to study it. It thus suggests to the researcher what specific research methods and strategies are best suited to conduct further inquiry. A design is a plan for conducting the research. It is implemented to attempt to find answers to the researcher's questions and/or to test any hypothesis or hypotheses that were formulated.

The design of a research study is a response to a series of questions. The major ones that it addresses are

- Where and when should the research be conducted?
- What data should be collected?
- From whom or what can it best be obtained?
- How should it be collected?
- What variables will need to be measured?
- How should they be measured?
- What other variables, if any, need to be controlled, and how should this be accomplished?
- How should the data collected be organized and analyzed?
- How should research findings be disseminated?

# The Purpose of Research Designs

The research design serves as a plan for the latter stages of the research. The answers to the preceding questions are not arrived at independently of each other. The decision-making process is made easier by the fact that these questions and their answers are interrelated. Having determined the answer to one or more of them, the answers to other questions often become quite predictable. For example, the selection of certain individuals to provide research data is likely to influence the general method of data collection that will be used. Similarly, the way variables are measured and the way that research participants are selected generally suggest the most appropriate type of statistical analysis to use. If one examines the ways that research has been conducted in the past, the interrelatedness of the preceding questions becomes readily apparent. Certain patterns emerge. Some of these patterns or ways of conducting research have been labeled. Some of them are universally recognized and understood; others are a little more ambiguous.

Over the years, certain design labels have been developed. They serve as a kind of shorthand for researchers to communicate to others the general characteristics of their research methods. For example, when a researcher states in a report or article that an experimental design was used, this says (or is supposed to say) that a package of related research methods was used. Knowing that the research design was experimental, a person knowledgeable about research will assume (usually correctly) that certain methods probably were used for selecting research participants, for addressing the problem of potentially intervening variables, or for interpreting the research findings.

Most designs that share the same label are more similar than dissimilar. Of course, every new research design is also unique in one or more ways. This is why a researcher is expected to do more than simply report the general design characteristics of the current research. As noted in Chapter 1, the scientific method requires that a researcher provide a detailed description of the research methods that were used so that others can attempt to verify the findings through replication. Research can be replicated only if a second researcher knows exactly how the original research was conducted.

# Broad Research Typologies

There are a number of broad descriptive terms that are used to convey the overall characteristics of one's research design. There are others that are a little more specific.

One broad categorization of research designs classifies research studies based on the number of times that measurement is repeated and the general purpose of the inquiry. It groups research designs into one of two general categories: cross-sectional or longitudinal.

## Cross-Sectional Designs

Most research designs use a single measurement of relevant variables. They are referred to as cross-sectional research designs. Ideally, all variables are measured simultaneously or as close in time as is possible. A kind of snapshot in time of what exists is taken and then analyzed for patterns and relationships between or among variables. Cross-sectional research is so common that it seems almost synonymous with the scientific method. It requires little explanation and is readily understood, so we will not devote much time to discussing it in detail at this point.

## Longitudinal Designs

A less common, more specialized alternative to cross-sectional designs is the longitudinal study. Like cross-sectional research, the term *longitudinal* should be used to describe one feature of a research design rather than as a design type per se. If the term *longitudinal* is not used in any way in describing a research design, we generally can assume that the design is cross-sectional.

All longitudinal research designs share a single characteristic—they entail the repeated study and measurement of the same variables over time at predetermined intervals. Longitudinal studies are designed to study change. But they try to find out more than simply if change occurred or how much change took place. They seek to identify exactly when change occurred and what phenomena were associated with it. Only longitudinal research can provide this type of useful knowledge.

Three additional adjectives are often used in describing longitudinal research. They reflect differences in the way that a sample of research participants is selected. One variety, the *trend study*, entails drawing a sample of participants on several different occasions from a group (pool) of potential participants. The pool tends to change over time. For example, a group of students may be selected at random from a social work program each year to participate in a study to assess changes in attitudes toward research. Although some students may be included in more than one stage of data collection (for example, they may appear in the sample selected during two or more different years), the total sample of students will be different each year from the sample selected any other year. An overall trend in changes in attitude within the program (but not within individual students) thus can be observed.

In a second variety of longitudinal research, the *cohort study*, the pool of potential research participants does not change, but the specific cases selected for study will differ during stages of data collection. For example, in a cohort study, a class of full-time students might be measured regarding their attitudes toward research over an academic year. Assuming that the class suffered no attrition or added no new members during the year, the class would be known as a cohort. Participants would be selected at random from the class on several occasions. No two groups selected for study would likely be identical in terms of which students would be included, but each group selected would represent the class at the various points of data collection.

In the third variation of longitudinal research, the *panel study,* the same group of research participants would be studied over time. In our example of a study to examine changes in student attitudes toward research, the same randomly selected students would be studied over their student careers to monitor any changes in their attitudes. Only attrition would result in any change in the composition of the group.

Longitudinal studies can last for a few days or a few weeks. More typically, they are conducted over a period of years. Some have gone on past the lifetime of the researchers who originally designed them and have been carried on by others; for example, studies on the status of women in the United States.

Most longitudinal studies are designed to document change. But they are also well suited to the needs of researchers who wish to document and learn more about the existence of a certain pattern of behavior and what is associated with it. A good example of longitudinal research of this type is the studies of a large number of terminally ill patients that were conducted by Elizabeth Kübler-Ross[1] and her associates over several decades. The researchers have been able to identify five predictable stages in the dying process and to describe them in detail. As a result, hospice social workers and others who work with the terminally ill now possess greater insight into their patients' behaviors and are better able to help them come to successful resolutions relating to their impending death.

The findings of other longitudinal studies in the area of grief and loss[2] have similarly proven invaluable to the social work practitioner. For example, we now know that the time around the first anniversary of the death of a loved one often is accompanied by depression and that anger at a deceased relative is a very predictable phenomenon at certain stages of the grieving process. Consequently, counseling now can focus on helping clients to anticipate and to deal with anniversary depression and to verbalize, better understand, accept, and work through their anger toward the deceased.

Longitudinal designs can acquire knowledge not readily acquired using other designs. Slowly developing changes and up-and-down fluctuations in behaviors and phenomena might be missed using cross-sectional designs. But they can be identified and plotted by using repeated measurements over long time periods. Longitudinal designs alone are able to tell us when changes occur and to help us to predict their occurrence with reasonable accuracy.

The major drawback to using longitudinal designs is their cost. Few researchers are willing to make the expensive, long-term commitment that is necessary to properly conduct them. Because they take so long to complete, researchers who hope to build an academic or scientific career around publication of numerous research papers or professional journal articles tend to shy away from them. One can spend a decade on a longitudinal study that can result in a single published scientific paper. However, such studies may be more substantive and may produce more definitive answers to research questions than many cross-sectional studies.

# The Knowledge-Building Continuum

One way to understand research design is to conceive of knowledge building in a given problem area as a cumulative process. As we suggested in Chapter 1, uncovering and disseminating knowledge is a systematic process that occurs over time. It is rarely (if ever) the work of one individual. That's why we tie our research to existing knowledge as reflected in the review of literature. We want to build on the work of others, and our findings will in turn help to facilitate the work of subsequent researchers.

Sometimes the process of movement toward answers and at least partial solutions to problems occurs relatively rapidly, but more typically, progress in knowledge building is slow work. It entails the use of a variety of methods (designs) that occur most often in a certain logical sequence.

When very little is known about a problem and there are many more questions than answers, certain types of research designs are indicated. As knowledge accumulates, other designs are both possible and indicated. They are in turn replaced by other designs that have the potential to provide more definitive answers to certain types of questions. Because there is a logical sequence in which different designs are employed in the study of a research problem, they can be placed on a continuum such as that shown in Figure 6.1.

As Figure 6.1 suggests, as a general rule, exploratory research designs tend to be the first kind of research conducted on a problem or question. They then form a basis for descriptive designs, which precede explanatory ones. At least that is the way it is supposed to happen. In the real world, the situation may be quite different. For example, in social work, our understanding of the phenomenon that is the focus of much of our research, human behavior, will always remain quite incomplete and fragmented. Consequently, much of the research that we conduct continues to be of the exploratory and descriptive types, no matter how long some type of behavior has been studied and no matter how many studies of it have been conducted.

Even if a sound base of research knowledge exists about a problem or question, we sometimes still find ourselves unable to move much further along the continuum for other reasons. We may never be able to conduct the most methodologically rigorous explanatory research studies. These designs (at least those that use human participants) are not always feasible for investigating certain questions, because to employ them would violate research and professional ethics (Chapter 2). Some questions—for example: What happens when clients are denied access to all help?—might best be studied by denying help to a randomly selected group of clients applying for our services and asking other organizations also to deny them assistance. Of course, such a practice would not and should not be tolerated. An alternative way of studying the question might

---

**FIGURE  6.1   The Knowledge-Building Continuum**

Exploratory ⟶ Descriptive ⟶ Explanatory

be the best that we could do, despite the fact that existing knowledge about the question might suggest that we are ready for explanatory research on it.

Orderly progress along the continuum is perhaps more of an ideal than a description of reality. There are numerous situations that suggest the need for exceptions. Sometimes, we mistakenly conclude that we have learned more about a problem than we really have. Explanatory research is conducted, and it presents us with surprises. It causes us to question the state of existing knowledge about a problem or question. Thus, we conclude that a return to descriptive or even exploratory research is indicated.

An important task for the researcher reviewing the literature is to locate just where on the continuum one's own research should fall. For example, if the literature review reveals that virtually all of the past research on a problem has been of an exploratory nature, then a more rigorous design, such as explanatory research, is clearly premature. Research that is designed to improve on the current description of the problem and the conditions that surround it would be more appropriate. Conversely, if the literature is replete with reports of research that used explanatory designs to successfully isolate the cause of the problem, additional exploratory or descriptive research would not seem appropriate. The existing level of knowledge would suggest that such research would be unnecessary and redundant and that rigorous research designed to test the effectiveness of methods of intervention (prevention or treatment) may be what is needed.

## Exploratory Designs

Exploratory research is appropriate when problems have been identified but our understanding of them is quite limited. It is conducted to lay the groundwork for other knowledge building that will follow. Exploratory designs are predicated on the assumption that we need to know more about something before we can begin to understand it or attempt to confront it using intervention methods with high potential for success. In exploratory research, we often don't even know what it is we need to know!

In an exploratory study, the researcher begins his or her inquiry without much insight into which variables may relate to the problem. But it is hoped that the research will narrow the list. Because the relevant variables cannot even be specified, there can be no hypotheses to test, and only the broadest of research questions can be examined. However, a frequent goal of exploratory research is to derive hypotheses for future research endeavors.

Similarly, selection of research participants or cases for study is usually not a very rigorous or exacting procedure when exploratory research designs are used. There may be few cases studied, or a large number may be selected in order to learn as much as possible about the problem. In either instance, there are no legitimate claims to their being representative of others not selected for study.

We do not wish to imply that persons who conduct exploratory research employ a more haphazard approach to knowledge building than those who use other designs. Good exploratory research is always carefully planned and conducted using specific methods and according to established guidelines. But researchers who conduct exploratory research must work within limitations not present within most other research designs.

Thus, exploratory designs are employed to begin the process of knowledge building about a problem or focused question. For example, prior to the 1960s, exploratory research was used appropriately for studies of child abuse. In the early 1980s, it was used for studying spouse abuse and the problems of people with HIV infection. These early studies simply tried to conceptualize exactly what the problem was, the degree to which it was recognized as a problem, what forms it took, and what variables might relate to it. As we entered the twenty-first century, exploratory designs no longer were appropriate for learning about most aspects of these particular problems, but they were appropriate for studying other, newly identified problems, such as the effects of managed care on medical treatment.

What are some of the forms that exploratory research can assume? We will describe three particular exploratory designs that are widely used in social work research. We will use standard notations to describe their elements as follows:

$X$ = exposure to the independent variable or treatment condition
$O_1$ = first measurement of the dependent variable
$O_2$ = second measurement of the dependent variable
$R$ = random assignment of persons to a group

**1. The One Shot Case Study.** The one-shot case study design, also called the one-group, posttest-only design, is the most basic of all research designs. Schematically, it is noted as

$$X \qquad O$$

where $X$ represents exposure to some variable (such as a program or intervention) and $O$ represents measurement of a dependent variable among participants. Let's look at an example of how this design may be used in a social work research study.

Suppose a social worker in a neighborhood community center wishes to determine if eight weeks of classes in English as a second language increases knowledge of the English language in a group of Spanish-speaking residents. The social worker identifies interested participants and arranges for them to receive the instruction. When the course is completed (eight weeks later), the group takes a brief paper-and-pencil test that measures knowledge of the English language. The social worker scores the tests and calculates the percentage of people who pass it. This provides the measurement of the dependent variable ($O$).

The major advantage of the design is simplicity. However, it does not provide any comparisons (for example, how much of the English language participants actually knew before exposure to the class, with how much they knew following the eight-week course). Thus, it is difficult to conclude from this design that the program itself (and not something else) brought about change in the participants' knowledge of English.

**2. The Cross-Sectional Survey Design.** The cross-sectional survey design entails measurement of some characteristic in a defined sample or group at a given point in time. It is diagrammed rather simply as

$$O$$

where $O$ represents one measurement of the dependent variable. For example, let's say the associate dean of a school of social work wishes to know what particular social work electives students might wish to take during the summer semester. A brief survey instrument identifying elective courses is developed and mailed to students to complete. A large percentage of these students complete the instrument and return it. The associate dean determines from their responses which courses should be offered during the summer semester ($O$).

The cross-sectional survey design, as used here, provides information about what individuals may want, feel, or believe at a given time. This is its primary usefulness. The alternative would be to guess what students might want for summer course work and run the risk of offering courses that no one is interested in taking or not offering courses that students may want or need.

**3. The Longitudinal Case Study Design.** In the longitudinal case study design, research participants are exposed to some independent variable (for example, as participants in a program) followed by several repeat measurements. Thus it is a form of longitudinal research. It may be diagrammed as follows:

$$X \quad O_1 \quad O_2 \quad O_3$$

Using our first example again, suppose the social worker wanted to determine if the knowledge of the English language acquired by participants is retained over a six-month period of time. $X$ represents the eight-week language course that participants take. $O_1$ is the first measurement of their knowledge of English taken immediately following the course. $O_2$ is the second measurement of their knowledge of English taken three months later, and $O_3$ is the third measurement of this same variable, at a six-month follow-up. From this design the social worker is able to determine if the knowledge gained by participants lasts over a six-month period of time following participation in the program and, if not, approximately when it starts to decline. This type of data would be useful for determining program priorities for the community center.

## *Descriptive Designs*

The accumulation of the findings derived from exploratory research makes it possible to use descriptive designs. Descriptive research has as its goal the measurement and description of relevant variables (those identified using exploratory research designs) and the distribution of their values. For example, research on the problem of child abuse moved beyond exploration and into description by the late 1960s and early 1970s. Studies sought to measure its patterns of incidence and severity and to chronicle its different forms. The major relevant variables had already been identified through exploratory research; it was now possible and desirable for researchers to measure how they were distributed and to see if there were any patterns of relationships between and among them.

Most descriptive research seeks to better understand and measure how variables are naturally distributed. It does not entail introducing or manipulating variables to see if other variables are affected. Thus, support for a relationship of causation between variables would not be possible using descriptive methods. Although seeking support for relationships between variables is not a major objective of most descriptive research, we sometimes see hypotheses tested in descriptive research designs. When we do, they generally predict a relationship of association or correlation.

Even when hypotheses are not formulated prior to data collection, relationships between and among variables sometimes appear to be obvious, especially in large-scale descriptive studies. For example, in one common type of descriptive study, the census, it is often possible to detect apparent associations or correlations that appear promising and are worthy of additional study. Statistical analysis can be performed to attempt to determine if the apparent relationship is likely to be the work of chance or sampling error (Chapter 12). It can be performed by the researchers who actually collected the data or by others who later have access to them.

In descriptive research, the researcher hopes to generalize from cases studied to those that are similar but were not part of the research study. Thus, it is critical that the researcher select and study cases that are typical of the entire group. Accuracy of measurement of variables also takes on great importance. Case sampling and measurement (the topics of later chapters) absorb a considerable amount of the time and attention of the researcher.

Descriptive research is only as good or as bad as the representativeness of the sample of cases that are studied and the accuracy of the description that it produces. Just describing, if performed well, is an exact science that requires a great amount of knowledge and skill. There are rules and procedures that govern the conduct of good descriptive research, just as in all other types of research.

Three different descriptive research designs that are widely used in social work research are described in the following sections.

**1. One Group Pretest–Posttest Design.** The one-group pretest–posttest design represents an improvement over many exploratory designs, as it adds an opportunity to compare pretest and posttest measures of the dependent variable. It is symbolized as follows:

$$O_1 \quad X \quad O_2$$

$O_1$ represents the first measurement of the dependent variable, prior to exposure of participants to the independent variable ($X$). Afterward, participants are again measured on the dependent variable, and their scores are compared. It is hoped that there will be a difference between performance at $O_1$ and $O_2$ and that this change may be attributed to the program or intervention ($X$). Let's look at our previous example and apply the one-group pretest–posttest design to it.

Using a paper-and-pencil test to measure knowledge of the English language in a group of Spanish-speaking clients at a neighborhood center, the social worker asks them to complete the test before the first session of the eight-week class ($O_1$). Following completion of this course, the participants complete the inventory again ($O_2$). The social worker then may make a comparison of how much change there was in knowledge of the English language from measurement 1 to measurement 2.

Because of the pretest measurement ($O_1$), it is possible to know how much change in the dependent variable actually occurred as a result of the intervention. This is the major advantage of the one-group pretest–posttest design.

**2. The Static Group Comparison Design.** The static group comparison design allows the researcher to compare two groups on their measurements of a dependent variable, following exposure of one group to the independent variable. It is symbolized as follows:

$$X \quad O_1$$
$$O_1$$

A brief example illustrates the usefulness of this design. A social worker wishes to compare two groups on their levels of anxiety following a behavioral treatment program designed to reduce the anxiety symptoms in otherwise healthy adults. Group 1 consists of those people who are selected for inclusion in the treatment program, a cognitive behavioral approach to treatment that lasts three months. Following completion of the program, the participants are measured on their level of anxiety using a standardized measuring instrument designed for this purpose. For comparison purposes, a group of similar adults who did not complete this program (perhaps they are on a waiting list for receiving this service) is measured using the same instrument. Then a comparison is made between those who completed the treatment and those who did not. If the group receiving the treatment shows a lower level of anxiety than the comparison group, then it may be concluded that the treatment had the desired effect. However, because there was no pretest for either group, we really do not know if the treatment group had a lower level of anxiety to begin with than the comparison group. This is the major limitation of the static group comparison design.

**3. Time Series Design.**  In the time series design, several measurements are taken on a dependent variable over time, typically before and after exposure to the independent variable (another longitudinal approach). A typical time series design looks like this:

$$O_1 \quad O_2 \quad O_3 \quad X \quad O_4 \quad O_5 \quad O_6$$

These symbols indicate that three measurements of the dependent variable were taken prior to exposure of the group to the intervention. Following intervention, three more measures (over time) were taken of the dependent variable. An example will help illustrate the usefulness of this design in social work research.

A group of men meet weekly at a local mental health center to work on issues related to anger expression. During week 1, week 2, and week 3, the level of expressed anger is measured using a standardized measuring instrument designed for this purpose. The social worker introduces a new model of treatment at week 4. The model requires several weeks of group process. When enough time has lapsed for the new treatment to have taken effect, the men's expressed anger is again measured for three consecutive weeks.

Several comparisons are possible using a time series design. First of all, the three pretest measures allow the researcher to establish a baseline measurement of the dependent variable. Baseline measures taken in this way allow a researcher to measure a variable as precisely as possible before intervention. The baseline measurement would be the average expressed anger score of the group over the three-week period prior to the introduction of the intervention in week 4. It probably would be a more accurate measurement of the dependent variable than a single measurement of it on just one day because the variable is likely to fluctuate naturally over time.

Following the intervention, the repeated measures allow the researcher to make at least two comparisons:

- Comparison 1: From the average pretest measure to an average posttest measure, to see if the intervention may have produced changes in expressed anger in the desired direction.
- Comparisons 2 and 3:  From $O_4$ to $O_5$ and from $O_5$ to $O_6$, to see if any changes that occurred in the desired direction endured over time.

In summary, descriptive designs allow the researcher to go beyond exploring and permit comparisons between groups on their measurement of the dependent variable, typically before and after participation in some intervention. Although they are an improvement over exploratory designs, they still fall far short of being able to tell us if the independent variable actually produced changes in the dependent variable.

## *Explanatory Research*

At some point, the knowledge about a problem may advance to a point where it is possible to justify the use of explanatory designs. Exploratory and descriptive designs seek primarily understanding of a problem and of factors that are associated with it. Some design variations give us hints as to which solutions might be effective. However, by using explanatory research, it is possible to arrive at more definitive answers as to what might cause the problem and what intervention methods are effective in treating or even preventing it.

When explanatory research designs are used, the researcher uses hypothesis testing to try to verify possible relationships between variables. The dependent and independent variables have been identified through exploratory research, and their distribution has been described through descriptive research. In explanatory research, cases are selected for study with utmost care, to be certain that they can be regarded as representative of all cases, including those not studied. The researcher hopes to be able to verify the presence of important relationships between or among variables. Whenever possible, other (intervening) variables that might somehow serve to misrepresent the true relationship between dependent and independent variables are controlled. This is accomplished either through their physical manipulation or, more frequently, through statistical methods. If they cannot be controlled, every effort is made to determine the degree to which they may have obfuscated the relationship between the independent and dependent variables.

Explanatory designs seek to uncover causal relationships between variables. As we indicated in the previous chapter, causality is a special kind of relationship. It goes beyond association and even simple correlation. A correlation is nothing more than the observation that certain variables relate to each other in a more or less consistent manner. In a causal relationship, exposure to an independent variable (and to its different quantities or qualities) actually brings about changes in the other (dependent) variable. There are three conditions that must be present in relationships in order to conclude that one variable ($x$) causes the changes in the other ($y$). These conditions are

1. $x$ must actually precede $y$ in time order.
2. $x$ and $y$ must consistently covary.
3. All other explanations for changes in $y$ must be ruled out.

All three of these conditions must be present in order to determine that $x$ brought about, or caused, the changes in $y$.

**Experimental Research.** Experimental designs are a specialized type of explanatory research. Experiments, like other forms of explanatory research, seek to explain the variations (different values) of a dependent variable in relation to one or more independent variables. But when reputable researchers use the word *experiment* to characterize their research, they are stating that their research design has several specific features. Thus, although all experiments can be described as explanatory, not all explanatory research is experimental.

Unfortunately, the word *experiment* has crept into the vernacular. It is tossed around rather loosely and sometimes used to describe almost any research or quasi-research endeavor. For example, we sometimes hear social workers talk about the experimental use of a new treatment method when what they have really done is simply to substitute the new method for another one. Sometimes *experiment* is even used to describe any action that a person performs deliberately just to see what happens. For example, we hear people talk about performing an experiment when they don't make the morning coffee one morning, in order to see if their roommate will make it or will wait for it to be made. Neither of these examples comes close to what true experimental research is.

An experimental research design is very rigorous. Its requirements make it the ideal design for generating cause–effect knowledge. However, these requirements also frequently preclude its use for logistical and ethical reasons. Why? In a true experiment, the following very demanding requirements must be met:

- *The independent variable(s) are introduced or manipulated, one at a time, by the researcher.* This means, for example, that the researcher wishing to study the relationship between enrollment in a specific job training program and success in seeking employment must control who is enrolled in the program and who is not. Or another researcher studying the effect of hours of treatment time on recovery in an inpatient psychiatric facility would have to tightly control the exact number of treatment hours given patients participating in the study.
- *There are one or more control groups that are not exposed to the independent variable.* In the first example just described, the researcher would select a group of individuals who would not enroll in the job training program (a control group). They would be identified but not given the training. Their success rate in finding employment (the dependent variable) would be measured along with that of those selected for the program for comparison purposes. In the second example, a control group would also be selected. Their number of hours of treatment time would not be influenced in any way by the researcher.
- *Research participants are randomly assigned to experimental and control groups.* This means that, in the first example, nothing (other than random assignment to the groups) would influence whether potential trainees would be enrolled in the job training program (experimental group) or selected for the control group. In the second example, assignment to either the experimental or the control group would also have to be totally random.

Why is randomization so important in an experiment? When experimental research designs are used, random assignment of research participants to experimental and control groups often is the primary vehicle used for control of intervening variables. Random assignment relies on the laws of probability and what is likely to occur in the long run. It depends on the equalization effect that occurs naturally within groups (subsamples) drawn from the same pool as more and more cases are added to them. As more cases are added to the two groups in a random manner, the groups become increasingly similar. In our first example, if the researcher assigned cases to the experimental and control groups randomly and if the two groups were reasonably large, the groups should be similar in all respects. This means that variables that we have reason to believe may affect success in finding employment, such as motivation level, work experience, health, intelligence, physical appearance, or verbal skills, will tend to be similar in the two groups when they are viewed in toto.

But what if the literature review failed to reveal one or more other intervening variables that might affect success in finding employment? They may be neither logical nor obvious, something that we might not have guessed to be potentially intervening variables (for example, number of siblings or birth order). Can these variables also be controlled through random assignment of cases to relatively large experimental and control groups? Can a researcher assume that if the experimental and control groups are fairly large, they will reflect comparable distributions of them? Yes. A highly desirable effect of random assignment is that, if performed correctly, it will control for the effects of all intervening variables, even those whose existence we have no reason to suspect! This is why randomization is such an important feature of experimental designs.

Randomization is so useful a method for controlling intervening variables that researchers frequently devise methods to use it in other ways within experimental designs. In our example of an experiment designed to measure the effectiveness of a job training program, the researcher might randomly select (from among available trainers) those who will be used in the program. This would increase the likelihood that it was the program and not the skills of the trainer that were evaluated. The researcher might also randomly select times of day to offer the training, rooms to be used, or any other potentially intervening variable that can be randomized without affecting the nature of the program being evaluated.

Even in nonexperimental research, randomization is sometimes used to improve the research design. Many potentially intervening variables can be randomized even if the researcher cannot physically control them. For example, a researcher can randomly select days or times to conduct measurements of client attitudes such as depression or anger, in order to minimize the likelihood that seasonal influences might bias the measurements.

- *The influence of all other, potentially intervening variables is controlled.* This is accomplished through some combination of their physical manipulation, statistical analysis, or, most frequently, through randomization. In the first example, a true experiment would require that the only difference between the groups of individuals in the experimental and control groups would be the fact that persons in the control group do not receive the training, whereas those in the experimental group do. In the second example, both groups would be comparable, except that the amount of treatment hours of patients in the experimental group would be controlled, whereas the treatment hours of those in the control group would not.

Experiments are the only research designs that possess the preceding combination of characteristics and requirements. They use the best available methods to help the researcher rule out the possible effects of intervening variables. Consequently, among the basic designs we have described, experimental designs do the most convincing job of providing evidence that a cause–effect relationship between variables exists. They can help the researcher conclude with reasonable certainty that the presence of a certain value of the independent variable caused a certain value of the dependent variable to occur. Because the independent variable was either introduced or manipulated by the researcher, it could not have been the other way around. Experimental designs also can prove that different values of the dependent variable could not have occurred because of one or more other (intervening) variables.

The term *quasi-experimental* is used by researchers to describe research designs that are similar to experimental designs but that fail to meet one or more of their requisite conditions. Frequently, researchers in social service organizations are able to constitute two groups, but they are unable to randomly assign participants to groups. Or, as indicated earlier in this chapter, sometimes it is ethically questionable to withhold treatment from a comparison (control) group. Whenever the conditions of the research design are such that any of these critical components is absent, we refer to the design as quasi-experimental to distinguish it from a true experimental design. Whole books have been written on various experimental and quasi-experimental research designs. The classic remains a 1963 volume by Campbell and Stanley.[3]

Because all true experimental designs require rigorous control over certain conditions (assignment of people to groups, exposure to the independent variable, and so on), it sometimes can be difficult to implement them because of ethical concerns. In human services, we are committed to delivering the best possible services to each client, regardless of what a research design may indicate as desirable. Research must be of lower priority than service. However, with careful planning, experiments can be designed and implemented within human service organizations. We will describe three experimental designs that are often used in social work research.

**1. The Classical Experimental Design.** The classical experimental design, also called the pretest–posttest control group design, does a good job of controlling for the possible effects of intervening variables. It is portrayed as follows:

| Group 1 | R | $O_1$ | X | $O_2$ |
|---------|---|-------|---|-------|
| Group 2 | R | $O_1$ |   | $O_2$ |

In this design, individuals are randomly assigned to one of two groups: an experimental group or a control group. The dependent variable is measured for both groups ($O_1$). The experimental group (group 1) is exposed to the independent variable, such as participation in a program. Following completion of the program, the dependent variable is again measured for both groups ($O_2$). Then the following comparisons can be made:

- Comparison 1: The researcher examines the $O_1$ scores for both groups, anticipating that these measures will be essentially equivalent. (They should be if randomization has been successful.) In addition, these measurements will be useful to compute changes in each group from $O_1$ to $O_2$.
- Comparison 2: The researcher examines the $O_2$ scores for both groups, anticipating that $O_2$ for the experimental group will have changed in a predicted direction, whereas $O_2$ for the control group will not. $O_2$ for the control group should not change, because this group was not exposed to the treatment program. Assuming the researcher finds the expected change in $O_2$ for the experimental group, with no real change in the control group, it can be concluded with some degree of certainty that the change is due to exposure to the independent variable rather than to some other factor.

The classical experimental design requires that the researcher has the authority to assign research participants to one of two treatment conditions. It also requires that both groups are pretested and posttested. Finally, the design requires that individuals in the control group not receive the intervention being tested—a requirement that might be regarded as professionally unethical and therefore unacceptable.

**2. The Solomon Four-Group Design.** The Solomon four-group design is very similar to the classical experimental design, but instead of using two groups, it uses four. The additional two groups are used to control for the possible effects of the pretest. The design is symbolized as follows:

| Group 1 | R | $O_1$ | X | $O_2$ |
|---------|---|-------|---|-------|
| Group 2 | R | $O_1$ |   | $O_2$ |
| Group 3 | R |       | X | $O_2$ |
| Group 4 | R |       |   | $O_2$ |

Although the design may appear complicated, it is actually quite simple. Groups 1 and 3 are both experimental groups; each receives exposure to the independent variable. However, group 3 does not receive a pretest. Groups 2 and 4 are both control groups; neither receives the independent variable. In addition, group 4 does not receive a pretest; in fact, the only thing group 4 receives is a posttest. Then at least four comparisons can be made:

- Comparison 1: $O_1$ and $O_2$ for both experimental groups. What the researcher hopes to find is a change in both experimental groups, with no difference between scores of the two groups. If there is a difference, it might indicate the effect of a pretest.
- Comparison 2: $O_2$ for both control groups. These measures ought to be similar, because neither group received the independent variable.
- Comparison 3: $O_1$ for groups 1 and 2. These measures ought to be similar as well, because random assignment has been used to assign people to groups, and no one at this point had received the independent variable.
- Comparison 4: $O_2$ for all four groups. If the intervention was successful, scores for the two experimental groups should be better than scores for the two control groups. However, unless the results of the first three comparisons showed the desired results, conclusions about the independent variable's causing changes in the dependent variable probably cannot be justified.

**3. The Posttest-Only Control Group Design.** The posttest-only control group design, sometimes called the randomized posttest-only control group design, uses random assignment of persons to either an experimental or control group to equalize them; neither group is pretested. The design is symbolized as follows:

$$R \quad X \quad O_1$$
$$R \qquad\quad O_1$$

$O_1$ is the first measurement of the dependent variable, which in this design is a posttest. The design allows the researcher to compare posttest measurements of the dependent variable by group. Specifically, the researcher is interested in discovering if the posttest measurement for the experimental group is either higher or lower than for the control group. It should be, if the independent variable had an effect. Even though there is no pretest to ensure equivalence of the groups prior to exposure to the independent variable, random assignment theoretically takes care of this. Pretests are required, however, when the measurement of the amount of change from pretest to posttest is important for the purpose of the study. In addition, pretesting is necessary if the groups are so small as to render randomization ineffective in creating equivalent groups.

## Internal Validity and External Validity

Of course, any design can contain major design flaws. They may contain methodological errors, such as poor measurement of variables, mistakes in the selection of a potential pool of research participants, or erroneous use of statistical methods for data analysis. If this occurs in explanatory research, any conclusions regarding relationships between dependent and independent variables (that is, claims about support for the research hypothesis) can be made in error. There is well-designed explanatory research and not-so-well-designed explanatory research. Similarly, there is good and bad descriptive and exploratory research. If any research contains major design flaws, its findings can be useless or, worse yet, misleading.

How can we judge when a research design has been well developed and implemented? Two criteria are widely used in evaluating the quality of certain research designs and the value of any findings generated by them. They are internal validity and external validity.

## Internal Validity

What does it mean if one states that a researcher's conclusions appear to have a high degree of internal validity? When is internal validity important? *Internal validity* refers to the amount of confidence we have that the independent variable and not some other variable or alternative explanation produced the variations that occurred in the dependent variable. Obviously then, internal validity is critical to any conclusions about causation drawn from explanatory research (but not for exploratory or descriptive studies). For example, suppose that a researcher asserts that, based on research findings, "in counseling victims of rape, counseling method A produces a higher rate of success than counseling method B." We will agree with this conclusion only if we are convinced that, based on the research design used, it is justifiable. We will be convinced only if the design seems to have internal validity; that is, if the differences in success rate that were observed appear to have been caused by the two counseling methods and nothing else. It was not client age, marital status, varying skill level of the social workers who counseled them, or any of the millions of other potentially intervening variables that produced the different rates of success. The research was designed so that they were all controlled in some way.

There are many factors that are generally acknowledged to threaten internal validity.[4] Although they are most relevant to experimental and other explanatory designs, some also have limited relevance to other designs. They include the following:

**Testing Effects.**   As we suggested in one of our earlier examples, the use of a pretest to measure the dependent variable may actually result in a change in measurements of the variable. So, theoretically, can any other measurement that is required. Participants can learn from or be otherwise influenced by the process of completing a questionnaire or other measurement procedures. If feasible and consistent with the type of research being conducted, the use of one or more control groups can help the researcher assess the extent to which testing effects might represent a threat to internal validity.

**Maturation or Passage of Time.**   Some behaviors and problems seem to have a logical life cycle or change naturally over time. For example, grief over the death of a loved one tends to subside over time with or without counseling. Any conclusion that the presence of long-term bereavement counseling may have resulted in improved survivor functioning would thus have to be tempered with an assessment of the degree to which time (the threat to internal validity) might have contributed to apparent treatment success.

**History.**   Events sometimes occur during the course of research that might have a major effect on the dependent variable. It may be a much greater effect than that of the independent variable. Such a historical event may never make the newspapers. For example, it may be the firing of a popular coworker or the implementation of a new personnel policy that affects the job satisfaction of a group of social workers much more than the presence or absence of a new attitude adjustment hour (the independent variable). Or the event may be truly historical in scope, such as the crash of an airliner or a terrorist bombing. We could sympathize with researchers who, for example, might have been attempting to prove that "type of counseling affects anxiety level of clients" if one of these disasters occurred in the community during the course of treatment. The internal validity of their findings would almost certainly be questioned.

**Statistical Regression.**   Sometimes it is desirable to select research participants who exhibit only the most extreme measurements of some variable. We might do this in order to be certain that our participants are those most in need of intervention and/or that they truly possess certain characteristics that we want to try to affect (for example, low assertiveness or a high level of hostility). Based on some measurement of the (dependent) variable, they will have exhibited the most dramatically high or low measurements of it. Following the introduction of intervention (the independent variable), the dependent variable generally would be measured again. The second measurement is likely to be less extreme than the first one. Would that mean that the intervention was successful? Maybe, but maybe not. Even if the intervention had no effect whatsoever, a less extreme measurement of the dependent variable might have occurred simply because participants were unlikely to repeat their extremely high or low measurement of the variable. There would be little room for their measurement of the variable to become more extreme, but plenty of room for it to moderate just based on its normal fluctuations.

The tendency of extreme measurements to regress or to become more moderate over time can obscure and obfuscate the results of research that uses participants who were selected because of their extreme measurements of a variable. If feasible, a control group consisting of others possessing equally extreme measurements can be used to determine whether statistical regression threatened the internal validity of research findings. If changes in the control group are found to parallel those in the experimental group, it was probably statistical regression and not the independent variable that affected the dependent variable.

**Instrumentation.** If there has been a pretest and a different version of the instrument was then used as a posttest, the researcher must be certain that any differences in the experimental and control groups did not result from differences in the instruments used. Were the pretest and posttest measurements equal in difficulty or otherwise comparable? Were the experimental and control groups given different versions, and were they comparable? Did they favor one group or the other? If not, any differences may have been caused by the different instruments used, not by the independent variable.

**Lack of Sample Comparability.** No comparison of an experimental group with a control group following the introduction or manipulation of an independent variable is fair if the two groups were not comparable to begin with. As noted, we use randomization in true experiments to ensure comparability. But in quasi-experiments or other explanatory designs, we often must use experimental and control groups in which participants were not randomly assigned. The samples may deliberately or unintentionally have been constituted in such a way that one group might have a higher likelihood of success (if that is the dependent variable). For example, what if we compare clients who attend a substance abuse counseling program with those who do not choose to participate after being referred for counseling? The counseling offered (the independent variable) may not explain the fact that those people in counseling had a lower rate of recidivism. Perhaps they were just more highly motivated, or some other factor might better explain both their wish to seek counseling and their lower recidivism rate than it would for those who did not attend.

**Experimental Mortality.** The fact that research participants or objects are lost to the researcher in the course of research can offer a threat to internal validity. This is particularly true in some forms of longitudinal research (discussed earlier in this chapter) but it can occur in other types of research as well. If the reasons that cases are lost are somehow related to the dependent variable, the results can be misinterpreted, and the findings may lack internal validity. For example, in a study of the effectiveness of a new method of addiction counseling, a control group (one that receives the usual treatment) could be used. Clients could be randomly assigned to one type of treatment or the other. At the time of the posttest interview, the experimental group (those who receive the new treatment) might reflect a much higher rate of success. But the experimental group has lost 40 percent of its cases (those who are no longer available to be interviewed), whereas all clients in the control group agree to participate in the posttest interview. The lost 40 percent may reflect the same rate of treatment success as the remaining 60 percent in the experimental group that were interviewed. But they also may not. They may have dropped out of treatment because the treatment was so successful that it became unnecessary. That is probably an overly optimistic interpretation of their behavior. It is also possible that they left because they concluded that their treatment was doing them no good, and they decided to devote the time that they had been wasting to better pursuit of their addiction!

If so, the conclusion that the experimental treatment was more successful than the usual treatment would be lacking in internal validity because of experimental mortality.

**Ambiguity about Direction of Causation.** Sometimes in nonexperimental research designs it could be argued that it was really the researcher's dependent variable that produced different values of the independent variable, rather than the other way around. For example, a researcher might observe that couples who completed a ten-week marital enrichment seminar have a higher level of marital satisfaction (the dependent variable) than those who dropped out before the seminar was completed. Does that mean that the seminar enhances marital satisfaction? Maybe. But perhaps satisfaction affected completion, rather than the other way around. Perhaps those who completed the seminar had fewer problems, making it easier for them to complete it, whereas those who had more problems had to drop out. As we can see in this example, this threat to internal validity is closely related to the previous one.

**Diffusion or Overlap of Intervention Methods.** If we hope to compare the effectiveness of two intervention methods, it is best if they are discrete and bear little or no similarity to each other. Unfortunately, this is not always the case. In the real world, blurring takes place over time, often because features of one intervention become imitated by practitioners of the other intervention method. Thus, any comparison is not a clean one.

For example, suppose a researcher wanted to find out whether support or confrontation is more effective in counseling spouse-abusing clients. Would the social workers assigned to use confrontation methods be able to stick to the method assigned to them? Would their treatment have elements of support? Would those assigned to be only supportive of clients occasionally lapse into a little confrontation? Perhaps both groups of social workers offering treatment will have learned over the years that certain elements of the opposite treatment method can be helpful on occasion and, consciously or unconsciously, they will inject them into their interventions. Then how will we be able to say that it was the treatment intervention (support or confrontation) that produced the different treatment success rates of the two groups of clients? Or if no difference in success rates were to be found, how do we know that the similarity between the two intervention methods used did not hide a real difference in the effectiveness of the methods?

These threats to internal validity should be regarded as potential problems to be aware of, rather than as a list of problems that can be avoided altogether. Perfect internal validity is rarely if ever assumed to exist. But the design of explanatory research can do much to enhance the likelihood of an acceptable level of internal validity. Experimental designs are more likely to produce findings with acceptable internal validity than other designs because of their characteristics. It should now be apparent why experimental designs help to reduce the various threats to internal validity.

## *External Validity*

When it is concluded in an explanatory study that a research finding appears to have a high level of internal validity, it is possible to conclude that variations of the independent variable (and not something else) may have caused variations within the dependent variable among cases (persons) studied. But how far can we generalize this relationship between variables? To all cases that were not selected for study? To all persons within the state who are similar in some way to those studied? To all persons everywhere who are similar? These are issues of external validity.

*External validity* refers to the extent to which findings are believed to apply beyond cases that were actually studied. Internal validity is necessary for a high level of external validity to be present. But it is not sufficient to guarantee its presence. To a great extent, external validity relates directly to the nature of the cases that were studied and to what degree they can be assumed to be representative of other cases that were not studied. Thus, it is an important issue to consider in descriptive research as well as in explanatory research. It is generally less an issue of concern in exploratory research.

To illustrate the concept of external validity, we might consider a hypothetical study of the effect of the career goals of child protection workers (the independent variable) on the quality of services that they deliver (the dependent variable). Let us assume that a carefully designed and implemented study of a sample of workers within Erie County in western New York State produces the finding that career goals of the workers in the study appear to directly affect the quality of child protection services within the county. On careful scrutiny of the researchers' methods, we conclude that the finding probably has internal validity; other variables and factors that might have caused the variations in the dependent variable were well controlled. To what degree does the finding have external validity? Is the relationship between the variables likely to be present among all child welfare workers (including those working in adoptions) within Erie County? Among all public welfare social workers in Erie County? Among all public welfare workers in all counties in New York State? Would it hold up for any county organization with a heavy urban population, for both BSW and MSW social workers, for staff whose average age is fifty-two years or older, for those with no formal social work education, or for some other group of workers who may differ from those actually studied in some other way? These are all questions that relate to the external validity of the findings of the research. Assessing the external validity of research findings and the design that produced them entails a judgment about the research sample that was studied. Specifically, it requires a conclusion about who (besides the people or objects in the research sample themselves) might also have the same characteristics of the people or objects in the sample. This is the issue of sample representativeness (discussed in detail in Chapter 9).

Obviously, good external validity (also referred to as *broad generalizability*) is important to the utility of explanatory research, which attempts to identify relationships between variables within research samples and provide evidence that the same relationships exist beyond those samples. If a representative sample is not used, research findings lose any credibility. However, external validity is also very important to researchers using descriptive studies, because they often study what they hope is a representative sample of people or objects in order to learn something about some larger group. In a descriptive study, a sample that is unique in some way can tell us little or nothing (or even mislead us) about the characteristics of people or objects not actually studied. But a descriptive study with good external validity can be very useful to the social worker. It can provide tentative knowledge about clients or other people who may never themselves have been studied by researchers.

External validity is not nearly as important in exploratory studies as it is in explanatory or descriptive ones. In fact, many exploratory studies make no pretense of studying a representative sample of people or objects, often because one simply is not available. (Internal validity, of course, is also a nonissue, because exploratory studies generally do not seek to find support for relationships between variables.)

As with internal validity, there are many threats to the external validity of a research finding. Many different phenomena can serve to make research participants unique. Any findings about relationships between variables found among them may not be generalizable to others. Their experience as participants in the research (for example, the attention given to them as research participants) may itself have made them different from persons who might otherwise be regarded as similar to them. The issue of just how much external validity a research finding possesses is not easily resolved. Certain methods of case sampling and the use of large samples can increase the likelihood that a research finding will have good external validity. But few, if any, findings constitute universal truths.

## External Validity and Cultural Issues

Research studies involving racial and ethnic groups raise some special concerns with regard to external validity. One issue is the use of generic labels when describing racial and ethnic groups in the United States. As the diversity of the American population continues to increase, the use of such labels in social work research is and will become increasingly problematic.

The term *Hispanic* is essentially a linguistic designation that refers to people from countries where Spanish is the dominant language and where cultural aspects such as religion, music, art, dance, and food are influenced by traditions emanating from Spain (usually as a colonial power). However, findings from studies on one Hispanic group may not be generalizable to other nationalities or ethnic groups that are included in this designation. There are distinct idiomatic differences, belief systems, and cultural patterns among and between groups, such as Cubans, Puerto Ricans, Dominicans, Mexican Americans, and Latin Americans, who make up the Hispanic mosaic in the United States. The failure to recognize these differences may lead to overgeneralizations from one group to another.

Within-group differences related to variables such as nationality, social class, education, religion, language, immigration patterns, and degree of acculturation influence responses in research and thereby determine the degree of external validity of a given research study. A similar issue must be addressed when using the term *black non-Hispanic,* which refers to people of African descent in the United States, South America, Africa, and the English-speaking Caribbean. The terms *American Indian* or *Native American* generally are used to describe 512 federally recognized tribes who speak more than 200 dialects. *Asian, Pacific Islander* refers to more than 60 separate racial and ethnic groups. The desire of demographers and researchers to reduce this vast complexity into a few easily applicable labels can lead to a false sense of security in generalizing findings across and within racial and ethnic subgroups.

Researchers are expected to help others assess the external validity of their research findings. In the research report, a detailed description should be provided of one's research participants and exactly how they were selected.

## What Is the "Best" Research Design?

The fact that experiments are characterized by rigorous hypothesis testing and methods that control for the effects of intervening variables often has led to the erroneous conclusion that they are always appropriate or are a standard by which to judge other research. Historically, there has been a pronounced bias in this direction. High school science teachers still sometimes denigrate any student research proposals that lack a control group when they are entered in science fairs (also known as "Annual Parents' Science Competitions"). The knowledge sought may suggest the need for an exploratory or descriptive study, or for a more qualitative approach to knowledge building, but the student who uses one may pay the price for using a design that is still regarded by some as unscientific or otherwise inferior.

Our profession has suffered from an experimental bias, too. It is the impetus for much of the criticism that has been leveled at social work research and the questioning of social work research findings. There is relatively little social work experimental research; therefore, our research isn't worth much, so say critics both within and outside our field. Admittedly, more experimental and other forms of explanatory research could be done with a little extra thought and effort. But such criticisms often fail to acknowledge the methodological and ethical difficulties (though certainly not the impossibility) of conducting such research within social work practice settings.

The common use of the terms *higher level* (for explanatory designs) and *lower level* (for exploratory or descriptive ones) over the years has been unfortunate. This terminology has often been construed as an indicator of quality in evaluating a research design, with lower-level designs viewed as sloppy or unscientific. But the choice of a design should be based on the type of knowledge needed and the degree to which it is already present. Any one type of design is not inherently better than any other. All can reflect rigor and the careful use of scientific methods. All have their uses and make valuable contributions to our knowledge building and to empirically based social work practice.

It should also be observed that some very good research designs seem to sit on the edge; they fall somewhere between two general categories. When this happens, a researcher might describe the general nature of his or her design using compound terms such as exploratory–descriptive or descriptive–explanatory to reflect the fact that a design does not quite fit cleanly into a single design category and that it contains elements of more than one.

Even the broad descriptions of research designs (cross-sectional or longitudinal and quantitative or qualitative) sometimes are not a perfect fit. Much research that is basically cross-sectional has one or more longitudinal components. It is also not at all unusual to have a sound research design that is a hybrid of quantitative and qualitative methodologies. The two components can be complementary, each serving to verify the other's findings. As long as there is consistency (see the following discussion) within the various components of a design, a hybrid design is acceptable, if not desirable. The researcher may simply be attempting to take advantage of the special features of different methods of knowledge building within the same study.

## Characteristics of Good Designs

The design selected by the researcher is described in the research report. Thus, it is vulnerable to critique. As we indicated in Chapter 1, this is a desirable characteristic of the scientific method.

Although no design is ever perfect (compromises are inevitable), the researcher strives to come up with the best design, given unavoidable limitations. The advantages of different design features must be considered. For example, the popularity of many cross-sectional designs is based in part on their potential to control several of the threats to internal validity. Such threats as history, maturation, and mortality can be eliminated when only a single measurement takes place.

Generally, an appropriate design can be recognized by the presence of certain characteristics:

- *It is based on the review of literature.* It should be obvious why the design was selected. The reader of the review of literature section of a report should not be surprised by any part of the research design. It should suggest that the researcher has learned from the methodological successes and failures of other researchers. A design may have come directly from a recommendation of the "Suggestions for Future Research" section of another recent study, or it may represent a needed replication of research conducted years earlier.

- *It is appropriate for the level of knowledge that exists.* The design should promise to advance knowledge about a problem or question. As such, it will generally fall at or slightly to the right on the research continuum of other recent scholarly research in the area. It should not threaten to either reinvent the wheel or represent a quantum leap by, for example, attempting experimental research on a problem that has barely been identified and adequately described. The design should suggest that the researcher has found the appropriate place on the design continuum.

- *It is internally consistent in each of its components.* As suggested earlier, certain design types can be recognized by groupings of characteristics. A design or design component should contain features that belong together, not a little bit of one and a little bit of another. For example, if a component of a design claims to be both quantitative and descriptive, and attempts to generalize from research participants to others, it should reflect careful attention to selection of a research sample that will represent the group being studied. The use of a group of participants selected less carefully than they might be in more qualitative, exploratory research would not be appropriate. Similarly, we would not expect to see a major concern with methods for the control of intervening variables as a part of the design, as it would be if the research component were explanatory or an experiment.

    Conversely, an experimental or explanatory design or design component would be expected to test hypotheses and contain strict control of intervening variables. Table 6.1 portrays what we are describing as internal consistency in research design formulation. It illustrates the point that one expects to find certain design features with certain designs or design components and not with others. When the researcher settles on a design type, the decision provides help in resolving such issues as the importance of obtaining a representative sample or the degree to which control of intervening variables is critical in conducting the research.

- *It is feasible.* The ideal research design may not be the best one. It may not be possible to implement. For this reason, the ideal design often includes a backup plan for those activities that might be expected to be encountered with some difficulty such as economic, political, ethical, or logistical obstacles. It may have to be compromised in order to deal with the realities that exist within the context of social work research. For example, descriptive research on gang members' use of cocaine that is otherwise well designed probably will have to rely on other sources of data if a cooperative climate suddenly deteriorates and gang members refuse to be interviewed by an outsider. A good backup plan might involve the substitution of interviews with community leaders or police officers who are closely affiliated with gang members. Such secondary sources, although probably not as good, would reflect a reasonable compromise.

**TABLE 6.1  General Characteristics of Types of Research Design**

| Characteristic | Design Type | | | |
| --- | --- | --- | --- | --- |
| | Exploratory | Descriptive | Explanatory | Experimental |
| Goal | Derive hypotheses, "know about" | Accurate description | Suggest association or causation | Demonstrate causation |
| Use of Hypotheses | None, but sought | Examine association or correlation | Imply possible causation | Test for causation |
| Sampling Rigor | Not important | Emphasis on representativeness | Rigorous standards | Rigorous standards |
| Knowledge of Key Variables | Little | Known and measured | Known, relationships examined | Known, relationships tested |
| Control of Intervening Variables | Variables unknown, sought | Not a major issue | Mostly statistical control | Controlled through randomization |

# Summary

In Chapter 6 we began our extended look at the topic of research design. A research design was defined as both a plan for conducting research and as a response to some important methodological questions.

A broad classification of research designs (cross-sectional or longitudinal) was presented, and key differences were highlighted. A descriptive overview of the research design continuum (exploratory, descriptive, explanatory) was presented. Knowledge building was defined as a process that continues over time. Internal validity and external validity were described as important evaluative criteria for assessing the quality of certain types of research designs. Internal validity is an especially important consideration in evaluating the methods and findings of those studies that seek to demonstrate a cause–effect relationship between variables. External validity is important in assessing the value of findings drawn from descriptive and explanatory studies, but usually much less of an issue in evaluating exploratory research.

Although some designs (explanatory and, especially, experimental) often are referred to as higher level, it was emphasized that this label should not suggest that one research design is inherently better than another. Various research designs are selected for use based primarily on the knowledge needs of social work practitioners and how far along the research design continuum knowledge building has progressed. Finally, criteria for the selection of the best research design for one's own research were presented.

# References

1. Kübler-Ross, E. (1989). *On death and dying.* New York: Macmillan, 38, 137.
2. Benoliel, J. Q. (1985). Loss and adaptation: Circumstances, contingencies, and consequences. *Death Studies, 9,* 217–233.
3. Campbell, D., & Stanley, J. (1963). *Experimental and quasi-experimental designs for research.* Chicago: Rand McNally.
4. See, for example, Rubin, A., & Babbie, E. (1997). *Research methods for social work* (3rd ed.). Pacific Grove, CA: Brooks/Cole, 277–282.

# 7

## QUALITATIVE RESEARCH METHODS

In Chapter 1, we introduced two broad categories of research that social workers conduct—quantitiative and qualitative—and described in general terms how they differ in purpose and approach. In this chapter and in the next one, we will discuss them in considerably more detail.

Distinctions between quantitative and qualitative research are not as clear-cut as we might wish. Both are used to produce generalized knowledge for our profession and to evaluate practice effectiveness. As we have noted elsewhere, many primarily quantitative studies contain qualitative components and vice versa. Further blurring the distinction between them, many of the same scientific methods are employed in both quantitative research and in qualitative studies. Deciding which methods should be discussed in this chapter and which in Chapter 8 was a difficult task. Thus, one could easily argue that some of them that we have labeled as predominantly qualitative could just as well be described as quantitative and vice versa.

In this chapter, our goal is to help the reader to better understand what qualitative research is all about. To accomplish this, it will frequently be instructive to describe how it differs from quantitative approaches.

## Interviewing in Qualitative Research

Interviewing of participants is an important part of many social work research studies. We will give it considerable attention in this chapter because it is so often the method of choice for data collection in qualitative research.

## Focus Groups and One-on-One Interviews

In qualitative research, participants sometimes are interviewed in a group, commonly referred to as a *focus group*. People who share a similar problem or who have experienced a similar life experience may be brought together where, led by the researcher, they discuss their experiences. For example, a focus group of openly gay teenagers could be formed to discuss how they experienced the attitudes of teachers and other high school students, or a group of Native American students might meet with a researcher to describe their perceptions of how they think they have been treated in a predominantly white community.

It is believed that a focus group has certain advantages over one-on-one interviews with researchers. Particularly if the experience was one that is difficult to talk about, the group can be a source of emotional support. Members are likely to be candid among others who have had similar experiences. The group also can be a stimulus for individual participants in another way. Members can be helped to think about and respond to issues (brought up by other members) that they might otherwise not have remembered. Focus groups also can be efficient for the researcher because the experiences of many participants can be collected in a relatively short period of time.

Are there negatives associated with collecting data in a group of research participants? Yes. A major one is that the influence of the group can easily produce data of questionable merit. It is difficult to know when participants are speaking honestly about their own experiences and perceptions, and when they are just joining in and revealing what they think the other group members expect them to offer. Because of the possibility of group influences on individuals, data collected in focus groups must be used cautiously.

One-on-one interviewing is used much more frequently than group interviews in qualitative research. There are many similarities between research interviewing of individuals within qualitative research studies and social work practice interviewing that is used in treatment of individuals, families, and groups. For example, both rely heavily on verbal and nonverbal methods of gathering data. Also, both require the establishment of some level of interpersonal relationship with those people being interviewed.

## Purpose of Interviews

Of course, the primary purpose of all research interviewing is to collect accurate data about some human phenomenon, usually the behavior, attitudes, perceptions, or beliefs of people. In qualitative research, the researcher hopes to find out how people experience some phenomenon or experience, to learn its meaning or its essence for them.

In contrast, quantitative research uses the interview to accurately measure some phenomenon. The researcher tries not to change or in any way influence the participants through use of the research interview. This is done for reasons of objectivity as well as because of ethical concerns (Chapter 2).

## Relationship with Participants

In a qualitative interview, the relationship with participants is likely to be close and even therapeutic, when needed. This type of relationship represents no particular problem, because there are few pretenses of objectivity in data collection and therefore little concern that it might be compromised.

Because of the nature of the relationship between researchers and participants in most qualitative research, requests for assistance are natural and expected. It is only natural to respond to them when they occur. They are handled promptly, as long as providing the type of assistance requested is perceived to be in the participant's best interests.

In a quantitative research interview, requests for advice or treatment also occur quite frequently, because the research participant generally knows that the researcher is a social worker. For example, it is difficult for a researcher to collect data about participants' methods of child rearing without advice being sought at some point during the research interview.

To a quantitative researcher, responding to requests for advice or counseling (or even ignoring them) can affect the participant's subsequent responses. It also can disrupt the flow of data collection, making it difficult to get the interview back on track. This is viewed as more problematic in more quantitative studies. The researcher, as a social worker, may feel a professional obligation to provide assistance, if able, but probably would not do so during data collection. A reply that "I will be happy to talk about that with you after we complete our interview" is appropriate and usually tends to be accepted by the participant. Naturally, such promises should be remembered and kept. Assistance may entail actually giving advice (but after data collection) or, more commonly, making a referral to an appropriate organization or helping person.

In qualitative research, displays of emotion by participants are not uncommon. In fact, sometimes the researcher encourages emotionality to help better understand how the participant is experiencing or has experienced some phenomenon. They may be helpful in achieving the researcher's objectives.

In contrast, emotionality in a more quantitative interview represents a problem for the researcher. Even when measurements of attitudes and feelings are sought, emotional behaviors are assumed to provide unreliable indicators of them. Besides, emotionality in a research interview can seriously interfere with the collection of other needed data.

## Structure

Usually, qualitative research interviews tend to involve relatively little structure and control by the researcher. Digressions by participants are expected and are generally regarded as useful because they lead into topics that often are more productive than those that the social worker might have introduced. Getting participants back on track is required only if it becomes apparent that they are avoiding topics that need to be discussed and that are believed to be within their emotional tolerance for discussion.

In more quantitative research interviews, major digressions by the participant may be viewed as undesirable. The researcher exerts fairly tight control over the flow of the interview. Too long or too frequent digressions can interfere with the completion of data collection. Research interviews that run overtime can result in fatigue for participants or the researcher; either may threaten the quality of data acquired. Unnecessarily long interviews can also cause other appointments to be missed or other potential participants to be in a less receptive mood for data collection.

## *Dealing with Sensitive Topics*

Both qualitative and quantitative interviews are likely to include discussion of behaviors or feelings of a personal or sensitive nature. Because this can provoke discomfort for participants, placement of such content within the interview is often an issue. In a qualitative research interview, they often are elicited early in the interview, when there will be plenty of time to explore them and to provide support. The researcher does not like to see discussions about sensitive issues begin as the interview is about to draw to a close and therefore does whatever possible to get to those issues early.

In more quantitative types of research, discussion of sensitive matters occurs only if necessary; that is, only if it relates to the research question and/or hypothesis. In such instances, it usually is planned near the end of the interview. Placed too early, there is a risk of losing potential participants who may decide that they have had enough, terminating the interview before much data have been collected. But if placed near the end of the interview, there is sufficient time for debriefing and for the interview to end on a less emotionally charged note.

## Research That Relies on Qualitative Methods

While the distinction between qualitative and quantitative research is often a little fuzzy and characterized by overlap, there are certain types of research that can be viewed as essentially qualitative in nature. They clearly rely heavily on observing and interviewing within an environment of sensitivity and trust, and they seek to answer questions that could not be answered if more traditional quantitative methods were used. The first three that we will discuss (unstructured systematic observation, ethnographic research, and cross-cultural research) are all closely related in their purpose and methods. All three employ a mixture of observation and participation by the researcher to attempt to find answers to research questions.

## *Unstructured Systematic Observation*

There are many instances in social work research where we may be interested in observing human behaviors. For example, we may wish to know more about parent–child interactions, group process, or task completion. Or, as part of a program evaluation, we may wish to learn what it is like to be a client in the program. If so, systematic observation is often the research method of choice. It provides the researcher with direct observations of the behavior of interest.

Unstructured observation is characterized by a lack of formal data-gathering instruments. Typically in unstructured observation, the researcher is either a passive observer or a participant observer. These methods are appropriate when the specific behavior being studied cannot be clearly specified in advance and when it is important to observe participants in their own environments rather than in a laboratory setting. For example, researchers who are interested in studying behavior of an identified group might choose to join the group and make observations over some period of time. Researchers in anthropology and social psychology have used unstructured observational methods in their studies of street gangs, homeless people, and various non-Western cultures.

In areas of inquiry where knowledge is limited, it often is best to observe behavior in an unstructured manner. In so doing, the researcher is not constrained by categories or checklists and is open to viewing all behaviors (or components of behaviors) that are displayed. Unstructured observation really falls somewhere between exploratory and descriptive research. It is used to learn more about a behavior, culture, or environment of interest, often to lay the groundwork for subsequent studies that are more structured.

Unstructured observation requires the researchers to maintain field notes. Usually they either make mental notes for later recording or maintain a recorded running account or description of the behaviors during the observation period. Developing and maintaining some kind of note-taking procedure is crucial; otherwise, at the end of the observation study, researchers would have to depend on their memory to recall what they observed.

Because unstructured observation tends to yield data that are primarily qualitative in nature, certain methods for presentation are generally used. Information collected often is presented in narrative rather than statistical form. Running accounts, case vignettes, and anecdotes are often used. Direct quotations from participants are frequently included.

We will use an example to demonstrate how unstructured observation might be used in social work research. Suppose that a researcher is interested in developing an understanding of the psychosocial needs of family caregivers of older people. Unstructured observation might be used to study caregivers and the older people to whom they offer care in their homes. During periods of observation, the researcher could carefully observe the needs and demands of older people, as well as the responses of their caregivers. The interactions between the two would be observed and characterized. The activities and emotional responses of the caregivers would be particularly noted. The application of an unstructured observational method would allow certain kinds of questions to be addressed. They might include

- Do caregivers seem able to perform the tasks required to provide needed care? If not, what are their emotional responses to not being able to meet the older person's needs?
- Do caregivers have opportunities to meet their own needs? What sacrifices do they appear to make in order to care for the older person? How able are they to verbalize anger or frustration because of the demands of caregiving?
- What assistance is available to caregivers? Are there other people who are part of the caregiving network? If so, which ones appear to be most helpful to caregivers, and why?

**Advantages of Unstructured Systematic Observation.**   Systematic observation is characterized by flexibility. During the observation period, researchers may take note of behaviors, reactions, or environmental features that may influence the behavior being studied. Trained, sensitive observers are able to record data about many variables of potential impact on it. During the course of an unstructured observation, researchers may become aware of the influence of other variables that were not originally identified or conceptualized. They may make the decision to include observations of these variables in their study or to make them the focus of some subsequent research study.

Findings from studies using systematic observation often can be generalized beyond those research participants who were studied. Especially in naturalistic observation—that is, in studies where data are gathered by observing participants in their own environments—external validity can be quite good. In systematic observation that occurs in the field (as distinguished from the laboratory), the researcher can be relatively confident that the behavior observed is characteristic of what people in that setting actually do. This is not always the case in other research designs, for example, in those that use questionnaires or other self-report measures that permit participants to tell researchers only what they wish us to know.

Of course, external validity in any research design is greatly dependent on the representativeness of the participants studied. In systematic observation, it also is affected by participants' reactivity; that is, the degree to which they modify their behavior in response to the presence of the observer. The possibility of reactivity's affecting the measurement process should be carefully considered in the design of a systematic observation study. It may be possible to select an observer role that will at least minimize the impact of reactivity while still providing the needed access to data.

**Disadvantages of Unstructured Systematic Observation.** Other disadvantages inherent in the use of systematic observation (besides reactivity) relate to the consistency and objectivity of measurement procedures. Both can seriously damage the credibility of one's research findings.

Consistency of data collection is a primary concern because, in unstructured observation, data collection is not standardized to any degree. When more than one observer collects data, variation in data collection procedures may be especially great. This is the issue of interrater reliability or agreement. The reliability of observational data can be enhanced by employing two or more observers to conduct the same measurement. Interrater reliability can be assessed by using a form of statistical analysis that estimates the percentage of agreement between two observers.

Fatigue or boredom can also negatively affect the quality of the observations that are made, because observation generally occurs over an extended period of time. The potential for this problem can be reduced by using several observers, with each responsible for relatively short time segments of observation.

Because observers must be sensitized to a behavior before it is described and recorded, the likelihood exists that selective perception will play a part in which data get noted or in the interpretation of what a behavior means. Training observers to increase sensitivity to the nature of the behavior of interest, to use appropriate observational techniques, and to use appropriate methods of recording data will minimize the major sources of measurement bias inherent in observation studies. However, subjectivity must be assumed to exist in all data collected using unstructured observation (and in other qualitative research studies as well).

## Ethnographic Research

One type of research that often takes a form similar to unstructured systematic observation is ethnographic research. It is especially well suited to facilitating an understanding of individuals within their context. But the purpose of ethnographic research is to allow researchers to do more than simply observe behaviors. It endeavors to help them understand beliefs, attitudes, values, roles, social structures, and norms of behavior in human environments that are different from their own.

Ethnographic methods were first developed in the field of anthropology to guide participant observation and qualitative field research of Western investigators studying behavior in primitive societies. However, ethnographic methods are now also used to understand subgroups within modern dominant cultures. Those subgroups may exist based on shared race, culture, class, religion, or some other characteristics that in some way differentiate the subgroup from the mainstream culture.

Two concepts embedded in ethnographic research methods are "emic" and "etic" perspectives. The *emic* perspective is that of the insider who is indigenous to the group being studied. This perspective is an experiential one based on an individual's having been socialized to daily living in the culture and participating fully in all its psychosocial aspects.

The *etic* perspective is that of the outsider—the stance traditionally assumed by researchers who study a culture that is not their own. An assumption of ethnographic research is that each perspective has advantages and disadvantages. For example, although the emic perspective permits an intricate understanding of even the most subtle cultural nuances, its familiarity with the cultural context may fail to raise critical questions about why things are the way they are or what maintains the status quo. Although the etic perspective may miss important cultural nuances, it allows researchers to raise questions of context and purpose that would never occur to an insider to ask. Ethnographic research attempts to blend these two perspectives by allowing the outside investigator to function as an insider, through participant observation and other methods that will enhance the understanding of the cultural context. As in other types of research that rely on participant observation, the extent to which the very presence of the outsider changes the natural order of the cultural dynamics of insiders (reactivity) is a potential source of distortion of data thus collected.

Goodson-Lawes[1] describes a particularly useful application of ethnographic methods in social work research. The researcher used ethnographic research to study families of Mexican and Vietnamese immigrants. Researchers lived with the families in order to understand the consequences of immigration for family functioning and family structure. They learned their language and took part in the daily life of the families. They became a normal presence in their homes. Events, reactions, emotions, and interactions were carefully recorded in detailed journals.

Although participant observation is the data collection methodology most often associated with ethnographic research, there are other methodological approaches that can help investigators to understand different cultures. These include ecomapping, formal and informal interviews, life histories, kinship charts, and analysis of religious practices, myths, music, and other forms of folklore. Some of these will be discussed in later sections of this chapter and in Chapter 8.

**Overcoming Obstacles to Ethnographic Research.** Because of negative historical and political encounters between ethnic communities and mainstream governmental or social welfare institutions, gaining access to study samples in ethnic communities may be problematic. Mistrust of motives for the research and fear of how the data may be used are frequently expressed concerns. Many ethnic communities have been used as study sites, with little or no feedback on study outcomes. Even when feedback has been given, it sometimes has not been in a form that is helpful in addressing community problems.

Many researchers conduct key informant surveys to assist them in conducting ethnographic research. They consist of unstructured interviews with knowledgeable individuals and community leaders or open-ended questionnaires mailed to them. They are used to gain the advice and support of people who can offer an insider's perspective on their research efforts. Such surveys may be especially useful when the researcher is undertaking exploratory investigation that requires an understanding of an unfamiliar research context or setting.

Who is a potential key informant? The answer to this question sometimes is hard to determine in ethnic communities. Leaders designated by funding sources or university advisory boards may not be regarded as leaders by the members of their ethnic group. Butler[2] notes, for example, that whereas funding sources may rely on academic credentials, work experience, or political connections to select leaders, members of the African American community are more likely to locate leadership in individuals who embody the community values of spirituality, wisdom, strength of character, and style. This suggests that key informants should be selected across social class strata in ethnic communities.

In conducting ethnographic research, key informants can be helpful in several ways. They can provide guidance on where to find information and resources on topics of study interest, how to access and gain participation of study participants, and how to interpret study findings. Key informant surveys are also a way of forging alliances with community leaders and influential citizens who can endorse the research enterprise.

Some ethnic communities have set up stringent review and approval procedures before permission to conduct research is granted. Notable among these are some of the Native American tribal groups. Any researcher wishing to conduct studies that are on tribal lands or that involve people who are members of their tribal group must be prepared to comply with their particular approval process. Typically, researchers must present a proposal before a tribal, community, or village governing body that frequently wishes to exercise some degree of control over the research process. Beauvais and Trimble[3] describe these as (1) assignment of a tribal or village member to monitor study implementation; (2) guidelines concerning respondent selection procedures; (3) community's right to review and edit questionnaires, interview schedules and field notes, and so on; (4) community's right to review and edit research reports and to restrict or prevent the circulation and distribution of findings; and (5) ownership of the raw data and findings granted to the tribe or village. There are a few tribes that forbid any outside research within their boundaries; as sovereign states, they can legally do so.

It is to the researcher's advantage to understand the specific historical and cultural traits of the target community to (1) anticipate the degree and nature of resistance to participation and (2) seek advice from knowledgeable individuals on overcoming resistance to participation. Kim and her colleagues[4] provide examples of recommended approaches in working with Asian American communities:

- Conducting data collection in private settings
- Providing refreshments (because of the importance of food and communal meals in social gatherings)

- Using personal contacts, such as telephone calls or word-of-mouth invitations, to invite participation in the study, rather than sending letters for formal appointments
- Compensating respondents for their time (because research and evaluation are less important to many Asian Americans than work in exchange for compensation)
- Providing transportation and child care (because many Asian American families are accustomed to having children present at semiformal gatherings)

## *Cross-Cultural Research*

Cross-cultural research is often an extension of intracultural research and seeks to test hypotheses related to the universality of findings across cultures or differences between cultures on variables of interest. It is being used more frequently than in past years due to a number of factors including the opening of previously sealed international borders, large migration streams, globalization of the economic market, international tourism, increased cross-cultural communication, and technological innovations that make communication and scholarship in other countries possible.[5] In cross-cultural research, investigators face some unique methodological challenges usually related to definitions of theoretical constructs and their valid measurement in different cultural contexts. Other problems relate to obtaining a representative sample and accuracy of translation of data collection instruments into foreign languages. Some of these are methodological issues unique to cross-cultural research, which will be addressed in more detail in later chapters in this text.

Social workers wishing to conduct research and/or practice in foreign countries will be especially interested in cross-cultural studies of human behavior, family systems, and other social organizations, as well as epidemiological studies of health and mental health disorders, and their treatment in various cultural contexts. Some of their findings may also apply to the study of ethnic and racial groups within the American culture.

Marin and Marin[6] offer several suggestions for researchers who plan to undertake cross-cultural research. They are designed to reduce the risk of *cultural encapsulation* (that is, depending entirely on one's own cultural frame of reference to formulate assumptions and define research constructs) and to increase *cultural relativity* (that is, the ability to understand behavior, attitudes, and values within the context of the culture in which it occurs). Suggested strategies include the following:

- Cultural immersion in the group to be studied
- Obtaining information directly from cultural minorities about values and normative behavior rooted in the culture (that is, what is normal and what is pathological for that specific culture)
- Collaboration with key informants from the culture to be studied on all aspects of the study design prior to initiating the study

## Case Studies

A case study combines observations of behavior with observations of attitudes and perceptions of research participants. Like many other forms of qualitative research, it employs methods of data collection that rely heavily on the interviewing skills of researchers and their capacity to establish relationships of trust. As we shall see, there are some good reasons for the case study's continued popularity among social work researchers.

Case studies have often been misunderstood and sometimes maligned. Misunderstandings about case studies have sometimes led to a belief that they are less than scientific methods for knowledge building. Part of this misunderstanding may be attributable to misapplication of the label to research that is poorly designed and implemented. For example, sometimes researchers have conducted some other type of research using a very small sample of research participants. In order to deflect criticisms of their work and the credibility of their findings, they have erroneously applied the case study label to their research design.

A case study is appropriate for situations in which certain conditions are present. They are that

- *Little is known about the area being studied.* Topics for which there already exists a substantive body of relevant knowledge are better studied using other research designs.
- *The area studied generally involves illegal behavior or at least a form of behavior that is not socially sanctioned.* Thus, the behavior is not available for study using more traditional research designs, such as surveys. Participants may be fearful about being found out and are usually very concerned about the confidentiality of what they reveal about themselves or their situation.
- *It is impossible to draw a representative sample of participants.* Because the research generally involves the study of illegal or other nonsocially sanctioned behavior, a master list of potential research participants does not exist. Consequently, participants are selected based on their availability and willingness to participate in the research. There is no way of knowing if they are typical of others who are involved in the same behavior.

Researchers conducting case studies collect their data from just one or a few cases. Usually the number does not exceed four or five. A case need not be an individual person; it can also be a family, a group, an organization, a community, or virtually any other system or entity that can be readily defined.

In a case study, interviewers must be receptive and nonjudgmental. They must be able to observe and interpret a wide variety of verbal and nonverbal communication, because data collected consist of both responses to preselected questions and the interviewer's observations of participants.

In a case study, acquiring the trust of participants is absolutely essential. Relationships of trust are not easily developed and nurtured because participants naturally tend to be guarded in what they say and to whom they say it. They have learned how to give evasive answers to sensitive questions and find it difficult to be candid. Social workers are ideally suited to conduct case studies. Their interviewing skills, nonjudgmental attitudes, and other professional values and ethics help to foster trust.

**Suitable Topics.**    There are many problem areas that are well suited to a case study design. Different aspects of substance abuse, sexual deviance, white-collar crime, and other forms of antisocial behavior come readily to mind. Many other gaps in knowledge that are the focus of social work research are not suited to case study designs, primarily because they do not involve behavior that is illegal or not socially acceptable.

Because what constitutes illegal or nonsocially sanctioned behavior tends to change over time, the list of problems that are suitable for study using a case study design is ever changing. One of the authors of this text supervised a case study of couples living together outside of marriage in the early 1970s. At the time and within the moral climate of the geographical locale in which the research was conducted, the case study was an appropriate choice of design. Just a few years later, research on the same topic could have and should have used other research methods because of a greater public acceptance of this alternate life-style. In 1988 he conducted a case study on "secret survivors," people who had experienced the sudden death of a partner in a long-term extramarital affair.[7] At that time, the case study was appropriate for a study of that problem. But less than a decade later, changing societal values and the accumulation of other exploratory studies of the problem or of similar ones (such as partners who die from AIDS) had moved our understanding of the problem beyond the point where a case study would be appropriate. Every year, problems emerge that are appropriate for research using a case study design, whereas others are deleted from the list.

**Strengths and Weaknesses of Case Studies.**    Case studies make it possible to achieve insights (such as how people feel about and experience certain phenomena) that are unavailable using more quantitative methods. They also are among the most interesting and gratifying types of research that can be conducted. A researcher conducting a case study can experience a feeling of being on the very cutting edge of knowledge building about a problem or question.

A major weakness of the case study is its limited capacity to generate knowledge that could be described as definitive. Any conclusions should be carefully qualified. Because the number of participants is small and because they cannot be considered representative, few real conclusions emerge from case histories. Often, the most that can be said about data collected is something like "These are some of the problems that were found," "These are some of the ways that some people experience them," or "These are what some people think can be done about them." A case study does not allow the researcher to generalize from participants to others who were not part of the study. Any such generalization would be presumptuous. Consequently, the external validity of a case study's findings is very low.

## *Grounded Theory*

One of the best known methods of qualitative research is grounded theory. It relies heavily on skillful interviewing and a specialized form of content analysis (a method of data analysis described in more detail in Chapter 8). Grounded theory research seeks to learn what meanings people give to certain events in their lives. Like most qualitative research, it seeks to generate hypotheses, not test them. Like many types of qualitative research, grounded theory also attempts to build theory from data (in contrast to quantitative research, which often tests theories using data). But it differs from other types of qualitative research in some important ways.

Researchers conducting grounded theory research constantly monitor and reshape their developing theories. The method involves a recurring process of proposing (based on analysis of completed interview data) and checking and verifying what has been proposed (within subsequent interviews). In grounded theory research, sample selection, data collection, and data analysis occur simultaneously rather than in a preestablished sequence. Analysis of early data guides and shapes subsequent sample selection and the focus of future data collection. Researchers use emerging theoretical categories to influence both the ways in which subsequent data collection will be accomplished and from whom. For example, in early interviews, researchers may begin by asking general research questions based on whatever clues the literature may provide as to what they might find. If some questions turn out to be irrelevant or nonproductive, they are dropped in subsequent interviews. Other, new ones, suggested by what they learned in earlier interviews may be added. Similarly, if certain types of participants seem to be providing more enlightenment for their emerging theories than others, subsequent interviews may target only those people who show the greatest potential to verify (or refute) their theories.

Despite its somewhat unconventional approaches to data collection and case sampling, grounded theory is definitely not a haphazard or unscientific method of conducting research. It employs a systematic sequence of steps. For example, after one batch of data is collected (often, interviews are videotaped), the process of analyzing and conceptualizing it, referred to as *coding,* is begun. In the early stages of analysis, a process called *open coding* is used. It entails broadly conceptualizing what the data seem to mean and beginning to categorize them. It requires a careful dissection of interviews, sometimes word by word. Questions such as "What is this?" or "What does this seem to mean?" are common at this stage of the data analysis.

Later, two other types of coding (which are a little too complicated to explain in this overview), axial coding and selective coding, are used. Eventually, as proposed relationships between categories gain support as more data are collected, the researcher produces what is referred to as a *story line*, a brief narrative description of what was observed. This is analyzed and distilled further to form what is called a *core category*. Finally, a theory or hypothesis emerges as a product of the research.

Grounded theory is based on the premise that the meanings that people give to events in their lives (for example, certain experiences or losses) are very important in understanding their responses and resilience to the events. It is based primarily on theories of symbolic interaction, which hold that people construct their own meanings for events based in part on their interactions with others. Grounded theory research thus seems especially well suited to acquiring the kinds of knowledge needed by social workers. Conducting it also requires many of the very attributes (interviewing skills, ability to form relationships, and so forth) that we possess.

## Oral Histories

Oral history taking is another method for collecting data that relies on skilled interviewing techniques. It is a unique opportunity for scholars to develop and present an understanding of peoples lives and experiences. Once completed, one or more oral histories may constitute a data source for historical research such as that described in Chapter 8.

Oral histories rely totally on firsthand accounts of individuals who have been there, not on artifacts. They are typically recorded (most commonly on videotape) for use by current researchers and for future generations. They often are designed to capture the firsthand experiences of people who are older or who otherwise may not be available to be interviewed at a later date. For example, oral histories have been made of veterans who fought in World War I, of former leaders of the American Civil Rights movement, of survivors of the Holocaust, of early labor organizers, of persons who worked in Franklin Roosevelt's New Deal programs, of men who were participants in the Tuskegee studies (Chapter 2), and others who either may already be dead or may soon not be alive to share their experiences with us.

Interviews generally are conducted and recorded during many sessions. Frequently, researchers conduct preresearch meetings with potential participants to develop comfortable relationships with them and to determine which questions might be most productive to ask when histories are being recorded. Then a research instrument is developed that is just a broad outline of the topics for discussion in the interviews. Once the data have been collected, they are often transcribed so that the data provided by participants (referred to as *narrators*) is readily available for study by others.

In oral histories, people have the opportunity to tell their stories and interpret the meanings of their actions. They are also encouraged to share emotional content with the researcher and to reflect on their feelings about their experiences.

Oral histories may be presented as single case studies of individuals, or they may be collected as a group of narratives provided by those sharing a common life experience. Oral history projects may also focus on organizations and groups, providing a record of the history of these organizations as seen through the eyes of those who were present in their earlier years. Thus, historical data about the organization are developed and preserved for future study.

As noted earlier in this chapter, oral histories sometimes are used in ethnographic studies. The oral history method was used in a study that examined life themes of native Hawaiian female elders.[8] The elders, known as *kupunas* to native Hawaiians, play important roles in native Hawaiian culture. Three themes selected for emphasis in the study were relationships with people, relationships with nature, and spiritual and religious beliefs. The data developed in interviews were transcribed and then analyzed according to the themes, and prepared in draft form for review by participants to aid in correcting any misinformation. Following the reviews, they were bound and preserved by the Center for Oral History at a university.

In another study, Martin conducted in-depth interviews of elderly African Americans living in a community in the southeastern part of the United States. She gathered and recorded oral histories from members of fifteen families.[9] The study evolved from Martin's concern with how the relative strengths of African American families are portrayed. It documented African American family adaptation systems.

Martin's interviewing schedule was an adaptation of Hartman's ecomap. A copy of the map was provided to all participants as a stimulus for discussion. The map was later used to help organize the oral history data that Martin had gathered.

Martin made extensive use of individual narratives to preserve the stories of her participants. All interviews were audiotaped and later transcribed. Themes related to adaptation, survival, and growth were identified in analyses of the transcriptions. The data were presented both in tabular form and thematically. Whenever possible, the respondents' own words were used to highlight important findings.

## Criteria for Evaluating Qualitative Designs

In the previous chapter, we described two criteria that are applied when evaluating explanatory and some descriptive research designs that test hypotheses about relationships between or among individuals. These criteria—internal validity and external validity—are often applied to studies that are primarily quantitative. However, we noted that they are not appropriate for other studies (exploratory ones and some descriptive ones) in which hypotheses are unlikely to be present and in which the goal is merely to learn more about some phenomenon and/or to describe it accurately. Most qualitative research designs fall into this latter category. So, how can we tell the difference between a well-designed qualitative study and one that contains major design flaws and whose findings thus lack credibility?

The criteria for evaluating a qualitative design are a little more vague and probably can best be stated as a group of related questions. Here are some questions we might ask:

1. Did the data collection methods seem to encourage research participants to discuss their experiences and perceptions honestly and candidly?
2. To what degree do the data reflect a diversity of experiences and perceptions?
3. Do the data reflect the "richness" that is sought when using qualitative methods?
4. Did the design yield data that can be evaluated in relation to existing knowledge found in the professional literature?
5. Did the research produce credible theories or hypotheses for future research?

# Feminist Research

There is a particular type of research, feminist research, that is neither qualitative or quantitative per se. We have chosen to include it in this chapter because it often uses the six methods that we have described, as well as other methods regarded as primarily qualitative. However, less frequently, it also uses some of the more quantitative methods described in Chapter 8. What sets feminist research apart from other types of research is not its methods, but its focus and purpose. It is designed to build knowledge about women, their unique problems, and the social institutions that affect them.

## *Goals and Assumptions*

In her work on feminist research[10] Shulamit Reinharz points out that feminist research relates to "women's ways of knowing," a concept developed by others who have observed that women acquire knowledge differently than men. Feminist research is designed to hear the voices and other communications that more traditional, male-oriented approaches to knowledge building may miss. It is conducted by people who generally identify themselves as feminists or at least are concerned with the status and well-being of women.

Feminist research should be regarded as research both for and about women. It is often a form of action research; that is, research designed to bring about change in women's lives by confronting sexism and attempting to alter those social institutions that may promote or perpetuate it. It results in consciousness raising and awareness of women's issues. The fact that feminist researchers study problems such as rape, sexual harassment, sexism, and salary equity stimulates reflection and discussion about these issues by others.

Feminist research rests on the assumption that the fact of gender is critical to understanding women and culture. Thus, gender is a central focus of it. It has produced a wealth of data about women. For example, within the past two decades, knowledge about domestic violence, marital rape, and women's work at home and in the community has been developed. Knowledge derived from feminist research is used to validate women's lives and experiences, and is useful for understanding their issues, problems, and strengths. It also has been used to suggest additional needed research relevant to women and to influence the development of social policy that directly affects women.

## Feminist Research as a Response to Traditional Research Methods

Similar to other qualitative approaches to knowledge building, knowledge that is developed through feminist research is contextual and relative. This is justified by feminist scholars based on the assertion that traditional approaches to scientific research assume an objectivity about the world that is irrelevant to women's lives.

More quantitative methods of inquiry are believed to ignore and distort women's realities. For example, many widely accepted measurement procedures were developed and standardized using males, thus making them of questionable value in understanding women's experiences. In addition, historically, many life experiences that are important to the lives of women, such as sexual harassment in the workplace, have been neglected by researchers using traditional research methods.

Feminist researchers have described the more traditional methods of inquiry (especially experimental designs) as being antithetical to the purposes of feminist research. For example, experimental research generally is conducted in the laboratory under tightly controlled research conditions. Feminists have argued that these types of designs have a sexist bias in the ways that questions are asked and answered and the way that data are interpreted. They assert that the artificiality of the research laboratory is not conducive to a true understanding of people and their relationships. In addition, it is asserted that traditional research methods have tended to exploit and objectify women.

Feminist research, with its emphasis on more qualitative approaches to interacting with research participants, is believed to be less exploitive in its approach to data collection than traditional methods. It is more egalitarian; the relationship between the researcher and the person being studied is more one of equality.

Feminist research is conducted within the context of an understanding of feminist perspectives of culture; it uses these perspectives to select methods for study of a research problem and for interpreting data. Feminist researchers also argue that their methods of conducting research allow them to critique knowledge developed by others using more traditional models of inquiry and to attempt to reconcile their findings with those of others. Doing this can put a whole new meaning on what a researcher learns directly, how the researcher interprets the findings of others, and how the data collection experience mutually affects the research participants.

## Design Features

Methodologically, feminist research has been described using such terms as *open, contextual, relative, interpretive, experiential, empowering,* and *social change–oriented.* These descriptors suggest the wide range of research designs used by and for feminist scholarship. There is no prescribed set of techniques or procedures in feminist research. It relies heavily on a variety of qualitative (and, less frequently, quantitative) techniques. Feminist research designs are sometimes hybrids, combining features of two or more approaches to knowledge building. For example, both quantitative and qualitative design features can be used in a single study. A variety of quantitative data can be collected and analyzed. But then participants also can be asked if they would like to meet with a member of the research team to discuss their experiences more fully in order to better understand their meaning to them.

Like some of the other forms of research described in this chapter, feminist methods are characterized by relatively open relationships between researchers and research participants. Researchers may get involved with the lives of participants by establishing relationships with them that go beyond simple data collection. They often serve as resources to participants by providing information about community resources or may assist them in bringing about social change. The relationship between researchers and their participants is viewed as critical to the development of knowledge about women. Questions asked often emanate from researchers' own concerns and experiences, rather than out of some previously developed interview schedule or agenda. The knowledge acquired through this kind of interpersonal interaction leads logically to an interpretive approach to data analysis which makes no claims of total objectivity.

Feminist research does not emphasize the testing of prespecified hypotheses. It focuses instead on the development of a wide range of information and understanding. It has been described as emergent; it is not highly controlled. It often seeks to gather a wide array of descriptive, contextual information in order to provide data that are as complete as possible for analysis. Thus, methods for collecting data are fewer than in traditional, quantitative research studies.

## Examples of Feminist Research

Virtually every research method has been used in the feminist approach. Based on our description, it should come as no surprise to the reader that some of the qualitative methods described earlier in this chapter (for example, grounded theory and oral histories) are frequently used. We will examine some other research methods not yet mentioned and describe some ways in which they have been used to build knowledge.

On occasion, feminist descriptive research has used quantitative methods such as fixed-alternative surveys and more open-ended, semistructured interviews (discussed in Chapter 8). Typically, large-scale surveys have been used to develop incidence data about a problem affecting women or to allow women to anonymously describe their attitudes, experiences, and beliefs about a women's issue. Vast amounts of quantitative data have been generated, statistical analyses performed, and findings publicized to attempt to promote social change.

Semistructured, open-ended questionnaires (administered by the researcher) are useful when the purpose of a study is to have participants respond to certain questions in their own words. Participants often become involved both in the interpretation of the meanings of their responses and in the refinement of data collection methods to be used in future research. Typically, this method of data collection entails the use of multiple sessions with participants. Because the researcher often cannot anticipate the type of information that will be shared, the interviews often are a process of discovery both for participants and for the feminist researcher.

What are some examples of past descriptive feminist research? Survey research studies with a feminist focus have been used to study date rape among college students. Prior to the mid-1980s there were few (if any) references to date rape in the social science literature. More quantitative studies on a variety of forms of abuse of women were developed partially as an outgrowth of earlier research and also because of changing societal definitions of what connotes permissible levels of violence. Two studies examining date rape as a form of violence against women were developed:

- In 1986, one of the authors of this book conducted a survey of over 600 college students at a large state-supported institution.[11] It produced incidence and prevalence data about date rape and compared the perceptions of men and women about the behavior. The study combined the use of a fixed-alternative questionnaire with a few open-ended questions. The fixed-alternative items were designed to develop incidence data and to describe how force was used by men and experienced by the women. The open-ended questions permitted participants to more fully describe any incident of date rape in which they had been involved. The researchers also offered suggestions for how to get help with these issues. Referral assistance was offered to those women wishing to be in touch with community organizations offering rape counseling services.

  The findings of the study demonstrated that there were sharp differences in how men and women define and report date rape, and in how they experienced the use of force. These were interpreted within a framework of discussion of stereotypical gender role differences and expectations for sexual favors.

- In a more recent survey, 209 male and female students from an ethnically diverse environment were surveyed.[12] The study also sought to estimate the incidence of date rape and to compare victimization rates by ethnicity.

Based on their findings, the researchers concluded that if they are to be effective, date rape prevention programs must be sensitive to cultural definitions of social role and to the different levels of acceptance of violence against women within different ethnic groups. Their recommendations were based in part on observations that Japanese women were less likely to label their victimization experiences on dates as sexual assaults than were Caucasian women.

Another good example of feminist descriptive research is provided by a study of work preferences and well-being among single African American working mothers. This population of women has largely been ignored by previous research on employment and welfare policy. Jackson (1993)[13] used semistructured interviews and a brief self-administered instrument with 111 single working mothers to explore how they cope with the demands of jobs and parenting. The data from this study were reported in relation to role strain, emotional well-being, perceptions of children, employment preferences, working hours, educational attainment, and gender of the child. Sophisticated quantitative analyses were used to analyze the data. The author found that mothers whose formal educational attainment was at the level of high school or below experienced greater role strain, greater depressive symptomatology, least favorable perceptions of children, and lower ratings of overall life satisfaction than those with more formal education. The study was noteworthy both because of the population of women the researcher chose to study and the use of a multimethodological approach to the problems under investigation.

Still another feminist descriptive study examined the experience of pregnancy and its relationship to attitudes regarding diagnostic testing. It was conducted using intensive, in-person interviews with thirty-one women to explore their experiences and perceptions of their pregnancies. Gregg[14] found that women experience pregnancy and identify being pregnant very differently. The women she interviewed talked about the risks and choices made in their pregnancies, including the use of diagnostic tests. The author used statistical analysis to develop topical categories and responses. She concluded that the medical/physiological approach to understanding pregnancy was inadequate for understanding the pregnancy experience.

A more qualitative approach to data collection and analysis—naturalistic inquiry (a form of unstructured systematic observation)—attempts to document and understand women's behavior as influenced by their social contexts. Observations may be made in a variety of field settings, such as women's health organizations, women's work and social groups, and other groups and communities to which women belong. The data in naturalistic inquiries, as in most qualitative research, are typically rich in detail. In naturalistic inquiry, the researcher allows the patterns and themes contained in the data observed to emerge.

There are many excellent examples of naturalistic inquiries in the literature. Many of these studies have been conducted by feminist sociologists and anthropologists. One study sought to better understand wife abuse in a rural community.[15] Based on the findings from the researcher's naturalistic inquiry of violence and social control, she conceptualized three categories of control. She then used them to assert that domestic violence is dependent on culture and social structures that condone men's domination of women and that, without them, violence would be less effective as a means of social control.

We have mentioned only a few of the forms that feminist research can take. As we noted earlier, it is the specialized purpose of feminist research, not any specific design or method, that gives it its identity. It is designed specifically to develop needed knowledge about women and the social institutions that impact on them.

## Using Qualitative Methods to Evaluate Practice Effectiveness

As we have illustrated, the research methods that we described in this chapter are often used to produce general knowledge to assist us in becoming more effective social work practitioners. But it should also be apparent that they can be (and often are) used for a more specific purpose: to evaluate the effectiveness of both our individual practice interventions and our social programs. For example, unstructured systematic observation, ethnographic research, cross-cultural research, or even a case study could be used to determine if a program is needed, is successfully underway, or has achieved its goal of serving a particular population-at-risk. In Chapters 13 and 14, we shall look more closely at how these research methods (as well as those quantitative methods described in the next chapter) are used for this purpose.

## Summary

In Chapter 1, we pointed out the basic differences between quantitative research methods and qualitative ones. In this chapter, we provided a more complete description of some popular qualitative research methods, how they differ from quantitative approaches, and on occasion, how they may exist side by side.

We emphasized the important role of interviewing in most qualitative studies and how it is used differently than in quantitative research. Then we discussed several types of research that, although they may have some quantitative elements, tend to be primarily qualitative in their methods of data collection and analysis. First, unstructured systematic observation was presented with both its advantages and its disadvantages. Special issues that must be addressed in the related types of research known as ethnographic and cross-cultural research were given special attention.

The case study was described as a design that is well suited to the strengths of the social work practitioner. Its greatest shortcoming is that its findings lack external validity. An overview of the nontraditional method known as grounded theory was presented. It is used to build theory from data using an ongoing process of proposing and verifying. Emerging theories are used to shape methods of data collection and to determine who should be asked to provide it as the research progresses. Oral histories were presented as both a method of data collection to help answer current research questions and as a way of preserving the firsthand observations of people for use by future researchers.

Finally, feminist research was described as a type of research that is distinguished more by its purpose and focus than by the uniqueness of its methods. It relies heavily on many of the qualitative approaches described elsewhere in Chapter 7 and, less frequently, on some of the quantitative methods described in Chapter 8. Numerous examples were offered to illustrate what makes feminist research unique.

# References

1. Goodson-Lawes, J. (1994). Ethnicity and poverty as research variables: Family studies with Mexican and Vietnamese newcomers. In E. Sherman & W. J. Reid (Eds.), *Qualitative research in social work*. New York: Columbia University Press, 21–31.

2. Butler, J. P. (1992). Of kindred minds: The ties that bind. In OSAP, *Cultural competence for evaluators*. Washington, DC: U.S. Department of Health and Human Services, 23–54.

3. Beauvais, F., & Trimble, J. E. (1992). The role of the researcher in evaluating American-Indian alcohol and other drug abuse prevention programs. In OSAP, *Cultural competence for evaluators*. Washington, DC: U.S. Department of Health and Human Services, 173–202.

4. Kim, S., McLeod, J. H., & Shantzis, C. (1992). Cultural competence for evaluators working with Asian American communities: Some practical considerations. In OSAP, *Cultural competence for evaluators*. Washington, DC: U.S. Department of Health and Human Services, 203–260.

5. Van de Vijver, F., & Leung, K. (1997). *Methods and data analysis for cross-cultural research*. Thousand Oaks, CA: Sage Publications.

6. Marin, G., & Marin, B. V. (1991). *Research with Hispanic populations*. Newbury Park, CA: Sage Publications.

7. Weinbach, R. (1989). Sudden death and secret survivors: Helping those who grieve alone. *Social Work, 34,* 57–60.

8. Mokuau, N., & Browne, C. (1994). Life themes of native Hawaiian female elders: Resources for cultural preservations. *Social Work, 39*(1), 43–49.

9. Martin, R. (1995). *Oral history in social work: Research, assessment, and intervention*. Thousand Oaks, CA: Sage Publications.

10. Reinharz, S. (1992). *Feminist methods in social research.* New York: Oxford University Press.

11. Yegidis, B. (1986). Date rape and other forced sexual encounters among college students. *Journal of Sex Education and Therapy, 12*(2), 51–54.

12. Mills, C., & Granoff, B. (1992). Date rape and acquaintance rape among a sample of college students. *Social Work, 37*(6), 504–509.

13. Jackson, A. (1993). Black, single, working mothers in poverty: Preferences for employment, well-being, and perceptions of preschool-age children. *Social Work, 38*(1), 26–33.

14. Gregg, R. (1994). Exploration of pregnancy and choice in a high-tech age. In C. Reissman (Ed.), *Qualitative studies in social work research.* Thousand Oaks, CA: Sage Publications.

15. Gagne, P. (1992). Appalachian women: Violence and social control. *Journal of Contemporary Ethnography, 20*(4), 387–415.

# 8

# QUANTITATIVE RESEARCH METHODS

In the previous chapter, we described research methods (qualitative ones) that are commonly used to better understand behaviors or phenomena about which we have only limited understanding. When used for this purpose, a research study can be described as exploratory. Less frequently, qualitative methods are used to describe a behavior or phenomenon that we already understand somewhat. Then the study is more descriptive. We would not expect to see qualitative methods used very often in explanatory research, because the conditions for testing hypotheses (for example, representative samples, control of extraneous variables, and so forth) are not characteristic of qualitative studies.

In contrast, more quantitative methods are often found in explanatory research studies. It is possible to test hypotheses in studies that entail more quantitative methods because they are characterized by (or at least should be characterized by)

1. Careful measurement of variables
2. Relatively large, representative case samples
3. Control of extraneous variables through randomization or some other method
4. Standardized data collection methods
5. Statistical analyses of data designed to determine the likelihood that sampling error might have produced an apparent relationship between or among variables

Quantitative methods are also employed in descriptive research. Descriptive quantitative research is used to provide accurate measurement of the distribution of variables and to identify associations and correlations between and among them. When associations and correlations have been identified, they can help

153

social workers to predict a measurement of one variable (the criterion) when they know the measurement of another variable (the predictor). For example, if quantitative research identifies a strong negative correlation between age of residents at admission to a long-term care facility and their length of survival, a social worker can use this knowledge to predict (with less-than-perfect accuracy) the number of days a given patient will survive based on her age at admission.

In this chapter, we will discuss some of the most commonly used quantitative methods for conducting research. As we shall see, some of these methods rely on the use of existing data, whereas others are best conducted by collecting original data that have not been previously collected for some other purpose.

# Research That Uses Secondary Data Analysis

Sometimes the time-consuming and expensive task of collecting original data for quantitative research studies is unnecessary. Many research questions can be examined using data that already exist, often within the social worker's place of employment. The reanalysis of selected information that was collected and stored for some other purpose is known as *secondary data analysis*.

## *Sources of Secondary Data*

Human service organizations store great amounts of information about their clients and programs. They can sometimes be used to examine research questions and to test hypotheses using quantitative methods.

Extensive data banks exist within public social agencies, both to meet government requirements and to facilitate service delivery to clients. Smaller private and sectarian organizations also store a substantial amount of information about clients and client functioning. Increasingly, information is stored and retrieved via computer data information systems. However, in some smaller organizations, it still is maintained manually in the form of written files and records.

There also are many sources of research data within the public domain that can be useful to social workers for conducting research. For example, census data are a rich source of data collected at great expense to the taxpayer. Generally, they tend to be underused by researchers. The public documents section of libraries stores a wide variety of other statistical data, some of which were listed in Chapter 4. Labor statistics and public health statistics are available through computer access and in public and university libraries. Federal grant reports and reports of demonstration projects also are available as documents and frequently contain useful data available for reanalysis. More and more data that were collected for some other purposes are appearing on the Internet each year. This information may be of use to a researcher. However, as we noted in Chapter 4, much of it may be untrustworthy because it usually has not been screened for accuracy.

Data that are within the public domain may be used (with appropriate citation from their sources). Researchers do not need permission to analyze census data or data published by the National Center for Health Statistics and other federal agencies. They can be used, for example, to chronicle social changes such as the rise and decline of various occupations, urban migration, or the increased presence of women in the workplace over the past century.

The NASW, the CSWE, and other professional organizations annually collect data about their members. Social workers interested in conducting research using selected characteristics of professional social workers, educators, schools, and students can obtain permission to reanalyze these data.

## Different Uses of Secondary Data Analysis

Secondary analysis is used in both descriptive and explanatory quantitative studies. It also is a component of many program evaluations (see Chapter 13). It is not used in experiments because, by definition, they require that the independent variable is either introduced or physically manipulated by the researcher. This would be impossible because, in secondary analysis, data were collected usually by someone else for some other purpose. Some examples may help to demonstrate the wide variety of ways that secondary analysis can benefit the social work practitioner.

- In an inpatient psychiatric hospital, a researcher may wish to describe the participation of institutionalized clients in making discharge plans. A secondary analysis of data drawn from available case records could be used.
- In a child protection agency, case record data could be used to compile a picture of the disposition of cases that are referred for investigation of possible child abuse. They could be used to create a composite picture of patterns of service delivery.
- As part of a program evaluation of a battered women's shelter, agency record data could be used to learn if clients served by the organization are representative of the community in age, income level, ethnicity, and so forth. Data could be compared statistically to county- or community-maintained data on the same social indicators.
- In a rehabilitation facility, secondary data analysis also could be used to seek support for the hypothesis that there is a positive correlation between clients' participation in a given program and changes in some aspect of their functioning. Data analysis might involve calculating the strength and direction of correlation between the two variables.

When data can be accessed by computer, it can be tempting for researchers to select data on many variables and to seek any relationships between them that can be found. We recommend caution in using this approach as a method of secondary analysis. For statistical reasons (beyond our discussion here) variables should be selected and analyzed only after the researcher has justified hypotheses about their relationships (based on the literature review). The computer should be used for statistical analysis of relationships believed to exist, not to engage in a fishing expedition.

## Tasks Required in Secondary Data Analysis

There are a number of activities that require special attention in research that employs secondary analysis of data. They include the following:

- *Operationalizing of variables.* Methods used to measure variables in the original data collection should be identified, and if at all possible, the same operational definitions should be applied in the current study. Also, some estimate of the degree of reliability and validity (Chapter 10) of the original measurement should be made.
- *Specifying the sampling plan used.* The source of data (case record, personnel file, monthly statistical report, and so on) and the strategy for selecting a sample of cases should be specified and justified.
- *Developing a data collection instrument and coding scheme for data collection.* Typically, this is accomplished by using a data collection instrument that has been developed specifically for the research. Data are drawn from the original documents and recorded on the instrument. The researcher may decide to have more than one person read and record the same data from the original source. If this is done, an estimate of the reliability of the data-gathering method can be made (Chapter 10).
- *Analyzing the data.* The appropriate level of measurement for each variable must be determined (based on information about how it was originally collected) before statistical analysis (Chapter 12) can be conducted.
- *Identifying the limitations of the study.* Although most research reports typically include a section describing limitations of the study, the inclusion of a limitations section is particularly important in secondary analysis. Due to the nature of the data being analyzed (they were defined and recorded for some purpose other than the current study and usually by people other than the researcher) there is a greater-than-usual likelihood that the data will have limitations.

## Advantages of Secondary Data Analysis

Secondary data analysis is appealing to social workers for a number of reasons. First, the financial costs associated with it often are minimal compared with other data collection methods. Second, it generally requires less time than other forms of data collection and analysis. The data are already collected and recorded; the researcher needs only to develop a sampling method and an instrument for coding and recording the data. If the data are already available in a form that is compatible with statistical analysis software, analysis can begin almost immediately following the literature review and the development of focused questions and/or hypotheses.

Secondary analyses are less intrusive than other methods that collect original data from participants. Permissions may not need to be secured, as people are not interviewed or observed in person by the researcher. However, when agency record data are used, clients' permission may be required because data were provided for use in treatment, not for research. Problems related to anonymity may not be an issue if data are stored by case number or some other method that ensures that the researcher cannot possibly know who provided which data when it was originally collected. As a general rule, one is less likely to encounter bureaucratic obstacles to conducting secondary analysis than when conducting other types of research that entail the collection of original data from clients or staff.

## Disadvantages of Secondary Data Analysis

Given the many advantages of conducting secondary analysis, why is it not used more frequently? For one thing, data available for secondary data analysis often are quite limited. When planning to do other forms of research, researchers learn from the literature review (Chapter 4) what variables need to be studied. Then, they simply collect whatever data are needed. In secondary analysis, the existing data may fall short of providing all that is required to answer a research question or to provide support or nonsupport for a hypothesis. If measurements of a variable are not in the record or document, the variable generally cannot be examined (unless it is possible to go back and measure it). The researcher's plans for studying a question or testing a hypothesis may need to be modified to fit existing data.

Another potential problem with the use of secondary analysis relates to the quality of measurement that was conducted. If the data are lacking in credibility, no amount of secondary analysis will improve their quality. A thorough examination of the context in which data were originally collected can help the researcher to determine whether they can be trusted. Some assessment of their quality should be made. Questions might include, for example: Who gathered them, using what kind of recording method? What hidden agenda may have influenced what was recorded and what was not? If the people who originally recorded the information are available to the researcher, they should be consulted on these and other issues.

## Some Specialized Methods of Secondary Data Analysis

Secondary analysis of data can take many forms. We will describe a few of the more popular ones.

**Quantitative Content Analysis.**  Content analysis involves the careful examination of human communication in such vehicles as magazines, journals, newspapers, and films. It also is used to analyze videotapes or transcriptions of audiotapes of social gatherings, meetings, and even research interviews.

Written documents such as newspaper articles, research papers, textbooks, and public documents all provide a rich source of data about people. In addition, photographs, television programs, magazine articles, tapes, films, and other representations of popular culture are available for examination and analysis. These sources can be very informative. They can be examined using content analysis to compare, for example, the portrayal of women and men, of Caucasians and people of color, of people with disabilities and other people, or of people across various sociocultural groups. The data can be analyzed either qualitatively or, more commonly, quantitatively, using a variety of methods.

Content analysis generally entails a categorization and counting process. Hypotheses about the association or correlation between certain variables can then be tested. We noted in Chapter 7 that feminist research sometimes uses quantitative methods to study issues important to women. Examples of feminist research questions that might be studied using quantitative content analysis include

- How many articles of relevance to women does a certain journal publish?
- How many papers have been published by women in a given journal or series of journals?
- How has the media's representation of women changed over the past ten years?

What is the usual sequence of events in conducting content analysis? It is similar to any other research that uses deductive methods. However, data are found within the communication sources analyzed. They are not collected directly from research participants. After the question is specified and a review of literature is conducted, a hypothesis usually can be formulated. Next, a small sample of the available communication sources is used to determine how best to measure the key variables. Then a larger, representative research sample is drawn, and numbers of cases that fall within the various value categories or values of the variables are counted. Statistical testing can be used to determine if it would be reasonably safe to conclude that there is support for research hypotheses. The results of the research can then be summarized in a research report, using tables, graphs, and/or narratives.

Two or three individuals often are used to measure the key variables. If the content analysis is performed well, there should be a high percentage of interobserver agreement among them. If there is a lack of consensus, data are regarded as suspect and may not be used.

There are many good examples of past research that has used content analysis. We will briefly mention just a few of them that would fall under the category of feminist research:

- Quam and Austin examined the coverage of women's issues in social work journals from 1970 to 1981.[1] The authors first conceptualized and operationalized what they meant by women's issues and then reviewed a total of 3,991 articles published in eight journals.

- Pugliesi examined the medicalization of emotion, a concept related to pre-menstrual syndrome (PMS).[2] She performed a content analysis of ninety articles published in popular magazines from 1976 to 1990. Her study provided an analysis of the meaning of PMS in popular culture.
- Rothman, Powers, and Rothman used content analysis of 146 top-grossing films from 1945 to 1993 to test their hypothesis that films produced during the conservative Reagan and Bush administrations were more sexist than those produced in other years.[3] The researchers demonstrated that since the 1960s there has been a marked increase in the representation of women in nontraditional roles and that, when they are, they tend to be presented in a sympathetic way. Thus, the researchers' hypothesis was not supported.

**Historical Research.** Another type of quantitative descriptive research that uses secondary data analysis seeks to describe not what is, but what was. Historical research involves the systematic collection and analysis of a wide array of historical data relevant to a research question and/or hypothesis. It requires reconstructing the past in order to address some current knowledge deficit or to answer some question or questions. For example, a historical research design might be used to study the original statements of missions, goals, and objectives of a social agency to try to find out what its founders had in mind for the organization at the time it was established. Or historical research might attempt to ascertain the original meaning of a social work construct by examining its usage in the professional literature when it first appeared fifty years ago.

Historical research, as a process, requires the development of a research question or hypothesis that can logically be studied by the analysis of historical documents and other sources that may illuminate the past. Once the question is defined, the researcher identifies sources of historical data that will begin to address the research question and/or hypothesis. Sources of data that may be consulted include interviews with key individuals who were present at an earlier time (oral histories), letters, memoirs, public records and documents, newspapers, agency memos, and reports.

Firsthand information, such as that given by key individuals or by their official records, is considered a primary data source. Secondary sources are those accounts that have been written by historians or other persons not directly involved in the historical event. Obviously, the source of the data used in a historical research study is a major factor in assessing the quality of its findings. Data that are biased or are of dubious quality make for poor historical research. Whenever possible, primary sources are preferred to secondary sources.

Once the data have been gathered, they must be synthesized. The researcher must determine what the data mean in relation to the research questions and/or hypotheses. Are there historical or conceptual themes present? How strong and pervasive are they? The final research report generally is written as a narrative that identifies the research questions and describes the method of inquiry (including an in-depth discussion of sources of data used). It then attempts to place the research findings in historical perspective.

When conducting historical research, researchers generally believe that current problems and questions often have their origins in earlier times. They are attempting to obtain a better understanding of the present by gaining a clearer understanding of how things were. Sometimes the past that the researcher hopes to reconstruct for this purpose may have existed many years or centuries earlier. Often, there are no survivors who might be interviewed, so data collection must rely on written records and documents to provide needed information.

The historical researcher frequently sets out either to provide additional confirmation for theories about what is believed to be true about the past or to attempt to dispel a common misconception about what existed. For example, Michael Byrd used historical research to study the attitudes of people toward the poor in colonial America.[4] He had observed that a common assumption among many historians is that the English poor laws were simply transferred from England to the colonies with very little modification. Thus, it has also been assumed that many of the harsh and punitive approaches to the poor that characterized life in England at the time also existed in the colonies.

Byrd conducted an extensive review of the literature. He then collected his data by a systematic review of approximately 2,000 carefully documented case histories of persons who sought financial aid during the years 1732 to 1775. All had requested assistance at St. Philip's Church, the major source of help for the poor in colonial Charles Town (now Charleston, South Carolina).

The researcher's findings bore little resemblance to what had been portrayed in history books. For example, he found that the poor were treated humanely and with dignity; no comments about their laziness or moral impoverishment were found. The poor also did not represent a distinct, stigmatized segment of colonial society. The community seemed to have worked together to provide them with opportunities to achieve financial independence.

Existing laws in Charles Town apparently were far less punitive than the English poor laws. They had been considerably softened to reflect the charitable attitudes toward the poor that were present at the time. Even those laws that might have limited assistance to some people who did not meet residency requirements often were circumvented in order to help those in need.

Any contention that the conservative and even punitive federal policies of financial assistance in the United States during the 1980s were somehow just an extension of what has always been in existence in America (that is, they are typically American) just does not hold up in light of Byrd's findings. These stereotypes and the stigmatization of the poor that is associated with them are relatively new; they are certainly not a part of the original value system on which the United States was founded.

**Meta-analysis.**   There is one form of secondary data analysis, meta-analysis, that is conducted using the results of other people's research as the data source.

In meta-analysis, the unit of analysis is not a case record or a person; it is a report of research. It examines all of the reports from a group of research studies that focused on the same questions or tested the same hypotheses. The reports may be found in professional journals, research monographs, program evaluation documents, theses, dissertations, or anywhere else that research designs and findings are described in sufficient detail to be critically analyzed.

Most meta-analysis is regarded as explanatory research. Thus, designs generally include hypothesis specification and testing, and statistical analysis of data. The designs can be highly rigorous and contain various methods to control for problems of design bias and intervening variables, some of which are unique to this type of research and some of which are common to other forms of secondary analysis.

A common use of meta-analysis is to try to ascertain what works (or does not work) in social work intervention. That in itself does not set it apart from other forms of research. But meta-analysis is used to attempt to answer questions such as: When we look at *all* of the evaluations of job training programs that have been used with welfare recipients, can we really say that training has been successful? or Based on available research studies, is it safe to use confrontation in treating clients who have been diagnosed as anorexic?

Because findings of meta-analysis are based on the reports of studies conducted by many different researchers in different settings, they are often based on data collected from very large numbers of research participants collectively. This has certain advantages. Although a particular design bias may have been in operation in one or two studies, it is unlikely to exist in all of them. Also, the large number of cases on which findings are based should make the likelihood of sampling error quite low. Thus, meta-analysis studies have the potential to possess a high level of both internal validity and external validity.

There are also several problems associated with the use of meta-analysis. Like all forms of secondary data analysis, meta-analysis studies are limited by the quality of data that are available. The report of one study may be very comprehensive; the report of another may be sketchy. This can cause problems in drawing conclusions about the credibility of their respective findings. Also, it is rare that two or more research studies that examined the same research question used exactly the same research methods. Because of this, we must ask: To what degree should they be compared or equated?

Another potential problem relates to the selection processes that sometimes influence what gets into print. Perhaps, as some people have suggested, professional journals may be more likely to publish articles where demonstration of support for directional or nondirectional hypotheses was found than those where variables were found to be unrelated. If this is true, it could result in a built-in bias within the data. Or when program evaluations are used in meta-analysis, they may be biased to show programs in a good light (or a bad one) if political pressure was applied. Certain statistical corrections and design features (beyond the scope of this book) have been developed to attempt to address the problem of bias in the use of meta-analysis.

Meta-analysis is growing in popularity among social work researchers. It is becoming more feasible as we begin to accumulate reports of research that are either replications of earlier research or are reports of research that are similar enough that they lend themselves to this type of research.

## Research That Collects and Analyzes Original Data

Of course, because of its limitations, secondary data do not allow us to adequately answer most of our research questions. We must collect new data in order to be certain that key variables will be measured well, using methods that we can trust.

### Experimental and Quasi-Experimental Research

In Chapter 6, we described experimental research and how it differs from other types of research. We also described several time-tested experimental designs. Whenever ethically and logistically possible, quantitative studies continue to employ experiments to test hypotheses, because they alone can produce cause–effect knowledge. That is why experimental designs are often the first choice of researchers seeking to know if one variable truly causes changes in some other variable. If a true experiment is not possible, a quasi-experimental design is often the second choice.

Experimental designs also are often the designs of choice for social workers conducting evaluations of program effectiveness. A carefully designed and executed experiment has a high level of both external validity and internal validity. Random sampling (see Chapter 9) increases the possibility that the sample will be representative of a larger group of cases from which it was drawn (external validity). Use of one or more control groups and random assignment to them help to increase the likelihood that the independent variable (and not something else) produced any change in the dependent variable (internal validity). Thus, it is possible when using an experimental design to conclude, for example, that it was the nature of a job training program and not the clients' motivation level, changes in the economy, or something else that produced a higher percentage of employment in a program's graduates (the experimental group) than among the graduates in a traditional program (the control group).

### Structured Observation

In quantitative research, experimental and quasi-experimental designs are often not feasible or desirable for one or a variety of reasons. Sometimes, they simply would not be effective in acquiring the kind of data we require. Especially if our goal is to accurately describe some behavior or phenomenon, other methods would be more effective. Structured observation is sometimes used for this purpose. In Chapter 7, we discussed unstructured observation methods as a form of qualitative research that entails making observations of behavior. But more structured forms of observation tend to be more quantitative. Structured observation requires identifying a specific behavior or set of behaviors and systematically observing them over a given time period. A data-gathering instrument is used. Because of the structure imposed by this method, data are more similar (on a case-by-case basis) and therefore more easily sorted and analyzed than those collected using less structured observation methods.

**Roles That Can Be Assumed.**   In designing any form of systematic observation, researchers must decide on the nature and degree of involvement with research participants that are best. The most appropriate role for a given study depends on the purpose of the study and the researcher's assessment of how the most accurate data can be obtained. Observer roles may be understood as being located on a continuum from complete observer to participant observer. Possible observer roles might include

- Concealed, nonparticipating (complete observer)
- Concealed, participating
- Not concealed, nonparticipating
- Not concealed, minimally participating
- Not concealed, participating (participant observer)

The two variables, concealment of the observer (usually the researcher) and degree of participation, can affect the quality of the data collected. When the presence of an observer is not concealed, participants may consciously or unconsciously alter their behavior. But when the presence of an observer is concealed from participants, they are more likely to behave in their usual manner. So why not simply conceal the fact that the researcher is an observer collecting research data? As was noted in our discussion of research ethics in Chapter 2, not allowing participants to know that they are being observed may be considered unwarranted intrusion on their privacy. It might not be permitted by an IRB on ethical grounds because participants had not voluntarily agreed to be part of the research. Even if participants had agreed to participate in research, but had not been told that they would be observed without their knowledge, that could be problematic. But if they voluntarily agreed to participate and were told that they would be observed but would not know exactly *when* they were being observed, this would not constitute deception and would probably be considered ethical.

How would the various roles be operationalized in social work research? An example might be helpful. Suppose a team of researchers is interested in studying the quality of interviewing skills of beginning social workers in a human service organization. If the researchers elect to observe the interview sessions of new workers from behind a one-way mirror, then they would be considered to be "concealed, nonparticipating." If the researchers observe from behind the mirror while utilizing equipment that would enable them to prompt the interviewers, then the observers would be "concealed, participating." They also could choose to observe a sample of client interviews conducted by beginning-level workers by actually sitting in on the interviews. If the researchers only record behaviors and do not influence the direction of the interview in any way, then they are "not concealed, nonparticipating." But if the researchers provide occasional sugges-tions to the workers, suggest approval or disapproval of the workers' interview-ing methods through nonverbal communication, or otherwise subtly influence them to conduct the interview differently, then the researchers are "not concealed, minimally participating." However, if the interviews are conducted jointly by researchers and workers, and the workers' skills are later evaluated, the re-searchers would be "not concealed, participating."

Sometimes the choice of an observer role can greatly affect the quality of the data that will be acquired. If researchers wish to gather data that will not be affected by their presence, then the observer should be concealed and nonpartici-pating. However, if the data are unlikely to be adversely affected by the ob-server's presence, then the observer need not be concealed.

**Steps in Conducting Structured Observation.**  There generally are seven steps in implementing a structured observational design. They are

1. *Define the behavior or list of behaviors to be studied.* In structured observation, the researcher decides what behaviors to study based on the literature review. They are those behaviors considered critical to an understanding of the research problem and to answering research questions and/or testing hy-potheses. Operational definitions of the behaviors are developed; they pro-vide the basis for observation. Characteristics of the behaviors to be measured are also specified, for example, their frequency, duration, intensity, and so forth.

2. *Identify a time frame during which the behaviors will be observed.* The researcher has to know when specific behaviors are most likely to occur. This knowledge also comes from a thorough understanding of the behavior under investiga-tion derived from the review of literature and personal or professional experience. For example, if we are interested in studying verbal abuse by caregivers of older people, the researcher should have learned which times of day are most stressful for caregivers. In addition to identifying a specific time during the day (or week or month) to observe, the literature review might also suggest a time interval during which the observation should occur. Will the observer observe for one hour at a time, for three hours, or for five minutes each hour? A time sample should be selected based on the nature of the behavior under study (when and how frequently it is most likely to occur) and on the physical and emotional capacities of observers to gather accurate data. If observers are required to gather data for long periods of time, the quality of the data may suffer (referred to as *measurement decay*). Observers get tired or bored; they require breaks and relief from their work.

3. *Develop a data collection instrument.* In structured observation, instruments typically take the form of behavioral checklists or category schemes. They

are designed so that, when a behavior is displayed, its characteristics can easily be recorded. The instrument may also include demographic data on participants being observed, such as name, age, gender, or other identifying characteristics. As is true for other new data collection instruments (Chapter 11), the instrument should be pilot tested before use. This is done to see how effective the instrument is in describing the behavior.

4. *Select an observer role.* The observer role most appropriate to the behavior being studied is selected. Logistical and ethical issues (as previously mentioned) are addressed.

5. *Train observers.* Structured observation requires the use of trained research personnel. Unless the researcher is conducting all observations personally (a potential source of bias), others usually are recruited or hired to observe. They need to be trained by the researcher in the method of observation to be used, and they need to gain experience with the use of the data collection instrument. Observers need to know what to look for, when to observe it, how to know if behavior is occurring, and how to record it using the instrument.

6. *Conduct the observations.* Observers apply the observational method, recording the data as they are obtained.

7. *Verify the data.* Data are checked for accuracy. It may be possible to use videotaping (with participant permission) to record behaviors. If so, an observer need not be present, and a team of trained reviewers can view the recordings and arrive at a consensus as to what occurred. If this is not possible, a second observer may be used. If there is a serious discrepancy between the data collected by two observers, the disputed data generally are discarded.

## *In-Person Interviews*

In the previous chapter, we discussed several forms of qualitative research that collect data using research interviews. Interviews (generally more structured than in qualitative studies) are also a useful way of collecting data in quantitative research. They are most appropriate when researchers are in need of data that can best be obtained through oral communication or a combination of oral communication and first-person observation.

Characteristics of research participants sometimes suggest that research interviews are the best way to obtain data. For example, very young children, some older people, people with learning disabilities, or other people with no or minimal literacy skills all may require the use of an interview.

Aspects of specific cultures also may favor the use of the in-person interview. Because cooperation in interpersonal interactions is important in cultures that are more collectivistic, research participants who adhere to these values may respond more favorably to in-person data collection approaches than to less personal data collection approaches, such as questionnaires or telephone surveys. In many Hispanic cultures, *personalismo* is valued; that is, time is taken for people to get to know one another and trust is established before information (especially that of a sensitive nature) is shared. The in-person interview is more conducive to this type of interaction and may increase rate of compliance with research protocols among people who hold this cultural perspective.

Whenever in-person interviews are used for data collection, researchers contact potential participants and acquire their permission to be interviewed. Then the interview is conducted at a time and a place that is mutually agreeable to both interviewer and participant.

As we have noted, in quantitative research interviewers attempt to minimize the opportunity for bias or distortion to affect the quality of the data gathered. They are careful not to influence the responses provided by research participants in any way, so that accurate measurement can be performed. For example, when a participant responds to questions, there is no indication provided in the form of either positive or negative reinforcement that would suggest that one response is preferable to another.

Unlike certain types of qualitative research (for example, qualitative forms of feminist research), the interviewer conducting quantitative research avoids the role of potential friend or some other role that might compromise the objectivity of the data collection process. Special attention is paid to dress, mode of communication, manner of presentation, and overall demeanor. The interviewer works to eliminate personal characteristics that may offend, intimidate, or otherwise influence the responses of participants. Of course, researchers cannot alter certain of their personal characteristics, such as age, gender, or ethnicity, but remain sensitive to them and attempt to determine how they may have influenced data collection.

**Advantages of Research Interviewing.**    Besides the fact that they allow the researcher to collect data from participants who might be unable to complete written data collection instruments, there are a number of other important advantages to collecting data using in-person interviews.

- *Opportunity to probe.* While talking with research participants, the researcher is able to initiate clarification about their responses by making such comments as "I wonder if you could tell me more about that?" or "What led you to that conclusion?" These comments provide participants with the opportunity to expand on responses more fully, thereby allowing the researcher to acquire more in-depth, accurate data. It may thus be possible to understand and measure an individual's attitude about an issue and perhaps even determine the origins of that attitude. This type of insight is less likely to occur if a mailed instrument or other method that does not allow for interaction between the researcher and the participant is used for data collection.
- *High completion rate.* Interviews usually permit researchers to secure a completed return. If participants agree to be interviewed, then interviewers usually are able to get them to complete the interview.

- *Access to supplementary data.* Interviewers are able to observe participants while they are responding to questions. Nonverbal communications may provide important data. They can indicate the participant's ease in responding, evasiveness in answering questions, or how seriously the participant seems to be taking the interview. They can be carefully observed, recorded, and used as part of later statistical analysis.

    Interviews can be conducted in a human service organization, a public place, or the participant's own home. If participants are interviewed in their home, additional variables can be measured and analyzed. For example, observations can be made about the home environment and about their interaction with significant others. These kind of data can provide the researcher with additional (in some cases, serendipitous) data which help to explain the participant's other responses more fully.

- *Opportunity to individualize data collection.* Interviews can be individualized as needed to facilitate data collection or to aid in obtaining complete data from participants. Of course, the more interviews differ, the more difficult it becomes to compare responses of participants.

**Use of Interviewing Skills.** Interviewing is a natural for social work researchers whose professional education prepares them to conduct interviews about a wide range of topics. Thus, interviewing takes advantage of their strengths.

**Disadvantages of Research Interviewing.** If interviews were the perfect way to collect quantitative research data, no other methods would be needed. But there are some major problems inherent in research interviews, especially in quantitive research. Although careful preparation can minimize them, it cannot totally eliminate them.

- *Influence of the interviewer.* The fact that the researcher is present and is posing questions directly to the participant may influence the responses of participants. (Qualitative researchers, we recall, regard such influence as inevitable anyway.) In some cases, participants may choose a response that they believe is sought by the interviewer. This type of distortion in responses is known as an *expectancy effect*. Participants also may choose a socially desirable response rather than provide their true response. Erroneous conclusions on the part of the interviewer can result.

- *Potential for recording errors.* The accuracy of data collected in an interview also may be negatively affected by the manner in which responses are recorded by the interviewer. Participants may provide truthful and accurate data, but if they are forgotten, distorted, misinterpreted, or recorded in error by the interviewer, data quality will still be low. Careful preparation for data collection that addresses how data are to be gathered and recorded can reduce the potential for recording errors. If interviewers other than the researcher are to be used, they should be carefully trained in order to have a thorough understanding of the expected role and demeanor of the interviewer and the purpose of the study and its overall design. They should be given supervised practice in use of the interview schedule and the correct manner of recording data.

Interviewer training can be expensive, but its cost is justified. If two or more interviewers are to be used, consistency in recording is enhanced if interviewers are trained together. They should be provided with the opportunity to ask any questions about the study that they may have. Interviewing simulations and role play can be part of the training package.

- *Measurement errors caused by demographic differences.* When interviewers and research participants are from different language, racial, cultural, or even socioeconomic groups, the possibility of biased responses due to either socially desirable responses or unwillingness or fear of providing frank answers to questions may be increased. This is especially likely to occur when the research topic touches on areas related to the nature of differences between investigator and participant (for example, racial prejudices and attitudes toward other groups).

Under certain conditions, it may be preferable to match interviewers and participants according to language, culture, and even socioeconomic status. Use of same-ethnic data collectors can increase rapport and trust. Communication also is enhanced when bilingual interviewers are used for participants who are not native English speakers. Bilingual and bicultural interviewers are more likely to be aware of idiomatic variations among particular ethnic or nationality groups, as well as subtle differences in meaning for the same or similar words. They are also more likely to recognize and understand nonverbal forms of communication, which may be more critical than what participants actually say.[5]

Butler[6] cautions that simply matching interviewer and participant by race or ethnicity may be insufficient to guard against measurement bias. She notes, for example, that many African American professionals are from the upper and middle classes or are trained in mainstream educational settings that remove them from the realities of fellow African Americans from different socioeconomic circumstances.

- *Expense.* Using research interviews for data collection can get expensive. If interviewers other than the researcher are used, salaries must be paid. If home visits are required, travel and related expenses (tolls, parking, and so on) add up quickly. If researchers conduct their own interviews, a valuable saving in the cost of interviewer training and salaries will be realized. But valuable time will have to be diverted from other activities both within and outside the research project. No matter who conducts them, research interviews are the most expensive method of data collection.

**Acquiring Complete Data.**  There are some practices that researchers try to follow to ensure that data received through interviewing are as complete and usable as possible. They include the following:

- *Provide complete identification.* Interviewers should appropriately identify themselves and remind the participant of the purpose of the study and of their agreement to be interviewed. An appropriate introduction helps to confirm that the study is legitimate and thus helps to make the participant more desirous of providing all requested data.

- *Promote pleasant interaction.* Respect and courtesy, of course, are appropriate in all research interviews. They are especially essential when interviews are conducted in the participant's own home, where the researcher is a guest. Research participants in quantitative research often give much more than they hope to receive; an interviewer's demeanor should reflect an appreciation of this fact.

- *Use data collection instruments.* Because quantitative research interviewing tends to be more structured than interviewing used in qualitative research, data collection instruments (sometimes referred to as *interview schedules*) generally are used. In interviews in which a high percentage of items are designed to be read to participants, the specific wording of an item and the sequence in which items are covered take on great importance. Any deviation from the wording or from sequencing of items could influence the responses that are received and could invalidate any comparisons made between research participants. (In less structured research, a schedule serves as only a general outline; wording and sequencing of items is less critical.)

- *Record unobtrusively.* The style of recording of research data and observations will vary from one interviewer to another and from one study to another. For some studies, it may be essential to circle the appropriate responses on a data collection instrument or to record verbatim what the participant says. It may be desirable to either audiotape or videotape the interview. Of course, if this mode of recording is selected, participants' permission should be solicited in writing. However data are recorded, it should be done as unobtrusively as possible in order not to disrupt the flow of the interview.

- *Specify the progress of the interview.* As the interview progresses, the interviewer should periodically let the participant know about what percentage of the interview remains to be completed. This may help participants avoid becoming frustrated about the time required, help them remain focused, and give them a feeling of better participation in the interview process. Interviewers might say something like "Now we have reached the halfway point" or "We have just two more questions to go" or "We're nearly through now."

## *Telephone Interviews and E-Mail Surveys*

Some data for quantitative studies can be conducted over the telephone or by e-mail. If the purpose of data collection is to acquire a small amount of mostly factual, not too personal information from a larger number of participants and the external validity of findings is relatively unimportant, they can be quick, relatively efficient methods. A fax machine is sometimes also used in these situations.

Two common examples of research that often use telephone interviews or e-mail surveys are client satisfaction surveys in human service organizations and alumni follow-up surveys in schools of social work. If an administrator is interested in determining to what degree a sample of clients is satisfied with services recently received, the phone can be used to contact former clients. Securing their responses to five or six questions can be performed quickly and inexpensively. Similarly, current students or faculty members can conduct a survey of a sample of a school's graduates to learn, for example, if they had difficulty in finding employment, what courses they found most useful in their practice, what curriculum changes they might recommend, and so forth.

When should telephone interviews be conducted? Common sense and experience would suggest that it is a poor idea to call between 5:00 P.M. and, say, 7:00 P.M., when many people are returning from work or having dinner. Similarly calling either late in the evening or very early in the morning is often resented by potential participants. Although these times are especially inconvenient for people to provide data over the phone, most any time that the researcher calls is likely to find potential participants doing something that they would prefer to do. Perhaps in earlier times people enjoyed unanticipated phone calls, but few do today. Finding a time that is convenient is a difficult but important task in telephone interviewing. Therefore, it is prudent to schedule telephone interviews with participants in advance whenever possible.

Even if a phone call comes at an ideal time, the recent increase in phone solicitation and marketing research has created a climate where any simple requests for information are now suspect. Telephone interviewers must overcome the annoyance and normal suspicions that people display when they receive a call from someone they do not know. The researcher can almost expect to hear "Okay, what are you selling?" or just a hang-up.

Unfortunately, pseudoresearch has been used as a device to make a sale or, even worse, to collect personal information to be used by the researcher for some self-serving (or even illicit) purpose. Telephone requests for information now have a poor reputation. Although virtually anyone can memorize a few questions to collect telephone data, overcoming resistance to providing information over the phone is the hardest part of telephone interviewing. It requires all the interviewing skills of the social worker.

Most of the same principles that apply to in-person interviews apply to the telephone interview as well. However, because participants may be naturally suspicious of why they have been called and of the true purpose of a caller whom they cannot see, telephone researchers have an especially hard sell. It is necessary that interviewers identify themselves and tell what organization is supporting or endorsing their research. They should also ask permission to conduct the interview. If a participant indicates that the call has come at an inconvenient time, a request to reschedule the interview should be made.

**Problems Related to External Validity.**   An important limitation of data gathered through telephone interviews and e-mail surveys is the difficulty of obtaining a group of participants who are representative of the group being studied. Therefore, the external validity of research that uses them often is regarded as poor.

Any time of day when telephone interviews are conducted has the potential to interfere with sample representativeness. For example, people employed outside the home tend to be unavailable during daytime hours. But representativeness of the sample can be hindered in other ways, too. An organization administrator might have access to all case records (containing phone numbers) to conduct a follow-up client satisfaction survey. But some former clients may have moved or had their phones disconnected and would thus be unavailable to be contacted. And they may be (disproportionately) the very people who either are doing very well and have moved out of state or are having the most problems and are most dissatisfied with their services. Similarly, an alumni follow-up survey might get the participation of only those alumni who are most satisfied with their education (and want to show their appreciation) or those who are most dissatisfied (and want to take the opportunity to vent about it). The alumni who are more neutral may have little vested interest in providing data. They are more likely to refuse to provide it and therefore will be underrepresented in the data collected.

Often, the researcher who lacks access to current agency or university records is even less fortunate. If it is necessary to dial numbers at random or select them randomly from a phone directory, a biased sample is almost certain to result. A telephone directory is not a very good source from which to draw a research sample. The phone book automatically excludes people who do not have telephones in their homes and those who do not have listed numbers. In addition, the widespread use of voice mail and answering machines (often used to screen calls) has made it difficult to get through to even many of those who have listed phone numbers. All of these factors can severely bias a sample in relation to occupation, gender, ethnicity, socioeconomic class, and other related variables that may be important to the research. Of course, many of these same variables are related to computer ownership and thus to who is available to participate in an e-mail survey.

## Mailed Surveys

Data collection by mail is widely used in quantitative social work research, especially in descriptive surveys. A mailed, self-administered data collection instrument can reach large numbers of participants quickly and at relatively low cost. However, for data thus acquired to be valuable, the instruments must reach the appropriate people, they must be completed correctly, and participants must return them as directed. In reality, what sometimes happens instead is that many mailed data collection instruments are either misplaced by recipients, discarded as junk mail, completed but never mailed back to the researcher, or completed incorrectly to the point that they must be discarded.

In order to increase the number of usable responses, it often is necessary to use a second or even third mailing of the data collection instrument. In order to reduce costs, instruments are precoded with an identifying number prior to the first mailing, so that when they are returned, the researcher can tell who has returned them and who has not. Then a second mailing is sent to those who did not return them. Given the virtual necessity of second mailings, data collection by mail is more costly than it might first appear. The costs of printing the instrument, of preparing the mailings, and of the postage required for two or more mailings can be appreciable. The major advantage of using mailed instruments is access to potential research participants. When they are used, large numbers of people who might otherwise be inaccessible for financial and/or logistical reasons can provide data.

### Problems with Data Collection by Mail

There also are several problems associated with the use of the postal system to collect data. We will discuss four of the major ones.

**Potential for Distortion.**   Distortion is likely to be present when any self-administered data collection instrument is used, but especially when data are collected by mail. When instruments are mailed to research participants, researchers do not know whether or not participants understood what was asked or if they responded honestly. A participant who does not need to face the researcher probably is more likely to misrepresent reality than one who participates in in-person data collection.

If inaccurate data are provided either accidentally or intentionally, researchers may not be able to detect it. They may have no way of knowing if the participant filled out the instrument carefully and thoughtfully or just put down anything to complete it. They do not know if its completion took an hour or two minutes. They also have no way of knowing the state of mind of participants when the instruments were completed. Researchers who collect their data using mailed data collection instruments must live with the specter of a group of participants sitting around together on a dull afternoon competing with each other to produce the most preposterous or the most amusing responses. Returned data collection instruments that contain clearly facetious or impossible responses can simply be discarded. But it is more difficult to determine what to do with a completed instrument that contains responses that are just a little unusual—it may contain valid data, or it may not.

**Identity of the Participant.**   When using a mailed instrument, it may be impossible to know if the person to whom it was sent completed it. Did it fall into the hands of a mischievous child? Or was it deliberately delegated to another for completion? The identity of the respondent is almost certain to be a problem with certain groups of people. For example, if a mailed questionnaire is sent to physicians, any research respondents are likely to be clerical staff members who work for the doctors and who complete all of their paperwork.

**Return Rate.** A common problem with data collection by mail is a low rate of return of completed instruments. It is just too easy for potential research participants to discard a request for data or, with all good intentions, to set it aside and forget about it. The researcher who uses mailed data collection asks much and offers little. There is no potential for a pleasant interpersonal exchange with the researcher, only a letter from a person who is most likely to be a stranger and whose motives for seeking participation in the research are likely to be suspect.

Although some research naturally draws a higher rate of return (for example, research on emotionally charged topics or requests for data sent to college alumni or people who are fellow members of religious or civic organizations), a typical rate for data collection instruments mailed to strangers and using at least one follow-up request is 30 to 40 percent. A return rate higher than that is considered quite good. One obvious implication is that if a sample of responses of a given size is needed, the researcher should either (1) send out at least three times that many instruments to ensure having enough completed ones for data analysis or (2) go to extraordinary lengths to attempt to increase the usual, expected rate of return.

The potential value of a well-designed study can be quickly negated if the researcher cannot generate a sufficiently large number of complete responses for analysis. There are ways to increase the likelihood of a satisfactory return rate. We will mention a few of the most effective ones.

- *Keep it short.* Excessive length probably results in more discarded instruments than any other cause. Few potential participants will complete a ten-page instrument, no matter what the topic or their interest in it. Ten pages worth of questions jammed onto both sides of four or five pages, or use of small print, will not fool anyone or fare any better. Such attempts at deception just make potential participants angry. Generally, if an instrument is longer than a few normally spaced, easily read pages, it probably is trying to collect too much data at a single time. The researcher also should use as many fixed-alternative items (see Chapter 11) as possible. People are more likely to make a check mark or an X than to write one or more words.
- *Avoid bad times.* Although there is no ideal time to ask research participants to complete an instrument, some times of the year have been found to be worse than others. The December holidays should be avoided. Among student participants, midterm and final examination times (and spring break) are not likely to result in a high response rate.
- *Provide incentives.* A small cash payment or some other small gift as payment for participation will almost always result in more instruments' being completed and returned. A promise of a reward after a completed instrument is received will be less effective in improving response rate than an incentive mailed out with the instrument and cover letter. Why are incentives not used more frequently? The costs of providing them may be great, and the costs may be more than just monetary. They may influence the responses received.

Are participants who are paid for their responses either consciously or unconsciously more likely to provide those responses that they think are being sought by the researcher? The answer to this question is almost impossible to determine. Another type of incentive that can increase response rate is an offer to share an outline or summary of the major research findings. If it is used, any requests for the summary (there are usually relatively few) must be honored, despite the cost of the additional correspondence. To not do so would be unethical.

- *Provide postage-paid, preaddressed return envelopes.* People are unlikely to return an instrument unless they can do it simply and with no cost to them. Given the usual rate of return for mailed instruments, it generally is more economical to use metered envelopes than to affix a stamp to the return envelope. The postage for each response will be a little higher than if a stamp were provided, but one is charged only for those that are mailed back. Postage also affects return rate in another way: Generally, more expensive mailing methods yield higher rates of response. First-class mail is more likely to result in completed instruments than third-class mail. High-priority methods such as overnight delivery yield relatively high rates of response, but their cost can be prohibitive.

- *Use a carefully worded cover letter.* The cover letter should tell potential participants how they were selected to receive the instrument and that their response is important to the success of the research. Especially if the research deals with sensitive matters (for example, sexuality, religious or political beliefs, or behaviors that are either illegal or not socially approved), potential respondents will need to know how the researcher got their names and how data will be used, and they will need to be assured that any confidentiality or anonymity promises will be kept.

  The cover letter should reflect the researcher's genuine interest in the research problem and the assumption that potential participants may share that interest. Potential respondents also will need to be convinced that the instrument is not just being sent to millions of people and that their responses are important to the success of the research. If the researcher personally signs each cover letter, this will help to reinforce this impression.

  Careful wording of the cover letter is very important. The wrong type of appeal for participation actually can reduce the rate of response. For example, a statement such as "I am a social work student who needs to collect data to meet my research course requirement" suggests that (1) the researcher probably is not really interested in the problem; (2) the researcher would not be conducting the research if it were not required; and (3) the findings are unlikely ever to be used for anything other than for helping a professor to assign a course grade. Why would anyone want to take the time to respond favorably to such an appeal?

- *Use return addresses and letterheads.* The return address on an envelope used to mail out a data collection instrument and the inside address on the cover letter can affect the rate of return of mailed instruments. A home or business address can lend credibility to a research study; generally, a post office box number can harm it.

The use of some agency return addresses and inside addresses can help to increase return rate; the use of others can decrease it. When an organizational affiliation is likely to increase response rate, permission to use agency envelopes and stationery should be sought. They suggest written endorsement of and support for the research. However, some organizations such as state departments of social services or state departments of mental health or corrections evoke certain emotional responses. Using their envelopes and stationery might negatively affect return rate and can even bias the data that are received.

**Response Bias.**  It can easily be determined if a researcher has the required number of cases to perform a certain type of statistical analysis. But a second and more difficult question that must be answered is whether the data that are available for analysis were collected from a representative sample of participants. Although a high percentage of responses to a mailing of an instrument (for example, 75 percent) is likely to produce a representative sample of those who were requested to participate, there is no guarantee that it does. The 25 percent who failed to respond may differ from the 75 percent who did in some important way that could still have produced a biased sample. Conversely, although not likely, even a very low rate of return theoretically could have produced a sample that is representative of the population being studied. The problem with using mailed instruments is that it is difficult to know whether those who did not return the instrument are similar to or different from those who did in some important way. Some follow-up calls to determine why the former group did not respond are sometimes informative. They can provide at least some insight into whether or not a response bias exists. However, they also can be perceived as harassment by those people who already indicated their unwillingness to be research participants when they did not return their data collection instruments.

In some research situations, a response bias is quite predictable. For example, a follow-up survey to assess the vocational success of people denied admission to a job training program would be expected to prompt a disproportionately high rate of return from three groups: (1) those who have been very successful and who wish to gloat about their success; (2) those who are still unemployed and who wish to blame their denial to the program for their failures; and (3) those who receive the instrument, perceive that it means that they are still being considered for admission to the program, and therefore are careful to complete and return it. A lower rate of return might be expected from other people who are employed, but have not been very successful in their careers or otherwise have less emotional investment in completing the data collection instrument.

A descriptive study of hazing rituals (emotional and physical abuse of students attempting to be admitted to membership in some group or organization) among high school and college students[7] provides a good example of how response bias can operate. In August 2000, many major newspapers reported that a large percentage of students had been victims of hazing. Although this conclusion was based on a study in which mailed questionnaires were completed and anonymously returned by a large number of students, the questionnaires represented only a 12 percent return rate; that is, only 12 percent of the questionnaires mailed out were returned. The low return rate was reason enough for us to question the external validity of any findings drawn from returned questionnaires. However, we also should ask who was most likely to return the questionnaires and who was not. Wouldn't students who had experienced hazing be more likely to take the trouble to complete and return them than those who had had no experience with hazing and thus had no particular interest in it? It would probably be safe to assume that generalizations from this sample (at least any about incidence of hazing) are very suspect.

When it appears that the use of the mail for data collection would be likely to result in response bias, other methods of data collection such as in-person interviews should be considered. A smaller (but more representative) sample of participants is almost always preferable to a larger, biased one.

## Using Quantitative Methods to Evaluate Practice Effectiveness

Quantitative research methods like those that we described in this chapter have been an important part of knowledge building for our profession for many years. Along with the more qualitative methods described in the previous chapter, they have helped to inform our practice decision making and to make us more knowledge-based practitioners.

Recently, as we have already noted, many of our research efforts have been directed toward evaluation of practice effectiveness—learning which interventions work (and which do not) for us as individual practitioners and evaluating both proposed and existing social programs. We mentioned earlier in this chapter how researchers might use an experiment to evaluate the effectiveness of a job training program. However, all of the other methods described in this chapter are used in evaluating practice effectiveness as well. When we look at this important role of research in social work practice in more detail (Chapters 13 and 14), we will see just how useful they can be.

## Summary

In this chapter, we took a more in-depth look at some of the more common methods employed for conducting quantitative research studies. We discussed several different alternatives for data collection. Secondary data analysis (using data acquired for some other purposes) can be a real time-saver for the researcher.

However, the data thus acquired often have serious limitations both in scope and in quality. Three specialized forms of secondary analysis were examined. Content analysis carefully breaks down and analyzes different forms of human communication. Historical research uses artifacts to attempt to re-create the past. Meta-analysis is used for testing hypotheses. It relies on the findings of many studies that examined the same research question or tested the same hypothesis.

Experimental and quasi-experimental research methods remain popular choices when we seek to learn if a cause–effect relationship between variables exist. Structured observation methods were examined, with special emphasis on the various roles that researchers can assume. We discussed a data collection method introduced in the previous chapter, in-person interviews, noting how they are conducted differently when used in quantitative research studies. In-person interviews also are very expensive to conduct.

Telephone interviews and e-mail were presented as inexpensive ways to acquire large numbers of responses to a limited number of questions. Their major weakness often is sampling bias, which seriously limits the external validity of findings.

Finally, we examined mailed data collection (usually in the form of a survey) as an option for collecting quantitative data. Although data collection by mail is widely used in social work research, it has many disadvantages. We discussed several of the more serious ones and suggested ways to minimize some of them.

# References

1. Quam, J., & Austin, C. (1984). Coverage of women's issues in eight social work journals, 1970–81. *Social Work, 29,* 360–365.
2. Pugliesi, K. (1992). Premenstrual syndrome: The medicalization of emotion related to conflict and chronic role strain. *Journal of Social Relations, 18*(2), 131–165.
3. Rothman, S., Powers, S., & Rothman, D. (1993). Feminism in films. *Society, 303*(203), 66–72.
4. Byrd, M. (1973). Ye have the poor always with you: Attitudes toward relief of the poor in colonial Charles Town. Unpublished MSW thesis. Columbia, SC: University of South Carolina.
5. Marin, G., & Marin, B. V. (1991). *Research with Hispanic populations.* Newbury Park, CA: Sage Publications.
6. Butler, J. P. (1992). Of kindred minds: The ties that bind. In OSAP, *Cultural competence for evaluators.* Washington, DC: U.S. Department of Health and Human Services, 23–54.
7. McQueen, A. (2000). Students humiliated by hazing. In *The State* (August 29, 2000). Columbia, SC, A1.

# 9

# CASE SAMPLING

As we examined methods for conducting qualitative and quantitative research, two activities, sampling and measurement, were frequently mentioned. Because of their importance, we will examine both of them them in some detail—sampling in this chapter and measurement in Chapters 10 and 11.

A sample can be either a group of research participants or a group of objects (for example, human service organizations, case records, and so forth). In most research designs that use human research participants to provide original data, a sample of participants is used in place of a much larger group of people. Especially in quantitative studies (and, to a lesser degree, in more qualitative ones), people in the sample are studied with the hope of learning something that can be generalized to others who were not part of the research. To state this in another way, researchers hope to produce findings that will possess good external validity.

In a sense, sampling is a shortcut to knowledge building—researchers hope to study a relatively small number of cases to learn something about a much larger group. However, for this to work, the sample must be a good one. The selection of a good sample (also sometimes referred to as *case sampling*) can help to produce findings that are useful to the social work practitioner and to other researchers. Conversely, a carelessly chosen or inappropriate sample can seriously weaken the usefulness of the findings of research that otherwise was well designed and implemented. If a sample is a poor one, it would be presumptuous to generalize any findings much beyond the sample or to conclude much else from it, for that matter.

## Sampling Terminology

When used in a discussion of sampling, some terms take on very specific meanings. Let us look at some of the most important ones.

**Case.**   A case (sometimes called an "element" if it refers to an inanimate object) is the basic unit of analysis in a given research study. If the unit of analysis is a person (as is often the situation in social work research), the term is used to denote each actual person who was selected for study. Collectively, those people selected as research participants for the study constitute the sample (see below). Of course, in research, the term *case* may refer to many different units of analysis other than individual people. For example, a study's cases or elements could be families, groups, organizations, communities, or even nations.

**Universe and Population.**   The word *universe* refers to the entire collection of people (or elements) that share some defined characteristics. A universe often is so comprehensive that there is no realistic hope that some people or objects within it could ever be studied by the researcher (for example, all incidents of child abuse among human beings during any given year). Another word, *population*, is sometimes used interchangeably with *universe*. But when we use the word *population*, it has a somewhat narrower connotation. It refers only to those cases that realistically might be selected as research participants, those that are potentially accessible to the researcher. For example, in one study a population may be all of the clients served by some organization's program. In another, it may be all students enrolled in a social work program at a given university. This is not to imply that a population for a research study is always relatively small or geographically limited. It may be possible to select cases from populations that are very large and/or widely dispersed. If, for example, there is a comprehensive list of all cases (such as the CSWE's list of all accredited BSW programs in the United States), the population may be both large and geographically dispersed. The definition of a research population is specific to a given research study and relates to such factors as budgetary constraints, methods of data collection, and time allocated to conduct the research. Thus, it must be carefully specified by the researcher.

**Sampling Frame.**   A sampling frame is the actual listing of potential cases from which some are drawn. Its elements may be identical to those of the population, but usually they are not. The researcher hopes that it will be at least a reasonable approximation of the population. But we all know that lists, no matter how meticulously they have been compiled, often are incomplete or contain some people or objects that should not be included. For example, if we are interested in studying some characteristic of social work students, then the population may be defined as all current BSW and MSW students at XYZ University, and the sampling frame may be an actual list of social work students supplied by the dean's office. It would not include all students who registered after the day the list was compiled, and it may contain the names of some students who recently have withdrawn from social work courses but have not completed the necessary paperwork or notified the dean.

A population is what we would like to use for selecting cases, whereas a sampling frame is an available list that is the next best thing to a population.

Frequently, a sampling frame is all that is available. Then one has no choice but to use a sampling frame, knowing full well that it is not a 100 percent accurate representation of the population. When researchers study some problem that carries a social stigma or is illegal, use of a sampling frame is usually inevitable. The sampling frame may not even be a close approximation of the population. For example, suppose that a researcher in Mississippi wishes to interview victims of date rape during the past six months, to determine what percentage of victims seem to be suffering from posttraumatic stress disorder (PTSD). No list of date rape victims in Mississippi for the time period may be available. But a sampling frame containing the names of at least some victims could be compiled with the help of local law enforcement officials within the state if they could be convinced that the researcher would protect participants' confidentiality and conduct the research ethically. The researcher might elect to use this sampling frame despite the fact that it probably differs in some important ways from the population of cases from which cases could be selected. For example, it would not contain the names of date rape victims who did not go to the police or refused to press charges against their attacker.

**Sample.**   We have used the term *sample* many times in this book. What exactly does it mean? A sample is a subset of cases selected for study from among people or objects within a defined population. It is chosen to represent the population. If there are two or more groupings of cases within a sample, they are referred to as *subsamples.*

Generally, researchers conclude that it is unfeasible or unnecessary to study the entire population or all potential cases. The population may be too large and/or too costly to study. Or researchers may conclude that it is possible to learn almost as much (and at far less cost) by studying only a portion of the population (or sampling frame). So they select a sample of cases.

**Representativeness.**   In the previous chapter, we mentioned the importance of using a representative sample in quantitative research. Although it is desirable in all research, it is less critical in most qualitative studies, which often do not seek support for hypotheses or otherwise hope to generalize their research findings from the sample to its population.

Representativeness is one of two criteria generally applied in evaluating the quality of a research sample. It refers to the degree to which a research sample is similar to the population from which it was drawn. Thus, representativeness should be regarded as a relative term. Ideally, researchers would like to study cases that are identical in all respects to the members of the population from which they were selected. Of course, the only way that this can happen is if they do not sample at all, but study the entire population instead. But if they did, the major benefit of sampling (conservation of research resources) would be lost. Fortunately, perfect representativeness in every respect within a sample is not really necessary—a sample can be sufficiently representative of a population if it resembles the population as a whole with respect to a limited number of relevant

variables, most often the dependent, independent, and any potentially intervening variables.

In Chapter 6, we mentioned three different sampling methods that are used
in longitudinal studies. Generally, sample representativeness is very important
in this type of research. It entails costly and time-consuming study of participants
who, it is hoped, will provide an accurate picture of changes that occur within
the population. A special problem in panel studies (which study the same group
of participants over time) is the likelihood that participants may drop out or
otherwise become unavailable as the study progresses. Because of death, participant mobility, or other forms of attrition ("experimental mortality"), the number
of participants who are available over the entire course of the study often is much
reduced from those who initially agreed to participate. If the causes for dropout
are not related to central research questions, the problem can be handled by
anticipating sizable participant loss and beginning with enough extra participants to absorb it. However, the participants who drop out may leave because of
factors relevant to the central focus of the research. If this occurs, their presence
can be missed and can bias the findings of the research.

**Size.** The second criterion that is considered in assessing the quality of a
research sample is size. We have chosen to discuss what may appear to be a
self-explanatory term because it has a special, narrow meaning within the context
of sampling. Sample size refers simply to the number of cases in the sample. A
sample is considered large, small, or somewhere in between based on how many
cases it contains, not on the percentage of the population or sampling frame that
it contains. This is an important distinction and one often misunderstood. Although it seems logical that a sample that includes only a small percentage of the
population could not possibly be a good sample, this is not necessarily true.
Political pollsters using large (1,800 to 2,200) samples have been remarkably
successful in recent years in predicting the results of most close national elections.
Yet their samples consistently include far less than 1 percent of registered voters.
Why have they been so successful? Because a sample of 1,800 to 2,200 is large in
the absolute sense. In addition, those cases within their samples were carefully
selected using methods designed to increase the likelihood of their sample's
representativeness.

An important factor to be considered in evaluating whether a sample size is
appropriate for a given research study is the statistical analysis used. We discuss
this in more detail later in this chapter. A sample can be considered too small if
it is smaller than the size for which a statistical test was designed. Conversely, it
is too large if it is larger than the size recommended for a given statistical test. If
a sample is concluded to be an appropriate size (for the statistical analysis used)
and has been selected in such a way that it produces a high likelihood of
representativeness, it is likely to be a good one.

**Sampling Error.** There are two reasons why a sample may differ from its
population (Figure 9.1). The difference that occurs naturally when a sample is

**FIGURE 9.1    Two Reasons Samples May Differ from the Population from Which They Were Drawn**

| | |
|---|---|
| 1. *Sampling bias* | The intentional or unintentional systematic distortion of a sample |
| 2. *Sampling error* | The normal tendency of a sample to differ from its population |

drawn from a population or sampling frame is referred to as *sampling error.* All samples, but especially smaller ones, are likely to differ from the population from which they were drawn. Even identically sized samples drawn from the same population (for example, two samples drawn independently from a class of social work students) are likely to differ regarding any characteristics that we may wish to study. The concept of sampling error is critical to an understanding of how certain types of statistical testing work (see Chapter 12). And it is often what can make variables appear to be related within the population when they really are not, and vice versa.

The relationship between sample size and the amount of sampling error present in a sample can be easily demonstrated by thinking of a class of fifty social work graduate students. Suppose the average age (referred to as the "mean" in statistical analysis) of the class is thirty, with most students being between twenty-seven and thirty-three. The oldest is thirty-nine, and the youngest is twenty-one. The ages of the students would form a bell shape, or normal distribution, if we were to form a frequency polygon of everyone's ages.

If we were to draw a sample of five students from the class, we would not expect the average age of the sample of five to be exactly thirty. It might be twenty-eight or thirty-two or even twenty-five or thirty-five. The difference between the mean of the sample and the mean of the class (population) would be the amount of sampling error in the sample. If we drew many repeated samples of five students from the class, rarely, if ever, would the mean age of a sample be exactly thirty. The average ages of the respective samples of five students would differ from the class mean (thirty) and from each other. Thus, most of the time, the mean age of any sample would be a poor estimate of the age of the class—the sample would not be very representative of the class for the variable age.

Now suppose that we had drawn samples of fifteen students from the same population (class) of fifty. We would still expect that the ages of the samples would rarely, if ever, be exactly thirty. However, we would expect that they would be closer to thirty than when we drew only samples of five. Why? Because with samples of fifteen, the law of averages would be more likely to take over than with samples of only five. A sample of five might contain, for example, five of the oldest students in the class. Then the sampling error might be large. In sampling fifteen students from the class, our first five selections might be the same five older students. But as we select more cases for the sample, the likelihood of drawing younger-than-average students (to balance off the first five) would be greater, because the average age of the remaining pool of students would now be less than thirty. As samples get larger, they begin to look more and more like their population. So, if we had drawn samples of forty-nine students each, we could expect that the samples might vary somewhat from the class average age of thirty and from each other, but not by very much. If we selected the entire population of all fifty students, there would be no sampling error. But this would defeat a purpose of sampling, which is to build knowledge in the most efficient way.

All samples are likely to vary from their populations. Thus, we cannot simply assume that measurements of a sample's characteristics (statistics) are the same as those of its population (parameters). But how much do they differ? We can assume that there is some degree of similarity between a sample and its population because the sample consists of cases drawn from the population. An estimate of the similarity of a sample to its population can help us gauge to what degree a drawn sample is sufficiently representative of the population in relation to one or more variables. But how similar can we expect a given sample to be to its population?

Statisticians have produced tables[1] and formulas to help us determine the minimum sample size that will produce an acceptable sampling error. It is important to remember that it is the number of cases in a sample (and not the percentage of the population that a sample represents) that is really important in evaluating the likely degree of sampling error within a sample.

**Sampling Bias.**  Even if a sample is relatively large and tables and/or statistical analysis reveals that the amount of sampling error is probably quite small, the sample still may not be adequately representative. It may contain too much sampling bias. *Sampling bias* refers to the systematic distortion of a sample. It can occur either intentionally or unintentionally. It is caused by such factors as the methods used to select a sample or when and where a sample was selected. A biased sample contains overrepresentation of some types of cases and under-representation of others (relative to the population from which it was drawn).

Biased samples can seriously limit the usefulness of the data collected by the researcher. If a sample does not represent its population, nearly anything we find out about cases in the sample will be of limited value. We may know a great deal about a particular (biased) group of cases, but we will be unable to generalize this knowledge to the population from which the sample was drawn. Thus, the external validity of findings generated by a study of a badly biased sample (or of one containing too much sampling error, for that matter) is low.

There are ways to decrease the likelihood that sampling bias will occur. By paying special attention to how and under what conditions a sample is selected, using strategies discussed later in this chapter, we can increase the representativeness of research samples.

**Statistic and Parameter.**  The terms *statistic* and *parameter* are closely related. Statistics are descriptions of the distribution of characteristics (variables) present in samples. Parameters are descriptions of the distribution of characteristics (or variables) present in populations. In research studies, we often secure statistics from our sample data that we hope will tell us something about the parameters of the same variables within the population that the sample is supposed to represent. For example, we may calculate the mean (average) age of people within the sample (a statistic) and hope to be able to use that statistic to estimate the mean age in the population (a parameter). In those less common situations in which we attempt to study the entire population, we would summarize the findings of the research study as parameters. For example, if we conducted a thorough analysis of active case records in a human service organization and then summarized the demographic characteristics of those clients currently being served, we would refer to our summaries as parameters.

**Random Sample.** A random sample is a sample drawn in such a way that all cases had an equal chance of being selected. There are distinct advantages to random samples. They control for sampling bias by making it impossible to distort the sample in some systematic way. In addition, although random samples cannot eliminate sampling error, with a random sample we can use the laws of probability to produce an estimate of the amount of sampling error within the sample and to statistically determine the probability that certain relationships between variables within the sample were the work of sampling error.

Random samples are sometimes used in social work research when a representative sample is important. However, several factors explain why they are not used more frequently. To draw a random sample, we must have access to a list of cases in a population or to a sampling frame that is a good approximation of the population. Even if a good sampling frame is available, the cost of acquiring a random sample may be prohibitive. Many organizations that maintain such lists charge researchers who may wish to use a list of cases drawn at random from them. Or it may simply be too expensive to collect data from cases in a random sample when they are geographically scattered and in-person interviews are the data collection method of choice.

There may also be ethical reasons why random samples are not used. For example, we could draw a random sample of current clients to receive an experimental treatment, but our knowledge of certain clients in the sample might suggest that they would more likely benefit from some other treatment or that they might likely be harmed by the experimental treatment. Ethically, such clients could not be included, and thus our sample would no longer be considered random.

We can now summarize how the preceding terms relate to each other in the context of research sampling:

*Universe* refers to the entire collection of people (or elements) that share some defined characteristic(s) that a researcher wishes to study. A *population* is that portion of the universe that is realistically accessible to the researcher. A *sampling frame* is an available list that approximates a population but usually differs from it in some ways. A *sample* is a group of *cases* drawn from either a sampling frame or a population that is actually studied in some way. The purpose of selecting a sample is to have available for study a group of cases that (to a greater or lesser degree) represent a larger number of cases within the population.

Two criteria used to evaluate the quality of a sample are its *representativeness* (the degree to which it resembles the population) and its *size* (the number of cases that it contains). Samples may tend not to be representative of the population because of (1) *sampling error*, which is the natural tendency of a sample to differ from its population or (2) *sampling bias*, which is the systematic distortion of a sample because of a variety of factors. In analyzing data collected from a *random sample* of cases, the researcher calculates sample *statistics* and conducts statistical analysis as a way of estimating population *parameters* or, in more quantitative studies, to determine the likelihood that sampling error might have produced a relationship between variables found within the sample.

## Probability Sampling

There are two general categories of sampling methods available to researchers: probability sampling and nonprobability sampling. In probability sampling, it is possible to calculate the statistical probability that any case within a sampling frame or population will be selected as part of the research sample. There are several methods used to select a probability sample.

### *Simple Random Sampling*

Simple random sampling is the most well known type of probability sampling. It entails randomly selecting some predetermined number of cases from the sampling frame or population. A researcher wanting to select 25 people from a sampling frame of 100 would write each person's name on an individual 3" × 5" file card and then randomly select 25 cards from some container. If the cards were identical except for the names on them and they were mixed in the container in a way that each had an equal probability of selection, a simple random sample would result.

For drawing larger samples, the researcher could consult a table of mathematically generated random numbers to assist in the selection of cases. To use a table of random numbers, each case is first assigned a consecutive number. Then the researcher enters the table at some random point (selecting any number off the chart arbitrarily) and moves through the chart systematically. For example, the researcher might decide to work down a given column of numbers until the required number of cases has been selected. The cases that are selected would be those that have the same numbers as those corresponding to the ones picked from the chart.

Another common method for selecting a simple random sample is to use a computer package designed to select numbers at random. Many statistics software packages now offer a random numbers function. All cases in the sampling frame or population are assigned consecutive numbers. Then the researcher enters the size of the sampling frame or population and the number or percentage of cases that will constitute the sample. The software produces a sample of random numbers as output. The researcher then selects the cases that have had those numbers assigned to them.

## Systematic Random Sampling

Systematic random sampling is popular because of its simplicity. No table of random numbers is needed, and no computer programs are required. It uses a three-step process. An example will help to explain how it works.

Suppose that a researcher wishes to conduct a client satisfaction survey using a 25 percent sample of all 100 active clients in a human service organization. That would be 25 cases. The case records for the active clients (the sampling frame) are stored in a locked file drawer. The first 25 case records in the file could be selected, but they would not constitute a probability sample. Such a sample might be biased. For example, because files are stored alphabetically, the first 25 cases could include only those cases whose last names start with a letter early in the alphabet—that might produce a bias in terms of ethnicity. So, a systematic random sample would be preferable.

How would a systematic sample be drawn? First, the necessary sampling interval (referred to as $k$) would have to be computed. The sampling interval is found by dividing the number of cases in the sampling frame by the number of cases needed for the sample. Because a sample of 25 would be 1 case out of 4 (100 divided by 25 = 4), the sampling interval ($k$) would be 4.

Next, the researcher would randomly select a number from 1 to 4 ($k$). Let us say that it is 3. The number thus selected (3) would be the starting point—the third case in the file would be selected. Then, the researcher would select every fourth case after that; that is, the seventh case, the eleventh, the fifteenth, the nineteenth, and so forth.

The initial, random selection of a starting point is an important step, and it cannot be ignored. It is necessary so that every case in the file would have had an equal chance of selection when the sampling commenced.

## Stratified Sampling

Stratified sampling can be used (1) to reduce the amount of sampling error when using a simple random sample or a systematic random sample, or (2) simply to ensure that there are enough cases within different values or value label categories of a variable for comparison purposes. For either purpose, a two-stage sampling method is used.

Stage 1 of stratified sampling requires the researcher to divide the population into homogeneous categories, or strata. That is, people or objects are placed in one of two or more strata (subgroups of the population or sampling frame) based on their measurement (value or value label) of a variable. Thus, within strata, members are homogeneous with regard to this variable (for example, all social workers in one stratum and all physicians in another stratum for the variable "profession," or all females in one stratum and all males in the other stratum for the variable "gender"). In the second stage, the desired number of cases are selected from each stratum by either simple random sampling or systematic random sampling.

There are two different types of stratified random sampling. They reflect (respectively) the two uses of stratified sampling that we mentioned previously. In *proportionate stratified random sampling,* the researcher elects to stratify based on a variable that could distort the research findings if not proportionately represented in the research sample (that is, one that is a potentially intervening variable). For example, a researcher wishing to study the effectiveness of treatment intervention on a group of clients who are clinically depressed might have good reason to stratify the sample by gender. There might be concern that client gender may be an intervening variable that relates to treatment success. Thus, a method is needed to ensure that the sample does not consist of a disproportionate (relative to the sampling frame) number of either men or women.

Let us assume that the sampling frame from which the sample is drawn consists of 1,000 cases, of which 900 are female and 100 are male. A 5 percent sample (consisting of 50 cases) is to be drawn. To draw a proportionate stratified random sample, the cases would first be sorted into two strata or groups consisting of (1) the 900 females and (2) the 100 males. Then 5 percent of the females (45 cases) would be selected at random, and 5 percent of the males (5 cases) would be selected at random. The sample, like the sampling frame, would thus be 90 percent female—perfectly representative regarding gender. The sample thus produced might be biased in some other respects, but it is definitely not biased regarding gender. And every case in the sampling frame had an equal likelihood of being selected (0.05, or 5 percent), so the sample is considered to be a random one.

But what if the researcher wished to determine if the treatment intervention is more effective with males or with females? If a proportionate stratified random sample were used, it would require comparing the clinical depression level of one subsample of 45 females (probably an acceptable size) with the other subsample consisting of only 5 males. The researcher might be uncomfortable with allowing only 5 males to represent all male clients. Could only 5 cases be representative of males? Five is a very small subsample; the likelihood of sampling error might be high, and certain potentially useful forms of statistical analysis that require larger samples would have to be eliminated.

An alternative method of sampling that also relies on the use of strata is *disproportionate stratified sampling.* It can be used to produce subsamples of comparable size for comparison purposes. For example, the researcher in the previous example might draw a random sample consisting of 25 females and 25 males from their respective strata. In this sample, there would be a disproportionate number of males (relative to the sampling frame). In the sample, 50 percent of the cases would be male, but in the sampling frame the percentage of males is only 10 percent. Males and females clearly would have a different probability of being selected for the research sample. But it is still possible to calculate the likelihood of their being selected for the research sample—thus, the sample would still be a probability one (but not a random one). Any male client would have a very high probability of being selected for the sample (25 out of 100, or 0.25); for any female client, the probability would be only 25 out of 900 or less than 0.03.

## Cluster Sampling

Cluster sampling involves a multistage process of listing and then randomly sampling groups of cases rather than individual cases. It is more likely to be used in large-scale survey research projects than in small, organization-based studies. There are some research situations where it is extremely useful for putting together a sample that is both representative and sufficiently large, while conserving the resources of the researcher.

In cluster sampling, researchers identify clusters of cases. Next, they randomly select a predetermined number of clusters. Then all cases (or, less commonly, a random sample of all cases) within each of the selected clusters constitute the research sample.

The following example should help clarify how cluster sampling is accomplished. Suppose a researcher wishes to identify and collect data from a random sample of battered women in residence at spouse abuse shelters within a state. For various reasons (including their safety), there is unlikely to exist a master list of these women. Thus, a simple random sampling method could not be used. However, a list of all shelters within a particular state may exist. Each shelter can be thought of as a cluster of cases. A random sample of these shelters (clusters) can be conducted. Then the administrators of the shelters selected could be asked to provide a list of all persons currently in the shelter (using numbers instead of names to preserve the clients' confidentiality). The list of numbers from each of these shelters could then comprise the research sample, or if the number of cases thus obtained were still too large, some form of random sample of the numbers could be selected.

Sometimes, even if a master list of potential research participants can be compiled, cluster sampling may still be the sampling method of choice. A major advantage of cluster sampling is that it allows the researcher to collect data in a timely and cost-efficient way, while not greatly increasing the likelihood of sampling bias. It allows a researcher to collect data on a large number of cases quickly and at relatively little cost. It is especially useful if the sampling frame or population consists of people or objects who are geographically scattered. In our example, the researcher would be able to collect data from a large number of participants in just a few locations (those shelters that were selected) using cluster sampling. Yet even if a simple random sample of all cases currently active in the shelters could have been drawn, a considerable amount of time and money would have been spent traveling around the state to interview just one or two cases in each of many different shelters.

# Nonprobability Sampling

In a nonprobability sample, it is not possible to calculate the likelihood that a given person or element will be selected. We assume that some cases will have a greater likelihood of being selected than others, so samples are not considered random. For some types of studies, methods that produce a probability sample cannot be used. This happens most frequently when no population list or even sampling frame is available from which to draw the sample. In such a situation, it would be impossible to calculate the likelihood of a given case's being selected. This was the case when one of the authors was involved in an exploratory study of women who delayed childbearing until after age thirty. No sample drawn could possibly be a probability one, because the population could not be identified or specified and no acceptable sampling frame was available.

Even when it is possible to draw a probability sample, it might not be the best sample to use to study a given problem or research question. A nonprobability sample may be preferable. In some of the types of research that we described in Chapters 6 and 7, sample representativeness is not as important as other sample characteristics. For example, in research studies where the emphasis may be on exploring the nature and impact of a problem, it may make sense to study only individuals who are likely to have the best in-depth understanding of the problem, whether or not they represent a cross-section of the population experiencing it. In this type of study, the researcher might deliberately exclude from the study those who might otherwise have been randomly selected as participants, but who may contribute little or nothing to an understanding of it.

Four commonly used nonprobability sampling methods have proven useful to social work researchers. All of these methods are suited to situations in which the researcher either (1) would prefer a representative sample but is unable to compile a population or sampling frame from which to draw one using probability sampling methods or (2) has decided that representativeness is less important to sample composition than one or more other characteristics.

## Convenience Sampling

One type of nonprobability sampling plan entails a very unscientific approach to sampling. It entails selecting cases for study primarily because they happen to be readily accessible to the researcher. It is this type of sampling that is most likely to have been used when we hear on the evening news that a "random sample" of residents of our community was interviewed about their opinions regarding some news event. In fact, the sample was not at all random! Generally, the people interviewed were all in the same shopping mall or were on a street corner near the television studio. They were selected mainly because of convenience. Clearly, some potential participants (those most readily available) had a greater likelihood of selection than others.

As is true of any sampling method, convenience sampling may produce an acceptable level of representativeness, but it is the method that is probably least likely to do so. The usefulness of convenience samples in social work research is limited. If the researcher is beginning to explore a new area of inquiry and it is hard to locate people with certain characteristics or obtain their permission to be research participants (for example, in some forms of qualitative research), it may be the only feasible alternative. But convenience samples present a major difficulty for researchers. How can they interpret the findings of their research? To whom do they apply? Under what conditions? Research designs that rely on convenience sampling have little or no claim to external validity. Findings generally are believed to be applicable only to those people or objects that were studied.

## Purposive Sampling

Sometimes cases are selected because they are believed to be able to give the researcher access to some unique approach to a problem or situation or a special perspective, experience, characteristic, or condition that we wish to understand. For example, suppose we wish to know more about the variations in coping strategies used by people diagnosed as HIV-positive. Although we might be able to produce a sampling frame of HIV-positive people who have recently been diagnosed and to draw a random sample from it, the sample thus selected might not be what is needed for our research. For our research objective, a purposive sample actually might be preferable to a representative one. It would be more likely to help us describe the wide variety of coping methods used.

How would we acquire a purposive sample of people recently diagnosed as HIV-positive? From informal conversations with medical staff, we might learn of a number of HIV-positive people being treated at clinics and hospitals who employ what staff perceive as unique coping strategies. We might then select those twenty people with what seem like the most unique ways of coping and ask them to voluntarily take part in in-depth research interviews. Our sample would not be representative of the population or even of the available sampling frame. It would not contain the same distribution of coping strategies (percentagewise) employed by others who are HIV-positive. For example, 40 percent of all HIV-positive people might all use the same coping strategy, but we might select only one person for our sample of twenty (5 percent) who use that strategy. Because we would be seeking to learn about the diversity of coping strategies used by people who are HIV-positive, there might be little value in interviewing more than one person who uses any one coping strategy. That would be redundant.

## Snowball Sampling

One method of nonprobability sampling does not select a sample at one point in time. The sample is compiled as the research progresses. When using snowball sampling, one or just a few people are identified as potential research participants. Then they are asked to provide the names of people they know or know about who, like themselves, have experienced some problem or who in other ways meet the necessary criteria for inclusion in the population. The next potential participants are contacted by the researcher to determine if they are indeed eligible for inclusion in the sample and whether or not they are willing to participate in the study. They may then be asked to provide the names of other possible participants. The process is repeated until enough participants agree to take part in the study.

Snowball sampling was used in the case studies described in Chapter 7 and in the previously mentioned research study that interviewed a sample of women who had given birth to their first child after age thirty. An initial sample of women was identified by placing an ad in the paper (hardly a random selection procedure). Women who responded to the ad were interviewed by a member of the research team to ensure they met the necessary criteria to be part of the research study and to attempt to complete an early draft of a research data collection instrument. At the conclusion of the interview, they were asked if they knew of other women who, like themselves, had borne their first child after age thirty. These prospects were then followed up by the research team. The use of snowball sampling was appropriate because (1) the purpose of the study was to develop a research instrument for a subsequent study of delayed childbearing and (2) the researchers were not attempting to accurately describe the population of women who delay childbearing.

## Quota Sampling

Another type of nonprobability sampling method is used to obtain a sample that is (1) as representative as possible and (2) of a specified size (quota). Quota sampling begins with establishing an accurate description of the research population regarding selected variables. This description is built into a matrix; that is, a table displaying the percentage of people in the population sharing each combination of characteristics. Then people are selected for study who have all of the characteristics described within each specific cell of the matrix. Sampling continues until there is a final sample of people selected that represents each of the cells. Quota sampling is the method of sampling that historically was used by political pollsters conducting exit polls. They have produced some accurate predictions but also some embarrassing, wrong ones.

Although quota samples are easy to implement, there is one major problem that frequently precludes their use. The researcher needs to have accurate data available about the population of interest in order to develop the quota matrix. If some data are missing or are not believed to be accurate, a representative sample cannot be obtained by quota sampling. Quota sampling should be used only when (1) the researcher has confidence that all data needed to establish a quota matrix are accurate and (2) some unbiased (perhaps random) method of selecting participants within each cell can be implemented after a matrix has been constructed.

## Selecting a Good Sample

When selecting the sampling method to be used and determining the appropriate sample size, a number of important, interrelated issues must be addressed. Some of them address practical matters that are easily understood; others are a little more technical. The major issues that the researcher needs to consider are (1) available resources for securing the sample, (2) the overall design and purpose of the study, (3) the type of statistical analysis that will be used, and (4) the level of representativeness that is required.

### *Available Resources*

If the study is being funded by a human service organization or some other organization that has contracted to have it designed and implemented, the size of the sample to be used may already have been specified. If this is not the case, the researcher is free to use judgment in selecting an appropriate research sample.

In general, larger samples are likely to be more representative of the population than are smaller ones. That is because, when larger samples are chosen, sampling error is reduced (a phenomenon that we will explain in more detail a little later in this chapter). But even in quantitative studies where sample representativeness usually is critical to the credibility of the research, there is a point of diminishing returns. A researcher gets to the point where an increase in sample size does not appreciably reduce the amount of sampling error that may be present.

Using large samples can be costly. It should be remembered that the processes of compromise and trade-off are ongoing activities in conducting social work research. Resources spent collecting data from a large number of research participants leaves less time and resources for performing other essential tasks in the research process. But if a smaller sample is used, some of that time and those resources can be used to perform those other tasks. The overall quality of the research might actually be better.

### *Overall Design and Purpose of the Study*

Generally, we expect to see different-size samples (and different sampling methods) with certain types of research. For example, qualitative research studies often use smaller samples than more quantitative designs and nonprobability sampling methods. Often a representative sample is impossible to obtain because of the absence of an adequate sampling frame. And it may not be considered important anyway if the research is primarily exploratory. However, large-scale descriptive studies that are primarily quantitative often use large samples (to reduce sampling error) and strive for representativeness by using random sampling methods, because the external validity of findings is considered very important. If, for example, the purpose of a study is to accurately describe the characteristics of some client population and a good sampling frame is available, then a randomly selected sample consisting of several hundred cases may be used in order to ensure the likelihood of a sufficiently representative sample.

Experimental and other forms of explanatory designs use samples of various sizes, usually depending on financial resources available to support the research and the number of cases available for study. Research whose objective is primarily to develop measurement instruments to be used in subsequent research studies may use relatively small samples but may use many different samples representing different subpopulations and/or different times and settings for measurement. If a researcher wishes merely to pilot-test a research instrument that will be revised and used to collect data, then a small nonprobability sample is likely to be used.

It is sometimes helpful to consult reports of other similar research and note how many cases were used. This kind of information can be used as a general guide, but it should be remembered that errors in sample size selection are quite common. We would not want to repeat another researcher's mistakes. For more in-depth discussion of sampling methods and issues, a text that is devoted solely to the topic of research sampling[2] should be consulted.

## Type of Statistical Analysis to Be Used

The size of a research sample and the type of sampling method used are important factors in the selection of the form of statistical analysis to be used. But sometimes it works the other way around. In some instances, the researcher knows in advance what analysis will have to be used—as, for example, when working under a contract that specifies which tests are acceptable or when replicating the research of others who used a specific form of statistical analysis. Then the size of the sample as well as the sampling method used (for example, probability or nonprobability) is tailored to the statistical analysis that must be used.

The relationship between types of statistical analysis and the most appropriate size are beyond the scope of this text. However, we should remember that sample size guidelines for various statistical analyses exist for a purpose. If a specific statistical test has been designed for a certain sample size, the sample size selected should neither be smaller than that number (usually a range) nor exceed it. As we suggested earlier, samples that are either larger or smaller than recommended for a given statistical test can result in misleading conclusions regarding relationships between variables.

## *Level of Representativeness Required*

As we noted earlier, quantitative studies place great importance on the representativeness of samples used. Whenever possible, they use random sampling methods to increase the representativeness of samples. In more qualitative studies where representativeness is impossible and/or unimportant, nonprobability sampling methods generally provide an adequate sample of cases.

## Summary

In this chapter, we focused on sample selection and its relationship to good research. Representativeness and size were identified as the two criteria most frequently used in evaluating the quality of a sample.

Sampling methods were characterized as either probability or nonprobability, depending on whether it is possible to calculate the mathematical probability that an individual person or object will be selected to be a case within the research sample. Random samples are often regarded as superior to nonrandom ones because they are more likely to be representative of the population from which they are selected and allow for the use of certain types of statistical analyses. Four types were described in this chapter: simple random sampling, systematic random sampling, cluster sampling, and proportional stratified random sampling.

For some research studies, probability samples may be neither feasible nor desirable. In some qualitative studies, for example, nonprobability sampling methods may yield samples that are exactly what is needed. Four common nonprobability sampling methods were described: convenience sampling, purposive sampling, snowball sampling, and quota sampling.

Finally, we discussed four major issues that the researcher needs to consider when deciding which sampling method to use and how large a sample is needed. They are (1) available resources for securing the sample, (2) the overall design and purpose of the study, (3) the type of statistical analysis that will be used, and (4) the level of representativeness that is required.

## References

1. See, for example, Rubin, A., & Babbie, E. (1997). *Research methods for social workers* (3rd ed.). Pacific Grove, CA: Brooks/Cole, 246.
2. See, for example, Jolliffee, F. R. (1986). *Survey design and analysis.* New York: Ellis Horwood; or Converse, J. M. (1987). *Survey research in the United States: Roots and emergence.* Berkeley, CA: University of California Press.

# 10

# MEASUREMENT CONCEPTS AND ISSUES

Once having decided on which people or objects will provide the needed data (sampling issues), researchers generally focus on measurement issues. Specifically, they decide (1) what data will need to be collected and (2) what instruments or methods will be used to collect it. These decisions are made (as are most other design decisions) based on what was learned from the review of the literature.

It is sometimes suggested that measurement issues should be addressed before participants are selected. Although there are compelling arguments for either sequence of activities, we think it makes more sense to make measurement decisions after sampling issues have been resolved. Until it is decided who will be providing data, it is difficult to know what type of measurement is possible and the best way to conduct it.

Measurement is the process of sorting and, if possible, quantifying information in some systematic fashion. It entails collecting data in relation to certain variables and assigning the appropriate value categories or values to individual cases. In the social work literature, there is disagreement as to how precisely it is possible to measure certain variables. Some writers have taken the position that, with enough effort, virtually all variables can be accurately measured.[1] They believe that most variables can be *quantified*, that is, a number can be assigned to accurately describe the exact amount of the variable present within a case. Other writers, especially those who espouse qualitative research methods, point out that because of the nature of many of the variables that are of interest to social workers, they cannot be quantified using standardized measurement techniques. Our position in this chapter is that for most (if not all) variables, a measurement strategy can be developed that will yield useful knowledge for researchers. However, we also acknowledge that many variables of interest to social workers do not readily lend themselves to quantification.

## Preparation for Measurement

Before any measurement can take place, two interrelated activities must take place. They are referred to as *conceptualization* and *operationalization*.

### *Conceptualization*

Conceptualization entails selecting and specifying what we believe to be the most important or relevant variables to measure and stating the value categories or values that each variable can assume. It also involves specifying as precisely as possible exactly what we will mean by those variables. In performing these tasks, we rely on both the review of literature and our practice knowledge and experience. For example, the literature may have suggested that abuse (or nonabuse) of medication by terminally ill patients may be related to whether or not hospice care is given. It may have suggested the hypothesis that "Terminally ill patients who have hospice care will be less likely to abuse medication than terminally ill patients who do not have hospice care." Two variables that clearly would need to be measured are (1) involvement (or noninvolvement) with a hospice and (2) the presence or absence of medication abuse. Specification of the predictor variable (hospice involvement/noninvolvement) would be no problem. But we would need to specify exactly what we mean by medication abuse (the criterion variable). Would it be any use of medication—accidental or intentional—other than exactly as prescribed? Should it include taking less of a medicine than prescribed? What about the use of additional nonprescription medication?

All of the preceding questions (and more) would need to be addressed before data collection could begin, so that cases could be correctly and consistently assigned to value categories for both variables. There are no right or wrong answers to the questions. A researcher can answer them any way that seems logical. Generally, the answers are summarized in what is referred to as an *operational definition*. An operational definition tells the reader of a research report exactly what criteria were used in measurement in the current study; other researchers might apply different operational definitions to the same term in their research. An operational definition says, in effect, "When I refer to a variable in this research, this is what I mean by it." For example, a researcher might construct the following operational definition:

> *Medication abuse = The intentional misuse of a prescribed, controlled narcotic substance on at least three occasions by a terminally ill person*

Generally, several operational definitions must be constructed. Operational definitions then are presented as a group (along with definitions of other terms that may need to be defined) at the end of a literature review or near the beginning of the methodology part of a research report. In our example, it would also be necessary to operationally define such terms as *terminally ill, hospice involvement,* and so forth.

## Operationalization

Operationalization is closely related to conceptualization. It refers to specifying the actual measuring devices or methods that will be used to measure the variables that have been conceptualized. Thus, it further clarifies the meaning of variables.

Generally, there are many different ways that a variable can be measured. For example, measurement of the variable "medication abuse" might entail actual observations by nurses, social workers, caregivers, or aides; it might also include social workers' impressions based on mental alertness or other symptoms, self-reports of patients, or something as specific as a count or measurement of the patient's available medication at regular intervals.

We noted that operational definitions of a term may vary from study to study. Similarly, different researchers may measure the same variable in different ways. Unless the researcher is replicating the research of others, that is fine. The only requirements for operationalization of a given variable are that it should be logical and justified (usually through the literature). Sometimes researchers choose to include the method of measurement (operationalization) of a variable in their operational definition of the variable. For example

*Medication abuse = The intentional misuse of a prescribed, controlled narcotic substance on at least three occasions by a terminally ill person* **as reported by the patient's primary caregiver**

**Cultural Sensitivity in Operationalization.** Certain theoretical concepts may have different meanings for research participants, depending on their different ethnic and cultural backgrounds. When this is the case, every effort should be made to operationalize a variable in a way that is consistent with the culture of those individuals who are providing research data. For example, what if a researcher needs to measure the educational attainment of a group of research participants? Traditionally, "years of formal schooling completed as reported by the research participant" is the operational definition of educational attainment. This definition, however, may underestimate the actual educational experiences and degree of knowledge attainment in certain groups of people. For example, for some African Americans, especially those from rural backgrounds, formal systems of education have not always been accessible. However, many African Americans (especially older ones) achieved both enhanced knowledge and skills through some combination of mentoring, apprenticeship, craftsmanship, and entrepreneurship. An accurate assessment of their educational attainment should include some measurement of these less formal avenues of education.

## Levels of Measurement

Levels (sometimes called "scales") of measurement refer to the degree of precision with which a variable is believed to be measured. Researchers must decide at what level each variable has been measured, sometimes based on the nature of the variable itself and more frequently on the method of measurement used. Determining what level of measurement a researcher has generated is an important decision. It is essential in deciding the most appropriate methods for statistical analyses of data (Chapter 12).[2] Researchers determine which of four labels is appropriate to apply to their measurement of a given variable. They represent a hierarchy of measurement precision.

**Nominal Level.**   Nominal-level measurement is the most basic form of measurement. It involves the use of a measurement scheme that simply sorts cases into different, mutually exclusive categories (value labels) of a variable. To be considered nominal level, a case must fall into one category (and only one) of the variable. The different value categories of a variable reflect only a difference in kind, not a difference in the amount of the variable present within a given case. Even if a number is used as a value label, the number has no quantitative significance. For example, in measuring the variable "gender," the researcher may use the number 1 for males and the number 2 for females, or the other way around. In either case, the numbers do not reflect a quantitative difference—just a qualitative one. They are merely labels, substitutes for words.

In measuring many variables, nominal measurement is all that is possible. Variables such as gender, whether one voted in the last election, whether one owns a car, undergraduate major, or religious affiliation are nominal by their very nature. (One might be interested in measuring the number of cars owned or degree of religiosity, but those are different variables, ones that have the potential for other, higher levels of measurement.)

**Ordinal Level.**   Ordinal measurement meets all the criteria for nominal measurement. In addition, the value labels possess a logical rank-ordering. The term *ordinal level* is appropriately assigned to variables that have been measured using a range of categories, such as "always," "sometimes," "rarely," and "never"; or "not improved," "slightly improved," "somewhat improved," and "greatly improved." Note that these categories (value labels) can be rank-ordered—we would all arrange them in the same sequence to reflect the different quantities of some variable that each represents. But the value labels are not very precise. For example, although we would all agree that "somewhat improved" reflects more improvement than "slightly improved," we cannot say exactly how much more.

Ordinal measurement is seen quite frequently in social work practice and research. For example, social workers may be interested in measuring the degree of cooperation displayed by families that have been court-ordered to receive treatment. They might categorize degree of cooperation as (1) highly cooperative, (2) cooperative, or (3) uncooperative. Of course, it would be necessary to specify the criteria by which a rating (1, 2, or 3) would be assigned. Note that the distance between successive points of measurement on the scale is not fixed. In other words, the distance between ratings of 2 and 3 on the scale is not assumed to be equal to the distance between ratings of 1 and 2. The numbers simply represent ranks.

Examples of variables in social work research that may be regarded as ordinal level include many sociodemographic variables such as age (when measured using the value categories elderly, middle-aged, young adult, adolescent, preado-lescent, and child); social class standing (upper, middle, lower, and so on); and degree of educational attainment (when measured by the highest degree completed). Many psychosocial variables that are measured using newly developed instruments generate ordinal level measurement. Examples may include degree of frustration, coping capacity, ability to use social support systems, or level of social functioning.

**Interval Level.**   Interval-level measurement meets all of the criteria for ordinal-level measurement and one additional one—the exact distances between categories of the variable are known and are equal to each other. The variable temperature, as measured on a Fahrenheit or centigrade thermometer, provides a clear example of interval-level measurement. The distances between points on the scale are fixed, so that, for example, the interval between 12 degrees and 13 degrees is the same as the interval between 35 degrees and 36 degrees. This kind of scale allows us to make interpretations of how warm or cold it is on a given day; a measurement of 75 degrees Fahrenheit on Tuesday represents a measurement that is warmer by 10 degrees than does a measurement of 65 degrees Fahrenheit at the same time on Wednesday. This kind of comparison could not be made if the measurement were regarded as only ordinal. We would know that Tuesday was warmer than Wednesday, but we would not be able to say exactly how much warmer.

Interval-level measurement may use a zero as one of its values (categories), but if it does, the zero represents just a point on a range of measurement rather than the absence of the variable. Again, using the example of temperature, 0 degrees Fahrenheit communicates extreme cold, but it does not denote the total absence of heat. Similarly, 0 degrees centigrade does not coincide with the absence of heat—it is merely the point at which water freezes.

Whether a measurement produces interval-level data is often debatable. (The same could be said for the other levels of measurement.) Generally, as long as the distance between successive points on the scale is fixed and equal, interval measurement can be assumed to exist. Depending on how precisely they can be measured, the same psychosocial variables used as examples in the previous section to demonstrate the use of ordinal level measurement (degree of frustration, coping capacity, ability to use social support systems, and level of social functioning) might be considered to be interval level. A newly developed method of measuring them would most likely produce measurement that could only be considered ordinal level. But over time and with repeated evaluation and refinement, an instrument might be developed that could safely be assumed to produce interval level measurement. When interval level measurement is attained, more precise data about the distribution of a variable can be acquired.

**Ratio Level.** Ratio-level measurement meets all of the criteria for interval measurement—values can be rank-ordered with fixed, equal distances between them. However, the ratio scale is characterized by an additional feature—zero has an absolute meaning; that is, it is used to indicate a point where there is no measurable quantity of the variable. For example, if the variable "income" were to be operationalized as the actual gross earned annual income of clients as reported on their prior year's income tax return, the variable could be regarded as ratio level. A value of zero would mean no earned income. In addition, a person with an income of $60,000 could be said to have an income three times that of another person with an income of $20,000. We could not make such statements about variables that are nominal, ordinal, or interval level.

In social work research, we might be interested in measuring how many children people have, how many social workers work on a case management team, how many other organizations have offered services to clients, or how many times a participant has been married. Each of these measurements could be regarded as ratio level.

# Criteria for Good Measurement

In previous chapters, we discussed two criteria used in evaluating overall research design (external validity and internal validity) and in assessing the quality of a research sample (representativeness and size). We have frequently alluded to the importance of the quality of measurement in good research. There are also two criteria that are used to assess measurement quality (see Figure 10.1). They are reliability and validity.

### FIGURE 10.1   Indications That the Measurement of a Variable Is a Good One

1. It has *reliability:* We can demonstrate that it produces consistent results (96, 96, 96, and so on) in a variety of situations and under different conditions.
2. It has *validity:* We can demonstrate that it actually measures what we claim that it measures (96 = high level of aggression, not of assertiveness).

*Note:* A measurement that is valid is both reliable and unbiased. Thus, a measurement that is valid is always reliable, but one that is reliable may not be valid.

## Reliability

Reliability is most closely related to the concept of consistency.[3] It asks the question: What is the likelihood that a measurement will produce the same results under various conditions? If the object or person being measured by it has not changed, a good measure should not produce different results under different conditions. For example, one type of reliability (test–retest, discussed in the next section) has to do with the extent to which a measurement produces the same results when measurement is conducted at one time as opposed to some other time. If there is no reason why a research participant's measurement of a variable (such as attitude toward capital punishment) should have changed, then measuring a person a second time using the same instrument as the first time should yield the same results. The results produced by the two measurements should be the same (consistent). If they are not, the measurement is not considered reliable.

The degree to which a measurement is reliable is usually expressed in what is referred to as a *correlation coefficient*. It is an indicator of how much a measurement of the variable on the instrument agrees (correlates) with some other measurement of the variable. A correlation coefficient reflects both the strength and the direction of the correlation between the two measurements. It consists of a number and a sign (– or +). Correlation coefficients range from –1.00 to +1.00. In using correlation coefficients as evidence of reliability, the researcher hopes to be able to produce correlation coefficients that are very high and positive (for example, .85, .92, and so forth).

Researchers and statisticians have developed ways to estimate the reliability of measurement. Generally, before an instrument is deemed appropriate for measurement within a given research study, some effort to estimate its reliability is made. We want to be reasonably certain that the method of measurement used will produce consistent results. There are five basic criteria employed for estimating the reliability of an instrument. We will discuss each method and explain how its unique focus suggests the reliability of a measurement.

**Test–Retest Reliability.**   An estimate of test–retest reliability (mentioned previously) requires testing the same participants twice, using the same measuring instrument and then comparing the two scores for each case. A correlation coefficient suggests the amount of agreement between the two sets of scores. The higher the (positive) correlation derived, the higher the reliability estimate.

Test–retest reliability tells the researcher how consistently an instrument performs at different times. A time delay may occur between the first and second measurements of the variable, or they may be scheduled immediately after each other. If a delay between measurements is to be used, it can be as great as a week or even several months. Longer delays are most often used if (1) there is reason to believe that participants' measurements of the variable do not change naturally over time and (2) the researcher is concerned with a testing effect, that is, the extent to which participants' second measurement of the variable might be influenced by the experience of the first measurement if the two measurements occur too closely to each other.

**Parallel Forms Reliability.**  An estimate of parallel forms reliability (also called "alternate forms reliability" or "equivalent forms reliability") involves the administration of two forms of the same test to the same participants. They are administered with or without a delay between administration. If the scores on the two forms of the same test are identical or nearly identical, parallel forms reliability has been demonstrated.

Parallel forms of a test are available for many standardized achievement and knowledge measures (for example, IQ tests, Scholastic Assessment Tests [SATs], or Graduate Record Exams [GREs]) as well as for tests designed to measure many attitudes or perceptions. They have been developed so that, no matter which form (variation) of the test a person completes, the score should be the same. In theory, a student can take one form of a test such as an SAT, and the persons sitting to the right and left could have different variations of the same test. None of the three would have an advantage over the others; their respective scores would provide a fair comparison of the variable being measured.

Parallel forms of a measurement instrument can be constructed only when the nature of the variable being measured is such that different versions of the measurement can be assumed to produce the same results. When they are used for measurement, proof of their statistical equivalence is generally expected. This is accomplished by demonstrating that the different forms produce measurements that are comparable. For example, the researcher might report that the different forms all produce distributions of scores that have the same or very similar means (averages) and the same amount of variability.

**Split Half Reliability.**  An estimate of split half reliability entails dividing a single measurement instrument into two equal parts and correlating the score on one half with the score on the other. The two halves may be derived by, for example, placing the even-numbered items in one group and the odd-numbered items in a second group. The reliability estimate derived from using the split half method is really an estimate of the internal consistency of the measure, that is, the degree to which half of the measurements within an instrument are correlated with the other half. It can suggest the degree to which the instrument provides a consistent measurement of the variable, but it does not provide an estimate of its consistency over time. Split half reliability estimates are widely used, in part because of their simplicity. Only one form of the measurement of the variable is required, and the measurement need take place only once.

**Coefficient Alpha.**  If a measurement instrument can be split in half, it also can be further subdivided into as many parts as there are contained within it. A better estimate of the overall reliability of the instrument than split half reliability may be obtained by securing the correlation between every pair of its parts (items).

Coefficient alpha is a statistic that summarizes the results of this kind of analysis. It provides an estimate of the reliability of a measurement instrument by generating the average correlation among all pairs of items. If the results of coefficient alpha analysis are a high positive correlation coefficient, responses to individual items or questions have been found to be highly correlated with each other. Most personal computers have a statistical software package that can perform this operation.

Some measurement instruments are designed to be multidimensional in nature—for example, occupational inventories or tests that measure different aspects or dimensions of personality. For these instruments, it would not be appropriate to estimate reliability by using a measure of internal consistency such as coefficient alpha or a test for split half reliability. One would expect to get a low correlation coefficient if they were used. Some other method of reliability estimation (such as the test–retest method) might be more appropriate, or each dimension of the variable could be treated as a separate variable using coefficient alpha or split half reliability.

**Interobserver Agreement.**   When more than one person collects data, another method of assessing reliability can provide an estimate of the reliability of the measurement process. Interobserver agreement can estimate the degree to which two or more observers agree in their measurements of a variable. As with other estimates of reliability, the higher the positive correlation between the measurements of two observers or interviewers, the greater the indication of consistency in measurement.

When is reliability considered to be very important to the quality of a research study? Traditionally, it has been more important in quantitative research than in most qualitative studies. That makes sense because findings about the relationship between variables are worthless unless the variables were measured in a way that provides consistent measurements. But reliability is important for qualitative measurement as well. For example, a grounded theory study (Chapter 7) may entail videotaping of in-depth interviews with research participants who recently experienced some loss in their lives. Then two or more judges can review the tapes and record how they think each participant experienced the loss. An estimate of the reliability of their measurements can be calculated (a correlation coefficient) using methods to estimate interobserver agreement.

Which reliability criterion is most important? It depends primarily on what variable is being measured, how it is measured, and how the measurement is to be used. Test–retest reliability might be desirable in many studies (especially quantitative ones), but estimating it may not be practical. For example, it may be too costly or too big an imposition on research participants to ask that they allow the same variable to be measured twice using the same method of measurement. Demonstration of parallel forms of reliability would be important and relevant (and possible) only in research that uses equivalent forms of the same measurement instrument. Split half reliability and coefficient alpha would be important for measurement of knowledge or attitudes where internal consistency of measurement is desirable. We might expect some demonstration of either or both if a new test or measurement instrument were being used. Interobserver agreement would be relevant and important when more than one interviewer is used to collect data as a means of estimating the effectiveness of interviewer training. We would want to know whether those collecting the data were comparably sensitized to the same behaviors or phenomena and whether they were recording their observations in the same ways.

Researchers may improve the reliability of measurement instruments by attending to a variety of factors. They include

- *Standardizing environmental factors during measurement.* Many factors besides the measurement instrument used can negatively affect consistency of measurement of variables. When conducting cross-sectional research, data should be collected in similar settings, at similar times, and in similar ways from all participants. In longitudinal studies, all measurements of the same variable should be conducted in similar settings.
- *Conducting a pilot study of the instrument.* In addition to its other uses (discussed in Chapter 11), the process of pilot testing a measurement instrument with a few individuals who are similar to the research participants can help to make measurement more reliable. For example, if a previously developed measurement instrument is to be used, pilot testing it can either confirm or refute the researcher's belief that the instrument is reliable when used with different research participants than those on whom it was developed. If indicated, another measurement instrument can be substituted or revisions in areas that appear to be unreliable can be made. Then the instrument can be pilot-tested again to see if problems have been corrected.
- *Increasing the number of items on a test or measurement instrument.* In general, for unidimensional measures (those measuring just one variable), adding items will improve the reliability estimate. This occurs because coefficient alpha is a function of both the average correlation among items and the number of items on a test or other instrument. Even for instruments that are not unidimensional, adding additional, clear items can sometimes help to improve the reliability of measurement.

## Validity

When evaluating measurement, *validity* refers to the degree that an instrument "adequately reflects the real meaning of the concept under consideration."[4] The presence of reliability is required for a measurement to be valid. But, as emphasized in Figure 10.1, reliability is not in itself sufficient to guarantee that a measurement is valid. For example, a measurement instrument may claim to measure assertiveness among people. It may produce consistent results (reliability). But it may, in fact, be measuring aggressiveness, not assertiveness. A valid measurement is both reliable and unbiased; that is, it contains no source of systematic distortion.

A commonly used example of a measurement that is reliable (consistent) but lacking in validity is a 36-inch cloth tape measure that has gotten wet and has shrunk by 2 inches, or a wooden yardstick that has had a 2-inch section (the first 2 inches) broken off. If the researcher were to measure a 34-inch table, either instrument would conclude that the table is 36 inches long. If the instruments were to be used to measure the table a month, a year, or ten years later (assuming no further change in the instruments or the table had occurred), they would again suggest that the table is 36 inches long. Other researchers could measure the table with the same instruments and arrive at the same conclusion about its length. It could be measured anywhere and under a variety of conditions, but the result of measurement would be the same—the table must be 36 inches long.

The fact that multiple measurements all produce the same results would suggest reliability (consistency), but valid measurement would not be present. The table would be 34 inches long and not 36 inches, despite what the measurements would suggest. Systematic distortion of the measures in the form of shrinkage and breakage served to make the instruments incapable of producing a true measurement of the table's length. Only the elimination of the bias would create a valid measurement.

Validity, like reliability, is not an all-or-nothing proposition. Validity often is a matter of degree. The researcher must be convinced (and able to convince others) that a measurement is sufficiently valid to produce an acceptable measurement of key variables within a given study.

Some instruments are more valid for conducting measurements with some populations than with others. For example, some measurements are believed to provide valid measurements of variables such as hostility in normal populations, but not with clinical populations.

Sometimes it takes a long time before it is concluded that an instrument measures what it claims to measure. For example, the SAT examination was long held to provide a valid measurement of scholastic aptitude. Critics asserted that although it provided a reliable assessment of "something" (some said scholastic achievement), it was not a scholastic aptitude measure. Not until the 1990s was the test's name changed to reflect this position.

Instruments are said to be valid for a given use and with a specific group when data are developed and presented to support these statements. Thus, the burden of proof is on the researcher to show that an instrument may be appropriately used in a given study. The researcher does this by either securing validity data that are available for existing instruments or developing validity data for new instruments.

If one cannot be sure that a given instrument will produce a reasonably valid measurement of a variable, it may be necessary to build ways to assess the validity of the instrument within the research design and report on the results of the assessment. Evidence of the validity of a measuring instrument is developed in relation to the purpose of the measurement instrument. Instruments can be categorized as serving one or more of three purposes:

1. To measure achievement in a content area. Tests of knowledge (examinations) have this purpose.
2. To predict performance in regard to some criterion. Examples would be aptitude tests or tests used to screen for admission into an educational program.
3. To provide a measure of a construct. Attitude scales or diagnostic instruments would be examples of instruments used for this purpose.

As with reliability, there are certain criteria that are employed to provide an estimate of validity. They are content validity, criterion validity, and construct validity. They correspond roughly to the three purposes of measurement instruments.

**Content Validity.**   Content validity involves an assessment of whether a measurement adequately covers all aspects or components of a particular body of content. It also involves a determination as to whether irrelevant or inappropriate content is present in the measurement. Content validity is the type of validity that is of special concern to the researcher when the purpose of a measuring instrument is to measure participants' learning or achievement in some content area. For example, to measure what participants learned in a workshop, seminar, or training session, tests need to be content-validated.

Tests of knowledge that are content valid pose questions that measure what was actually covered in a course, training session, or other curriculum package. They do not ask questions that do not relate to the curriculum's content. For example, an item on a test on this chapter that tested the student's understanding of reliability in the context of measurement probably could be assumed to possess content validity; one that asked the names of the authors of this text (an old favorite among some professors) would not.

Tests are generally judged to be content valid based on how they were developed. Content validity is achieved by defining a hypothetical domain (or universe) of test items. Items then are randomly selected so that they are believed to be representative of the domain. Researchers may not actually develop a hypothetical domain of test items (sometimes called a "test bank"). They simply define each content area, identify its major categories, and then write items that correspond to the various categories or facets of the content area. This process is known as constructing a blueprint of the measure. When this is carefully done, it improves the likelihood that the measure will be content valid. Researchers reporting on the content validity of a measure are expected to describe the procedures used in instrument development that support their claim of content validity.

The use of content experts is also extremely helpful in providing evidence of the content validity of an instrument. They may be used to help define the content area so that a useful blueprint will emerge. In addition, content experts might be asked to evaluate a draft of the instrument to assess the usefulness of specific test items. Or they may be used to examine the completed instrument to state how content valid the test appears to be. In truth, this assessment really does not provide hard evidence of the content validity of the test. What it provides is information about the *face validity* of the measure, that is, that the test looks valid on the face (or surface).

**Criterion Validity.**   Evidence of criterion validity is important when the purpose of an instrument is to predict behavior or to measure some characteristic of research participants. Evidence of criterion validity is achieved by demonstrating that scores on the measuring instrument are consistent with scores on another, accepted indicator of the same variable. The second indicator (which may or may not be a standardized measurement instrument per se) is known as the criterion. As with reliability, evidence of criterion validity usually is presented statistically as a correlation coefficient.

There are two subcategories of criterion validity: concurrent validity and predictive validity. *Concurrent validity* is demonstrated by producing a high positive correlation between two measures—the measurement instrument and the criterion—both of which are made at approximately the same time. For example, one might correlate scores on a newly developed measurement of student test anxiety with scores on some other well-accepted measure of anxiety. If the new measure has concurrent validity, statistical correlation with the older measurement instrument should be high and positive. In a somewhat less scientific way, a researcher who has developed an instrument presumed to measure charisma might demonstrate its concurrent validity by pilot-testing it with two groups: people generally acknowledged to possess charisma and those who are believed to lack it. If the instrument has concurrent validity, the first group should receive high scores, whereas the latter group should receive low measurements of the variable.

*Predictive validity* provides evidence of the correlation between a measure and some future performance or behavior. To develop evidence of predictive validity, data on the criterion are gathered. For example, newly developed screening inventories to predict abusive behaviors might be correlated with the results of follow-up studies of research participants who completed the inventories to determine just how well the instruments were able to predict abusive behaviors.

One example of the concept of predictive validity that is well known to students is the use of standardized tests such as SATs or GREs to predict how students will perform in college or in graduate school. The measure of how students actually perform in school is the criterion. Educational researchers interested in providing evidence of criterion validity for standardized tests must attempt to demonstrate a high correlation between scores attained by students on these tests and their later performance in school (usually as measured by grade point average or whether a student graduated).

**Construct Validity.** In some social work research, the researcher develops an instrument to measure a variable that really is a construct. A construct is something that is defined primarily through a cognitive process—it usually cannot be directly observed. Many psychiatric diagnostic categories are constructs. For example, anorexia nervosa, bipolar disorder, and schizophrenia are constructs. Their presence is inferred when certain conditions exist (as described in the *Diagnostic and Statistical Manual of Mental Disorders*, Fourth Edition). For example, schizophrenia is said to exist only when a certain group of symptoms or behaviors is identified as present (certain thought disorders, inappropriate affect, and so forth).

If an instrument is to provide a valid measurement of a construct, it must measure the essential components of the construct. Thus, if a researcher designed a data collection instrument to classify participants as either schizophrenic or not schizophrenic, the instrument should include items that cover all of those symptoms or behaviors that together constitute the construct of schizophrenia. If, for example, the instrument provides no indication of whether the participant has hallucinations, that would suggest that the instrument is probably lacking in construct validity.

Evidence of construct validity involves the use of several related types of information. Construct validity demonstrates that the construct being measured exists within a theoretical framework, thereby explaining the construct itself and how it relates to other variables. In a sense, a test of construct validity becomes both a measure of the construct and a test of its underlying theory as well.

Concurrent validity data can help to provide evidence of the construct validity of an instrument. For example, the researcher could examine how people who have been diagnosed as schizophrenic score on the instrument. If the instrument shows a pattern of relationships with criterion measures (the diagnosis), then evidence of the meaning of the construct is provided. Similarly, face validity, the fact that it is logical to conclude that a measurement really measures what it claims to measure, helps to support claims of construct validity.

There are other ways in which construct validity overlaps somewhat with concurrent validity. If the conceptualization of a variable leads a researcher to the expectation that two groups should differ on their measurements of the construct (for example, people diagnosed as schizophrenic and those diagnosed as not having a schizophrenic thought disorder), then this expectation of difference can be tested. If the two group measures are significantly different (as we would expect), then the implication is that the test really measures the construct and hence demonstrates construct validity. In short, assembling evidence of construct validity involves, in part, the collection of other kinds of validity data and the drawing of appropriate inferences from these data about the meaning of the construct.

# Cultural Issues in Measurement of Variables

Caution should be exercised when instruments are to be used with research participants who are different in important ways from groups with whom the existing instruments were developed and normed. Before using an existing measurement instrument, social work researchers need to be familiar with how and on which population group(s) the measurement was constructed. It should never be assumed that established norms and benchmarks on which scoring is based apply uniformly to all participants across all settings and cultural contexts. When conducting cross-cultural research, efforts should be made to find instruments normed on a variety of cultural groups or nationalities, or to look for instruments developed in a variety of cultural contexts that attempt to measure the same underlying construct. Such instruments are difficult to find. A few examples of instruments designed for and/or normed on specific ethnic and racial groups are

- Acculturation Rating Scale for Mexican Americans (ARSMA) by Cuellar, Harris, and Jasso (1980), which measures degree of acculturation for normal and clinical populations of Mexican Americans
- Hispanic Stress Inventory by Cervantes, Padilla, and Salgado de Snyder (1990), which measures psychological stress in immigrants from Latin America and in Mexican Americans
- TEMAS (Tell-Me-a-Story) by Constantino, Malgady, and Rogler (1988), which is a thematic apperception test developed for African American and Hispanic children

Special concerns about the preservation of reliability and validity arise when instruments are translated from one language to another for use with linguistically diverse study populations. The nonequivalence of research instruments can limit the usefulness of data obtained in cross-cultural research. Many authors suggest ways to increase the likelihood that reliability and validity will be maintained throughout the translation process. Five such suggestions are

1. Attempt to understand one's own values and cultural perspectives and how they might influence the researcher's definitions of key constructs that the instrument is designed to measure.
2. Consult with members of the group of interest to determine the cultural relevance of constructs of interest within the target population and to assess the face validity of the instrument items for measuring constructs of interest in that culture.
3. Translate the instrument from the first language to the second language, using skilled, bilingually fluent translators working individually, sequentially, or as a team. (The translators should be aware of idiomatic subtleties related to geography or social class.)

4. Translate the instrument from the second language back into the first language, using skilled translators. The back-translation should then be compared to the original version to determine the accuracy of the original translation.
5. Field-test the translated instrument using bilingual participants, in order to establish equivalence through parallel forms reliability coefficients.

## Summary

Chapter 10 presented the concepts basic to measurement of variables. Two early tasks of the measurement process were identified: conceptualization and operationalization. Another measurement task of the researcher involves deciding just how precisely a variable can be measured. The four levels of measurement (nominal, ordinal, interval, and ratio) were differentiated.

The criteria used to evaluate the quality of measurement were discussed. Reliability relates to the degree to which a measurement is consistent in the way that it measures a variable. Validity refers to the degree to which a measurement is successful in actually measuring what it has claimed to measure. A measurement that is valid is reliable, and it is also unbiased. Methods that social work researchers may use to estimate the reliability and the validity of a measurement instrument were described. Their relative importance for different types of measurement and for different research objectives were identified.

Finally, we examined a few ways in which reliability and validity of measurement may be influenced by cultural differences.

Chapter 10 provided merely an overview of the very critical area of measurement. Other issues related to measurement are discussed in Chapter 11.

## References

1. Rubin, A., & Babbie, E. (1997). *Research methods for social work* (3rd ed.). Pacific Grove, CA: Brooks/Cole, 129–131.
2. Leedy, P. (1997). *Practical research: Planning and design* (6th ed.). Upper Saddle River, NJ: Prentice Hall, 30.
3. York, R. (1998). *Conducting social work research.* Boston, MA: Allyn & Bacon, 69.
4. Rubin, A., & Babbie, E. (2001). *Research methods for social work* (4th ed.). Belmont, CA: Wadsworth Publishing Company, 177.

# 11

# USE OF DATA COLLECTION INSTRUMENTS

In almost all research studies, researchers use some form of data collection instrument to record their measurements of variables and to organize their data into a more or less standard format. Data collection instruments vary widely in structure and content. In exploratory, qualitative studies, they may be nothing more than a group of questions or topics to be covered in some order during the course of an interview. At the other extreme, in highly standardized, quantitative research, they may be long, carefully worded documents designed to be read or administered in one very specific way.

As Figure 11.1 suggests, data collection instruments usually consist of some combination of (1) individual items, each of which provides a measurement of a single variable, and/or (2) a group of items that together provide a measurement of a single variable. We will look at the less intricate of these—one item, one variable—first.

## FIGURE 11.1 The Components of Data Collection Instruments

1. One item; one variable
   A. Open-ended items
   B. Fixed-alternative items
2. Two or more items; one variable
   A. Indexes
   B. Scales,* for example, Likert, Thurstone, Guttman, semantic differential, and so forth

*A scale may contain subscales, each of which contains two or more items. Each subscale may measure a different variable.

## Fixed-Alternative and Open-Ended Items

Some variables can be measured using only a single item or question on a data collection instrument. These items may be classified as either fixed-alternative or open-ended. An example of a fixed-alternative (also called closed-ended) item is

*Please indicate your current legal marital status by circling the letter of one response below:*

*a. married*
*b. single never married*
*c. separated*
*d. divorced*
*e. widowed*

In contrast, open-ended, less structured items are those for which participants provide their own responses in their own words. For example, an open-ended item would be

*In your own words, please briefly describe your experience with marriage and your current attitudes toward it.*

_____

_____

_____

As a general rule, fixed-alternative items are used in instruments when the range of responses to the item can be anticipated; that is, when the researcher is quite sure what the range of different responses will be. They are also sometimes used when the researcher simply wishes the participant to consider certain responses that the participant might otherwise fail to consider. They often include an "other" category for any unanticipated responses.

In contrast, open-ended items are more likely to be used when the range of responses is likely to be great and/or the researcher cannot possibly anticipate them all. A researcher may also select an open-ended item format to avoid suggesting possible responses to research participants. Open-ended items also allow the researcher to collect data in the form of direct quotations. Sometimes these can be very meaningful in presenting participants' attitudes or opinions.

It is not unusual for a researcher to develop the first draft of a data collection instrument using an open-ended item to measure a variable. After pilot-testing the instrument (discussed later in the chapter), it is observed that answers tend to fall within a small range of categories. Consequently, a fixed-alternative item is substituted in the final draft of the instrument. Conversely, a pilot-testing of a data collection instrument that uses a fixed-alternative item to measure a variable may produce a larger number and range of responses than anticipated. Many of them may be in the "other" category. Then the researcher may decide to revise the instrument to substitute an open-ended item to measure the variable.

Open-ended items provide a more in-depth understanding of a topic than do fixed-alternative items. They are especially useful when the purpose of an item is to secure qualitative data. However, this advantage may be offset by a number of potential disadvantages that must be considered.

- Participants are less likely to complete items that require them to write out their responses. Thus, the overall return rate may be low.
- The researcher cannot precode response categories for computer data entry because open-ended items do not presuppose the use of certain responses by participants.
- The researcher may experience difficulty in analyzing data that reflect wide variation and are not readily amenable to quantitative analysis. Although there are now data analysis software programs for analyzing qualitative data, they are less numerous than those designed for use with quantitative data.

## Indexes and Scales

Although it is often possible to measure a variable by asking a single fixed-alternative or open-ended question, many variables are not so easily measured. For example, attitudes and behavioral patterns generally cannot be accurately measured by a response to a single question or item. They require that the researcher use multiple items in order to accurately measure them. The items constitute what is referred to as an *index* or a *scale*. In an index or scale, the response to each item contributes to the researcher's understanding of the participant in relation to the variable being measured. Ultimately, all the relevant responses (viewed as a whole) make it possible for the researcher to assign the research participant to one category (value) of the variable.

Indexes and scales (especially the latter) tend to be highly structured and highly refined. They are used both as independent data collection instruments and as one component of a larger instrument. Although indexes and scales both perform measurements of complex variables, they do it in different ways.

### Indexes

An index consists of a number of items that are believed to be important indicators of the variable being measured. In general terms, the more items that participants indicate as applying to them, the greater the quantity of the variable they are presumed to possess. An example of an index to measure depression might be

*Place a check mark in front of each feeling that you have experienced during the past week:*

_____ sadness
_____ hopelessness
_____ powerlessness
_____ just not caring
_____ wanting to be alone
_____ anxiety

In the preceding index, a score would range from 0 to 6, depending on how many responses a participant checked, with a 0 reflecting the lowest level of depression, and a 6 reflecting the highest. The measurement produced by an index is generally acknowledged to be ordinal level (Chapter 10). A participant who checked five items is considered more depressed than one who checked only four; a participant who checked two is more depressed than one who checked one, and so forth. But the intervals (categories as denoted by the number of check marks present) are not considered to be equal, and no claim is made that each symptom is an equally good indicator of the presence of depression. Some may be better indicators than others. The number of symptoms checked, however, would allow participants to be rank-ordered for the variable depression.

Indexes provide a better measurement of some variables than a single item could provide, but they are still a little crude. They sometimes are used as the first step in the development of a more precise, multiple-item form of measurement: the scale.

## Scales

Whereas an index asks research participants to respond to each item in a dichotomous manner, indicating how many of the items apply, a scale asks for a more precise answer. Scales might ask, for example, how frequently or to what degree each item applies. Several identical response options are made available for each item, thereby greatly increasing the range of scores among participants.

**Linear or Summative Scales.**  A common form of scale, known as the linear or summative model, is similar to an index in that it allows the researcher to derive a sum score for each participant by adding up the responses to individual scale items. An example of a linear scale to measure depression would be

*Indicate how often you experienced each of these symptoms by circling the appropriate number.*

|              | Never |   |   |   | Often |
|--------------|-------|---|---|---|-------|
| 1. sad/down  | 0     | 1 | 2 | 3 | 4     |
| 2. hopeless  | 0     | 1 | 2 | 3 | 4     |
| 3. powerless | 0     | 1 | 2 | 3 | 4     |

|  | *Never* |  |  |  | *Often* |
|---|---|---|---|---|---|
| 4. *apathetic* | 0 | 1 | 2 | 3 | 4 |
| 5. *withdrawn* | 0 | 1 | 2 | 3 | 4 |
| 6. *anxious* | 0 | 1 | 2 | 3 | 4 |

On the preceding scale, participants would be asked to circle a number for each item, and these numbers would then be totaled. Thus, the highest possible score that could be attained would be 24, and the lowest possible score would be 0. On this type of scale, lower scores are operationalized to mean a lower level of the variable being measured (depression); relatively higher scores indicate a higher level of it.

Linear or summative scaling is very popular among researchers in social science research. Many variables that researchers are interested in studying can be scaled using this model. It is appropriate whenever the researcher can construct multiple items that reflect comparable dimensions of the variable. The items are designed to provide (in toto) a measure of a variable.

Researchers often use a specific kind of summative scale known as a *Likert scale* (named after its developer) when attitudes are measured. A set of attitude items is supplied. Participants indicate their level of agreement with each item. For example, a Likert scale might be used to measure client satisfaction with worker services.

*Indicate your level of agreement with each of the items listed below:*

|  | *Strongly Agree* |  |  |  | *Strongly Disagree* |
|---|---|---|---|---|---|
| 1. *My worker was prepared for sessions.* | 1 | 2 | 3 | 4 | 5 |
| 2. *My worker tried to be prompt.* | 1 | 2 | 3 | 4 | 5 |
| 3. *My worker seemed preoccupied.* | 1 | 2 | 3 | 4 | 5 |
| 4. *My worker acted professionally.* | 1 | 2 | 3 | 4 | 5 |
| 5. *My worker did not care about me as a person.* | 1 | 2 | 3 | 4 | 5 |
| 6. *My worker tried to understand me.* | 1 | 2 | 3 | 4 | 5 |
| 7. *My worker really wanted to help me.* | 1 | 2 | 3 | 4 | 5 |

Likert scales generally contain a mixture of items that are so-called positive and negative. Positive items are those where a high level of agreement with the item would reflect a high quantity of the variable being measured and where a low level of agreement with the item would reflect a low quantity of the variable (such as items 1, 2, 4, 6, and 7 in the preceding example).

Negative items (such as items 3 and 5) are worded in such a way that a high level of agreement with the item reflects a low quantity of the variable being measured, and vice versa. In scoring negative items, scoring is reversed; that is, responses of "strongly agree" are given a 1; "strongly disagree," a 5; and so forth.

Why do researchers include negative items in a scale? They are included primarily to determine whether the participant has answered honestly. When negative items are included, an individual completing the scale is less likely to determine what is being measured, gauge about where they fall in relation to the variable, and then simply circle the same number for all items. To further ensure honesty, the researcher would not want to simply alternate positive and negative items, a pattern that could soon be identified by the participant. A random mixture of positive and negative items allows a researcher to determine whether participants really read and carefully considered each item before responding to it. If they did, a consistent pattern of responses (reflecting a measurement of the variable) should be evident in both types of item (internal reliability).

**Thurstone Scales.**   A Thurstone scale uses judges to evaluate the early drafts of scales and asks them to assess the relative importance of individual items being measured. Based on these ratings, eventually each item is assigned a *weighting*, a number reflecting its relative importance to measurement of the concept. The items are then placed randomly within the scale. The weightings are not known to research participants who complete the scale, but they are used by the researcher in calculating participants' scores; responses to different items "count" more or less than others. For example, a Thurstone scale might be constructed to measure the severity of behavioral problems reflected by preadolescent children. It might ask parents if their child had engaged in any one of ten behaviors during the past six months. Based on the opinions of experts and a long, time-consuming series of tasks leading to its development, the scale would contain different weightings for different behaviors reflecting their severity. For example, "fought with siblings" or "disobeyed your rule" might get a low weighting, say, 1.2 or 1.3. In contrast, a behavior judged to be more symptomatic of serious difficulties such as "tortured animals" or "set fires" might have a weighting of, say, 4.5 or 5.2. Because Thurstone scales are very time consuming to develop, we do not see them too often in social work research.

**Guttman Scales.**   A Guttman scale also is developed by ranking items, but the items are placed in order (rather than randomly) in the final product. For example, a Guttman scale might use a rank-ordering of statements about welfare recipients, ranging from most negative to most positive, and ask participants to indicate with which statements they disagree. Then it would be noted at what point (after how many items) in the scale a participant would first register disagreement. The point of disagreement would be important because we could generally assume that once a participant disagreed with one statement, there also would be disagreement with the other, more positive ones that followed.

A *Bogardus Social Distance scale* is a special form of a Guttman scale. It measures to what degree people would be willing to interact with people who are different from themselves, such as people of a different ethnic group or people with a different sexual orientation. Participants would review in sequence a rank-ordering of statements, each of which describes a closer interaction with the other group than the previous one. They would indicate if they would be willing to tolerate each level of interaction. The researcher would note at what point each participant would "draw the line" on a form of interaction and, it is assumed, on all of the interactions described after that one. The number of tolerable interactions would, with a single number, give a good indication of each participant's willingness to interact with others.

**Semantic Differential Scales.** A semantic differential scale presents the participant with a list of word opposites (for example, soft/hard, clean/dirty, old/new, dull/interesting, simple/complicated, and so on), which often seem to be of only vague or indirect relevance to the concept or phenomenon (for example, lawyers, food stamps, or capital punishment) that the participant has been asked to describe. The opposites are placed on opposite ends of a line, and the participant is asked to place an X on the line to indicate a response to the concept or phenomenon in relation to the two opposite words. In some semantic differential scales, the participant is asked to place a check mark under one of several columns with words above them such as "frequently," "sometimes," "rarely," or "never." Semantic differential scales are a kind of word association game. The participant is assumed (sometimes somewhat unwillingly) to reveal true feelings or attitudes about something and thus to provide a measurement of a variable. For example, nurses might be asked to respond to a series of opposites including strong/weak, good/evil, firm/soft, and so forth, to indicate their attitudes about social workers.

There are many other types of scales, often named after the individuals who developed the methods for constructing them. They are used less frequently in social work research, but each has specialized uses to which they are ideally suited. We have mentioned only some of the most well known ones. They and other types of scales are discussed in greater depth and with examples of each in Miller[1] and in some of the other texts mentioned in Figure 11.2.

Figure 11.2 is a listing of reference volumes that describe instruments available to measure variables that frequently are of interest within social work research. In addition to these books, professional journals in psychology, education, and social work often contain articles that report on the development of measurement instruments.

Unlike indexes, there is a lack of consensus among researchers (and authors of textbooks) as to the level of measurement that is produced by some scales. Thurstone scales, in part because they are developed using a long, painstaking method, generally are acknowledged to yield interval data. Guttman scales

**FIGURE 11.2    References for Scales, Tests, and Other Types of Measurement Instruments**

---

Beere, C. A. (1990). *Gender roles: A handbook of tests and measures.* New York: Greenwood Press.

Beere, C. A. (1990). *Women and women's issues: A handbook of tests and measures.* San Francisco: Jossey-Bass.

Buros, O. (1978). *Eighth mental measurements yearbook.* Highland Park, NJ: The Gryphon Press.

Corcoran, K., & Fischer, J. (1987). *Measures for clinical practice: A sourcebook.* New York: The Free Press.

Corcoran, K., & Fischer, J. (1994). *Measures for clinical practice* (2nd ed.). Vol. 1: *Couples, families and children.* Vol. 2: *Adults.* New York: The Free Press.

Goldman, B. A. (1978–1995). *Directory of unpublished experimental measures.* Vol. 1–6. New York: Human Sciences Press.

Holman, A. M. (1983). *Family assessment: Tools for understanding and intervention.* Newbury Park, CA: Sage Publications.

Hudson, W. W. (1982). *The clinical measurement package.* Homewood, IL: The Dorsey Press.

Miller, D. (1991). *Handbook of research design and social measurement* (5th ed.). Newbury Park, CA: Sage Publications.

Rauch, J. (1994). *Assessment: A sourcebook for social work practice.* Milwaukee: Families International Incorporated.

Touliatos, J., Perlmutter, B. F., & Straus, M. A. (1990). *Handbook of family measurement techniques.* Newbury Park, CA: Sage Publications.

---

(including Bogardus Social Distance scales) generate only ordinal level, as (by general consensus) do semantic differential scales. Some authors of Likert scales (especially those that have undergone many years of development and refinement) claim that their scales produce interval measurement. Others say that any Likert scale does, but there is no general agreement on this point.

The issue usually centers most around those scales that are fairly newly developed, have not undergone extensive statistical analysis, and are relatively simple; that is, they contain no weighting or other indication of the reality that not all items are probably of equal importance as indicators of the variable being measured. Generally, any scale that has only recently been developed by the researcher is less likely to be regarded as capable of yielding interval-level measurement than one that has been many years in its development. The presence or absence of words provided alongside all or just some of the response numbers in a scale (referred to as "anchoring") is another issue in the debate over the level of data that a scale generates. If only numbers are used, a scale is more likely to be considered interval than if it is anchored, because we can agree that the distances between intervals are equal. However, we have more difficulty in drawing that conclusion when words are used. In the interest of the researcher's credibility, it is often best to err on the conservative side by claiming only ordinal measurement from a scale, unless there is substantial evidence that a claim of interval-level measurement can be justified.

## Construction of Scales

Scales generally are developed by researchers following rigorous rules and procedures. Many scales have been developed, tested, and repeatedly revised and honed over decades.

The specific methods employed in constructing the various types of scales mentioned in this chapter are beyond the scope of this book. Scale building is an exact science. It is the focus of graduate courses in statistics and measurement. Only rarely would a social worker attempt to construct a new scale as part of a research study. But to gain an appreciation of the effort that goes into their construction, we will briefly mention the general way that it is done.

1. *The variable to be measured is operationally defined.* The definition should refer to all relevant aspects of the variable. A clear definition enables the researcher to write an *item pool*, a preliminary set of items that may be included in the scale. The item pool should be as exhaustive as possible; one generally starts with many more items than are necessary, so that less relevant items later can be eliminated while leaving enough items to constitute the scale. The items should be reviewed by content experts, people who are subject matter specialists. Their role is to evaluate the items for clarity, relevance, appropriateness, and ease in responding. Then items should be revised as needed. A draft instrument is produced, and a pilot test of the instrument is conducted. Pilot test participants are asked to respond to the questions and to provide a critique of the items. They are encouraged to make comments about the items themselves, for example, which items are not clear, which contain words that they do not understand, and so on.

2. *Data from the pilot test are analyzed.* This is accomplished using a correlational statistical process known as *item analysis*. The process typically involves the calculation of two statistics by computer: item-to-total-scale correlations (for each item) and a reliability coefficient that provides a measure of the internal reliability of the scale (such as coefficient alpha). They are calculated to ensure that all of the items that are to comprise the scale are measuring the same construct and that the items, when taken together, represent a unidimensional measure.

   The item-to-total-scale analysis determines how responses to each item correlate with how participants responded overall to the scale. (It is similar to the item analysis that professors sometimes use on multiple-choice or true/false tests to eliminate bad test items—those that were missed by students who did well on the test overall and/or were answered correctly by students who did poorly.) A researcher would want to retain only items with the highest positive item-total correlations. Items with low or negative item-total correlations are usually deleted. The analysis required for item-total correlations is conducted using statistical software packages specifically designed for social science data. When this is done, a reliability estimate of the scale describes the statistical effect of deletion of individual items. This assists the researcher in deciding which scale items to keep and which ones to delete.

Coefficient alpha, we will recall, reflects the degree to which individual items correlate with each other. Scales that are designed to measure a unidimensional construct should reflect a high degree of internal consistency. Scales that are multidimensional in nature (for example, the MMPI [Minnesota Multiphasic Personality Inventory]) would not be expected to reflect it, but their various subscales would.

3. *The scale is modified as needed.* Items are deleted or revised. If items are added at this stage, they should be subjected to pilot testing and further statistical analysis. Once the scale is fully developed, data about the reliability and validity of it and of individual scale items are retained for reporting and for future analysis.

After undergoing this process, a scale (or at least a portion of it) often is published in a book of data collection instruments or in a professional journal. The process of its development is described, along with a description of the people who contributed data for its development. Conclusions about its reliability and validity (based on statistical analyses) as well as about their limitations are noted. For example, we might read that "The scale was found to have a test-retest reliability of .89 among Latinos under age sixty-five who reside in the United States and Canada for whom Spanish is a first language. However, its reliability among other Spanish-speaking people was only .45."

## When Are Existing Instruments Appropriate for Use?

When we discussed data collection methods in Chapter 8, we suggested that secondary analysis of data collected for some other purpose can be a real time- and effort-saver in some situations. Similarly, if it is possible to use a data measurement instrument developed by another researcher, a great deal of time and effort can be saved. The process of developing new instruments often represents a discrete research project in and of itself. Thus, where appropriate, researchers should consider using instruments or portions of instruments that have already been developed.

In determining if an existing measurement instrument would be appropriate to use in one's research study, a number of issues need to be examined. First, the researcher needs to determine if the instrument can appropriately be used with the population of interest. Is it likely to provide reliable measurement with the researcher's participants? Measures are developed for specific uses with specific research populations. The researcher will need to determine if the proposed research participants are similar enough to the participants with whom the instrument was developed and tested, so that it will yield reliable data.[2] Cultural differences, especially the meaning of words within subcultures or within different ethnic groups should be given special attention.

The question of validity requires a comparison of conceptual definitions. Before using an instrument developed as part of another study, we would want to be sure that what the instrument purports to measure is the same variable that we need to measure. In order to use an existing measure, a researcher has to (1) find one that was developed using the same (or similar) conceptual definition of the variable that needs to be measured or (2) adapt a current conceptual definition to that which was used in the development of the existing instrument. For example, a researcher interested in measuring parenting skills could try to find a measurement tool that was developed using a conceptual definition of parenting skills that is the same as the conceptual definition suggested by the researcher's review of the literature. If this proves to be impossible, the researcher might still be able to find a measurement tool that seems to measure most aspects of parenting skills of interest and then conceptually redefine the variable to be consistent with the conceptual definition of parenting skills used by the developer of the instrument. Fortunately, reference material regarding specific measures often includes the conceptual definition of the variable that was used by the author of the instrument.

There are a number of reference volumes in university libraries that provide a listing and description of indexes, scales, and other available measures. Information about the instrument may include how to contact the authors of the measure or how to obtain it. If the instrument is copyrighted (most indexes and scales are), it may have to be purchased from the publisher or directly from the author. If it is not copyrighted, it can usually be used with the author's written permission. Of course, if the instrument is in the public domain, it may be used without permission of the authors.

## Use of Revised Instruments

If the researcher is unable to locate an existing measure that is appropriate for use in a given study, there may exist an instrument that, it appears, could be modified and used. For example, an instrument may be available that measures client satisfaction with services received from an out-patient mental health clinic. If the researcher is interested in measuring client satisfaction with services received within an in-patient mental health setting, it may be possible to modify the existing instrument for use. Several items may be borrowed from the instrument exactly as written and others reworded for use in the current study. This "new" instrument should then be pilot-tested with a sample of participants who are similar to the intended study group, to see if measurement problems may have been introduced by the revision.

If the research study is exploratory of if the instrument to be used is just a guideline for use by the researcher (for example, in a qualitative study in which data collection is conducted using unstructured interviews), modifications of existing instruments can be made with little concern about the effects of the changes. When these data collection methods are used, parts of different instruments may be freely borrowed and changed as deemed appropriate. There is little reason to be concerned about how a change in wording might affect reliability and validity of measurement. Instead, an assessment of the quality of measurement is often based on the researcher's judgment of the degree of candor and truthfulness that participants seemed to display.

In more quantitative studies that rely heavily on accurate measurement of variables in order to test hypotheses, rewording of existing instruments or changing them in any way should be undertaken with extreme caution. When using revised instruments, advice regarding the possible effects of the modifications in wording on quality of measurement may be obtained by contacting the original instrument's author. If large sections of a data collection instrument are borrowed from an existing instrument (especially if it is copyrighted), the researcher also must gain permission to use the instrument from the author or publisher. If only a few items are used, and if the original wording is substantially altered, permission is usually not necessary.

When borrowing items from an existing instrument, the researcher should remember that assessments of its reliability and validity were based on the instrument as a whole. Thus, it would not be correct to borrow and alter items and then to assume that those assessments are necessarily still accurate. Indexes and scales are especially sensitive to revision. Adding or deleting items or changing even a word or two can threaten their capacity to provide valid measurement.

## Constructing New Instruments

If it is not possible to find an existing measure or to revise one to yield useful measurements of one or more variables, then a new data collection instrument may have to be developed. In those more qualitative studies that rely on a data collection instrument to standardize data collection methods (at least to some extent), it is often simplest to create a new instrument from scratch, rather than to try to revise an existing one that is likely to have been developed to study some other question with some other group of research participants. The process of developing such an instrument may be relatively simple. It may consist primarily of thinking through and discussing with others what areas should be explored, within the context of an in-person interview, focus group, and so forth, as well as, perhaps, the best sequence in which to explore them.

In more quantitative studies that rely more on careful, standardized measurement of variables, construction of a new data collection instrument is an exacting and demanding task.[3] Whichever formats and methods are selected, the task requires careful attention if one is to derive measurements that are regarded as reliable and valid.

## Issues in Development of New Instruments

There are a number of issues that should be considered in developing a new data collection instrument for use in quantitative research. They relate to its intent, formatting, and sequencing of questions, as well as to its length, clarity, wording, and presentation. Although they are most relevant to mailed or participant-completed instruments (discussed in the next section), most of them are equally relevant to data collection in which participant responses are recorded by the researcher.

**Intent of Items.** The researcher should ask: Is an item or series of items designed to measure (1) knowledge, (2) attitudes or beliefs, or (3) behaviors of participants? The intent of an item determines the way in which a question or item is worded. An example of a knowledge item is

> *Can a doctor be sued for reporting suspected child abuse that is later proven to be unfounded?*
>
> _____ *yes* _____ *no*

An example of an attitude or belief item is

> *How helpful was your social worker?*
> _____ *very helpful*
> _____ *somewhat helpful*
> _____ *not helpful*

An example of a behavior question is

> *During the past month, how many times have you attempted to talk to your social worker by phone?*
> _____ *never*
> _____ *once or twice*
> _____ *three times or more*

**Clarity of Items.** If items are not clearly understood by participants, their responses may not provide an accurate measurement of a variable. The best items generally are those that ask participants for a simple response, are unambiguous, and are phrased positively rather than negatively. People do not always notice a qualifying word in a question (for example, words such as *hardly, never, not,* or *barely*); therefore, they are best not used.

**Use of Contingency Instructions.**   Contingency instructions are sometimes appropriate. They are used to direct the participant through the instrument in an efficient manner (or, if it is administered by the researcher, to assist him or her). They also provide a way to reduce the number of items that participants are asked to respond to and to avoid asking participants to answer items that are not applicable to them. They reflect consideration on the part of the researcher and help to organize the data that are collected. An example of a contingency instruction is

> *If you answered "yes" to question 2 above, please respond to questions 3 through 7; if you answered "no" to question 2, please skip down to question 8.*

**Sequencing of Items.**   In developing new instruments, there are two perspectives on sequencing of questions. Some researchers prefer to begin with the most general (and least controversial or personal) items and then move to the more specific ones. General-to-specific sequencing may be preferable if the researcher has reason to believe that participants will be more comfortable with this sequence of item presentation. Placing demographic and/or less threatening items first may help to gain the trust and confidence of the participant. It also may be helpful to the researcher to have some understanding of the participants being studied prior to covering more specific items. The more personal or more threatening items can then be placed near the end of the instrument.

If the researcher is not concerned that some items in the instrument might be offensive to or otherwise alienate participants, the specific-to-general sequence may be preferable. Then the most important and the most specific (to the study) items are placed first. The more general data (often, demographic information) can be secured at the end. An advantage of this sequencing pattern is that if the instrument is not fully completed, some of the more important data will still be available to the researcher.

**Instructions for Responding.**   In securing useful data, the wording of instructions is equally as important as the wording of the items themselves. Participants must understand how they are expected to respond to items. This seems self-evident; however, researchers frequently assume that the correct method to respond to items is as obvious to the participant as it is to them. Consequently, they fail to provide complete instructions for responding. If there are two or more distinct sections and/or question types used, separate instructions should be included directly above each section or question type.

**Length of the Instrument.**   The length issue is perhaps best addressed through use of common sense. As we suggested in Chapter 8, the longer the instrument, the less likely people are to complete it. The researcher needs to collect enough data to be able to answer research questions and/or to test hypotheses. Necessary items must be included, but unnecessary ones should be omitted. Frequently, the length of an instrument can be reduced through the elimination of demographic items that are not relevant to the focus of the research. As we indicated in Chapter 5, there is no such thing as a "usual" or standard group of demographic variables that must be included within every instrument.

**Presentation.** A self-administered data collection instrument should not appear crowded. Leaving adequate space for people to respond to items and not crowding questions together helps participants to complete it. In addition, instruments should be error free. The goal is to make their completion a pleasant (or at least a nonstressful) experience, so that a high percentage of fully completed responses will be received.

**Pilot Testing.** Even though the researcher may think that all of the preceding issues have been addressed, newly developed data collection instruments almost always produce some surprises. Not even very experienced researchers are able to anticipate just how items on a data collection instrument will be perceived or interpreted by the participant or how a participant might respond overall to the instrument. A panel of experts consisting of people very knowledgeable about instrument construction can provide good advice and suggestions. But what these individuals can contribute may be no substitute for the feedback provided by people like the research participants themselves. A pilot-testing of an instrument provides information on many different factors that relate to the quality of a data collection instrument. Feedback is likely to provide insights about the following:

- Clarity/misinterpretation of wording of items
- Juxtaposition of items that may bias measurement
- Potential offensiveness of items
- Redundancy that may annoy participants
- Indication that more structure is needed
- Indication that less structure is needed
- Time required to complete the instrument

Some of the preceding feedback can be gleaned from the way that the pilot study participants complete the instrument. Some of it may require one or more additional broad questions that are not a part of the measurement instrument per se. For example, the researcher might add an extra question—What parts of the instrument were difficult for you to complete and why?—and leave space for pilot study participants to write in whatever they may choose. Another good question is: Do you feel that the instrument gave you an opportunity to represent yourself accurately and, if not, why not? Such questions reflect an awareness of the possibility that the newly developed instrument may somehow lead participants to answer in certain ways or that questions or items that should have been included as part of the measurement process may have been inadvertently omitted. A good pilot test and the thoughtful revisions that it generates can result in fewer problems and better measurement when data are subsequently collected from research participants.

There is an ethical issue that often comes up when using people as participants in the pilot-testing of a data collection instrument. If no additional questions are added to the proposed instrument (that is usually a "giveaway"), participants might not be aware that they are not "real participants" unless they are told so. Should they be told why they are being asked to complete the data collection instrument or be allowed to misunderstand their role? To not tell them seems dishonest and deceptive, but to tell them may influence the seriousness with which they approach the task. Besides, in many instances, the pilot test includes giving participants the same introduction or cover letter that will be given to other participants, in order to see how effective it is. And that is almost certain to mislead them. Sometimes the data that pilot study participants provide can be aggregated along with that of other participants, thus avoiding the issue. But in other situations, the researcher must decide what is the most ethical way to approach it. It may entail telling participants in general terms what their role is, stressing the importance of their unique contribution to the research effort, and asking them if they still wish to participate in it.

## Use of Self-Administered Instruments

Self-administered data collection instruments are used when the primary purpose of the study is to gather descriptive data about research participants. They are commonly associated with one form of descriptive research: the mailed survey. In surveys, the researcher generally is interested in aggregating data about the characteristics, behaviors, feelings, attitudes, or opinions of a given population. The term *questionnaire* is widely applied to self-administered instruments when they are used in surveys.

Other types of knowledge building (besides surveys) also use self-administered instruments. They are used to collect data for all levels of research. Social work practitioners also use them to secure a measurement of some aspect of client functioning. For example, a clinician may wish to get an objective measure of the level of depression that clients are experiencing and may either find or develop a data collection instrument that clients can complete without any in-person instructions or supervision.

### Advantages of Self-Administered Instruments

Because they are highly structured, self-administered instruments have several advantages. They include the following:

- *Presence of the researcher is not required.* Once the instruments have been developed and distributed, the researcher is free to work on other research tasks while awaiting their return.
- *Responses and response categories can be precoded.* Analysis of the data is greatly facilitated when the researcher collects data that are presorted into computer-ready categories.
- *Data can be collected using fixed stimuli.* All participants are asked to respond to the same questions, worded in the same way. Thus, at least one aspect of data collection is standardized. This is especially important in quantitative studies.
- *There is the perception of anonymity.* Even though instruments may be precoded with identifying information, generally participants do not write their names anywhere on them. The appearance of anonymity (if not the reality of it) is thus maintained. This may increase participants' willingness to provide data. Most research that uses questionnaires for data collection reports data in aggregate form, at least enhancing confidentiality of responses. Participants can be reasonably confident that their individual responses cannot be attributed to them. This is an advantage to the researcher, both for securing truthful information and for increasing the likelihood of a larger percentage of completed questionnaires.

## Supervised Administration of Self-Administered Instruments

Many self-administered instruments combine the use of both fixed-alternative and open-ended items, and may also contain scales and/or indexes. They can be mailed to research participants who never see or meet the researcher. However, even when an instrument can be self-administered, there may be certain advantages for researchers to be present while it is being completed.

A major reason for supervising data collection either individually or in a group situation is a high rate of completion. If the researcher is present and distributes and collects the data collection instrument from participants, more fully completed instruments will be received than if the instrument were mailed out.

There are sometimes other reasons researchers wish to be present during data collection; for example, to clarify the intention of items or to observe whether the instruments were completed conscientiously or in a haphazard way. This latter determination would be impossible if data collection by mail were used.

Supervision of data collection may take place using an individual, one-on-one method. When data collection by individual participants is supervised, participants may be able to complete the instrument in their place of work, at home, or at some other place and time convenient for both the participant and the researcher. If so, appointments are made. When individual data collection is supervised, the participant receives the instrument and is asked to complete it. Once completed, it is either given directly to the researcher or placed in a sealed envelope or some other receptacle. Of course, participants are thanked for their contribution to the research. But other interaction with the researcher is limited to what is absolutely necessary to facilitate data collection. In this way, it is hoped that the data collected will be a response to the data collection instrument and not to the researcher. Of course, as we have suggested, just the researcher's physical presence may be enough to introduce error into the measurement process. This is especially likely to occur if the researcher already knows the research participant in some other capacity, for example, as a coworker or therapist.

Supervised individual completion of instruments can produce a high completion rate. But if comparisons of participants or hypothesis testing is part of the research design (as in most quantitative research), individualized data arrangements may not be desirable. Then the same setting should be used for data collection with all research participants. This ensures that the setting of data collection will not constitute an intervening variable.

The individual instrument administration method is very time consuming and expensive. Securing data from a large sample would be impractical. An alternative to the one-on-one, supervised method of data collection is instrument completion in a group setting. For example, the researcher might supervise the completion of an instrument by all members of a support group or by all participants in a workshop. Or a group consisting of the research sample might be constituted specifically for the purpose of data collection. When group supervision of data collection is used, instruments are distributed, participants complete them at their own pace or within a prescribed time limit, and they are collected. The major benefit of this kind of administration is efficiency—a large amount of data can be collected in a relatively short amount of time. Its relatively low cost and high rate of return are advantages that the researcher should consider when selecting a data-gathering method. However, like individually supervised completion of data collection instruments, the researcher's presence can still have the potential to influence the data received. In addition, responses may be influenced by the reactions (for example, anger, embarassment, boredom) of others in the room.

# Summary

In this chapter, we looked at data collection instruments as tools for use in data collection. Some variables can be measured with a single item or question. It can be either a fixed-alternative or open-ended item, depending on the specific data needs of the researcher. We discussed the use of other instruments that require many items to measure complex variables: indexes and scales. An overview of the most common types of scales was presented. Construction of indexes and scales was described as a highly complex process that generally is beyond the scope of a social work research study.

Issues in the use of existing instruments or of modifying those of others were presented. We examined many of the issues that must be addressed in constructing new instruments. Finally, the option of individual or group-supervised completion of self-administered data collection instruments (as opposed to use of the mail) was discussed. Group administration is more cost-efficient than individual supervised data collection, but when using either method, the researcher's presence can have the effect of biasing data that are collected.

# References

1. Miller, D. (1991). *Handbook of research design and social measurement.* Newbury Park, CA: Sage Publications.
2. *Standards for educational and psychological testing.* (1985). Washington, DC: American Psychological Association.
3. Nunnally, J. (1978). *Psychometric theory.* New York: McGraw-Hill.

# 12

# ANALYZING DATA AND DISSEMINATING FINDINGS

Data can take many forms. For example, in more qualitative studies data may take the form of audiotapes or videotapes of interviews, or field notes of interaction with participants. In secondary analysis, they may be completed data collection schedules compiled from case records or some other source. In meta-analysis, they may be the findings of many studies that examined a similar problem or question. Or, when a mailed survey method of data collection was used, they may consist of a stack of completed questionnaires.

No matter what form data assume, they must be organized, summarized, and analyzed, most frequently with the help of computer-assisted statistical analysis. Generally, we associate statistical analysis of data with more quantitative research methods. However, methods for statistical analysis of qualitative findings have also been developed. A number of software packages are now available to assist researchers in the tasks of classifying, ordering, and analyzing qualitative data.[1]

## The Data in Perspective

In order to begin to make sense of the data collected, it helps to first understand their source by asking certain questions. The answers to these questions and other related ones help to put any research findings in perspective. For example, if original data were collected from research participants,

- Who were they?
- Under what conditions did they provide data?
- What assurances about anonymity or confidentiality were given?
- What understandings did they have about how data would be used?
- What prior relationship, if any, did they have to the researcher?

- As a research sample, do they appear to be representative of the sampling frame or population from which they were drawn?
- Was the sample biased in some way?
- How might any possible bias affect the quality of the data?
- How much might sampling bias have affected the quality of the data, given the size of the sample?

When appropriate, a good place to start is to calculate the percentage of completed responses, also called *response rate*. This is done by dividing the actual number of cases for which there are reasonably complete data by the potential number of cases (all cases that the researcher sought to include in the sample). However, as we discussed in Chapter 9, whereas a high percentage of completed responses is more likely to produce a representative sample than a low response rate, even a high percentage of responses does not guarantee representativeness. Generally, it is also helpful to try to identify patterns of response. Certain questions can be helpful in this regard. For example,

- From among potential cases within the sample, which ones contain complete data and which do not?
- Do they differ in any meaningful way?
- If so, does this difference suggest the presence of a sampling bias that should be reported and discussed, or is the difference one that is probably unrelated to any research findings?

Most researchers summarize the most relevant characteristics of their data sources in a separate section of their reports. The summary helps both researchers and the readers of their reports to attempt to estimate whether their data sources were typical of the sample selected or the population or sampling frame from which they were drawn. If research participants provided the data, a description of them often is presented in group form; that is, as a broad demographic profile of who they were. Sometimes, a profile of a typical participant is provided.

A demographic profile of research participants can help the researcher put the findings of a research study into perspective. It can suggest their degree of external validity. For readers of a research report to be able to assess the relevance of the research findings to their own specific practice situations, a clear picture of those who provided data is necessary. For example, a report of a study based on a sample of low-income mothers needing assistance in developing parenting skills might include a demographic summary of the research participants in relation to the variables age, income, presence of a father or father figure, number of children, and degree of support from extended family. Readers of such a report can assess how closely the participants resembled their own clients and thus can help them determine whether the findings may be of relevance to them.

For similar reasons, researchers generally describe the setting in which the research was conducted. It allows readers of their reports (1) to judge to what degree the setting in which data were collected might have influenced findings and (2) in the case of organization-based research, to assess whether the nature of the organization in which the research took place (and its services) are similar enough to their own that the findings of the research may be helpful in informing their own practice in some way. For example, readers of a report who work in an outpatient clinic, where managed care limits reimbursement for services to only four treatment sessions, may quickly conclude that a research finding that individual treatment is more effective than group treatment is of little relevance to them. They would base this conclusion on the researcher's description, which states that the research was conducted in a private, inpatient psychiatric setting that offers primarily long-term intensive psychotherapy.

## Preparing for Statistical Analysis of Data

Prior to conducting statistical analysis and attempting to draw conclusions and findings from it, it is helpful to review the purpose of the study. It suggests the general type of statistical analysis that would be appropriate. For example, was the research designed to assess the effectiveness of various treatment interventions for addressing a problem that clients were experiencing? Or was it designed merely to describe the effects that the problem has on specific client groups? In the first instance, the researcher would be expected to conduct and report on statistical analysis that would provide evidence of the relative effectiveness of the various intervention methods. In the second, only statistical analysis that provides a clear description of the range of effects of the problems observed and some indication of their distribution within the research sample might be required.

The presence of still other research purposes would suggest other approaches to analysis of the data. For example, if the purpose of a study was to describe group performance before and after exposure to some independent variable, or to compare two or more groups in relation to some behavior or attitude, a statistical test that is especially well suited to accomplishing these tasks would need to be used. If the study's purpose was to determine to what degree several variables, viewed together, may explain or predict some problem or phenomenon, then a very different form of statistical analysis would be appropriate. Or if the purpose was to assess how effective an individual's or a program's intervention was, still other tests might be used.

A review of how research questions and hypotheses were stated can help a researcher in selecting the most appropriate method of statistical analysis. For example, sometimes questions are posed in such a way that it is clear that differences between or among groups are being sought; other times, it is clear that the degree of association or correlation between or among variables is being investigated.

There are a number of other interrelated issues associated with the choice of methods used to answer research questions and/or to seek statistical support for hypotheses. They require the researcher to recall and review many aspects of the research design that produced the research data. Once again, certain questions can be helpful. For example,

- Was the purpose of the research to generate knowledge for the profession or to evaluate individual or program effectiveness?
- If the former, what general category of sampling was used (probability or nonprobability)?
- How many samples or subsamples were used?
- How large was each sample?
- How (specifically) was each selected?
- Are the variables of interest believed to be normally distributed within the population, or is their distribution badly skewed?
- What levels of measurement were generated for each variable that will be used in statistical analysis?

## Statistical Analysis of Research Data: An Overview

An in-depth discussion of methods of statistical analysis is beyond the scope of this book. However, we will examine the conceptual underpinnings that are critical to understanding how statistical analysis is conducted and how it assists the researcher in drawing conclusions based on research data.

If the volume of data being analyzed is small and the type of statistical analysis that is to be performed is relatively simple, researchers sometimes choose not to use a computer to assist in data analysis. However, because of the many user-friendly statistical software packages[2] available for use with personal computers and because of easy access to mainframe computers, statistical analysis by hand has now become quite rare.

Complex statistical computations are performed flawlessly when a computer is used for data analysis, assuming that the data have been entered accurately and the appropriate method of statistical analysis has been selected. Probably, in the past, the most time-consuming step in statistical analysis has always been data entry. However, even this tedious operation may soon be eliminated as technology allows us to merely scan the data into a computer for analysis. Once data are entered into the computer, a wide variety of statistical analyses can be performed, each in just a matter of seconds. The results can be a real source of gratification to researchers who have been eagerly waiting to learn how their research turned out.

The ease with which statistical analysis can be performed by a computer represents both a bonanza and a danger for the researcher. Statistical tests that would have been outside the mathematical competence of many researchers just a few years ago are now possible for anyone with even average data-processing skills. However, because hundreds of different statistical analyses can be performed very easily and quickly, there is a real danger that either (1) findings will not be interpreted correctly by researchers or (2) they will be misleading to readers of research reports. Unfortunately, computer programs cannot always determine if a given statistical analysis has been used appropriately. They also cannot know whether a researcher has even a beginning understanding of how the results of statistical analysis should be interpreted in light of the research question or hypothesis. They cannot know how the nature and size of the sample that provided the data may have affected results. They also cannot warn the reader of a research report when a researcher has stumbled on a spurious (that is, not real) relationship between variables simply by trying an almost infinite number of combinations—something that is now quite easy to do because of the ease with which computer analysis of data can be performed.

There are a few basic understandings that are central to the successful use of statistical analyses by the researcher. We will present an overview of them in this text and suggest that they be studied in greater depth elsewhere.

## The Uses of Statistical Analysis

Researchers often use statistical analyses at several points in the research process to assist in decision making. They play an important role (1) in the design of research, (2) in summarizing the distribution of variables within research data, and (3) in drawing conclusions and interpretations about answers to research questions and the presence or absence of support for hypotheses. In this chapter, we will only briefly mention the first of these uses while focusing most of our discussion on the second and third.

**Designing Research.** Some statistical methods are very helpful to the researcher for making decisions related to the design of research. For example, statistical analyses can tell us when a sample is sufficiently large that the impact of sampling error is acceptably low, or they can tell us the mathematical probability that a selected sample is sufficiently representative of a known population in relation to some variable.[3] Statistical analyses also are used to help design and refine data collection instruments such as scales and indexes. They perform operations such as coefficient alpha to help assess the overall reliability of a data collection instrument. They also can be used to identify items in the instrument that appear to measure the same component of a variable, items that may be redundant or unnecessary, or that can be used to construct parallel forms of the instrument.

**Describing Distribution of Variables.** A second type of statistical analysis, descriptive statistical analysis, is used to provide a concise summary of data accumulated about and from those persons or cases that were studied.[4] When it is used, no attempt is made to imply that whatever was found to exist for cases in the sample would be true of other persons who were not a part of the research sample. We use descriptive statistical analyses (sometimes referred to as *data* *reduction*) simply to try to reduce large amounts of data to a manageable size, so that the researcher (or the reader of a research report) will be able to visualize the major characteristics of the participants and the data that they provided.

Descriptive statistical analyses may involve the construction of frequency distributions or graphs. A frequency distribution is a table displaying how many participants or cases fell in each value category or value (measurement) of a variable. The frequencies are displayed alongside the various value categories or values of the variable. Also, if the variable is at least ordinal level, frequency distributions may include additional columns for cumulative frequencies (how many cases had a measurement larger or smaller than a given value). Another column may reflect percentages of all cases represented by the cases in a given value category or what percentage of all cases had a measurement above or below a given value (cumulative percentages). Sometimes values are grouped; that is, ranges of values are used instead of individual values, in order to make a frequency distribution table smaller. When this is done, the researcher seeks to make the table simpler to understand without giving up too much detail.

Graphs also are frequently used to describe the distribution of variables within a sample or population of cases studied. They can be very simple or very complex. The simplest forms just portray the same data that is contained in frequency distributions; that is, the distribution of values of a variable. Some commonly used examples are bar charts, line diagrams, histograms, and pie charts. Bar charts and line diagrams use bars or lines of lengths that are proportional to the number of cases that possess a given measurement of a variable. Thus, for the variable number of children, if twice as many research participants had two children as had four children, the bar or line for the value 4 (children) would be half as long as the bar or line for the value 2 (children).

Histograms are graphs that portray the shape of the distribution of a variable. They can be created simply by connecting the tops of the lines or bars in a line diagram or bar chart to form a shape (a polygon). Then the overall distribution can be described in summmary form. For example, if the shape thus created is essentially bell-shaped, the variable is regarded as normally distributed within the sample or population that provided the data.

Pie charts use areas of a circle or some other figure to correspond to the percentage of all cases that were found to have a given measurement of a variable. If 20 percent of participants in a study had four children, a pie chart for the variable number of children could be constructed in which a slice that is 20 percent or 72 degrees (360 degrees × .20 = 72 degrees) of the "pie" would be labeled with the value 4. If 40 percent of participants had two children, the slice containing the value 2 would be twice as large—it would occupy 40 percent or 144 degrees of the pie (a circle) and so forth.

Another commonly used graph is a scattergram. Unlike the other graphs that we have described, it portrays the distribution of two variables simultaneously. Each dot on the graph represents a case and its measurement for each of two variables. The overall pattern of dots can be used to suggest whether the two variables may be correlated and, somewhat crudely, how strongly they may be correlated.

Another way of describing the distribution of a variable within a data set is to report what was found to be a typical value category or value among its measurements. Several different options are available for this purpose. They are collectively referred to as *measures of central tendency*. One or more measures of central tendency for variables of interest are computed and included in the research report. The most commonly used ones include the following:

1. The *mode* = the value category or value that had the largest frequency (occured most often) within the data
2. The *median* = the midpoint in a rank-ordered distribution of an ordinal-, interval-, or ratio-level variable
3. The *arithmetic mean* = the average of the values of all cases for an interval- or ratio-level variable

In describing the distribution of a data set, it is also helpful to describe to what degree cases were homogeneous (similar) in relationship to a variable and to what degree their value categories or values reflected heterogeneity (difference). Descriptive statistics (or parameters) that do this are collectively referred to as *measures of dispersion* (or measures of variability). When reported along with one or more measures of central tendency, they offer a fairly complete summary description of the distribution of a variable among cases in a research sample or population. Some of the more commonly used measures of dispersion are the range, interquartile range, variance, and standard deviation. Statistics books provide the formula for their computation, describe how they differ, and provide criteria for determining when each should be used.

**Answering Questions and Testing Hypotheses.**   When exploratory research designs or some forms of descriptive research are used, descriptive statistics are often all that we would expect to see in the research report. They provide exactly what we seek—a clear, easily comprehensible picture of something that we previously were unable to describe accurately. But in other research designs, such as descriptive research that seeks to document the existence of association or correlation between variables, and, of course, in explanatory research, the researcher generally wishes to do more than simply describe the characteristics of the participants. The existence of a relationship between variables has been predicted and stated as a hypothesis. A sample of research participants has been selected to represent members of the population, and they have been studied in some way to determine if there is support for the hypothesized relationship.

Perhaps, on first blush, there is an apparent relationship between variables—it can be seen within the data collected from the research sample. Is that sufficient proof of the relationship? Before researchers can conclude that a relationship is a real one that probably exists within the population from which the sample was drawn, they must be reasonably certain that something else did not cause the apparent relationship.

Let us consider a rather typical scenario in which there appears to be support for a researcher's hypothesis that an experimental treatment is more effective than a traditional one. Within the data collected from a sample of clients, the experimental intervention method seems to have produced better results than the traditional one. For example, researchers might have observed that one group of ten randomly selected alcoholic clients receiving an experimental counseling method reflected a 60 percent rate of treatment success (operationally defined as alcohol abstinence for one month), as compared with members of a control group who received the usual treatment and who reflected only a 40 percent success rate.

Suppose that the research was carefully designed and implemented. The researchers are reasonably confident that their design has good internal validity, that is, they are reasonably certain that something else besides the different treatments (the independent variable) did not cause the different results (the dependent variable). Another way of saying the same thing would be to say that "All threats to internal validity were adequately controlled." Does that mean that the relationship between the variables is a real one that exists beyond the sample? Not necessarily. What about sampling error? Wouldn't we expect to produce some difference in success rates with any two relatively small groups of clients selected randomly, even if the two treatment methods were really equally effective? Yes. Only sampling bias was controlled by randomization.

The question is: Is the difference in the success rates of the two groups of research participants (the experimental and control groups) large enough that it can safely be assumed that it is not simply the work of sampling error? Statistical analysis can determine how safe it would be to make generalizations about the relative effectiveness of the two treatments that would go beyond the participants in the current research. This third use of statistical analysis employs methods that are broadly referred to as *inferential statistical analysis.*

Using a theoretical concept called a *sampling distribution,* inferential statistical tests can tell the researcher the statistical probability that the apparent relationship between or among variables that can be seen in the research data is the work of sampling error or if it probably is indicative of a true relationship that exists within the population. They are based on mathematics and the laws of probability. They can tell us whether the difference between a 60 percent success rate and a 40 percent success rate using two groups of only ten participants each is really no big deal, that it is probably just the result of sampling error. Thus, inferential statistical analysis can be used to help us draw conclusions about the relative effectiveness of the treatment methods used in our hypothetical research example. Any one of several tests (there is usually one that is most appropriate) could be used to determine the exact probability that a 20 percent difference in success rate would occur with two subsamples of ten cases drawn at random just because of sampling error. If statistical analysis can successfully discredit it as a likely explanation for the apparent relationship between treatment and success rate among our research participants, we would be able to conclude that the relationship might be a real one.

Most of the time, being more than 95 percent certain that an apparent relationship within a research sample is not the work of sampling error is good enough for researchers to claim support for a relationship between variables. (As we noted in Chapter 1, all scientific knowledge is tentative anyway.) Of course, as in our example, reseachers also must be reasonably certain that the threats to internal validity have been adequately controlled by the research design.

When inferential statistical analysis demonstrates that the probability of sampling error's having produced an apparent relationship between variables is less than one time in twenty (referred to as $p < .05$), we customarily describe the relationship between variables as *statistically significant* (see Figure 12.1). Of course, the researcher may (with justification) set the level of statistical significance at some other level (referred to as a *rejection level* or *alpha level*), such as .025, .01, or even .001. If so, statistical significance would require demonstration that the likelihood of chance's having produced the apparent relationship between variables is less than the level selected.

It is possible to imply whether a statistically significant relationship was found to exist without actually using the words *statistically significant*. For example, in a report, a researcher might summarize the findings of a study simply by stating, "Among low-income women without extended family support, women who used casework services were more likely to possess a higher level of awareness of the medical needs of infants than those who did not use casework services. However, clients who used casework services were no more likely to use outpatient medical facilities for their babies' treatment than those participants who did not receive casework services."

It is important that we not make too much of a finding of statistical significance. First of all, as we have suggested, a finding of statistical significance, like all of the findings of scientific inquiry, is only a tentative conclusion based on reasonable certainty. It says only that sampling error is a very unlikely explanation of the apparent relationship between or among variables that occurred among cases that were studied. It never totally rules it out.

## FIGURE 12.1  Statistical Significance: What It Is and What It Is Not

*It is* mathematical evidence, based on the laws of probability, that the relationship between or among variables within a sample is very unlikely to be the work of sampling error (chance).

*It is not* 100 percent proof that the relationship within the sample was not the work of sampling error.

*It is not* 100 percent proof that the variables are related.

*It is not* proof that something else (some threat to internal validity) did not cause the relationship.

*It is not* proof that the relationship is necessarily a strong one.

*It is not* proof that the relationship is necessarily a meaningful one.

As we also suggested, even if there is a statistically significant relationship between variables, a true relationship between them or an important one still may not exist. A finding of statistical significance says nothing about the other possible causes of the apparent relationship within the research sample (besides a true relationship) that might make the dependent and independent variables appear to be related. For example, some other variable or variables or a badly biased sample may have produced it.

Sometimes, statistically significant relationships between or among variables that are not the work of sampling bias or any of the other threats to internal validity are real. But they still are not terribly valuable! They reflect real relationships, but they are relationships between or among variables that are virtually worthless because they are not very strong.[5] This phenomenon is especially likely if the researcher is using relatively large research samples. Statistical significance is achieved quite frequently and easily if very large samples are used. But statistical significance thus achieved may be of limited or no practical value to the social work practitioner. Researchers can minimize the likelihood of achieving significance when the relationship between variables is so weak as to be meaningless if they use a sample that does not exceed the size recommended for a given type of statistical analysis. The choice of statistical analysis to be used relates to the issue of practical application. A good question to ask is: If a relationship between variables is found, how strong would the relationship have to be, to be considered meaningful?

Finally, meaningless statistical significance also is sometimes achieved even when the recommended sample size is used and the analysis is performed correctly. The problem is, the research finding is nothing new or unexpected! This occurs fairly frequently when tests are used to determine if a correlation between two variables is probably a real one. Some correlations are valuable; but many others are not, even if they are real. For example, among a group of human service organization clients, we could almost certainly demonstrate a statistically significant positive correlation between income and the amount of money spent on social activities. But would such a finding be valuable? It is highly predictable, because one generally has to have money (or at least good credit) to spend it. Besides, would the finding help us to be more effective in our intervention with human service organization clients? Probably not.

All statistical tests have assumptions that underlie their use. These assumptions should be carefully reviewed and understood. Even the selection of a frequency distribution, graph, or other descriptive statistic to report central tendency or dispersion is not always simple. It requires that the researcher be knowledgeable about rules and conditions that must be met. It also requires an ethical commitment to portray the distribution of variables as accurately as possible. As we all know, it is very easy to lie with statistics by selecting a type of analysis that portrays the data the way we want them to look. There also are certain situations in which the usual requirements for the use of a statistical test ethically can be ignored. In order to understand the assumptions of a test and select an appropriate one, a statistics text or a statistician should be consulted.

Fortunately, even the process of selecting the correct statistical analyses is becoming easier thanks to advances in computer technology. Software packages are now available that use a series of questions to help the researcher narrow down the list of analyses that might be appropriate for a given situation. However, even they require a good conceptual understanding of statistical analyses and research design.

## Interpreting and Reporting the Results of Statistical Analysis

Once statistical analyses have been performed, the results still must be interpreted by the researcher. Any limitations of the methods of statistical analysis used should be identified and interpreted as to their possible effects.

The results are first examined in relation to the focus of the research. What do the results suggest about the answer to the research question or questions? What do they indicate about any hypotheses? Were they supported? If so, what does that mean? If not, how could the researcher's prediction have been wrong? How can the results of statistical analyses be used to better understand the research problem or even to suggest effective prevention or intervention methods for alleviating it? What are the implications for the social work practitioner who is seeking to provide better social work services?

The statistical analysis of research data generates many different findings. Often they can be interpreted in a variety of ways. The specific meaning of the results of each individual statistical analysis must be ascertained. This often requires researchers to make use of their practice experience. It also often requires them to look again at the relevant literature in an attempt to reconcile their findings with those of other researchers. Eventually, they must use their best judgment, knowing that they might be wrong in their interpretations.

When research participants provide data, it is often a good idea to build into the research design a strategy for early feedback of study results to participants and their communities. Researchers can share major study findings with study participants and their communities (in nontechnical language) and enlist their help in interpretation. This occurs before publication of the results in formal reports or scholarly journals. There are several advantages to doing this, especially in cross-cultural research. First, people who know the community well offer a unique perspective on a study's findings. They can often suggest differences in interpretation that might never occur to the researcher. They can also help to determine how best to use the study findings to address community concerns and problems. Finally, sharing the data prior to dissemination to the professional community reinforces the notion of partnership in the research enterprise and communicates respect for study participants and the communities they represent.

Interpreting research findings is not easy. For example, how do we interpret the descriptive finding that adolescents have such widely differing attitudes toward the use of contraception to prevent unwanted pregnancies? Or that the staff perceives a program to be highly successful while community leaders express resentment about it? Or that a software program that is used to perform content analysis of transcribed conversations with college students shows that anti-Semitic attitudes still persist among them? Or that a test of statistical significance supports a hypothesis that two groups of research participants really are different in relation to some variable? Or that another statistical finding that one variable really is associated with another in some consistent pattern? Does it suggest that the predictor variable really is contributing to variations in the criterion variable? Is the strength of the correlation really all that strong?

Because of the difficulty of drawing definitive conclusions from research data, researchers sometimes simply report findings, suggest several possible interpretations, and let the readers of their report draw their own conclusions. When inferential statistical analysis has been used, both findings of statistically significant relationships between variables and findings of nonsignificance can be equally valuable to readers. Both should be reported.

## Disseminating Research Knowledge

A major reason for conducting research is to contribute to the social work knowledge base. In order for this to occur, research findings must be interpreted and communicated to interested audiences. As we have emphasized throughout this text, the researcher has an obligation to the research and practice communities to communicate the results of research to those individuals who can use it to improve their work. All research findings from soundly designed and implemented research are potentially valuable to others. For example, even the finding that "No support was found for a relationship between type of treatment and treatment effectiveness" can help other researchers to avoid the mistake of believing and acting on an erroneous belief that one treatment method is superior to another. It can help practitioners to avoid believing what logically ought to be true, but is not. Thus, it can help them to make better decisions.

There are many vehicles that can be used to share research findings. We will mention some of the more commonly used ones.

### Reports and Monographs

If research is sponsored (funded) by some organization or if it is designed to meet a graduate degree requirement, it is expected that it will be written using a fairly standardized format and bound. The written report generally is quite lengthy. In the case of funded research, the report may be distributed to interested parties in what is generally referred to as a *research monograph*. If the research was a degree requirement, it may be called a *thesis* (master's degree) or a *dissertation* (doctorate). The report is placed in the library of the university where the student completed the degree. It is also made available to others through interlibrary loan systems in either hard copy or via electronic communication. Whatever its distribution and no matter what it may be called, a complete research report provides a detailed description of the entire research process, including the methods used. Sufficient information is offered so that readers can either replicate the research and/or evaluate whether the researcher's conclusions and recommendations appear to be justified and appropriate for implementation in their own practice.

Usually, there are eight sections to a research report. Sometimes two or more are combined, but the researcher is expected to provide sufficient detail about each of the eight areas. Although the reports of qualitative studies vary somewhat from the reports of more traditional quantitative studies, they still tend to follow the same general format. At this point in our discussion of social work research methods, the components of the research report should seem very predictable and familiar. They should serve to summarize much of the content in earlier chapters.

1. *Introduction.* The historical background of the study is described, and the origin of the researcher's interest in the topic may be noted. The research problem is specified and a description of its scope and its significance is stated and documented. The broad research question that was the focus of the study is stated.
2. *Review of the Literature.* A summary and synthesis of literature relevant to the research question is presented. The literature assembled is used to summarize what is already known about the research question and to identify how the current research study promised to build on and extend the knowledge previously available. It provides the rationale for research hypotheses and/or more specific research questions, and for the design of the research.
3. *Statement of Research Questions and Hypotheses.* Related to the purpose of the study and following logically from the review of the literature, a specific set of research questions and/or hypotheses that were examined are stated. Operational definitions of key terms (also derived from the review of literature) may be included here, or they may appear early in the next section.
4. *Methodology.* A detailed description of the research design is presented. It includes the methods of selection of research participants or objects that were studied and, frequently, the rationale for that method. Methods for conducting measurements of key variables are described, including a discussion of the selection and/or development of any data collection instruments that were used. The methodology section reports in detail what was done, to whom or what, and by what method(s). The rationale for all major methodological decisions is presented (sampling, measurement, data collection methods, and choice of methods for statistical analysis). The section enables the reader of the report both to assess the credibility of the researcher and the research findings and to replicate the research, if desired.

5. *Results.* The principal findings derived from the research are presented. Outcomes of statistical analysis are summarized and interpreted. The findings section generally contains tables, graphs, or other methods of summarizing the results of analyses to help the reader to visualize what was found. In qualitative research, the findings section is likely to contain case vignettes; long, verbatim quotations, or other formats containing data derived directly from research participants.

6. *Discussion, Conclusions, and Implications.* The findings are discussed in relation to the research questions and/or hypotheses. Answers to questions are proposed, and, if applicable, evidence of support or nonsupport for hypotheses is presented. Findings are also discussed in relation to the literature. Findings that corroborate those of other researchers and theoreticians are identified, and findings that conflict with what has been reported elsewhere in the literature are discussed and, where appropriate, reconciled. The implications of the findings for social work practice are an especially important component of this section of the research report. In qualitative research, this section may contain a theory or hypothesis that may later be tested by researchers using more quantitative methods.

7. *Limitations.* Shortcomings of the design are discussed. No research is perfect—all research tends to be limited somewhat by one or more design constraints. For example, an explanatory design may contain inherent problems because of the ethical impossibility of using a control group or because of the researcher's need to draw a sample from a sampling frame rather than from the total population. Limitations also can result as a function of other methodological difficulties, such as the need to use a data collection instrument that had not yet been demonstrated to be reliable with the participants used in the research or because of constraints on the kinds of data that could be collected. There are many issues in research that prevent studies from being designed or executed flawlessly. The reader requires an honest description of these limitations to know how to interpret and evaluate findings. A useful format for the discussion of each major limitation consists of (1) a specific description of the nature and scope of the limitation; (2) an explanation of why the limitation was unavoidable; (3) the researcher's speculation on how the limitation may have negatively affected the research and its findings; (4) a description of what, if anything, was done to minimize the potential negative effects of the limitation on the research; and (5) an assessment of how successful the effort was.

8. *Conclusions and Recommendations.* A description of how the study is believed to have advanced knowledge in the problem area is presented. The researcher also identifies needs for further research and suggests ways in which it might be designed and implemented both to build on the achievements of the current research and to avoid its shortcomings. Generally, the researcher also makes specific suggestions as to how the findings might be implemented to improve the delivery of services to social work clients; that is, what changes in intervention methods appear to be indicated based on the findings of the study.

## *Internal Correspondence and In-Service Training*

There are many reasons why one may choose to disseminate research findings through internal correspondence or in-service training sessions. For example, research studies with limited external validity, research on unique client populations, or unreplicated evaluation studies all may be appropriately disseminated through mechanisms internal to the organization. Many organizations, particularly larger ones, have monthly or semiannual newsletters. Their editors are looking for materials to include. As vehicles to disseminate research findings, these outlets have several advantages for researchers. When they submit a summary of their research (emphasizing its findings) to the editor of such a publication, it is almost certain to be published, especially if an inquiry to see what form it should take has been made in advance. If published, the summary is very likely to be read because staff members generally like to read about what is going on in their work setting. In addition, the findings will be read and put to use with only minimal time lag following completion of the research.

If the researcher's organization also has a program of regular in-service training or staff development, such a forum can also be a good place to disseminate the results of research. Some organizations prefer to do this informally, for example a voluntary-attendance, brown bag lunch program where staff take turns leading discussions about various work-related issues. This type of program attracts those who have a genuine interest in a researcher's findings and produces a likelihood that findings will be disseminated quickly and put to use.

## *Major Conference Presentations*

Research findings of a more general interest can be disseminated through presentations at professional conferences and symposia. As we observed earlier in Chapter 4, many national and international social work organizations—for example, NASW, American Public Welfare Association, Child Welfare League of America, CSWE, The International Federation of Social Workers, and the Group for Human Services Technology Applications (HUSITA)—hold conferences at various locations throughout the United States and (in some instances) the world. Some of them sponsor conferences that may be more geographically limited or more narrowly focused, such as conferences relating specifically to services to people with HIV infections, family support and preservation programs, long-term care, family violence, homelessness, or some other specialization within social work. In addition, there are still more (hundreds) of other major conferences in related fields, such as psychology, sociology, public health, public administration, or education, that are held regularly or sporadically and that generally include presentations that are of multidisciplinary interest.

The largest and most prestigious conferences usually solicit proposals and abstracts for presentations about a wide range of topics that are loosely related to a theme. A "call for abstracts" or "call for proposals" and a deadline for their receipt is published in professional journals or newsletters, or mailed to the organization's members along with advertisements for the conference. Typically, a prospective presenter is asked to write a brief overview and/or abstract of what is to be presented and to indicate in which area of the program it would best fit. Many major conferences now have a separate grouping for proposals for presentations that are empirically based and another for those that are more conceptual or theoretical in nature. Proposals for presentations of research generally are expected to follow an outline that is provided—usually a miniversion of a traditional research report—plus descriptions of the methods for presentation. The author may be asked to indicate those individuals who would be most likely to benefit from and be interested in the presentation. The presentation overview or abstract itself generally does not include any identifying information, thus allowing it to be reviewed anonymously. A separate or detachable cover page usually is required. It includes the proposed presenter's name and affiliation, phone number, fax number, and other identifying information.

Generally, the major conference planning committees receive many more proposals for presentations than there are places for them on the program. It is not unusual for a major conference to accept only 10 or 20 percent of all proposals received. The review process takes time. Often there is about six months between the proposal's receipt (acknowledged on a postage-paid card supplied by the proposer) and notification of a decision by the planning committee.

The major conferences tend to use a large number of volunteer reviewers. A proposal may be read anonymously by two or three professional peers who provide a numerical rating on a scale devised by the conference planning committee. The system is likely to give points for such criteria as the proposal's relevance to the conference theme, the potential interest of conference participants in the topic, the quality of the research described, or how well the proposal is written or conforms to guidelines. The review criteria to be used usually are listed in the call for abstracts.

All proposers are notified at the same time of the decision of the planning committee. Those who are invited to present are asked to respond in writing whether or not they can commit to attend. Audiovisual equipment can be requested, if needed, usually at some cost to the presenter, or what is needed sometimes can be brought from home.

Presentations can take a number of different forms. A researcher may be asked to write and present a formal paper, leaving time for discussion and questions from those in attendance. Although it is possible to simply read the paper, this is not very enjoyable for anyone involved and is now rarely done. The single-paper presentation is less popular today than it once was. Now it is more common to group two or three related papers in one session where each individual has an allotted period of time to present. A moderator introduces the presenters, monitors the time, and generally makes sure that all presenters are treated equitably. Presenters offer a brief overview of their work, usually in an informal manner. Especially in international conferences, presenters tend to use slides or computer-assisted presentation methods such as PowerPoint. If these aids are not used, handouts summarizing major findings for those in attendance usually are expected.

Another format is the poster session. It is similar to how high school students showcase their research in science fairs (only without the seedlings, household products, or batteries!). The presenter is located in a large hall with many others who are also there to present and discuss their work. Typically, they are provided with a mobile display board to visually exhibit their research methods and findings. Conference attendees come by to talk with them about their research.

No matter which type of presentation method is used, presenters generally are expected to pay for travel expenses, and accommodations or to get their employers to pay for them. Only invited speakers and those who give keynote addresses are usually reimbursed for expenses by the conference sponsor. Some conferences provide a reduced registration fee for those who are presenting; some do not even offer that.

Presentations at major conferences, particularly those that report on research, can be good public relations for organizations and universities. Thus, professional travel assistance from one's employer may be forthcoming, depending on available funds and policies. If the research was funded by some outside source, there may be money for knowledge dissemination at conferences in the grant that funded it.

Even if presenting at a major conference costs the researcher some money, the expenditure may be justified and productive. It can be intellectually stimulating to discuss your research with colleagues, some of whom invariably challenge some aspect of the research design and/or question the findings and recommendations. Those individuals who choose to attend a researcher's presentation generally have shared interests and may even be doing research in the same problem area. Opportunities to share findings and even to collaborate in some future research project can develop. In addition, a researcher learns a great deal about research from attending others' presentations.

The presentation of research at a prestigious conference can enhance a social work career. This is especially true for academicians or for those who work for research-oriented organizations such as teaching hospitals. In addition, continuing education units (CEUs) can be obtained and applied to help meet state licensure requirements. Because major conferences also tend to be held in interesting places, there are also opportunities for sightseeing and recreation. Attending them can be just plain enjoyable.

Many conferences also help with the dissemination of research knowledge in another way. Presentations or a summary of them often are put together in audiotape or monograph form and are sold (or sometimes distributed at no charge) to members who either attended the conference or were unable to attend. If the sponsoring organization has its own professional journal or journals, presenters may be asked to submit (for publication consideration) a paper based on their presentation.

## Other Professional Gatherings

There are many other smaller conferences—for example, local and regional meetings—where researchers also can disseminate the results of their research.

Getting on the program of, for example, a state NASW symposium or regional conference may be a less prestigious achievement than presenting at a major national or international conference. However, especially if the findings are primarily of local interest, a local or regional conference may be the perfect vehicle to share newly acquired knowledge.

Local and regional meetings have certain advantages. They generally are less expensive to attend than the major national ones. Costs associated with presentation (travel, registration fees, lodging, and so forth) tend to be lower at smaller conferences that have fewer attendees and that are held in less exotic locales. Opportunities to meet and network with fellow professionals may be better in some respects. At local and regional conferences, researchers can interact with those individuals whose help may be valuable for meeting daily job responsibilities or for acquiring needed support for future research projects. In addition, most of the other benefits available at major conferences are also available at local or regional ones.

## Publication in Professional Journals

The most traditional and a potentially effective way to disseminate research knowledge is through the publication of an article in a professional journal. On the surface, we might think that a published article will ensure that one's findings will be widely disseminated and used. Not necessarily. A few such journals have very wide circulations, but most do not. Besides, there is no way to know if, just because someone receives a copy of a journal, a given article in it will be read. As we observed in Chapter 1, many social work practitioners tend not to read and use reports of research within the professional literature.

Despite the fact that publication of the results of research does not guarantee that they will be read, publication means that, at least potentially, the results can be read by many others. Professional journals are purchased by libraries, where they are available to students, scholars, and researchers to use in the development of their research literature reviews and thus in their own research on a problem. They remain available for use for many years, long after a conference presentation has been forgotten.

Getting an article published in a professional journal can be a very tedious, time-consuming, and sometimes frustrating experience. Many more prospective articles are submitted than are accepted for publication. It is not easy to publish in the most prestigious and widely read journals. Many people want to publish in them. Academicians want and sometimes even need to be published in them to maintain or advance their careers. Thus, they publish only a small percentage of articles submitted for publication. In contrast, some of the more narrowly focused and less well known journals may accept up to 50 percent of articles submitted, or even more.

There are good reference books available to help prospective authors find the journals most likely to publish a report of their work.[6] Colleagues who have been published (especially academicians) often are another good resource.

Many journals have printed pamphlets or fliers that explain the procedure for submission of an article for publication; others describe the procedure in each issue of the journal. The procedures are more alike than dissimilar. Those that use a "blind review procedure" use a group of consulting editors (usually relatively accomplished academicians and other professionals who serve limited terms). They have agreed to anonymously read those articles that appear to have some publication potential or, in some cases, all articles submitted. Two or three reviewers, selected by the editor based on their expertise or interest in the topic of an article, read and critique the article and recommend to reject it, revise it, or accept it as is. The final decision, however, generally remains with the editor, a small committee, or an editorial board.

Often, a journal editor provides the writer with anonymous feedback from those who reviewed the article. Even if the article is rejected outright, suggestions for improving it may still be made. It is fairly common for reviewers to read an article, see publication potential in it, and then recommend specific revisions. When this occurs, authors are provided with the suggestions and asked to reply indicating whether they plan to revise their article as suggested by a certain date and resubmit it. Resubmission following revision is no guarantee that an article will be accepted, but if conscientious revisions were made as requested, acceptance is fairly likely.

An article should be sent to only one journal at a time. Anything else is considered unethical. Most journals use volunteer, unpaid reviewers who give of their time as a service to their profession. It would be a major imposition for an author to send an article to several different journals simultaneously, perhaps getting it accepted by two or more. Because only one ultimately can publish it, the reviewers from the other journals would have wasted their time reviewing and critiquing it. However, once one journal indicates that an article has been refused, it is ethical to send it elsewhere. It is not unusual for an article to be rejected by several journals until finally accepted by one.

Although the quality of the article and of the research methods employed are major considerations in whether an article is accepted for publication, luck and timing also play roles. For example, assuming that the article is a good one or has the potential to be, its acceptance may depend in part on when it is submitted to a journal. Its chances are enhanced if it arrives when the journal needs another article to complete an upcoming issue. If the journal already has accepted but not published some other article on a similar topic or issue, that could be fortuitous, or it could work against the researcher. The journal may decide to accept the article along with the previously accepted one, to complement it or even to make the topic the focus of a special issue including still other articles related to the same problem area. But the other, already-accepted article on the issue or topic may also work to the researcher's detriment. The editor may decide that the article that the researcher submitted, although otherwise publishable, is simply not needed.

There are intrinsic rewards for having an article published in a professional journal. There is something very gratifying about seeing it in print and perhaps cited in someone else's work, and to at least be able to hope that it is being read, appreciated, and used by others. But journals do not pay authors for their articles when they publish them; in fact, publishing an article can be expensive (the costs of postage, word processing, and photocopying). Unfortunately, publication in journals also does not promote rapid dissemination of research findings. Getting an article accepted can take a year or more. Once accepted, it may not be published for another year or two. Despite these disadvantages, publication of one's research methods and findings in a professional journal probably remains the most generally accepted acknowledgment that a researcher has met an obligation to the scientific community.

# Summary

Chapter 12 described the processes involved in analyzing research findings and disseminating them so that they can be used to inform practice. Some of the more commonly used methods of data reduction (frequency distributions and graphs, measures of central tendency and dispersion) were described. It was emphasized that the researcher has an obligation to accurately describe the research sample or population from which data were collected. Results of descriptive statistical analysis usually are reported to portray participants' relevant demographic characteristics.

If hypothesis testing is undertaken (as is the case in most quantitative studies), inferential statistical analysis of data is undertaken to determine the likelihood that sampling error may have produced a relationship between variables within a research sample. An overview of both the theoretical underpinnings and the limitations of statistical testing was presented. The limited meaning of statistical significance was discussed. It was explained how, in some situations, a finding of a statistically significant relationship between variables may be of little practical value. All statistical tests of significance have assumptions; they must be understood by the researcher so that an appropriate test can be selected and used.

The eight sections of a typical research report were described. The research report or monograph was proposed as just one vehicle that researchers use to communicate research findings to interested audiences. Other alternatives for research dissemination that were discussed are internal correspondence and in-service training, major conference presentations, other professional gatherings, and publication in professional journals.

# References

1. See, for example, Tesch, R. (1991). Computer programs that assist in the analysis of qualitative data: An overview. *Qualitative Health Research, 1*(3), 309–325.

2. See, for example, Statistical Package for the Social Sciences, SPSS, Inc. (1994). *Base system user's guide.* Chicago, IL: SPSS.
3. Sudham, S. (1976). *Applied sampling.* New York: Academic Press.
4. Weinbach, R., & Grinnell, R. (2001). *Statistics for social workers* (5th ed.). Needham Heights, MA: Allyn & Bacon.
5. Weinbach, R. (1989). When is statistical significance meaningful? A practice perspective. *Journal of Sociology and Social Welfare, 16,* 31–38.
6. See, for example, NASW Press Staff. (1997). *An author's guide to social work journals* (4th ed.). Washington, DC: NASW Press; or Beebe, L. (1993). *Professional writing for the human services.* Washington, DC: NASW Press.

# EVALUATION RESEARCH

# 13

# EVALUATING PROGRAMS

The qualitative and quantitative research methods that we have described to this point are probably best known for their ability to contribute to our professional knowledge base. Fortunately, these same proven methods are equally effective for a second important activity: providing feedback on the effectiveness of our practice interventions. This is the area of evaluation research that we have frequently referred to in earlier chapters.

Evaluation research can be defined as "any research designed and implemented to evaluate the effectiveness of some form of social work practice." It might also be helpful here to recall that practice consists of both programs and services. Programs (and methods for evaluating them) are the focus of this chapter. In the next chapter, we will examine useful methods for evaluating the effectiveness of services.

Programs are subunits of organizations, constructed in a unique way to address some social program. They are more or less self-contained. What they hope to accomplish should be consistent with the organization's mission and its vision statement. However, programs generally have their own goals, objectives, policies, rules, procedures, strategies, services, staff, budget, space, and so forth, which may differ from those elsewhere in the organization.

For social workers, the pressure to evaluate the effectiveness of programs is increasing. Many of these pressures come from those who finance them. Taxpayers and people who contribute to umbrella organizations such as United Way want to know if their contributions are producing desired results. Managed care and other efforts to reduce the cost of human services are increasing the need to demonstrate that what we do really works. Consumers (clients) also are among those who have a legitimate concern about the usefulness of programs in which they participate.

Conscientious professionals have still another reason for evaluating programs. It goes beyond the need to be accountable to those who often pay our salaries. We want and need to know whether the programs we provide are effective. If they are, we want to do more of whatever it is that works. If they are not, we need to know why and to find other, more effective methods to use.

## What Is Program Evaluation?

Program evaluation is applied research; that is, research designed to accomplish some task rather than to simply build knowledge. The task of program evaluation is to test the theoretical models that underlie social programs. Most programs "sound good"—they seem like they ought to get under way easily and accomplish their objectives. But a program that sounds good "in theory" may not be what is actually needed in the real world.

Program evaluation occurs at all stages of program development. It occurs when programs are in the planning or formulation stage. Then the goal of the research is to accurately describe the need for a program and to tailor the program to meet that need. Once programs are underway, other forms of program evaluation look at how well a program has been implemented. Still other forms of program evaluation look at accountability issues—How well did the program achieve its objectives? The results of these evaluations are often used for making decisions about whether a program should be continued, modified, or terminated.

Although program evaluations can be undertaken at any time in the life cycle of a program, certain events often precipitate them. For example, a politically prominent critic of the program may have questioned the need for the program, professionals or clients may have exposed doubt about its effectiveness, or a funding organization may have determined that extended funding will not be offered until it has demonstrated its ongoing accountability.

Not all program evaluations occur because of pressure from some outside force or the concern of those critical of a program. Program evaluations are also internally driven. An ongoing monitoring of a program by its own staff is often an important part of good program management.

Program evaluation is an important and specialized research enterprise. There are individuals who specialize in it, and there are many books and articles that focus on it.[1] They go into great detail about the specific methods for conducting it. In this text, we will focus on developing a good general understanding of what program evaluation is, what different focuses it can assume, and how it relates to our discussion of social work research in earlier chapters.

Program evaluation seeks to improve the quality of social programs. The programs may be involved in social action, prevention, treatment, or any other form of intervention that improves human conditions.

Program evaluation is a relatively new form of research, first receiving widespread attention after World War II. The need for it became especially great in the 1970s and 1980s, when conservative government leaders carried through on election promises to take a careful (some would say hypercritical) look at social programs that were accused of having failed to solve problems like poverty, unemployment, delinquency, and substance abuse. Other constituencies also began to voice demands for accountability at about the same time. Members of the general public contribute financial support to many human service organizations through tax revenues. They wanted to know how their taxes were being spent, and they sought documentation of the success of social programs that they were supporting. The consumer movement that surfaced in the 1960s and 1970s also produced another group of people—clients—who wanted proof that programs were accomplishing their objectives. Even helping professionals themselves began to recognize the importance of evaluating the success of programs. Faced with threatened and real funding cutbacks, they sought methods to help them to use limited resources in the most economical and productive ways.

At the time when demands for program evaluation first began to occur, social workers were fearful that it would result in a loss of many valuable programs. Although some programs were lost, the fears proved to be mostly unfounded. By now we have become quite comfortable with program evaluations as a part of responsible practice. We recognize both their necessity and their value. We recognize that many programs within human service organizations receive funding through grants and contracts with government organizations and private charitable organizations, and we acknowledge that these organizations have a right to know if the money that they provide is being used productively. We are no longer surprised that almost all such agreements now require that the recipient provide a rigorous evaluation of the way that monies are spent and some documentation of a program's success. Besides, if a program is not effective, we would like to know it anyway, so that we can revise it or drop it and spend our time and energy on some other program with greater success potential.

## Planning/Evaluation Models

Programs occur (or should occur) as a response to a perceived need. They are a response to a problem. Thus, there is a certain logical sequence that is common to program evaluation models.

Many models of program evaluation have been developed. One of the best known of these is the rational planning model,[2] which was conceptualized by Robert Mayer. The model describes nine interrelated phases that summarize the major tasks associated with program planning and evaluation. The model suggests a linear process; that is, one that emphasizes the accomplishment of a series of sequential tasks. On more careful examination, however, it can be observed that some of these tasks can be conducted simultaneously; others are closely linked to previous tasks.

First, a needs assessment study should be conducted to better understand the nature of the problem that the proposed program seeks to address. In response to the findings of a needs assessment, proposed program goals are revised; that is, planners of a proposed program reconsider what general outcomes are sought.

As a result of both analysis of needs assessment data and the establishment of program goals, specific program objectives are articulated. Once objectives are articulated, various program alternatives are designed. They are supposed to contribute to the achievement of these objectives. The possible consequence of each program alternative is anticipated, for example, "If we do this, then such and such may occur." Ultimately, one program alternative is selected for implementation, and subsequently its success is evaluated. These evaluation data are used as feedback to the planning process. Whatever data are learned about the program and about program outcomes are used as input into the ongoing planning/evaluation process.

When conceptualized in this fashion, program evaluation becomes an integral component in the ongoing activities of program planning and implementation. It is not merely a research activity that seems tacked on at the conclusion of a program.

While the planning/evaluation process is continuous, there are three identifiable stages within it. They are referred to as (1) needs assessment, (2) program implementation, and (3) program outcomes. We will examine each of them in the sequence in which they occur.

## Needs Assessment

In the broadest sense, the purpose of a needs assessment is to determine by objective methods if a program that is being considered is really needed or if an existing program is still needed. Typically, a needs assessment defines the problem of concern, describes actual conditions and how they differ from what is desired, identifies unmet needs, and diagnoses the obstacles that might prevent a program from being effective in meeting them.

What type of questions does a researcher try to answer in conducting a needs assessment? The most basic question is: Is the problem that we think exists a real one? Documentation of the existence of a problem, whom it affects, its magnitude, the forms that it takes, and the costs that result from it are extremely useful for the program planner or administrator.

A second question to be asked is: What services are needed to address the problem? Also, because we know that simply offering relevant services within a program does not guarantee the program's success, another question must be answered: Which of these services would be likely to be used, and to what degree? Corollary questions are: What are the potential sources of resistance to use of services? How can services be offered to increase the likelihood that they will be fully used? and How might offering the program affect other programs within the organization and outside of it?

Accurate answers to these and other related questions are absolutely essential if the findings of a needs assessment are to have value. A needs assessment can be a valuable planning tool, or if it contains major design flaws, it can be a real liability to the achievement of the goals of a program. A poor needs assessment is worse than none at all. It can mislead an administrator into making decisions based on an inaccurate reading of the environment for a program. Poor decisions will occur. Valuable resources will be misdirected and wasted.

One way to increase the likelihood of accurate answers to questions is to obtain several different perspectives, a process that researchers sometimes describe as *triangulation*. It means, essentially, collecting data from three (or more) sources, each having different perspectives on an issue. It usually can be assumed that no one group, influenced by its own concerns, priorities, experiences, and vested interests, can provide a totally accurate assessment of any situation. In triangulation, the different sources help to verify or to refute each other. Although any one source may be misleading, when data from all sources are examined together, the truth will emerge.

How might triangulation work in a needs assessment? Suppose a needs assessment is being conducted in preparation for the development of an AIDS prevention program within a community judged to be at risk for high incidence of the disease. Politicians, medical professionals, public educators, clergy, elders, and potential direct recipients of services who might be surveyed or interviewed (either individually or in focus groups) might provide very different answers to the same questions. Collectively, these people might be described as "key informants." Still other answers might be suggested through an analysis of organization records, community data, and other sources of data collected for a variety of specialized uses.

Somewhere within all of the conflicting data collected, there would be found the knowledge needed to create and implement a successful program. The researcher conducting the needs assessment would have the difficult job of finding it and conveying it accurately to whomever has sponsored the research. The sponsor would expect the researcher to take the data, to carefully weigh them, and to synthesize them in a report that contains both an accurate description of conditions as they really exist and recommendations designed to improve the proposed program.

Needs assessments have been and will remain one of the most valuable types of applied research. They can greatly increase the likelihood of programs' success. They also can avoid failure for programs that should not be implemented—those that seem logical but lack some key element.

Needs assessments require a researcher who knows how to gather data from a variety of both primary and secondary sources. They also require the ability to process vast amounts of data drawn from many sources and to be able to sift through them to see the total picture. Social workers are well suited to conducting this type of research. They know and understand individual behavior. They understand the dynamics of families, groups, organizations, and communities. They also understand the political processes that impact on the success of social programs and services.

Although needs assessments are most often associated with programs that are in the planning stage, they also are conducted when programs have been in existence for a while, sometimes for a long time. They can be used (1) to answer the basic question: Is this program still needed? or (2) to determine what changes in the program are necessary for it to retain its relevance. Conditions that contribute to the need for a program change over time. A program that was once needed and made a valuable contribution to a society may now be questioned, thus suggesting the appropriateness of a needs assessment.

What clues may suggest that a needs assessment of an existing program should be designed and implemented? Certain client groups may have stopped participating in the program, or the nature of the community (its economic well-being, ethnic mix, and so forth) may have changed. Perhaps other organizations may have begun similar programs that now compete with the program, or technological changes may have occurred that now make the program appear old-fashioned or even obsolete. These and other changing conditions may suggest that it is time to conduct research that can be used either to justify continuing a program, to modify it, or to phase it out completely. Data from needs assessment also can be used to convince others of the continued need for a program, or to budget for either an expanded or scaled-down program. They can also help in marketing a program if it is concluded that it is still needed, and for planning for future changes designed to keep the program viable.

## Evaluating Program Implementation

Evaluating program implementation involves securing data about whether a program is operational as plannned and, if it is, how well it is operating. This form of program evaluation is referred to as a *formative evaluation.* In formative evaluations, the evaluation is designed to determine if the program is on schedule and doing what it was intended to do. It seeks to generate suggestions for overcoming obstacles to program implementation and to recommend ways to improve how a program is operating.[3] Evaluating program implementation generally yields three kinds of data: (1) documentation that the program is really in operation as planned; (2) data designed to help program planners know how well program activities are being managed; and (3) data about program design defects or undesirable unintended consequences of the program.

In many formative evaluations, the researcher's role is very close to that of consultant. Feedback to the sponsor of the research is likely to be regular and ongoing. Regular reports along the way may be provided, in addition to a final written report of the evaluation. As problems are identified, changes are made and their success is then evaluated.

Formative evaluations often require the researcher to collect new data from a variety of sources. They might include many of the same sources that are used in conducting needs assessments, such as telephone surveys, mailed questionnaires, focus groups, use of key informants, structured and unstructured firsthand observation, and other methods that were described elsewhere. However, secondary data analysis is often part of a formative evaluation, too.

For example, the daily maintenance of attendance sheets might provide the evaluator with data about how well a program is monitoring clients' use of group treatment services. What is a problem with this type of evaluation focus? Critics have suggested that what good monitoring is can be a subjective judgment; no two evaluators may agree on its definition.

Another form of formative analysis that relies heavily on secondary data analysis is referred to as *social accounting*. Program records are examined for duplicated counts of recipients of services, ambiguous definitions of categories of service, and the program's overall accuracy of record keeping and reporting. Social accounting is based on the assumption that good programs keep accurate records, know exactly whom they serve, track their progress, and specify the type of services provided. Therefore, the quality of a program can be assessed by examining the quality of its records. There is one major problem with this focus—good records are not always synonymous with successful programs. Although good records are often characteristic of good programs, they are no guarantee that the program is really doing what it was intended to do. In fact, obsessive record keeping sometimes can absorb so much of a program's resources that there are not enough time and resources left to be able to accomplish program objectives!

Other program records that are created specifically for a formative evaluation, such as activity flow sheets and time sheets for staff, provide yet another focus for some formative evaluations. They tell the evaluator about how clients move through the program and how staff time is used. Based in part on the business invention of *time-and-motion studies,* evaluations look at how much of staff time is devoted to productive activities as opposed to other activities that appear to contribute little or nothing to goal attainment. Wasted time and unanticipated use of time in undesirable activities are identified. We can visualize the evaluator with notepad, pencil, and stopwatch. The "efficiency expert" is forever stopping staff (sometimes on the way to the rest room) to ask them what they are doing, why they are doing it, and sometimes how they could be better using their time. Various staff activities may be timed, and the time required for one staff member to complete a task may be compared with the time it takes for another staff member to complete the same or a similar task.

When time-and-motion studies are conducted, the evaluator may not be physically present, but other, sometimes bitterly resented methods may be substituted. Staff may be required to keep extensive logs of their daily activities and to justify the relationship of each of their activities to program objectives. Besides the staff animosity that these evaluation methods can generate, their critics quickly point out that the time required for answering questions or completing logs represents a serious drain on a program's resources. Staff may argue that, if they did not have to spend so much time and effort reporting on their activities, they might be able to contribute more to program success! Social workers also argue that the concepts of "productive" and "nonproductive" are not easily differentiated in our professional practice. Some of what may appear to the outside evaluator as wasted time may in fact be time that contributes to attainment of program goals. For example, a chat over coffee with a supervisor from another unit could enhance valuable communication networks, or a few minutes of daydreaming may be an absolute necessity to clear one's mind in order to be of help to the next client.

Still another type of formative analysis, the *administrative audit*, looks at a program's policies, rules, procedures, job descriptions, and other management tools, and evaluates their appropriateness and effectiveness. The underlying assumption of an administrative audit is that good programs are well managed, both internally and in relation to other programs and organizations. Therefore, the success of a program is reflected in how well managed it is. One problem with this line of thinking and with evaluation designs that result from it is that it may give insufficient recognition to one inescapable truth—a well-managed program that was poorly conceived still may be struggling. Too much emphasis on its management may not provide the data needed to improve it.

All of the specialized types of formative analysis that we have described have been criticized for their narrow focus. Each is likely to miss something important that can offer useful feedback to administrators. For that reason, a formative evaluation design often contains a combination of several of them, along with original data collected from several different sources. The researcher can then try to sort out all of the data to try to see the bigger picture. This is a variation of the triangulation method that we discussed in relation to needs assessments.

Formative evaluations can provide a formal documentation of the existence of an operational program. They can offer decision makers data about program difficulties. When data are sought for the purpose of improving program functioning, formative evaluations can provide it.

A formative evaluation is designed to provide feedback (more accurately, "feedforward") to program administrators. The researcher who conducts a formative evaluation hopes to identify strengths and weaknesses of a program in its early stages and to recommend needed changes while the program is still in its earliest stages of development. When a similar evaluation is conducted later in the life cycle of a program, sometimes even when the program is nearing completion, a different term, *process evaluation,* is more appropriate. A process evaluation also relies on a mixture of qualitative and quantitative data to gain insight into the functioning of a program. However, whereas a formative evaluation might try to learn what is working and what is not working, a process evaluation would be more of a post mortem. It would try to learn why an objective was not achieved or why one component of a program was successful whereas another was not, so that other programs (rather than the current program) can learn from the current program's mistakes. Because the goals and methods of formative evaluations and process evaluations are so similar, the two terms are often used interchangeably.

## *Evaluating Program Outcomes*

Outcome evaluations remain the best-known form of evaluative research. Because, as we have noted, their findings have the potential to threaten the existence of programs and the careers of people who work in them, they are sometimes also the most feared form of evaluation research. However, there are many benefits to outcome evaluations. They are beneficial to future clients by increasing the likelihood that they will receive services that work and will not receive services that are ineffective. Outcome evaluations also are more likely to provide general knowledge for the profession than the other types of program evaluation that we have discussed thus far. Why? When the results of an outcome evaluation are disseminated to others not involved in the program but working in the same area of practice, they are likely to learn something that is potentially useful to them in their work. If a program is found to be successful, they may then wish to try the same type of intervention or adapt it to meet the needs of their own client population.

If a program is found to be unsuccessful in achieving its objectives, other professionals can still learn from its failings in important ways. For example, they might learn that the program was not well conceived in the first place. Or the program, though theoretically good, might have failed to successfully address the problem for a variety of logistical reasons or because cultural issues were inadequately addressed. Another possibility is that the program was unsuccessful because the problem was not what it is generally believed to be. When this occurs, not only is something learned about the possible solution to a problem, but also our understanding of the problem itself can be enhanced. Learning about why a program was unsuccessful can be very useful to other professionals seeking to address the same problem—it can keep them from making some of the same mistakes.

Until relatively recently, the success of programs was evaluated based on their outputs. For example, the conclusion that "This program offered services to 140 hospice patients and their families during the past year, an increase of over 22 percent over the previous year" was adequate evidence that a program had been successful. However, recent accountability pressures now require that documentation of how many people were served, and similar outputs are no longer adequate evidence of a program's success. Now the emphasis is on outcome; that is, the degree to which a program has been successful in achieving its objectives at a reasonable cost. Thus, this kind of evaluation often involves a dual-focused emphasis on program effectiveness (achievement of objectives) and program efficiency (the relationship of outcome to expenditure of efforts and resources).[4] These two evaluative criteria cannot be viewed independently. The quality of a program must be assessed in relation to both. Comparisons between two related programs often are helpful in this regard. They might reveal that one program may be achieving its objectives, but at an extremely high cost, whereas another program may be achieving the same objectives, but at a much lower cost. Thus, both are effective, but they get very different marks in efficiency. We will use an example to show how this could occur and how it is often difficult to determine which is the better program.

Suppose that program A and program B are both job training programs. Program A carefully selected three clients and offered each client room, board, full tuition, and expenses to attend a junior college for two years, as well as free weekly counseling. At the end of two years, all three clients have found good jobs (a success rate of 100 percent). The total cost of program A was $150,000, or $50,000 per client.

The total cost of program B was only $45,000, much lower than program A's. It was able to keep down costs by designing and offering its own intensive job training course. But program B also had a much lower success rate; only three of twelve (25 percent) of its graduates found good jobs. However, program B could claim that it had been successful in placing three clients (the same number as program A) and at a cost of only $15,000 per client!

It could be argued that program B was more efficient than program A, because the cost of each success in program B was less than one-third the cost of each success in program A. It could also be argued that program A was more effective because of its higher success rate. Or it could be argued that it was equally as effective as program B (but less efficient), because both programs successfully helped three clients to find good jobs. So, which was the more successful program? It is hard to say. We probably would be concerned about the per capita cost of helping people find employment under program A. But we also could not help being concerned about the low success rate of program B. What about the human costs related to those nine clients who completed the program, hopeful of getting good jobs, who were not successful in finding employment?

The interaction between success (and failure) and their costs is never a simple one. Weighing the relative merits of effectiveness and efficiency objectively is one of the most difficult tasks faced by the program evaluator. Studying program outcomes typically requires the evaluator to assess client gains and losses, the side effects and unintended consequences of the program, and the costs (including economic, social, and psychological) of operating it. As we have found with other forms of research, good outcome evaluation studies must rely heavily on the knowledge, skills, and professional values possessed by the social worker.

## What Is the Appropriate Design for a Program Evaluation?

There are many different ideas about what constitutes a fair yet rigorous evaluation design for a social program. It is probably safe to say that a design developed for any one program is ill suited for another. That is why no two are alike. In order to design an appropriate evaluation, one must first identify the stage of program development of the program.[5] Is it in the planning stages, laying the groundwork for future services? Is it offering some services but still seeking to expand through outreach and publicity? Or are most activities devoted to services that are in place, well known, and relatively stable? The stage of development of a program is determined by such factors as the activities of staff and how they spend most of their time, funding priorities within the program, and the kind of data (records) collected and used by it. It is not synonymous with how long the program has been in existence. A program could be decades old but still actively seeking community sanction and client acceptance. Conversely, a program that is only a year or two old may devote most of its energies to the delivery of needed and legitimized services.

The pressure for accountability of social programs in recent years has produced a wide variety of different evaluation designs and strategies. As suggested earlier, many have been borrowed from the business and corporate sectors and modified to a greater or lesser degree to adapt them to social organizations. Some have come into fashion quickly and fallen out of fashion about as quickly. We will not attempt to examine individual evaluation models (presented in many books and government documents, and a topic for advanced study). However, we will offer some general principles relating to the design of evaluation studies in each of the three categories that we have discussed.

Needs assessments typically combine elements of both quantitative and qualitative research. Frequently, the methods employed are both exploratory and descriptive. For example, the open-ended question—Do you think there is a need for an HIV infection prevention project in our community?—might be asked of people representing a wide variety of backgrounds and perspectives in either one-on-one interviews or in a focus group. Or the same question (along with others) could be part of a mailed survey sent to community leaders. Much of the data required in needs assessments also can be found through secondary analysis of social indicators, census data, and other sources of data collected for some other purpose.

Formative or process evaluations tend to be primarily descriptive. For example, the evaluator may wish to gather a wide array of descriptive data (including personal observations) to evaluate how well a program seems to have gotten off the ground and to make recommendations for needed changes. Descriptive designs also may be used to answer other questions about program implementation, for example: Are the clients who were targeted for services actually being served? Confidential, in-depth interviews with clients and staff may be conducted and the content of interviews examined using content analysis.

Outcome evaluations tend to be explanatory. They are designed so that it can be learned not only whether or not a program achieved its objectives but also whether or not the program can "take credit" for any achievements. Therefore, they test hypotheses about program effectiveness by using inferential statistical analyses to learn the probability that the relationship between the program and some indicator of success was a real one, and not just a function of sampling error. When outcome evaluations employ experimental and quasi-experimental designs that rely on random assignment of clients to programs (and to control groups), it is also possible to conclude that it was the program, and not something else, that produced any successes (the issue of internal validity).

Although qualitative methods are sometimes used to gather data or as a kind of validity check on data that have been compiled using more quantitative measures, researchers conducting outcome evaluations try whenever possible to rely on measurement that is as objective as possible. If experimental or quasi-experimental designs are ethically feasible and if program outcomes have been well stated and quantified (for example, "Following completion of the program, clients who completed the program will have a lower rate of rehospitalization that those who did not participate in the program"), the determination of whether or not the program achieved its objectives is a relatively simple, statistical one. However, if the objectives of the program were never well formulated, then hypotheses about anticipated outcomes of the program will be difficult to state, and the process of evaluation becomes much more difficult. When this happens, someone (often another evaluator) may first have to examine the program's activities and, based on them, use an inductive process to identify and specify the program's mission, goals, and objectives. Then an outcome evaluation becomes possible.

When the major thrust of an evaluation study is an outcome analysis, the evaluator must have a clear understanding of the anticipated outcomes and be very careful in the selection of appropriate outcome measures. If judgments are to be made on the basis of its outcomes, then rigorous but fair outcome measures are needed. Often they are already available in the form of standardized indexes or scales. But it may be that, in the interest of fairness, original evaluation instruments will need to be developed for the evaluation. If this is necessary, then the researcher must use instrument development procedures that will ensure that measures will be valid (see Chapter 10).

One notable trend has been evident in recent years. Increasingly, evaluations of existing programs are being required, by outside funding sources, to include input from consumers of services (clients). This trend generally has met with little resistance from social workers since, when asked (or, perhaps, because they are asked) clients generally report a high level of satisfaction with programs and services. However, in some fields of practice (for example, protective services or the juvenile justice system) where clients are "involuntary," some have argued that consumer satisfaction is an unfair yardstick for measuring program success.

## Other Types of Evaluation Research

There are still many more specific designs for the evaluation of social programs. We will briefly describe three of them. They are cost-benefit analysis, analysis of program impact, and analysis of program structure. Each of the three has a very specialized use, and, like all forms of program evaluations, each has been widely criticized. Nevertheless, because they are still widely used, often as components of a multifaceted evaluation design package, social workers need to be familiar with them.

### Cost-Benefit Analysis

Cost-benefit analysis attempts to identify the benefits of a program, both tangible and intangible, as well as its direct and indirect monetary costs. Thus, it places a heavy emphasis on the efficiency of a program. The ratio of benefits to costs provides an indicator of the return that society receives from its investment in a program. In theory, any program's benefits should be greater than its costs. Cost-benefit analysis is a structured method for determining whether this is the case.

Although it may be possible to quantify the inputs and resources used in a program (its costs), it is often much harder to quantify program outcomes and benefits. As social workers, we are well aware that the ultimate benefits of our intervention are difficult to ascertain. They often are even more difficult to quantify, especially in dollars and cents. For example, can we really say that completing an intensive counseling program is the reason why a spouse is no longer abusive? Even if we can be reasonably certain that the program caused the behavioral change, can it be accurately determined just how much it saved the taxpayer in treatment services? Probably not.

Cost-benefit analysis has been around for quite a while. Over the years, specific methods have been developed that are of some assistance in estimating the dollar value of the benefits of a program. However, they remain rather imprecise.

## Program Impact Evaluations

Most evaluation designs focus on short-range success (outcome). However, there has been concern that they do not adequately address two issues: (1) the program's success may not hold up over time and (2) they give inadequate attention to the impact of the program on other programs and services—the unintended consequences of the program. In response to these concerns, some evaluation models have attempted to address them. They are broadly referred to as *program impact evaluations*. They determine whether programs have resulted in permanent desirable changes. For example, they might ask if job training graduates remained employed and continued to advance within the workplace following graduation, or whether street crime rates and unemployment rates stayed low or declined even more following the introduction of athletic and recreational programs for youth.

Program impact evaluations also seek to look beyond a program itself to examine how the program's presence may have affected other programs or phenomena. They are a recognition (consistent with systems theory) that almost any change or innovation within a system is likely to produce both anticipated and unanticipated changes within other system components. For example, if this type of evaluation were used to evaluate a hospital's new bereavement program for caregivers of terminally ill patients who have recently died, many questions that would go beyond whether the program itself was effective would be asked. They might include, for example,

- How has the program changed the daily activities of social workers in the hospital's existing hospice program?

- How has the morale of the hospice social workers been affected?
- How has the new program's presence changed the informal power structure of the social work department?
- How has reallocation of funding affected the work of other staff?
- Are former caregivers more likely to serve as volunteers (after the required waiting period) than they were prior to the existence of the program?

Evaluating program impact requires the evaluator to extrapolate from the data collected in program outcome studies and to creatively use current social indicators. A problem with impact evaluation studies is the presence of a multitude of other variables that can affect the dependent variable, especially because these studies generally employ a longer time framework for conducting an evaluation. So many different events and circumstances can intervene that it becomes very difficult to attribute any apparent impact directly to the effects of a program. In our previous example, it would be very hard to attribute changes within the hospice social work program directly to the presence of the new bereavement program rather than to other events or phenomena. For example, staff turnover, the lack of pay raises in more than three years, or burnout might have been the real reasons for any changes. Perhaps no changes were produced by the program at all. Or they might have been even more dramatic if the bereavement program had not been implemented!

The difficulty of isolating the impact of a program and of determining how other (intervening) variables may relate to any apparent program impact is certainly not unique to social work research. For example, impact studies in the 1980s were used to examine the relationship between lower speed limits and rate of traffic fatalities. But how can people say (as many do) that fewer fatal accidents in the 1970s and the early 1980s were the result of federally imposed 55-mile-per-hour speed limits or that an increase in fatalities in the late 1990s occurred because speed limits were relaxed? One would need to control for many other possibly intervening variables, such as gasoline prices, number of miles driven, the work of Mothers Against Drunk Drivers (MADD), inconsistent punishments for driving while under the influence of alcohol or drugs, changes in automobile safety equipment, changes in size and design of automobiles, the advent of cellular phones, and literally hundreds of other variables that may contribute to traffic fatality rates.

## Program Structure Evaluations

Program structure evaluation relies heavily on what most people would regard as outward measures of the success of a program. The rationale for this focus is that the programs that are generally regarded as good tend to have certain characteristics, for example, attractive facilities; private offices; well-educated professional staff; numerous, well-trained support staff; state-of-the-art electronic communications and data storage and retrieval systems; and a full menu of services. So why should we not evaluate other programs using these criteria?

The argument is logical and, in certain types of facilities such as hospitals, it may even have some validity. But, as we noted early in this book, researchers have learned to become suspicious of logic.

Critics have pointed to the superficiality of structural indicators and noted that some of the best social programs would rate as very poor if they were to be used as indicators of quality. Other, unsuccessful programs would tend to look good if structural evaluation criteria alone were applied. Evaluations that emphasize structural factors also have been blamed for wasteful use of a program's limited resources. Administrators have had to upgrade unnecessarily in certain areas in order to address the focus of structural evaluations, while neglecting other important program areas. Structural evaluations also can lead to unnecessary duplication of services and equipment. For example, an emphasis on structure in evaluations of hospitals has resulted in some situations where administrators in several hospitals in the same city all felt compelled to purchase the same, very expensive diagnostic equipment, even though demand for its use was so low that it was used only a few hours per week in any one hospital. The equipment could easily have been shared, but then only one hospital would have received "credit" for having it, come evaluation time.

## Who Should Conduct Evaluative Research?

When the decision is made to conduct some type of evaluation study, the question of who should conduct the evaluation must be addressed. Sometimes there are organization staff members with expertise in program evaluation, and other times, such persons must be recruited from the outside. We will discuss the relative advantages and disadvantages of using in-house or external evaluators and describe one evaluation method that seeks to combine the best features of both.

### Use of an In-House Evaluator

The person who has expertise in research and evaluation methods and who is already part of the organization's staff in some professional capacity may be a good choice to design and implement a program evaluation. An advantage of using such individuals is that they are already familiar with the organization's functions, policies, programs, people, and politics. There is little need to acquaint in-house evaluators with any of these aspects of an organization; they can hit the ground running. Because they are in-house, they also should have sensitivity to the client populations served and some sense of the organization's purpose and direction. This knowledge should help them in selecting or developing appropriate and sensitive methods of measuring key variables. Assuming that in-house evaluators also have expertise in data analysis and interpretation or have access to resources for these purposes, the evaluation study can proceed smoothly and at minimal cost to the organization. Because they are already on the payroll of an organization, no additional expenses are incurred. However, there still is a cost. In-house evaluators must be given release time from their usual duties. Other staff may need to be hired to cover for them while they conduct their program evaluations.

Of course, there also are disadvantages to using an in-house evaluator. One relates to a given evaluator's experience and expertise in program evaluation. Many individuals claim to be knowledgeable in the areas of research and statistics, and some are. But program evaluation is quite different from most other forms of research, and few persons who are employed within organizations perform program evaluations on a regular basis. Unless the person is competent to perform all necessary research tasks, the quality of the evaluation may suffer. Of course, outside consultants may be hired to help perform specialized tasks; this may be necessary to successfully implement an evaluation that uses an in-house evaluator.

A second disadvantage involves the extent to which in-house evaluators can be objective about the findings of a program evaluation in the organization where they are employed. Evaluation involves making judgments about programs; these judgments should be based on the data collected and on nothing else. In-house evaluators may have difficulty being objective (an understandable difficulty if the evaluator has had even minimal involvement with the program or has acquaintances or friends who have). Or, as an employee of the organization, the evaluator might feel pressured to present findings in a way consistent with the wishes of administrators—an ethical dilemma that a nonemployee would be less likely to face. If, for whatever reason, the evaluator's objectivity is compromised, the quality and value of the research will be severely damaged.

A third disadvantage involves the way that other staff may perceive the in-house evaluator. Suddenly the evaluator may appear to have been elevated in status (perhaps with justification). The evaluator may have the power to influence the functions and even the job status of coworkers. This may result in staff resentment and resistance (more than if an outside evaluator were to be used), and it may prompt staff to be uncooperative or even to sabotage the evaluator's work. After completing the evaluation, the in-house evaluator may find relationships with coworkers to be negatively affected or even irreparably damaged. This can be costly to the organization as well as to the individuals involved.

## *Use of an External Evaluator*

Contracts and grants that fund a program often require that organization administrators use evaluators who are not employed by their organization. But even if it is not required, an administrator or board of directors may choose to hire outside evaluators for a program evaluation. Expertise and objectivity are two major advantages to using outside evaluators. Unfortunately, there are also distinct disadvantages to using them.

Hiring an outside evaluator requires an organization to find the money to pay someone to design and conduct a program evaluation. Given the austere budgets that often characterize human service organizations, hiring outside evaluators may be economically prohibitive.

Outside evaluators generally are paid well for their time and expertise, and they may require more time to conduct an evaluation than would an in-house evaluator. Before they can even begin to design and implement an evaluation, an external evaluator first needs to learn about the organization and its programs. If this is not done, an evaluation design that is inappropriate and unfair may result. The amount of time needed to educate an outside evaluator varies with the complexity of the organization and its programs. But it is always necessary for an outside evaluator to spend time trying to understand what a program is trying to accomplish (its goals and objectives), the ways in which it goes about trying to accomplish them, and the stage of development that the program is in.

A third potential disadvantage concerns the extent to which external evaluators (particularly those who are not social workers working in a related practice setting) are likely to be insensitive to certain realities within which a program must operate. They may have difficulty understanding the many sources of resistance that confront clients seeking to change some aspect of their lives or the hostile task environment that exists for many unpopular programs that social workers offer. For example, they may not understand that programs designed to protect children from abuse or to prevent the spread of sexually transmitted diseases are often resented by community members who may create obstacles to their success. An outside evaluator also may have difficulty developing appropriate evaluation instruments and standards to assess the success level of such programs. Can an outside evaluator understand that a 30 percent success rate for a program to train the chronically unemployed may constitute an acceptable level of success? Or that treatment programs for chronic sex offenders have historically had a very low rate of success? Of course, if the program has clearly articulated realistic objectives from the outset and if the program is evaluated based on them, this problem can be greatly reduced.

## Empowerment Evaluation

Empowerment evaluation is an approach to program evaluation that combines the use of in-house and external evaluators in a unique way. It has the expressed purpose of helping program staff evaluate themselves and their programs in order to improve practice and foster self-determination.[6] It employs both qualitative and quantitative methodologies. Program staff conduct their own evaluations using a form of self-evaluation and reflection; it is very process oriented. An outside evaluator acts as a coach or facilitator depending on the capabilities of program participants and staff.

Empowerment evaluation is consistent with social work professional values. It is being used in a variety of human service organizations in many different countries, particularly with those that serve more powerless and historically disenfranchised populations. Zimmerman[7] describes the empowerment process as one in which attempts to gain control, obtain needed resources, and critically understand one's social environment are fundamental. Through this type of evaluation, people develop skills to become independent problem solvers and decision makers. Because all of the program staff (and, to a lesser degree, clients) are involved with the evaluation from its inception and form a team with the external evaluator, some of the power dynamics and areas of distrust typically associated with external evaluations are minimized.

The assessment of a program's value is not the end point of empowerment evaluation, but part of an ongoing process of service and quality improvement. The goal is to have program staff internalize and institutionalize self-evaluation practices. It allows them to practice ongoing program evaluation and improvement in the face of population shifts, changing knowledge about practice, and evolving external political forces that affect the social welfare environment.

Fetterman identifies several facets of empowerment evaluation: training, facilitation, advocacy, illumination, and liberation.[8]

*Training.* Skilled evaluators teach program staff how to conduct their own evaluations with a focus on mastery and internalization of evaluation principles and practices as an integral part of program planning.

*Facilitation.* Skilled evaluators serve as coaches to help program staff conduct their own self-evaluations. Tasks include goal setting, specifying of performance indicators, establishing baselines, developing rating scales, and monitoring goal attainment.

*Advocacy.* Program staff are helped to use the findings of the evaluation to gain more leverage over resources and to participate in the political process. Advocate evaluators use findings to try to change public opinion and influence the policy decision-making process.

*Illumination.* Program staff are helped to gain new insights and understanding about program dynamics and roles of various stakeholders.

*Liberation.* Liberation is the ultimate outcome of empowerment evaluation. It is a process through which program staff are freed from preexisting roles and constraints as they learn more about what works and what does not work. They are helped to discover new opportunities, to use existing resources in innovative ways, and to redefine the roles they play in continuous program improvement.

## The Political Context of Program Evaluation

Program evaluation is research designed to generate knowledge for decision making and action. In the case of an established program, it seeks to provide decision makers with data about how well the program is achieving its goals and objectives.

Usually, social workers and other professional staff are asked to be involved in the implementation phase of a program evaluation. They may be involved in data-gathering activities, such as submitting work documents to the evaluation team, completing questionnaires or interviews, or asking their clients to provide evaluative data. Both professional and nonprofessional staff members may express concern and skepticism when they are asked to supply data that will be used for evaluating a program. They may be fearful both for the future of the program and for their own welfare.

One possible recommendation of a program evaluator is that a planned or existing program should be terminated or significantly modified. Although the decisions that are to be made about a program aren't usually of the "continue" versus "terminate" type, staff are aware that the process of evaluating always entails making a judgment (either directly or implicitly) about the value of a given program. They also know that good outcome measures are sometimes difficult to develop and that the real, lasting achievements of a program often are hard to assess. Thus, they fear that what they perceive to be a valuable program may show up in a bad light.

There also may be concern that an individual staff member's work performance will be assessed by the evaluator using data provided, and then shared with administrators or supervisors. The study design may, in fact, require that individual workers submit time sheets, activity logs, and other process documents. However, a goal of program evaluation studies typically is not to evaluate individual work performance (although they almost always reflect on the performance of a program's top administrator). Individual employee performance evaluations are generally conducted at regularly scheduled intervals (often, annually or semiannually) by the worker's supervisor and are separate and unrelated to program evaluation studies. The evaluator is likely to receive better cooperation from staff if they are reminded of this.

A program evaluation also should be viewed as part of a greater political process for two major, related reasons. The first has to do with the purpose of the study, and the second concerns the use and potential misuse of evaluation data. Usually, program evaluation studies are conducted at the request or mandate of organizations that have provided funding for a program. They are conducted to address accountability concerns or to assist in answering some question, for example: Should the program be funded for another year or cycle?

In addition, program evaluations can legitimately be requested by boards of directors and funding organizations at any time. Unfortunately, such a request may not always be based on a desire for constructive feedback or other evaluation data designed to improve the program being evaluated. There may be other hidden agendas. Sometimes evaluations are requested because boards of directors simply wish to secure damaging evidence about an unpopular program or its administrator. For example, an evaluator may be hired because the board is seeking documentation to justify the firing of a program's director. Or, if a program provides desirable employment for friends or relatives, the board may be seeking justification to continue it, despite the fact that it is known to be ineffective. As we suggested earlier, an outside evaluator is likely to have more credibility and is assumed to be more objective than an employee of the organization where a program is based. Thus, they are especially vulnerable to being "used" unless (1) they are politically astute and (2) they adhere to ethical standards and insist on reporting their findings in a way that presents a complete and accurate picture of a program.

When evaluators are sought from outside (or even within) an organization to conduct program evaluations, they should be aware that there are reasons why evaluations are sought and why they have been selected to conduct them. Potential evaluators attempt to determine these reasons before agreeing to conduct program evaluations. They often ask questions about the purpose of proposed evaluations and explore what possible uses may be made of the data. If it appears after some inquiry that something other than an honest evaluation is being sought, ethical evaluators refuse to participate in it.

## Ethical Issues

There are ethical issues in any type of research. We discussed some of the more general ones in Chapter 2. They apply to program evaluations as well as to research that is designed to build general knowledge for our profession. For example, confidentiality, anonymity, and informed consent issues must be addressed, because people who provide data for program evaluations often are vulnerable to retaliation if they are critical of a program and the source of their comments is revealed to administrators. When conducting program evaluations, however, there are also some very specific ethical dilemmas that must be confronted. Because the evaluator usually has a considerable amount of latitude in making certain critical decisions about how the research will be conducted, it is quite easy to influence the results of an evaluation.

Suppose that you have been asked to conduct an outcome evaluation of a program that was established to provide assistance to couples and individuals seeking to adopt children from Russia and China. The program is a new one to the agency, which had not previously offered international adoption services. If you were unethical, how could you "stack" the evaluation so that the program would look highly successful and so that your friend who works in the program can remained employed? Or, conversely, how could you design the research to make the program appear ineffective?

Evaluators make a number of important design decisions, sometimes with the "help" of powerful people like administrators, but often unilaterally. Most likely, the program has several objectives, some of which have been achieved and some of which have not been achieved. By choosing to focus on those where you know the program has been successful (for example, in expediting paperwork) and either not addressing or deemphasizing those where it has not been successful, it is possible to make a program look better than it really is. Conversely, a focus on the program's shortcomings (for example, its failure to attract single parents) could make it appear worse than it really is.

Similarly, the decision of who will provide data can distort results. Interviewing parents of newly adopted children (as opposed to those who dropped out before the adoption was completed) can make the program look good. Interviewing staff from agencies that compete with the program for clients can make it look bad. Or, knowing what we do about different methods of data collection (for example, that in-person interviews have very high completion rates but mailed questionnaires have lower, often biased completion rates), it would be possible to get whatever results are sought. Statistical analysis and interpretation of findings also would provide opportunities to deliberately misrepresent the results of the evaluation.

In contrast, an ethical researcher would strive to produce an evaluation that is feasible given budgetary constraints and given the need not to disrupt client services, but also one that is fair and accurate. Fairness might entail getting a wide array of perspectives on the program and reporting them in a way that no group feels that their input was ignored. Accuracy would relate to the reliability and validity of the data, as well as to the correct use and interpretation of statistical analyses.

## Reports of Program Evaluations

As we have repeatedly emphasized, the purpose of a program evaluation is a little different from that of other kinds of social work research. Although (like other research) it seeks to acquire needed knowledge, the knowledge sought is specific in nature. Consequently, research findings are also reported somewhat differently.

There are some special characteristics of reports of program evaluations that relate to the nature of evaluative research.[9] Because program evaluation is action-oriented research which is typically conducted for the purpose of making one or more decisions about the future of a program, the report of a program evaluation is written to reflect the kind of decisions that the evaluator is attempting to facilitate. Typically, there are six sections in the report of a program evaluation.

1. *Executive summary.* The executive summary presents the essential elements of the total report, including why the evaluation was conducted. It highlights the major findings and recommendations, is brief (typically about one page), and usually is written after the rest of the report has already been prepared. In some respects, it may be the most important part of the report of a program evaluation. Like the abstract of a journal article, it may be the only part of the

report that is read by all concerned. The executive summary should be written with great care, so that it captures the main points of the report and serves as a kind of teaser to the reader to examine in greater detail the researcher's findings in the rest of the report.

2. *Program description.* The program description includes data about the development of the program, its goals and objectives, data about the client population the program is intended to serve, and (for existing programs) an account of what happens to clients after they first enter the program (the flow of activity). Data about program staffing is also included. After reviewing this section of the report, the reader should have an understanding of why the program is proposed or already exists, what it intends to accomplish, and how it would achieve or already is attempting to achieve its goals. The program description section of the report can be quite long, but the author of the report usually tailors this section of the report to the intended audience. Readers who already are very familiar with the proposed or existing program will require less data in each area than, for example, a board of directors consisting of several new members who may be only marginally knowledgeable about it.

3. *Program evaluation design.* The third section of the report states the specific purpose for which the study was conducted, along with the type of evaluation design used (for example, needs assessment, formative, or outcome evaluation). Any data collection instruments that were used are described, and the reader is referred to the appendix of the report where they are included. Any available data regarding their reliability and validity are provided. The methods of data collection are described in detail. Any limitations inherent in the evaluation design (for example, time constraints or limited access to needed data) are specified and discussed, much as they are in any other research report.

4. *Results.* In the fourth section of the report, the evaluator generally addresses each of the evaluation questions in sequence, through a discussion of relevant data. Descriptive data are presented in tabular or graphic form. Results of the use of statistical analyses generally are presented in as straightforward a manner as possible, with numbers and statistical notations kept to a minimum. If administrators or others ask the evaluator to give an oral report of the results of an evaluation study to select groups such as the board of directors, it is this section that forms the basis for such a report. But the evaluator generally adapts the way findings are presented to the anticipated interest area of the group (but not the findings themselves).

5. *Discussion.* The overall results of the study are discussed in the report's fifth section. If the evaluation was a needs assessment, efforts are made to reconcile conflicting data sources. If it was more process oriented, then the discussion of results would be more likely to address the apparent success of development or implementation of the program to date. If it was intended to be outcome oriented, then there is a discussion of whether the program seems to have had the desired effect or impact on program participants. The

researcher is careful also to note those areas of evaluation where, because of lack of data or other methodological limitations, no definitive conclusions could be drawn.

6. *Recommendations.* In a recommendations section, the evaluator proposes a course of action as suggested by the data. If it has been made clear that specific recommendations are sought, recommendations are made in descending order of importance. Direct and persuasive language is appropriate. The evaluator's objective input has been solicited to help make one or more decisions about the program; candor is both sought and appreciated by those who authorized and paid for the evaluation.

When data have been conflicting or otherwise inconclusive, recommendations for additional evaluation may be appropriate. In those evaluation studies in which the evaluator has determined that specific recommendations are not being sought by the person or group that commissioned the evaluation (because they wish to formulate their own recommendations), this section is deleted and the evaluator's report concludes with the discussion section (part 5).

# Summary

This chapter provided an overview of program evaluation research. It is a specialized type of research conducted to evaluate both proposed and existing programs. It often is used to demonstrate accountability in the use of resources within existing programs and to modify and improve them.

In a general sense, program evaluation can be understood as a critical component in an ongoing planning process. There are three major types of evaluation studies: needs assessments, studies of program implementation (formative evaluation), and studies of program outcomes (outcome or product evaluation). They each have their own specific data needs, research designs, and data-gathering techniques. Researchers sometimes also evaluate programs using a more specific focus, such as the cost-benefit ratio, impact, or structure of a program.

When the option is available, the decision as to use an in-house or an outside evaluator to conduct program evaluations is a complex one. Both alternatives have advantages and disadvantages. An alternative that uses both in-house and outside evaluators—empowerment evaluation—was presented as a compromise that often combines the best features of both.

Program evaluations are action-oriented and decision-oriented research; decisions about programs and their continuation are likely to be made as a result of them. This fact and others were discussed in the context of political and ethical factors that can affect the researcher's capacity to design and conduct program evaluations.

Finally, the unique purposes and characteristics of reports of program evaluations were noted. They provide knowledge and recommendations that are specific to a given program. Some evaluations (especially those that examine program outcome) also can contribute to our professional body of knowledge.

# References

1. See, for example, Gabor, P., Unrau, Y., & Grinnell, R., Jr. (1998). *Evaluation for social workers* (2nd ed.). Boston, MA: Allyn & Bacon; or Royse, D., et al. (2001). *Program evaluation: An introduction.* Chicago: Nelson-Hall Publishers.
2. Mayer, R. (1985). *Policy and program planning: A developmental perspective.* Englewood Cliffs, NJ: Prentice Hall.
3. Worthen B., & Sanders, J. (1973). *Educational evaluation: Theory and practice.* Belmont, CA: Wadsworth Publishing Company.
4. Cheetham, J. (1992). Evaluating social work effectiveness. *Research on Social Work Practice,* 2(3), 265–287.
5. Tripodi, T., Fellin, P., & Epstein, I. (1978). *Differential social program evaluation.* Itasca, IL: F. E. Peacock Publishers.
6. Fetterman, D. M., Kaftarian, S. J., & Wandersman, A. (Eds.). (1996). *Empowerment evaluation.* Thousand Oaks, CA: Sage Publications.
7. Zimmerman, M., Israel, B., Schulz, A., & Checkoway, B. (1992). Further explorations in empowerment theory: An empirical analysis of psychological empowerment. *American Journal of Community Psychology,* 20(6), 707–727.
8. Fetterman, D. M., Kaftarian, S. J., & Wandersman, A. (Eds.). (1996). *Empowerment evaluation.* Thousands Oaks, CA: Sage Publications.
9. Morris, L., Fitz-Gibbon, C. T., & Freeman, M. F. (1987). *How to communicate evaluation findings.* Newbury Park, CA: Sage Publications.

# 14

## EVALUATING INDIVIDUAL PRACTICE EFFECTIVENESS

In the previous chapter, we examined one type of evaluation research: program evaluation. We saw how many of the research concepts and methods that we discussed in earlier chapters are also useful for monitoring and evaluating the success of social programs. However, social work practitioners also need to know how well they are doing in their individual practice interventions; that is, in the services they offer to clients and client groups. We require regular feedback if we are to be knowledge-based practitioners. In this chapter, we will look at how research methods can be used to provide it.

## Alternatives to Single-System Research

As we have suggested repeatedly throughout this book, there are many potential sources of research data. The data that social workers need to assess their effectiveness also can come from a variety of sources. We will briefly mention a few of them and then shift our focus to what we believe to be an especially good way to evaluate individual practice effectiveness.

### *Supervisor Feedback*

Historically, a good potential source of data for feedback has been the social worker's line supervisor. In supervisory conferences, social workers were encouraged to objectively evaluate their progress with individual clients or larger client systems. Along with the supervisor (often a very experienced, accomplished practitioner), achievements were identified and applauded, and shortcomings were analyzed in order to find better ways to accomplish the goals of intervention. At least, that is the way it sometimes worked. Unfortunately, supervisory conferences sometimes had other agendas that got in the way of useful feedback. One major problem was that supervisors were also asked to perform annual or semiannual performance evaluations of their subordinates, with little knowledge of their work other than what they learned during supervisory conferences. Not surprisingly, social workers were not always totally candid when discussing their interventions. They were unwilling to jeopardize salary increases or promotions by describing situations in which they appeared to be less than totally effective. Thus, they were deprived of the feedback that might have been most useful in their work.

In recent years, trends within our profession have made the line supervisor an even less likely source of valid feedback. Cost-cutting measures in many settings, such as hospitals and psychiatric facilities, have eliminated many supervisory positions. If a social worker has a supervisor at all, it is likely to be someone who is seen only rarely, is unfamiliar with the supervisee's work, and may belong to another professional discipline. In other settings, alternative models of supervision (for example, group supervision, peer supervision, or even supervision via the Internet) have sometimes replaced the former supervisor-supervisee relationship which at least had the potential for providing good, honest feedback on social worker intervention effectiveness.

The annual or semiannual performance evaluations of supervisors also have limited value as indicators of practice effectiveness. They are not the reports of careful research on worker effectiveness conducted by the supervisor. If data collection instruments are used at all, they rarely have undergone validation using scientific methods. Often, written evaluations consist of subjective judgments based on occasional firsthand observations, data provided by the individual being evaluated, and the impressions of other employees. Content analysis of case records also may be used. Overall, the lack of standardized methods for evaluation of a social worker's effectiveness make them of extremely limited value as feedback to the social worker. They are useful primarily for justifying personnel actions.

## Consumer Feedback

If there are obstacles to feedback from supervisors, why not get it directly from those consumers who are supposed to benefit from our interventions? Aren't they in the best position to tell us if we are helping or making a difference in their lives? Yes, but unfortunately, our clients often fail to provide honest answers.

Suppose, for example, that a social worker decided to draw a random sample of past and/or active clients and to construct and mail out a brief questionnaire asking them to evaluate the services received. Would this provide an accurate assessment of the social worker's effectiveness? Probably not. First, those clients most likely to return the data collection instrument would be those most satisfied with services and, perhaps, a smaller number who were least satisfied with them—an uneven, biased response rate. Others who might really be less than totally satisfied might still report that they were satisfied, simply because they were impressed that the social worker cared enough to ask. For a variety of reasons, the presence of a past or present helping relationship with individual clients and client groups tends to influence the results of a client satisfaction survey. We alluded to this problem in the previous chapter when we referred to client satisfaction surveys as a dubious, positively biased source of data for evaluating programs.

Another important problem with asking clients about their satisfaction with services is that satisfaction is not synonymous with successful intervention. We may be measuring the wrong thing. A client might be satisfied with intervention because it was convenient or inexpensive, because the social worker seemed to really "care," or for any number of other reasons, even though no progress on a problem was made. Conversely, dissatisfaction may have occurred because the social worker offered some needed but unpleasant form of intervention (for example, confrontation) that ultimately proved effective or because of some negative transference relationship. Even if clients are surveyed in such a way that questions focus on client progress rather than on satisfaction, it is almost impossible for satisfaction issues not to influence the results. (This same phenomenon often occurs when students are asked to evaluate the teaching effectiveness of their professors.)

Despite their problems, client surveys sometimes can provide some useful feedback of individual and program practice effectiveness. They are most likely to yield useful data when current clients (as well as former ones) are surveyed, when carefully developed data collection instruments are used, and when open-ended questions (for example: Describe any changes that have occurred that you think are related to our meetings) are included, along with fixed-alternative items or scales.

## Goal Attainment Scaling

Another method of evaluating the success of an individual social worker's intervention methods, goal attainment scaling (GAS), also relies on consumers (clients) to provide data. However, the data reported are client behaviors, rather than their satisfaction with services. Thus, it is believed to be less vulnerable to bias.

GAS is nothing new; it was first used back in the 1960s among therapists working with psychiatric patients. Since then, it has been used in a wide variety of settings where social workers are employed. When using it, a social worker identifies (along with the client or client system) a small number (usually, three to five) of specific client problems. Because they are easiest to measure, it is best if they are problem behaviors of the client or client system or, if appropriate, the lack of desirable behaviors. They should be problems of importance to the client and ones for which it is reasonable to expect that social work intervention might produce some positive changes. Although we normally associate GAS with the treatment of individual clients, it is also applicable for working with problems within groups, families, institutions or communities, as long as the problem and its incidence can be easily quantified. For example, a social worker employed in a community agency might use it to assess her effectiveness in increasing the percentage of the local population who register to vote in an upcoming presidential election.

Once having identified and specified a small number of problems and the goals of intervention associated with them, a range of five levels of goal attainment are specified and listed in rank order. They are assigned a number between –2 and +2. Zero is assigned to what will be the expected outcome if intervention is successful. Plus scores are assigned to goal attainment that is greater than expected and minus scores to goal attainment levels that are less than expected. To return to our previous example—the social worker attempting to increase voter registration prior to a presidential election in a community where current registration is only 20 percent—might use the following scale:

| | |
|---|---|
| Most unfavorable outcome (–2) | 20% |
| Less than expected outcome (–1) | 21–25% |
| Expected outcome (0) | 26–30% |
| More than expected outcome (+1) | 31–35% |
| Most favorable outcome (+2) | over 35% |

The decision as to which percentage of registration would represent expected outcome (0) and which percentage would be appropriate for the other four levels would be based on an assessment of what was realistic, given the time available for the intervention, and what past experience has taught the social worker about the likely impact of the intervention. Setting them at the appropriate levels requires a good understanding of both the client group and the likely impact of the intervention method being used.

The results of goal attainment in addressing different problems can be combined mathematically to suggest, overall, how effective a social worker has been in working with a client or client system. The different problems can also be weighted to reflect their relative importance. Methods are even available to convert results to a scale with scores ranging between 1 and 100.

GAS is designed for use with well-motivated clients who will work to set realistic goals and honestly report their behaviors, as well as with larger client systems where valid measurement of behaviors is possible. It also is designed for social workers who want honest feedback about their effectiveness, not social workers who just want to appear successful. If, either unintentionally or deliberately, the different levels of success are scaled too high or too low or if the measurement of success is inappropriate for some other reason, the results of GAS will be of little value as feedback to the social worker. For example, if both the social worker and an adolescent with a problem of severe shyness in social situations set an expected goal of two Internet chat-room conversations per week (+2 = four; –2 equals none), a 0 level or even a +2 level might be accomplished. It would make the social worker appear successful, but would this really represent successful intervention for the client's shyness? Probably not, because the goal levels were set so low that they could easily be achieved. In addition, the goals may have been inappropriate, because there is little reason to believe that increased Internet conversations might help the problem of shyness in social situations.

# Single-System Research

Single-system research (also referred to as $n = 1$, single-case time-series, single-subject research, and idiographic research) refers to a collection of research designs that are both similar to and different from the traditional group research designs that we examined in earlier chapters. Unlike group research, single-system research does not have as its primary goal building generalized knowledge or uncovering relationships between variables that may be of use to many other people. In that sense, it is more similar to program evaluation. (See Figure 13.1 in the previous chapter.) It does not seek to provide the broad assessment of programs that program evaluation designs produce (Chapter 13). It simply seeks answers to the questions: Does what I am doing with this client or with this client system seem to be making a difference? and If it does seem to be making a difference, is the change consistent with my intervention goals?

As in all other research, social workers conducting single system research collect, record, and analyze data, and then they interpret it for use in practice decision making. Their research has some (mostly superficial) resemblances to some of the specific designs that we have discussed. Like program evaluation, it seeks to evaluate practice effectiveness. Like longitudinal research, it entails the repeated measurement of the same variable over time. It even introduces an independent variable and uses a variation of a control group. Because of these latter characteristics, some writers have even gone so far as to describe certain single-system research designs as experimental. However, there is some disagreement on this point.

There also are many differences between single-system research and the other forms of research that we have examined. Other research designs often use research specialists who do little else but conduct research studies. When practitioners conduct other types of research (especially quantitative studies), they tend to leave their role as practitioner behind and assume the role of researcher. In contrast, single-system research is conducted by practitioners for their own use (feedback). Often the research is integrated with the practice intervention.

The unit of analysis in single-system research, the case or research participant, can be any entity that is normally the target for social work treatment or intervention; that is, any client system. Although it can be (and most frequently is) an individual client, it also can be a couple, a family, a group, an organization, or a community.

Single-system research is best suited to those situations in which (1) a primary treatment goal is change in some client behavior, attitude, perception, or other characteristic; and (2) whatever the social worker is seeking to change can be easily and accurately measured. Because easy, accurate measurement is required and behavior is relatively easy to measure, most single-system research has focused on changes in client behavior. When something other than behavior is the target for change, self-administered indexes and scales are often used to measure it. For simplicity, we will use the term *behavior* throughout the rest of this chapter, but it should be understood that we could just as well be talking about research that examines practice effectiveness in attempting to change an attitude, perception, or some other client characteristic. We will also use only examples involving interventions designed to affect changes in behavior. The behavior that the social worker may be attempting to influence can be a dysfunctional one for the client. Or it can be a desirable one that the social worker wants to enhance or foster. A consistent pattern in the behavior is desirable (stable, increasing, decreasing, or even fluctuating, but in a consistent manner).

Whenever possible, it is preferable to define the goal of intervention in a positive way. This is consistent with practice values that stress our building on client strengths (the "strengths perspective"). For example, it would be preferable to define our goal as "increasing the number of self-esteem–enhancing comments made by Ms. X to her son" rather than "decreasing the number of deprecating comments made by Ms. X to her son."

As we have suggested, single-system research is not appropriate for evaluating the effectiveness of all practice interventions. In order to use it, the researcher/practitioner must be able to specify exactly what change is sought and the method used to attain it. If there are multiple goals for intervention, if progress toward attainment of a single goal cannot be easily measured, or if the intervention method cannot be easily specified, single-system research may not be appropriate. For example, a social worker providing counseling focused on reducing verbally abusive behavior by a spouse, using a specific new method of intervention, could use single-system research to evaluate practice effectiveness in influencing that client behavior. But the same social worker might not be able to use single-system research to evaluate overall practice effectiveness with a client where a variety of methods are used to provide the client with assistance in addressing several different problems. However, it might still be possible to use it with just one component of her treatment, such as a specific intervention to influence just one of the problem behaviors of the client. The target for change need not be the central problem. It can be just one symptom of the problem or even some behavior that may be only tangentially related to the central problem but is still creating difficulty for the client.

Over the past few decades, researchers and theoreticians have greatly expanded the number of practice situations where single-system research can be used. Progress has come from at least two sources. First, social work researchers have created and refined scales for the measurement of such hard-to-measure variables as marital adjustment and family relations.[1] The instruments have been shown to possess both reliability and validity when used repeatedly with the same clients or client groups. Second, other scholars have designed highly sophisticated single-system research designs. There is now a design that is suitable for nearly every practice situation.[2] Researchers have even developed computer software to make the recording and analysis of data nearly effortless for the practitioner.[3]

An assumption underlying the use of single-system research designs is that, if an intervention makes a difference, a client or client system will show a response to it (change). With most designs, we are expecting (hoping?) that the behavior that is the target of the intervention will fluctuate when the intervention is introduced and, in some instances, even after it is removed. The stronger the pattern of agreement between the presence of intervention and changes in the behavior, the greater the evidence that the intervention makes a difference. If a pattern continues during repeated introductions of the intervention and another pattern occurs during removal of it, the evidence that it makes a difference is especially strong. Such consistent patterns would constitute an unlikely coincidence, one that would defy the laws of probability. They would suggest that the intervention and the client behavior are related. Of course, we would hope to demonstrate that intervention is accompanied by a *desirable change* in the behavior of the client, one that is consistent with intervention goals. But the observation that the presence of intervention is accompanied by undesirable change or even that it makes no difference would still be valuable feedback to the practitioner. Either would suggest that the intervention was not successful, at least not with that particular client or client system.

In single-system research, specific terminology is used. A *baseline* or *A phase* is a block of time in which the effects of the intervention whose effects are being evaluated is not present. During an A phase, measurement of the behavior that the social worker is attempting to influence takes place. Other forms of assistance to the client (the usual treatment) may also be initiated or may continue during an A phase. An A phase sometimes can be created retroactively. If good records have been kept or reliable observations and measurement of the behavior already have been made and are available, the usual pattern of the behavior can be determined. However, this entails secondary data analysis, which, as we have discussed, can have serious limitations. Among other things, it is dependent on the ways in which the behavior was conceptualized and operationalized, and how conscientiously it was measured, often by someone else.

Another period of time (of predetermined length) in which the intervention is present is called an *intervention phase* or *B phase*. It is identical to an A phase except for the presence of the intervention whose effect is being studied. The behavior or other phenomenon that the social worker is seeking to influence is called the *target problem* (or target behavior) and is regarded as the dependent variable for research purposes. The specific treatment or intervention that is used serves as the independent variable.

Advocates of single-system research suggest that, in certain designs, A phases serve the same function as control groups do in experimental research designs. They provide a source of comparison by indicating what occurs with the target problem when the intervention (1) either has not been introduced or (2) is withdrawn following a B phase. It has been suggested that in single-system research a case thus serves as its own control (during an A phase).

The B phases are then regarded as being comparable to the experimental groups in an experiment. Although this may have some theoretical justification, the lack of a true control group creates a need for some other way to control for threats to internal validity. Researchers need to know that it was the intervention and not something else that produced changes in the target problem.

As we shall see, different single-system designs are also used to compare the effectiveness of different interventions (always introduced one at a time) and to examine whether a given intervention seems to work more effectively with one target problem than with another. In the latter situation, only one problem at a time receives the intervention. This is a cardinal rule of single-system research—during a B phase, there is only one intervention and one target problem. If this were not the case, it would be almost impossible to know which intervention was associated with change in which target problem.

When using single-system research designs, changes in the target problem are carefully monitored over the course of the research. Ideally, the monitoring involves using more than one observer or some other method to ensure that the measurements of the behavior are reliable and valid. Measurements are recorded as they are made, usually using standard graph paper or a computer software package designed to produce the recording graphs that are characteristic of single-system research. The presence or absence of intervention at the time of each measurement is clearly indicated on the graph by labeling time intervals as either A (for an A phase) or B (for a B phase). The measurements of the target problem are displayed along the vertical axis, and units of time are displayed along the horizontal axis. Thus, each dot on the graph reflects a measurement of the behavior that is being charted and the point in time when the measurement took place. The dots are connected to form a histogram.

Behaviors that are likely to occur frequently are usually measured using small time intervals, such as days, hours, or even minutes. For example, certain speech mannerisms or involuntary behaviors, such as repeated throat clearing, may occur so frequently that the entire research study might be completed in an hour or even less time. If the target problem occurs less frequently, larger units of time are used. The research may take place over a longer time period, for example, over a period of weeks, months, or even years. Figure 14.1 displays the planned efforts of a social worker to get a legislator to consult with the social worker about pending social legislation. The intervention consisted of regular mailed reminders of the social worker's availability for consultation. Note that the effects of the intervention appear to be rather minimal over the 27 months in which the single-system research occurred. There was relatively little change in the legislator's behavior when the intervention was introduced (B phase).

Like any other variable, there are many different ways in which a target problem can be measured. Four common ways used in single-system research are

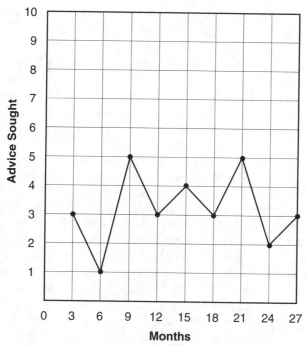

**FIGURE 14.1   Number of Times Advice Was Sought
on Pending Social Legislation**

1. *Frequency.* For example, we might measure the number of times that an inpatient psychiatric patient attends recreational therapy each week.
2. *Duration.* For example, we might measure the length of time that family members spend eating their evening meal together over a two-month period.
3. *Interval.* For example, we might measure the length of time between incidents of racial conflict within a community during five years.
4. *Magnitude.* For example, we might measure the amount of research grant money coming into a human service organization over a ten-year period.

Which type of measurement of the target problem is most appropriate for a given research study? The answer to this question relates in part to research issues and in part to treatment ones. The availability of measurement instruments for one or the other type of measurement may be an important consideration, especially if the target problem is one that is not easily measured, for example, an attitude or belief. It may also be more feasible to conduct one type of measurement than another. For example, the frequency of certain behaviors, such as substance abuse, may be difficult to measure with precision or may not be particularly relevant to intervention goals. But the interval between occurrences may be both.

The goal of intervention is an especially important consideration in determining how the dependent variable will be measured. For example, a practitioner may conclude that increasing the number of times that two parents discuss child-rearing practices or decreasing the interval between discussions is not consistent with intervention goals. This might be the case if, in the past, such discussions have always been superficial and brief. A more appropriate treatment goal might be to increase the duration of discussions of child rearing instead. Thus, it would be their duration (rather than their frequency or the interval between them) that would be measured and recorded.

As we discussed in Chapter 10, good measurement is both reliable and valid. However, in single-system studies, other issues must be considered. Measurement of a variable should be sensitive enough that it will record meaningful changes, yet not so sensitive that it will record changes that are meaningless in relationship to the goals of the intervention. It also should be as nonobtrusive as possible so that it does not interfere with the intervention itself.

Measurement also must be acceptable to the client or client system. This is in part an ethical issue. Because a power differential exists and because they fear displeasing the social worker, clients might agree to provide data that they would prefer not to provide or to permit measurement in a way that they might otherwise resist. Thus, it is the social worker's responsibility to ensure that both the measurement itself and its method of collection are acceptable to the client or client system.

## Conducting Single-System Research

We have presented an overview of what single-system research is and some of the issues that are considered in designing it. There is a general sequence of steps that are followed. They are presented in Figure 14.2.

Notice that seven of the eleven steps in Figure 14.2 are conducted before the research data are collected. As we have emphasized in other types of research, careful planning is critical to research success. With single-system research, steps 2 and 4 take on special importance if we are to learn about our practice effectiveness. We need to know exactly what our intervention is and what it is that we hope it is influencing. Otherwise, any findings are of little practical value. The importance of the other steps in Figure 14.2 will become more evident in our next discussion.

## Design Alternatives

Just like the research designs that we discussed in earlier chapters, different single-system designs have been created to answer different questions. Some are exploratory. They lack an A phase and seek simply to answer the question: Do

### FIGURE  14.2    The Usual Steps in Single-System Research

1. Describe the client's problem (or at least its symptoms).
2. Specify the target problem—the behavior, attitude, and so on (the dependent variable) and how you propose to measure it.
3. Identify the pattern of the dependent variable believed to exist (stable, rising, falling, and so forth).
4. In no more than fifty words, specify the treatment or intervention to be used (the independent variable) and how it will relate to other, ongoing services to the client.
5. Locate and specify professional literature that suggests that your treatment may produce the desired results.
6. Select from among the various single-subject designs the one that you will use. Justify why it is best, given such factors as time, ethical constraints, need to control for other variables, treatment goals, and so on.
7. Determine which pattern of the dependent variable would indicate that your intervention may be related to a desired effect with your client, that is, the treatment goal. Determine which pattern(s) would suggest the possibility that your intervention may have promoted unhealthy dependency or some other unintended consequence.
8. Conduct the research, carefully graphing measurements of the dependent variable over time.
9. Carefully analyze the results of the research relative to step 7.
10. If the intervention appears to have been associated with success, replicate the research with other similar clients or client groups who might also benefit from it.
11. Disseminate the results of the research to colleagues who might benefit from knowing them.

An earlier version of this figure appeared in Compton, B., & Galaway, B. (1999). *Social work processes* (4th ed.). Pacific Grove, CA: Brooks/Cole, 472.

changes occur with the presence of an intervention? Others are descriptive. They contain a baseline A phase and are used to answer the question: How *much* change occurs when an intervention is introduced? Still others are (at least loosely) described as experimental. They contain a series of alternating A and B phases, and attempt to answer the question: Does the intervention *cause* changes in the dependent variable? Experimental designs tend to be the most complex because they must attempt to control for threats to internal validity. We will look at examples of all three types, paying special attention to their specialized uses.

## B

The most basic of exploratory designs is the B design. It consists of the introduction of the intervention and then the monitoring of any changes that occur in the target problem during a predetermined time period. It is exactly what most responsible practitioners already do to some degree. However, if the monitoring were conducted as single-system research, (1) careful measurement (quantification) of the target problem would take place; (2) the research would end at the predetermined time (which may precede the termination of treatment); and (3) the measurements would be graphed and carefully interpreted. Other exploratory designs are BC or BCD, in which different interventions are tried in a predetermined sequence.

## AB

An AB design is just slightly more complicated than B and is considered descriptive. It consists of just two phases—a beginning baseline phase during which the intervention whose effectiveness is being evaluated is not offered, followed by an intervention phase when intervention is present (Figure 14.3). It cannot answer two important questions: (1) How do I know that it was the intervention and not something else that occurred at the same time that caused any changes (or lack of change) in the target problem? and (2) What would happen if I were to discontinue the intervention?

**FIGURE 14.3   AB Design: Patient Violence toward Staff**

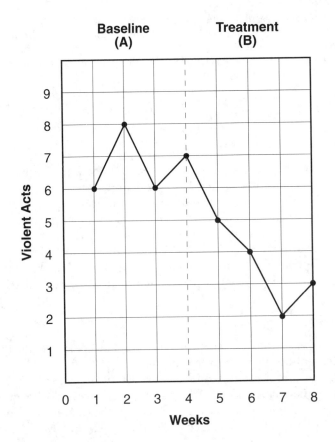

When using an AB design, the intervention being evaluated is not offered until a baseline phase of measurement (A phase) occurs. Thus, a social worker might have an ethical objection to using an AB design with a client or client system that is in imminent danger because the target problem is life threatening or otherwise destructive. For example, we might not want to use an AB design to see if a promising intervention is effective in reducing the number of times that a new client who is at high risk for contracting an HIV infection engages in unsafe sexual practices. We could not ethically justify waiting to offer the intervention just because we preferred to use an AB design. However, if we already have or can acquire valid data on the client's sexual practices prior to seeking treatment, we might be able to use them as our baseline.

AB is often the design of choice when permanent learning or nonreversible behavior or attitudes are a likely consequence (and a goal) of the intervention. Some behaviors, once learned, are not likely to spontaneously revert back if intervention were to be withdrawn. Perhaps, the behavior is even self-reinforcing. Then an AB may be appropriate. For example, a social worker may select a specific intervention to increase the frequency of assertive behaviors in a client. The intervention may be accompanied by an increase in these behaviors, as reflected in the B phase of the design. The AB design may be all that is needed to know that the intervention worked. The literature and our experience would tell us that the client is likely to continue assertive behaviors when appropriate, because they promote desired results.

In all single-system research designs, the dependent variable (target problem) must be measured accurately. But it should not be measured so narrowly that another similar behavior can simply be substituted for it. In the example portrayed in Figure 14.3, where intervention was used to attempt to reduce or eliminate physical attacks on staff within an inpatient psychiatric setting, we would not have wanted to use the variable "attacks on nurses" as the target problem, even if that is exactly what the target behavior was. A dramatic decline in the dependent variable during the intervention phase might have suggested successful intervention. However, during the time that the patient stopped attacking nurses, increased attacks on social work staff may have occured! This phenomenon is referred to as *symptom substitution*. In the example (Figure 14.3), we might question whether the possibility of symptom substitution has been fully eliminated. The patient's decline in violent behavior toward staff conceivably could still have been redirected toward other patients. This undesirable behavior would not be measured in the social worker's research because of the way the target problem was conceptualized and operationalized. It might have been even better to define the target problem as "physical attacks on other people," thus including other patients and even visitors as well.

When using descriptive designs such as AB (or ABC or ABCD), a social worker does not control for other variables (besides the intervention) that might produce change in the target problem. In the research portrayed in Figure 14.3, for example, the decrease in attacks on staff during the B phase may have been the effect of the intervention, but it is impossible to know for sure. It may also have been the result of changes in the patient's diet or medication, help offered by other staff, visits from the patient's relatives, pressure from other patients, the passage of time, and any of hundreds of other factors working alone or together.

Perhaps the A phase was just an atypical time for the patient (sampling error) and the B phase is simply more typical of the patient's behavior. Then the B phase did not really reflect change. Descriptive single-system designs can only answer the question: How much change occurred? if they have good baseline measurement which describes accurately what conditions are typical prior to the introduction of the intervention.

If measurements of the target problem in an A phase constitute what is believed to be a good baseline, simply "eyeballing" the data on a graph can provide a pretty good idea of how much change occurred and whether it is in the predicted direction. But it is possible to do even more. In descriptive studies where there is a baseline A phase followed by a B phase (also the case in explanatory designs), statistical analyses of the data can be used to determine the mathematical probability that any differences in the dependent variable between the A and B phases represent nothing more than normal fluctuation. There are several easily computed tests (beyond the scope of this book) that can tell us if the difference between the measurements in the A phase and the subsequent B phase is statistically significant; that is, it is large enough that the probability of its representing just normal fluctuation over time is quite small.

## *ABA*

If a second phase of observation and measurement is used following an A phase and then the introduction of an intervention, we have an ABA design. This experimental design is an effort to increase internal validity. If the target problem shows improvement during the B phase and then it seems to get worse during the second A phase, this may provide further evidence of the effectiveness of the intervention. It also can suggest what may be an undesirable dependency on the intervention, because the problem only seems to get better during the presence of the intervention.

What if, for example, the intervention goal is to reduce marijuana usage? This occurs during the B phase, but it increases again during the second A phase, as illustrated in Figure 14.4. The amount of marijuana usage and the presence or absence of intervention seem to be related in a desirable direction. However, does this observation provide evidence that intervention has been successful? Maybe, maybe not. Some treatment methods (for example, those used by Alcoholics Anonymous) actually promote dependency or, perhaps more accurately, seek to substitute one form of dependency for a more desirable one. If, in our example, this was a goal of our intervention, we might conclude that it was successful.

Other interpretations of the findings also could be made. Perhaps the intervention would have produced permanent change, but it did not continue long enough to be successful. Perhaps a longer period of intervention might be

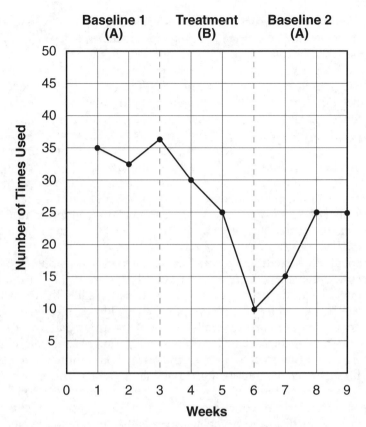

**FIGURE 14.4   ABA Design: Marijuana Usage**

indicated. That would be a useful and generally positive interpretation. But another way to interpret the findings is that, because desirable behavior occurred only when the client experienced the intervention (and not following it), the intervention may not have been successful. If the social worker/practitioner had hypothesized that the single intervention would be so effective that it would permanently reduce heavy marijuana usage, there is a lack of support for this hypothesis. The results of research that uses an ABA design (as well as those of many other designs) must be interpreted with special attention to the issue of the desirability of client dependency on the continued presence of an intervention.

Most likely, the social worker in our example hoped to see a further decline in marijuana usage or at least no increase in it during the second A phase. That would have been what single-system researchers refer to as *treatment carryover*. If a previously established (during the B phase) pattern continues or if not much change occurs in the transition from the B phase to the second A phase of an ABA design, it is often hard to know just how to interpret the results of the research. It may be that it makes little difference whether the intervention continues past a certain time; that is, the social worker has achieved the goal of most social work intervention: permanent change without ongoing dependency.

The second A phase of the ABA design (and of other designs that use more than one A phase) can be characterized by either withdrawal of the intervention, or reversal, a deliberate attempt to reverse the pattern of the target behavior within the prior B phase. Withdrawal generally is the method used in second and subsequent A phases in single-system research. Not surprisingly, many social workers object to the use of reversal methods during later A phases. Could a social worker ethically attempt to increase marijuana usage or some other behavior that, in treatment planning or contracting with the client, was identified as a problem? Or, ethically, should a social worker attempt to decrease the frequency of a client behavior that is judged to be in the client's best interests, just to attempt to find further evidence of the effect of a treatment intervention on it? For ethical as well as logistical reasons, ABA and other designs that use reversal are quite rare in social work research.

Although an ABA design can tell the researcher what happens to a behavior after the intervention stops (which an AB design cannot do), it is not a favorite among social workers. This is probably because it both begins and ends with an A phase in which the intervention believed to be effective is not given. Unless good data are already available about the prior pattern of the target problem, it requires the social worker to wait a period of time before offering a promising form of intervention. Later, the research is completed in a second A phase, during which the intervention is again not offered. This may make some social workers uncomfortable because it does not parallel the natural course of treatment in many social work practice settings. For example, patients hospitalized with acute medical and psychiatric problems often are in the greatest need of intervention from social workers just after entering and just before leaving the hospital.

There are two common misunderstandings that probably contribute to a reluctance to use ABA and other designs that begin and end in an A phase. First, some people mistakenly think that all assistance or services to the client or client system are denied during an A phase. This is not correct. During A phases, only the specific intervention that is the independent variable within the research (often an adjunct to the usual services) is not provided to the client. Usual services continue to be offered. Second, there is no reason why the course of a single system design has to coincide with the course of social work treatment. The research does not have to start at the time that treatment is begun; it can begin later. Nor does it have to end at the time of treatment termination; it can end (and often does) while the client is still being offered services. Thus, a treatment that appears to have been successful based on an evaluation using an ABA design can be reintroduced and continued indefinitely after the second A phase has been completed and the research has ended. A social worker would be very likely to do this because the research seemed to indicate that the intervention was beneficial to the client.

## *ABAB*

The addition of one or more alternating A and B phases helps to provide additional evidence for a cause-effect relationship between the dependent and independent variables. Figure 14.5 is the graph of an ABAB design that a social worker used with a client whose problem was an inability to make decisions. The social worker sought to increase the frequency of the client's independent decision making through an intervention method that had been devised. As Figure 14.5 suggests, the intervention appears to have produced more independent decision making, but the frequency of the dependent variable declined when the intervention was withdrawn during the second A phase. The client's desirable behavior seemed to be very much dependent on the presence of the intervention by the social worker. Can this finding really be interpreted as an indication of success in treating a client whose problem was one of excessive dependency to begin with? Very likely, no.

**FIGURE 14.5    ABAB Design: Independent Decisions
              Made by Client**

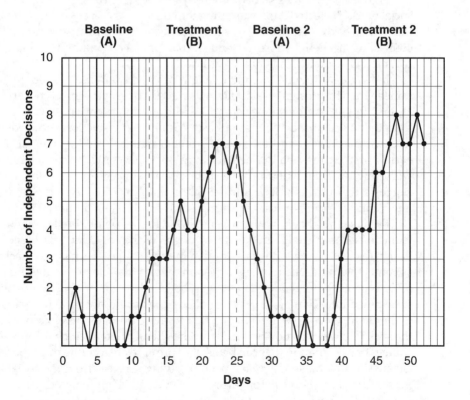

An ABAB design can readily detect whether dependency on the presence of an intervention occurred. Thus, it is appropriate in intervention situations where client dependency is viewed as desirable and where the social worker wishes to see if it has been established or with an already-dependent client like the one in our example, where there was concern that an undesirable dependency might occur and the social worker wanted to know whether it did.

Unlike the ABA design, the ABAB ends in an intervention (B) phase. This is considered a plus by those social work researcher/practitioners who, justifiably or not, have misgivings about using those designs that end in an A phase.

## BAB

BAB designs are quite popular experimental designs among social work practitioners. They begin and end in an intervention (B) phase, characteristics that appear to be consistent with social work practice values and ethics. They are especially well suited to crisis situations where the social worker believes that conducting a baseline measurement prior to offering the intervention would be unethical, but where it is believed that the intervention can safely be withdrawn after a short period of time.

Figure 14.6 illustrates a BAB single-system research design. The public health social worker selected it for examining the effectiveness of a "shock" intervention method (weekly discussions of rising disease rates in nearby communities) in counseling a client whose current sexual practices put him at high risk of contracting sexually transmitted diseases.

In single-system research, the length of A and B phases generally is determined when the design is selected. In using a BAB design, ethical concerns center around the timing of the decision to withdraw intervention; that is, the move from the first B phase into the A phase. Without extensive foreknowledge of the research participant and the target problem pattern (unlike when an A phase occurs first), it may be difficult to know when it could be considered safe to withdraw the intervention. What if the social worker's professional judgment suggests that ethically it would be detrimental to the client to withdraw the intervention at the time that the design calls for it to be withdrawn?

Because they begin without benefit of a first A phase, BAB designs are less likely to be completed than the other designs we have already discussed. A BAB design (as well as other designs, for that matter) sometimes has to be "scrapped" as contact with the client or client system reveals that the problem is either more or less of an emergency than it was believed to be or that removal of the anticipated intervention at the prescribed time would not be in the best interest of the client. Of course, the lack of a first A phase does not necessarily mean that the social worker has no knowledge of the client. There may be records or other sources of information that can be used to provide an accurate description of the client. The client also may have been receiving services from the social worker for some period of time before the research design is implemented. It is not at all unusual for a social worker to decide to conduct single-system research with a

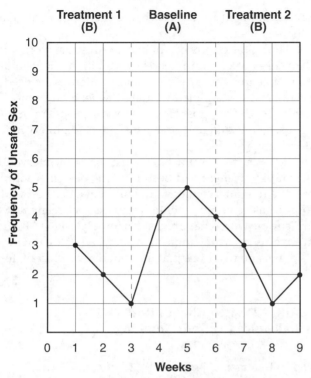

**FIGURE 14.6 BAB Design: Client Practice of Unsafe Sex**

client who has been known for some time. Often, observation of a client problem over time is the impetus for conducting single-system research. As we have already emphasized, whether a single-system design to evaluate the effect of a specific form of intervention begins in an A phase or a B phase, the course of the research does not have to coincide (chronologically) with the course of treatment.

## ABCD

Sometimes, as practitioners, we know of several different interventions that may be effective, but none of them is clearly indicated to be the most effective. We seek some general guidance as to which may be best or, to be more precise, which one or series of them seems to work best with a given client or client system. (Remember, as we emphasized in our discussion of case studies, that any generalizations based on very small, unrepresentative samples are ill advised.) The ABCD design examines several different interventions introduced one at a time. It thus is used to examine the relationship among several independent variables (interventions) and a single dependent variable (a target problem). An ABCD design can provide a beginning indication of the relative effectiveness of several different interventions. Several of them, used with different clients who have the same problem, can also begin to tell us what sequence of treatments may be associated with the best results.

Figure 14.7 illustrates the efforts of a public health social worker to evaluate the relative effectiveness of several interventions with a client in a smoking-cessation program. Note that three different interventions were used in succession. Each intervention was attempted for the same length of time. That is not always the case with ABCD designs. However, if different-length intervention phases had been used, the different lengths allotted for interventions might constitute an intervening variable.

Note that in the research (Figure 14.7) three different interventions were introduced (B, C, and D). If there had been four, the design would have been ABCDE; if there were five interventions, it would have been ABCDEF, and so forth. Figure 14.7 also has no nonintervention A phases between interventions. If they had been present, we would have had still another design (ABACAD). Such a design would give us a clearer indication of whether treatment carryover occurred. But, its downside would be that the cumulative effect of, for example,

**FIGURE  14.7   ABCD Design: Client Effort
to Reduce Cigarette Smoking**

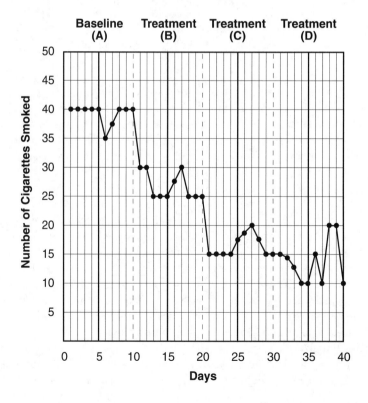

treatments B, C, and D would not be as easy to determine because of the presence of A phases between them. One question to ask in the selection of a research design is always: Exactly what is it that we want to know? The answer to that question suggests the most appropriate design.

The lack of an A phase between successive interventions is why ABCD designs are not very useful for learning which of several interventions is most effective in influencing the target problem. The potential for treatment carryover from one phase into subsequent ones can make it difficult to determine just which intervention produced the most change in the dependent variable (target problem). For example, the continuation of a desired behavior at approximately the same level following the shift from one intervention to another, as in the D phase in Figure 14.7, may mean that interventions C and D are equally effective. It may also mean that the effects of intervention C continued on through the D phase. If so, it may be this carryover and not intervention D that produced the level of the desired behavior in the D phase. Another interpretation may be that intervention D may simply be ineffective or may even promote smoking. If this is true, the social worker would have even further support for the effectiveness of intervention C. But how can we know this is what happened? The possibility of treatment carryover can severely limit any conclusions about the relative effectiveness of different interventions when ABCD designs are used. If such conclusions are sought, an ABACAD design would be preferable.

ABCD designs like the one reported in Figure 14.7 can still provide some useful information about the sequence of interventions that is associated with the best results. The researcher who conducted the smoking-cessation research could use the same participant again (or another one with a similar problem), again use an ABCD type design, but reverse the order of interventions. This time, the researcher could begin in an A phase but then introduce interventions C, B, and D in sequence. Then the sequence might be interventions D, C, and B, and so forth. It might be possible to use the same participant over and over again in our example, given what we know about smoking recidivism ("Quitting smoking is easy I've done it at least a hundred times"). Eventually, the best sequence of two or more treatments might be identified, especially if the research were to be replicated many other times with similar participants. Obviously, this use of ABCD designs would not be possible with many types of target problems; it would not be suitable where a problem or behavior does not tend to reoccur. But unfortunately, problem recidivism does occur in our work. In situations where it tends to happen (for example, family violence, substance abuse, truancy, delinquency), the repeated use of the ABCD design can sometimes be quite enlightening.

Ethical concerns related to use of ABCD designs are not as great as with some other designs. One issue sometimes voiced relates to withdrawing an apparently successful intervention in order to substitute one that may not be found to work as well. But this is not as problematic as it might first seem, because the withdrawal of an apparently successful intervention most often is immediately followed by another promising intervention, not by an A phase. Besides, the most successful intervention can always be reintroduced after the research is completed at the predetermined time.

## Multiple Baseline

Sometimes the social work practitioner may use an intervention method that may be suited to influencing two or more (usually related) target problems. There is a need to verify its overall effectiveness, but also to find out if it seems to influence one target problem more effectively than the other. In this situation, the social worker has one independent variable (the intervention method) and more than one dependent variable (target problems). Then a multiple-baseline single-system design may be the design of choice.

When using a multiple-baseline design, an A phase precedes the introduction of the intervention. During that phase, baseline measurements of the two or more dependent variables are taken. Then the intervention is introduced to attempt to influence one of them. Generally, it is applied first to the target problem that has reflected the clearest pattern of occurence during the initial baseline measurement (A) phase. As the intervention is offered (the first B phase), baseline measurement of the other target problem(s) continues, thus creating an extended A phase for it. Following efforts to influence the first target problem with the intervention (the first B phase), a second B phase occurs. During it, intervention shifts to the second target problem, while a second A phase occurs for the first target problem—the intervention is no longer applied to it. If there are more than two dependent variables, the intervention then shifts to the third variable, while the first remains in an extended second A phase and the second enters a second A phase, and so forth.

Figure 14.8 illustrates an application of a multiple-baseline design that had only two target problems. The researcher, a social worker assigned to a home health program, was trying to get her patient, a 64-year-old woman who was recovering from a stroke, to be more involved in the activities that she had enjoyed prior to her illness. It was believed that renewed participation in them would be physically therapeutic and would also help the patient to feel more self-confident and thus improve her overall attitude toward life. The patient identified two such activities: crocheting and meal preparation (the dependent variables). The intervention (the independent variable) consisted of bringing along magazines and other written materials on one and then the other activity to weekly home visits and spending a minimum of fifteen minutes each visit discussing them with the patient. The patient kept a record of her involvement in both activities for the duration of the research and shared it with the social worker at each weekly visit. The social worker graphed both activities as in Figure 14.8. During the first four weeks, only the usual counseling took place. It formed the baseline phase (A) for the first target problem (crocheting) and the first half of an extended baseline phase (A) for the second target problem (meal preparation). During weeks 5 through 8, materials on crocheting were brought and discussed (intervention). However, no similar discussion of meal preparation

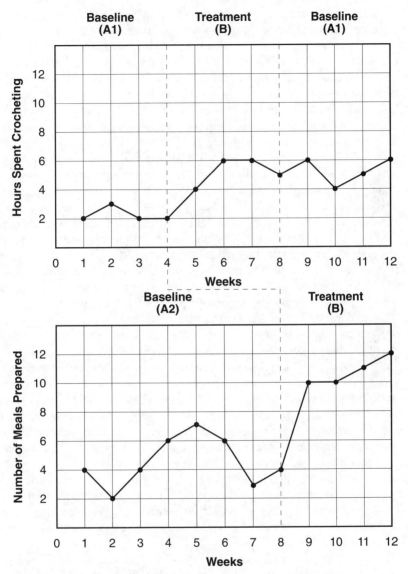

**FIGURE 14.8   Multiple-Baseline Design: Crocheting and Meal Preparation**

took place. Discussion of meal preparation materials (recipes, cooking magazines) provided by the social worker did not take place until weeks 9 through 12. During that time, no crocheting literature was provided or discussed. Thus, a second baseline phase (A) was established for crocheting during weeks 9 through 12, because efforts to influence crocheting activities had been withdrawn.

How might we interpret the data displayed in Figure 14.8? At first blush, it appears that the intervention was accompanied by more success when applied to meal preparation than to crocheting. But if we examine the graph a little more carefully and apply our knowledge of social work practice, many other possible interpretations might be proposed. Some of them relate to possible interaction between the two dependent variables. For example, notice that during weeks 2 through 5, meal preparation was already on the increase, even though the intervention had not yet been applied to it. We might speculate that the decline in meal preparation during weeks 5 through 7 was related to the patient's increased involvement in crocheting during that time. Perhaps the crocheting actually made it more difficult for the patient to prepare her meals, a logical conclusion. We might also question whether the dramatic increase in meal preparation during weeks 9 through 12 was not just a resumption of the trend that had been evident during weeks 2 through 5. Perhaps it was not the intervention that produced it, but just the patient adjusting to the increase in her crocheting activity. Or perhaps the increased amount of time spent in meal preparation during weeks 9 through 12 may have been the result of the intervention. It also may have limited any further increase in time spent crocheting. Still other interpretations of changes in both target problems are possible.

Interpreting findings from any single-system research requires a heavy dose of logic and an awareness of treatment goals. It also entails a recognition of the client or client system's limitations and wishes. We know that, during the time the patient in our example was crocheting, she could not be preparing meals, and vice versa. There also was a limit to how many meals the patient might reasonably have been expected to prepare in a week (probably twenty-one, if she had no physical limitations). There was a less obvious limit to the amount of time we might have expected her to spend crocheting. Was it six hours a week? Ten? What was reasonable, and what would have been therapeutic for her? What was her pattern of behavior before she had the stroke? What was she capable of and desirous of doing at the time of the research? At what point would she have been spending too much time crocheting or cooking meals? What would have been the optimal amount of time spent in either activity, given any limitations that she had and the need for other activities such as physical therapy or just resting or socializing?

Regardless of which activity may have been influenced more by the intervention, one interpretation of the research might be that the social worker may have demonstrated at least some degree of overall success in helping the patient become more active. Of course, there is no way to know even this for certain. The patient's greater activity during the latter weeks of the research may have been more attributable to improved health, a relative's cajoling or threats, or some other threat to the internal validity of the research design rather than to the social worker's intervention.

Multiple-baseline designs are well suited to situations where two or more related target problems can be measured and where a single intervention shows promise for influencing either or both of them. Primarily because of the fact that this combination occurs so frequently in social work practice settings, they have been widely advocated for evaluating individual social work practice. Unlike some of the other designs that we have discussed, multiple-baseline designs in this example do not present as many ethical issues related to withdrawing an intervention that may have been accompanied by some success. Once an intervention is introduced, it is continued in a related form. Of course, because it shifts from one target problem to another, there is the potential for treatment carryover. This produces some of the problems that we encounter in attempting to interpret findings. One way to reduce the likelihood of treatment carryover is to add an A phase between each introduction of the independent variable where it is not applied to any target problem. Of course, doing this results in a different and even more complicated design.

There are many different ways in which multiple-baseline designs can be used; we have mentioned just one of them. In addition to situations in which there is one intervention and two target problems, they can also be used when there is one intervention and two or more similar settings. For example, we could use a multiple baseline to attempt to answer the question: In which setting is the intervention most effective? We could also use the same design (with the same graphing methods) if we have one intervention but two or more similar clients whose problem is the same. Then we could use it to answer the question: With which client does the intervention work best?

## Strengths and Weaknesses of Single-System Research

Single-system research is not new. It has been discussed in the social work literature for more than thirty years. During the 1980s, it was rediscovered and touted as a logical bridge between research and practice, two activities that, as we suggested in Chapter 1, all too often have occurred independently of each other.

An objective assessment of the place of single-system research would probably conclude that it falls somewhere between those of its most vocal advocates and critics, recognizing that it has both strengths and some very definite weaknesses. On the positive side of the ledger, single-system research designs are inexpensive to implement. They cost very little in time and other resources, something that generally cannot be said of group research designs. They are easily comprehended; a short staff development program is all that is needed to get staff started in using them to evaluate their practice. They offer almost instantaneous feedback regarding a social worker's practice effectiveness. There is no need to wait months or even years to acquire and disseminate research findings—a phenomenon that is more typical when group research designs are used. In single-system research, data are collected and are interpreted on an ongoing basis while practice intervention continues. Application of findings is thus easily and quickly accomplished.

Findings from single-system research are never obscure or esoteric; they are in a form that is amenable to utilization. They can provide useful early feedback about new or experimental intervention methods. The methods can be quickly evaluated and either discarded or, if they seem to be promising, evaluated more thoroughly using group research designs.

Single-system research provides good feedback for evaluating the effectiveness of practice intervention methods, especially those that are primarily task centered or problem solving in nature. Sometimes a series of studies using the same dependent and independent variables, the same designs, and participants with the same behaviors or problems can begin to suggest knowledge that transcends any one case. This method (replication) is the only way that single-system research can make any claim to generalized knowledge building or to producing findings with external validity. However, any such claim is a tenuous one at best, given what we know about the uniqueness of all people and their situations.

A lack of external validity of findings is single-system research's greatest limitation. Without careful replication (and sometimes even with it), single-system research fails to even begin to suggest groups or categories of persons with whom an intervention will or will not be effective. As we suggested when we discussed case studies in Chapter 7, it is presumptuous to attempt to generalize findings that were derived from studying a unique sample of one. Such a sample is so small that sampling error is a virtual certainty. It also is not randomly selected. Thus, it cannot be considered representative of anything but itself.

Single-system research also cannot be used to evaluate all individual practice effectiveness. It is frequently unsuitable for evaluating a social worker's practice in many situations where intervention success cannot be equated with specific, easily measurable changes in some target problem. Even where it is appropriate for use, it often must depend on a client's own measurement and self-report of target problems (especially when used anywhere other than in institutional settings). The accuracy of self-reported measurement can easily be questioned. However, this potential problem is no stranger to the social worker. Almost all intervention must rely heavily on the fact that what others tell us is truthful and accurate.

Another problem related to single-system research is that it cannot be used productively unless work environments support its use. Even though the research requires relatively little time and effort on the part of the practitioner, problems can occur unless administrators and supervisors are convinced of its value. A supervisor who fails to share a commitment to it and who does not understand it may view it with suspicion and even perceive a supervisee to be wasting time conducting it. No one will want to conduct single-system research if a supervisor demands to know why the social worker is "fooling around with those graphs when you should be seeing clients or keeping your records up to date."

If single-system research is not understood and valued by administrators and supervisors, an even worse problem can occur. A supervisor may attempt to use a social worker's research findings (including graphs) as evidence of the supervisee's competence (or lack of it). They may be used for annual or semiannual performance evaluations or to support personnel actions. This practice can be tempting for supervisors seeking "objective" criteria to justify their actions. But it is a gross misuse of single-system research. The research is not intended as a vehicle to assist the supervisor in evaluating the researcher; it is intended primarily as feedback for the researcher/practitioner. Any other use will quickly discourage a social worker from conducting it. However, on occasions when a supervisor has understood and appreciated the purpose of single-system research, some supervisees have been able to discuss their findings safely and productively in case supervision conferences designed to help them use their research findings to become more effective practitioners.

## Ethical Issues

We have alluded to a number of ethical concerns that have been voiced regarding the use of single-system research. However, most of them, when examined carefully, are really nonissues. For example, as we noted, contrary to some misconceptions, A phases need not be time periods when no services are offered; only the intervention that is being evaluated is withheld. Similarly, a design that ends in an A phase does not mean that a client cannot later receive an intervention method that was associated with a desirable change in the target problem. Duration of treatment can be longer (on both ends) than the duration of the research.

Even the strongest advocates of single-system research would never suggest that the research should take precedence over the welfare of those we are committed to help. Suppose that a single-system design calls for a change, for example, the removal of an apparently successful intervention or the introduction of one that, based on new knowledge of the client, may prove injurious. If so, the research may simply have to be terminated or the design altered, despite the fact that either decision may result in less valuable feedback to the social worker. Or, if the design calls for no change to occur and the current A or B phase appears to not be in the client's best interest, the research design also may have to be discarded. Practice values should always take precedence over the researcher's need for knowledge. This same principle applies in all forms of research. However, when single-system designs are used, the cost of ending the research prematurely or changing the design for ethical reasons is rarely great. In contrast, in large-group designs, it can be very expensive.

There are a few ethical issues that have yet to be resolved. They relate to what we discussed back in Chapter 2. Some people claim that conducting research with one's clients comes dangerously close to a dual relationship and may therefore be unethical. Others suggest that the only way to avoid this conflict is to have clients sign consent forms, thus ensuring that the principle of voluntary informed consent has not been violated. Still others content that single-system research is just part of good practice; it is not research per se. Thus, a signed consent form is not necessary. They see nothing unethical about using a method to systematically monitor and evaluate one's practice in order to ensure that the best possible interventions are offered. In fact, they suggest, it would be irresponsible for a professional not to do so.

Different agencies have different rules and policies on the use of consent forms and the necessity of review of single-system proposals by institutional review boards (IRBs). Administrators in some settings (for example, teaching hospitals) contend that a client receiving services has already agreed to participate in research and that no additional requirements must be met. Other settings may require one or both for their legal protection. Even universities have different policies on the issues. The university where one of the authors of this book teaches requires professors of students conducting single-system research to submit a summary of all proposed studies to an IRB for approval and that students request their research participants (clients) to sign an informed voluntary consent form. At the university where the other author teachers, there are no such requirements, because single-system research is seen more as a part of social work practice than as research.

Because there is a lack of consensus on a number of ethical issues related to single-system research, a social worker must be careful to check out what rules and policies are in force in the agency or other institution under whose auspices the research will be conducted. Generally, any rules or policies in effect are not very prohibitive and should not discourage anyone from conducting this valuable type of research.

## Summary

In this chapter, we examined several alternatives for practitioners who wish to receive feedback about their practice effectiveness. The one that relies most on the research methods discussed in this book, single-system research, involves a careful monitoring of changes in certain behaviors, attitudes, perceptions, or other characteristics of clients or client systems. Design variations are employed to attempt to answer different questions, to control for the effect of other variables, and to be able to conduct research in a way that is not in conflict with professional values and practice ethics. We discussed only a few of the simpler designs that can be used, stressing their specialized usage and individual strengths and shortcomings. We demonstrated the importance (and the complexity) of interpreting research findings.

Single-system designs are intended for the use of the individual practitioner. They are not appropriate for evaluating some types of social work intervention. They also are of very limited use in contributing to our generalized body of knowledge. However, through replication it is possible to build knowledge that is not merely specific to work with an individual client or client system.

# References

1. Hudson, W. (1982). *The clinical measurement package: A field manual.* Homewood, IL: The Dorsey Press.
2. See, for example, Gabor, P., Unrau, Y., & Grinnell, R., Jr. (1998). *Evaluation and quality improvement in the human services.* Needham Heights, MA: Allyn & Bacon; or Bloom, M., Fischer, J., & Orme, J. (1999). *Evaluating practice: Guidelines for the accountable professional.* Needham Heights, MA: Allyn & Bacon.
3. Bloom, Fischer, & Orme (1999).

# POSTSCRIPT

We began our discussion of research methods for social workers by noting the gap that has often existed between research and social work practice. We ended it with a discussion of research methods whose findings have immediate practical use for the social work practitioner. This was not unintentional. We wanted to end this book by reminding the reader that practice utilization of research findings is not an unachievable goal.

In the past, the publication of a researcher's findings in a report or some other method of dissemination has been far from a guarantee that the findings would be used for practice decision making. Thousands of potentially useful research reports have been archived in a library or some other repository where they have never been read by anyone. Sometimes it has seemed as if the purpose of conducting research has been to say that we did it to address some problem rather than to acquire knowledge. Even program evaluation documents have been known to have little influence on practice methods and client services. Once having served their political and/or economic purposes, few if any of their recommendations have been implemented.

Social workers who have attended research presentations at in-service training or professional conferences often have failed to apply the findings of the research to their practice or even to see a connection between what they learned and their day-to-day activities. They seem to go about their business pretty much as before, uninfluenced by the researchers' efforts. Even the findings from single-subject research probably have been ignored on occasion, especially if they are contrary to the practitioner's wishes and beliefs.

Since 1991, when the first edition of this book was published, we have observed that the old scenario of research nonutilization in social work has changed. Since the previous edition of this book was written, progress toward empirically based practice has been even more visible. Increased emphasis on qualitative research has provided many social workers with research methods and findings to which they could easily relate.

A commitment to use the findings of research in our practice will continue to occur only if individual social workers hold the belief that research and practice are more similar than dissimilar, and that the two activities have much to offer each other. When social work practitioners decide to use research findings for practice decision making, they make a statement about the value of empirically based practice as well as a commitment to provide the best possible services to their clients.

Knowledge building through the use of scientific methods is highly consistent with all forms of good social work practice. Research utilization can flow naturally and productively from an understanding of research methods, once they are shown to be logical and complementary to practice. We hope that we have been successful in helping to develop this important linkage among the readers of this book.

# ADDITIONAL READINGS IN RESEARCH METHODS

Abrahamson, M. (1983). *Social research methods.* Englewood Cliffs, NJ: Prentice Hall.

Alter, C. F., & Evens, W. (1990). *Evaluating your practice: A guide to self assessment.* New York: Springer Publishing Company.

Anastas, J. W., & MacDonald, M. L. (1994). *Research design for social work and the human services.* New York: Lexington Books.

Atherton, C. R., & Klemmack, D. L. (1982). *Research methods in social work.* Lexington, MA: D. C. Heath and Company.

Babbie, E. (1998). *The practice of social research* (8th ed.). Belmont, CA: Wadsworth Publishing.

Babbie, E. (1990). *Survey research methods.* Belmont, CA: Wadsworth Publishing Company.

Bailey, K. D. (1994). *Methods of social research* (4th ed.). New York: The Free Press.

Barlow, D. H., & Hersen, J. (1984). *Single-case experimental designs: Strategies for studying behavioral change.* New York: Pergamon Press.

Bausell, B. R. (1994). *Conducting meaningful experiments: 40 steps to becoming a scientist.* Thousand Oaks, CA: Sage Publications.

Beebe, L. (1993). *Professional writing for the human services.* Annapolis: NASW Press.

Berg, B. L. (1989). *Qualitative research methods for the social sciences* (2nd ed.). Needham Heights, MA: Allyn & Bacon.

Black, T. (1993). *Evaluating social science research.* Thousand Oaks, CA: Sage Publications.

Bloom, M., Fischer, J., & Orme, J. (1995). *Evaluating practice: Guidelines for the accountable professional* (2nd ed.). Needham Heights, MA: Allyn & Bacon.

Bouman, G. D. (1995). *A handbook of social science research* (2nd ed.). New York: Oxford University Press.

Camilli, G., & Shepard, L. A. (1994). *Methods for identifying biased test items.* Thousand Oaks, CA: Sage Publications.

Campbell, D., & Stanley, J. (1963). *Experimental and quasi-experimental designs for research.* Boston: Houghton Mifflin.

Cliff, N. (1996). *Ordinal methods for behavioral data analysis.* Mahwah, NJ: Erlbaum.

Cook, T. D., & Campbell, D. T. (1979). *Quasi-experimentation: Design and analysis issues for field settings.* Chicago: Rand McNally.

Corcoran, K., & Fischer, J. (1987). *Measures for clinical practice: A sourcebook.* New York: The Free Press.

Cortazzi, M. (1993). *Narrative analysis.* Washington, DC: Falmer Press.

Craft, J. (1990). *Statistics and data analysis for social workers* (2nd ed.). Itasca, IL: F. E. Peacock Publishers.

Creswell, J. (1994). *Research design: Qualitative and quantitative approaches.* Thousand Oaks, CA: Sage Publications.

Dawson, B., Klass, M., Guy, R., & Edgley, C. (1991). *Understanding social work research.* Needham Heights, MA: Allyn & Bacon.

Denzin, N., & Lincoln, Y. (1994). *Handbook of qualitative research.* Thousand Oaks, CA: Sage Publications.

DePoy, E., & Gitlin, L. N. (1994). *Introduction to research: Multiple strategies for health and human services.* St. Louis: Mosby–Year Book.

Dey, E. (1993). *Qualitative data analysis: A user-friendly guide for social scientists.* New York: Routledge.

Dixon, G. R., Bouma, G. D., & Atkinson, B. J. (1987). *A handbook of social science research.* New York: Oxford University Press.

Eisikovits, R. A., & Kashti, Y. (1987). *Qualitative research and evaluation in group care.* Binghamton, NY: The Hawthorne Press.

Feldman, M. S. (1995). *Strategies for interpreting qualitative data.* Thousand Oaks, CA: Sage Publications.

Fink, A., & Kosecoff, J. (1985). *How to conduct surveys.* Thousand Oaks, CA: Sage Publications.

Fischer, J., & Corcoran, K. (1994). *Measures for clinical practice* (2nd ed.). Vol. 1: *Couples, Families, and Children.* Vol. 2: *Adults.* New York: The Free Press.

Fitz-Gibbon, C. T., & Morris, L. L. (1987). *How to design a program evaluation.* Newbury Park, CA: Sage Publications.

Fowler, F. J., Jr. (1993). *Survey research methods* (2nd ed.). Thousand Oaks, CA: Sage Publications.

Gabor, P. A., & Grinnell, R. M., Jr. (1994). *Evaluation and quality improvement in the human services.* Needham Heights, MA: Allyn & Bacon.

Gilbert, N. (1993). *Researching social life.* Thousand Oaks, CA: Sage Publications.

Gilgun, J., Daly, K., & Handel, G. (1992). *Qualitative methods in family research.* Thousand Oaks, CA: Sage Publications.

Gillespie, D. F., & Glisson, C. (1993). *Quantitative methods in social work.* Binghamton, NY: The Haworth Press.

Ginsberg, L. (1995). *Social work almanac* (2nd ed.). Silver Spring, MD: NASW Press.

Glaser, B. G., & Strauss, A. (1967). *The discovery of grounded theory: Strategies for qualitative research.* Hawthorne, NY: Aldine de Gruyter.

Grasso, A. J., & Epstein, I. (1992). *Research utilization in the social services: Innovations for practice and administration.* Binghamton, NY: The Haworth Press.

Grinnell, R. M., Jr. (1997). *Social work research and evaluation* (5th ed.). Itasca, IL: F. E. Peacock Publishers.

Goldstein, H. (1969). *Research standards and methods for social workers.* Northbrook, IL: Whitehall.

Guy, R. F., Edgley, C. E., Arafat, I., & Allen, D. E. (1987). *Social research methods: Puzzles and solutions.* Needham Heights, MA: Allyn & Bacon.

Hall, L. D., & Marshall, K. P. (1992). *Computing for social research: Practical approaches.* Belmont, CA: Wadsworth Publishing Company.

Hamel, J. (1993). *Case study methods.* Thousand Oaks, CA: Sage Publications.

Hammersley, M. (1993). *Social research.* Thousand Oaks, CA: Sage Publications.

Hart, C. (1999). *Doing a literature review.* Thousand Oaks, CA: Sage Publications.

Hedderson, J., & Fisher, M. (1993). *SPSS made simple* (2nd ed.). Belmont, CA: Wadsworth Publishing Company.

Herzog, T. R. (1996). *Research methods in the social sciences.* New York: Harper- Collins.

Hoover, K., & Donovan, T. (1995). *The elements of social scientific thinking.* New York: St. Martin's Press.

Hudson, W. (1982). *The clinical measurement package: A field manual.* Homewood, IL: The Dorsey Press.

Humphreys, L. (1975). *Tearoom trade: Impersonal sex in public places* (2nd ed.). Chicago: Aldine Press.

Jayartne, S., & Levy, R. (1979). *Empirical clinical practice.* New York: Columbia University Press.

Jones, J. H. (1982). *Bad blood: The Tuskegee syphilis experiment.* New York: The Free Press.

Judd, C. M., Smith, E. R., & Kidder, L. H. (1991). *Research methods in social relations* (6th ed.). Fort Worth, TX: Harcourt Brace.

Katz, J. (1972). *Experimentation with human beings.* New York: Russell Sage Foundation.

Kazdin, A. E., & Hussain, A. (1982). *Single-case research designs.* San Francisco: Jossey-Bass.

Kerlinger, F. N. (1986). *Foundations of behavioral research* (3rd ed.). New York: Holt, Rinehart and Winston.

Kish, L. (1965). *Survey sampling.* New York: John Wiley and Sons.

Kish, L. (1987). *Statistical design for research.* New York: John Wiley and Sons.

Labaw, P. (1985). *Advanced questionnaire design.* Cambridge, MA: Abt Books.

Langbein, L. I. (1980). *Discovering whether programs work: A guide to statistical methods for program evaluation.* Santa Monica, CA: Goodyear Publishing Company.

Lavrakas, P. J. (1993). *Telephone survey methods.* Thousand Oaks, CA: Sage Publications.

Lee, R. M., (1993). *Doing research on sensitive topics.* Thousand Oaks, CA: Sage Publications.

Leedy, P. (1997). *Practical research planning and design* (6th ed.). New York: Macmillan Publishing.

Lofland, J., & Lofland, L. (1995). *Analyzing social settings* (3rd ed.). Belmont, CA: Wadsworth Publishing Company.

Majchrzak, A. (1984). *Methods for policy research.* Newbury Park, CA: Sage Publications.

Mark, R. (1996). *Research made simple: A handbook for social workers.* Thousand Oaks, CA: Sage Publications.

Marlow, C. (1998). *Research methods for generalist social work* (2nd ed.). Pacific Grove, CA: Brooks/Cole Publishing Company.

Marshall, C., & Rossman, G. B. (1995). *Designing qualitative research* (2nd ed.). Thousand Oaks, CA: Sage Publications.

Mayer, R. (1985). *Policy and program planning: A developmental perspective.* Englewood Cliffs, NJ: Prentice Hall.

Meenaghan, T. M. (1994). *Policy analysis and methods: Political and ethical considerations.* Chicago: Nelson-Hall Publishers.

Mendelsohn, H. (1992). *An author's guide to social work journals* (3rd ed.). Washington, DC: NASW Press.

Miles, M., & Huberman, M. (1994). *Qualitative data analysis.* Thousand Oaks, CA: Sage Publications.

Miller, C., & Treitel, C. (1991). *Feminist research methods: An annotated bibliography.* New York: The Greenwood Press.

Miller, D. (1991). *Handbook of research design and social measurement* (5th ed.). Newbury Park: Sage Publications.

Monette, D. R., Sullivan, T. J., & Dejong, C. R. (1998). *Applied social research* (4th ed.). Forth Worth, TX: Harcourt Brace.

Morris, J. M. (1993). *Critical issues in qualitative research methods.* Thousand Oaks, CA: Sage Publications.

Morris, L., Fitz-Gibbon, C. T., & Freeman, M. F. (1987). *How to communicate evaluation findings.* Newbury Park, CA: Sage Publications.

Nachmias, C., & Nachmias, D. (1992). *Research methods in the social sciences* (4th ed.). New York: St. Martin's Press.

National Association of Social Workers. (1985). *Encyclopedia of social work* (19th ed.). Silver Spring, MD: NASW Press.

Neuman, W. L. (1997). *Social research methods: Qualitative and quantitative approaches* (3rd ed.). Needham Heights, MA: Allyn & Bacon.

Nielsen, J. (1990). *Feminist research methods.* Boulder, CO: Westview Press.

Nunnally, J., & Bernstein, I. H. (1994). *Psychometric theory* (3rd ed.). New York: McGraw-Hill.

Nurius, P. S., & Hudson, W. (1993). *Human services practice, evaluation, and computers: A practical guide for today and tomorrow.* Pacific Grove, CA: Brooks/Cole Publishing.

Patton, N. Q. (1990). *Qualitative evaluation methods.* Beverly Hills, CA: Sage Publications.

Pecora, P. J., Fraser, M. W., Nelson, K., McCroskey, J., & Meezan, W. (1995). *Evaluating family-based services.* Hawthorne, NY: Aldine Publications.

Polansky, N. (1960). *Social work research.* Chicago: University of Chicago Press.

Posavac, E., & Carey, R. (1997). *Program evaluation: Methods and case studies* (5th ed.). Upper Saddle River, NJ: Prentice Hall.

Powers, G., Meenaghan, T., & Toomey, B. (1985). *Practice focused research: Integrating human service practice and research.* Englewood Cliffs, NJ: Prentice Hall.

*Publication manual of the American Psychological Association* (4th ed.). (1994). Washington, DC: American Psychological Association.

Pyrczak, R., & Bruce, R. (1992). *Writing empirical research reports.* Los Angeles, CA: Pyrczak Publishing.

Ragin, C. C. (1994). *Constructing social research: The unity and diversity of method.* Thousand Oaks, CA: Pine Forge Press.

Rauch, J. (1994). *Assessment: A sourcebook for social work practice.* Milwaukee, WI: Families International Inc.

Reid, W. J., & Smith, A. (1989). *Research in social work.* Irvington, NY: Columbia University Press.

Reinharz, S. (1992). *Feminist methods in social research.* New York: Oxford University Press.

Reissman, K. (1994). *Narrative analysis.* Thousand Oaks, CA: Sage Publications.

Reissman, K. (1994). *Qualitative studies in social work.* Thousand Oaks, CA: Sage Publications.

Reynolds, P. (1982). *Ethics and social science research.* Englewood Cliffs, NJ: Prentice Hall.

Rose, S. D., & Feldman, R. A. (1987). *Research in social group work.* Binghamton, NY: The Hawthorne Press.

Rossi, P., & Freeman, H. E. (1993). *Evaluation: A systematic approach* (5th ed.). Beverly Hills, CA: Sage Publications.

Rothman, D., & Rothman, S. (1984). *The Willowbrook wars.* New York: Harper and Row.

Rothman, J., & Thomas E. J. (1994). *Intervention research: Design and development for human service.* Binghamton, NY: The Haworth Press.

Royse, D. (1995). *Research methods in social work* (2nd ed.). Chicago: Nelson-Hall Publishers.

Royse, D., & Thyer, B. (1996). *Program evaluation: An introduction* (2nd ed.). Chicago: Nelson-Hall Publishers.

Rubin, A., & Babbie, E. (1993). *Research methods for social work* (2nd ed.). Pacific Grove, CA: Brooks/Cole Publishing.

Runcie, J. F. (1980). *Experiencing social research* (2nd ed.). Homewood, IL: The Dorsey Press.

Scheaffer, R. L., Mendenhall, W., & Ott, L. (1986). *Elementary survey sampling* (3rd ed.). Boston: Duxbury Press.

Sherman, E., & Reid, W. J. (Eds.) (1994). *Qualitative research in social work.* New York: Columbia University Press.

Shontz, F. (1986). *Fundamentals of research in the behavioral sciences.* Washington, DC: American Psychiatric Press.

Silverman, D. (1993). *Interpreting qualitative data.* Thousand Oaks, CA: Sage Publications.

Singleton, R. A., Jr., Straits, B. C., & Margaret, M. (1993). *Approaches to social research* (2nd ed.). New York: Oxford University Press.

Smith, M. J. (1990). *Program evaluation in human services.* New York: Springer Publishing Company.

*Standards for educational and psychological testing* (1985). Washington, DC: American Psychological Association.

Stern, P. C., & Kalof, L. (1996). *Evaluating social science research* (2nd ed.). New York: Oxford University Press.

Sudham, S. (1976). *Applied sampling.* New York: Academic Press.

Traub, R. E. (1994). *Reliability for the social sciences.* Thousand Oaks, CA: Sage Publications.

Tripodi, T. (1983). *Evaluative research for social workers.* Englewood Cliffs, NJ: Prentice Hall.

Tripodi, T., & Epstein, I. (1980). *Research techniques for clinical social workers.* New York: Columbia University Press.

Tripodi, T., Fellin, P., & Epstein, I. (1978). *Differential social program evaluation.* Itasca, IL: F. E. Peacock Publishers.

Tutty, L. M., & Rothery, R. M. (1996). *Qualitative research for social workers: Phases, steps and tasks.* Boston: Allyn & Bacon.

Tyson, K. (1995). *New foundations for scientific, social, and behavioral research: The heuristic paradigm.* Needham Heights, MA: Allyn & Bacon.

Videka-Sherman, L., & Reid, W. J. (1990). *Advances in clinical social work research.* Silver Spring, MD: NASW Press.

Vogt, P. (1993). *Dictionary of statistics and methodology.* Thousand Oaks, CA: Sage Publications.

Wechsler, H., Reinherz, H., & Dobbin, D. (1981). *Social work research in the human services* (2nd ed.). New York: Human Sciences Press.

Weinbach, R. W., & Grinnell, R. M., Jr. (2001). *Statistics for social workers* (5th ed.). Needham Heights, MA: Allyn & Bacon.

Weiss, C. (1972). *Evaluation research.* Englewood Cliffs, NJ: Prentice Hall.

Welch, S., & Comer, J. (1988). *Quantitative methods for public administration.* Chicago: The Dorsey Press.

Williams, M., Unrau, Y. A., & Grinnell, R. M., Jr. (1998). *Introduction to social work research.* Itasca, IL: F. E. Peacock Publishers.

Wolcott, H. F. (1994). *Transforming qualitative data.* Thousand Oaks, CA: Sage Publications.

Worthen, B., & Sanders, J. (1973). *Education evaluation: Theory and practice.* Belmont, CA: Wadsworth Publishing Company.

Worthen, B. R. (1997). *Program evaluation: Alternative approaches and practical guidelines* (2nd ed.). New York: Longman and Co.

Yin, R. K. (1993). *Applications of case study research.* Thousand Oaks, CA: Sage Publications.

Yin, R. K. (1994). *Case study research: Design and methods.* Thousand Oaks, CA: Sage Publications.

# Index

AB design, 292–294
ABA design, 294–296
ABAB design, 297–298
ABACAD design, 300
ABCD design, 299–301
ABCDE design, 300
ABCDEF design, 300
Accountability, 20–21
    defined, 20–21, 263–264
    program evaluation and,
      264–266
Administrative audit, 264
Advocates, use of, 38
AFDC recipients, 12–14
AIDS research, 29–31
Alpha level, 241
Alternate measures, 204
Anchoring, of scales, 219
Anonymity, 40–41
    in mail surveys, 40
    questionnaires and, 229
Antecedent variable, 89
A phase, 287–288
Association, 90–91
Authority,
    responses to, 32–34
    as source of knowledge, 12

B design, 291–292
BAB design, 298
Bem, Daryl, 78
Between group designs, 110–111
Bias
    in research interviewing,
      175–176
    return rate, 173–175
Bio-data. See Demographic
    variables
Bogardus social distance scale, 219
B phase, 287–288

Briar, Scott, 6
Byrd, Michael, 160

Case, defined, 180
Case sample. See Sampling
Case studies, 139–141
    advantages, 140
    conditions for use, 139
    defined, 139
    misuse of data from, 139
    topics suitable for, 140
Causation, 89–90
    defined, 89–90
    internal validity, 118, 121
    research design and, 109
Cause-effect relationships, 90
Census data, 154
Central tendency, 239
Clinical scientist model, 6
Closed-ended questions, 214–215
Cluster sample, 189
Codes of ethics, 42
Coefficient alpha, 204–205, 221–222
Cohort study, 103
Computers,
    data bases and, 67
    statistical analysis and, 236–237
Concealment, 163–164
Concentration camps, 27–28
Conceptualization, 198–199
Concurrent validity, 209
Conferences and symposia,
    as sources of literature, 72–73
    as vehicles to disseminate
      research findings, 247–249
Confidentiality, 40–41
Consistency of measurement. See
    Reliability
Construct, defined, 210
Construct validity, 210
Content analysis, 157–159

Content experts, 221
Content validity, 208–209
Contingency instructions, 226
Contingent variable, 88–89
Control groups, 113
    pretesting and, 115–116
Convenience sample, 190–191
Correlation, 91–92
    negative, 91–92
    positive, 91–92
Correlation coefficient, 203
Cost-benefit analysis, 268–269
Council on Social Work Education,
    3, 4
Cover letters, for mail-out
    surveys, 174
Credibility, 75–76
    in review of literature, 75–76
Criterion validity, 209
Criterion variable, 86–88
Cross-cultural
    journals, 69–70
    research, 138
Cross-sectional research design,
    103
Cross-sectional survey design, 108
Cultural encapsulation, 138
Cultural issues, external validity
    and, 123–124
Cultural relativity, 138
Cumulative frequencies, 238

Data analysis, 233–244
    describing objects of the study
      and, 237–239
    interpreting results of, 243–244
    statistical, 236–244
Data collection instruments,
    162–177, 213–231
    construction of, 221–222
    indexes, 214–215, 221–222

Data collection instruments (*cont.*)
  pre-existing measures, 215–221
  research interviews, 165–169
  revised instruments and,
    223–224
  scales, 215–222
  for structured observation,
    164–165
Degree of participation, 163
Demographic variables, 85–86,
  234–235
Dependency, client, 294
Dependent variable, 86–88, 242
  defined, 87
  pretesting and, 110
Descriptive design, 109–110,
  129–150
  one group pretest-posttest, 110
  program process, evaluations
    as, 262–264
  secondary analysis of data in,
    154–160
  static group comparison,
    110–111
  structured observation in,
    162–165
  time series, 111
Descriptive knowledge, 9
Descriptive statistics, 237–239
Design. *See* Research design
Direction of causation, 121
Dispersion, 239
Disproportionate stratified
  sample, 188
Dissemination of findings, 19–20
Distortion, in data collected,
  167–168
Drugs, in medical research, 30–31
Duration of behavior, 289

Empirical knowledge, 4, 15
Empowerment evaluation, 273–274
Ethics, 25–43, 296, 307–308
  abuse of human research
    subjects and, 26–36
  credit for research and, 42–43
  dual-role relationship, 29
  informed consent and, 36–38
  obligations to others, 42–43
  in observation studies, 163–164
  of single subject research,
    307–308
  standards for treatment of
    participants, 36–41
Ethnographic studies, 135–138
Evaluative research. *See* Program
  evaluation
Executive summaries, 277–278
Existing instruments, 222–224
  appropriateness of, 222–223

indexes as, 215–216
  scales as, 216–221
Expectancy effect, 167
Experience survey, 144–145
Experimental design, 113–117
  characteristics of, 113
  classical experimental design,
    115–116
  outcome analysis and, 114
  posttest only control group
    design, 117
  pretesting and, 115–116
  random assignment in, 114
  Solomon four group design,
    116–117
  testing for causation in, 115
Experimental mortality, 120–121
Explanatory design, 112–117
  secondary analysis of data in,
    155
Exploratory design, 106–109
  needs assessment as, 260–262
  nonprobability sampling in,
    106
  one shot case study, 107–108
External evaluators, in program
  evaluations, 272–273
External validity, 122–124
  of case studies, 140–141
  cultural issues and, 123–124
  described, 122
  factors affecting, 122
  of single subject designs, 306
Extraneous variable. *See*
  Intervening variable

Face validity, 208–209
Feasibility, of research design, 126
Feminist research, 144–149
  defined, 144
  features of, 146
  types of, 146–149
Fernald Science Club, 38–39
Fixed-alternative items, 214–215
Focused research questions, 81–83
Formative evaluation. *See*
  Program evaluation
Frequency, defined, 86
  of target behavior, 289

Garvin, Charles, 6
Generalizability. *See* External
  validity
Goal Attainment Scaling, 283–285
Graphs, 238
Gregg, R., 148
Grief, longitudinal studies of, 104
Grinnell, Richard M., Jr., 7–8
Grounded theory, 141–142

Group administration, of
  questionnaires, 229–230
Guttman scale, 218–219

Historical research, 159–160
History, as a threat to internal
  validity, 119
Homosexual behavior, 34–35
Human subjects, terminology
  discussed, 26
Human subjects review team, 36
Humphreys, Laud, 34–35
Hypotheses, 83–85
  appropriate uses of, 93–94
  construction of, 94–97
  criteria for, 94–96
  defined, 83–85
  descriptive design and, 109
  directional and nondirectional,
    92
  null, 92–94
  subhypotheses, 96–97
  testing with statistical analysis,
    239–243
  types of relationships expressed
    in, 89–92
  wording of, 94–96

Impact evaluation, 269–270
Independent variable, 86–88
  defined, 86–88
  pretesting and, 113
Indexes, 215–216
Inferential statistical analysis, 240
Informed consent, 36–39
In-house evaluators, in program
  evaluation, 271–272
In-person research interviews,
  165–169
  advantages of, 166–167
  data collection instrument for,
    168–169
  disadvantages of, 167–168
In-service training, 247
Institutional Review Boards, 36
Instrumentation, as a threat to
  internal validity, 120
Instruments. *See* Data collection
  instruments
Internal consistency (of design),
  126
Internal correspondence, 247
Internal validity, 117–121
  described, 118
  external validity and, 117–118
  factors affecting, 118–121
Internet, as a source of knowledge,
  67–68
Interobserver agreement, 164–165,
  205

Interval, between target behaviors, 289
Interval level measurement, 201–202, 218
Intervening variable, 88–89
Interviews
focus group and one-on-one, 130
purpose of, 130–131
and qualitative research, 129–132
relationship with participants, 131
and sensitive topics, 132
as sources of literature, 71–72
structuring of, 131–132
Item analysis, 221
Item pool, 221

Jackson, A., 148
*Journal of Social Work Education*, 68

Kirk, Stuart, 5
Knowledge, 8–14
descriptive, 9
predictive, 9–10
prescriptive, 10
problems with nonscientific, 10–14
sources of, 10–14
Kübler-Ross, Elizabeth, 104

Levels of measurement, 200–202
interval level, 201–202
nominal level, 200
ordinal level, 200–201
ratio level, 202
Likert scale, 217–218
Limitations, of research, 246
Linear scale, 216–218
Literature review. *See* Review of literature
Logic, as a source of knowledge, 10–12
Logical positivism, 16
Longitudinal case study design, 108
Longitudinal research, 103–104
advantages of, 104
described, 103
disadvantages of, 104
single subject research and, 285
types of research, 103–104
types of studies in, 103–104

gazines and periodicals, as sources of literature, 74–76
out surveys, 171–176
vantages of, 171–172
ymity and, 172

disadvantages of, 172–176
distortion and, 173
representativeness and, 173–176
return rate and, 173–175
Maturation, 118–119
Measurement, of variables, 197–212
components of, 198–199
cultural issues and, 211–212
evaluating quality of, 202–212
levels of, 200–202
in single subject research, 289
Medical research, 27–31, 39
in concentration camps, 27–28
on disadvantaged populations, 27–28, 30–32, 38–39
Meta-analysis, 160–162
Milgram, Stanley, 32
Multiple baseline designs, 302–305
Multiple-item measures, 215–222
indexes, 215–216
scales, 216–222

National Association of Social Workers, 4, 21
code of ethics, 42
Naturalistic inquiry, 145
Needs assessments, 260–262
Negative correlation, 91–92
Newspapers, as sources of literature, 73–74
Nominal level measurement, 200
Nonprobability sampling, 190–193
accidental or convenience sample, 190–191
purposive sample, 191
quota sample, 192–193
snowball sample, 192
Nuremberg trials, 27

Obscuring variable, 88–89
Observation research. *See* Structured observation
Open-ended items, 214–215
Operational definition, of variables, 199
Operationalization, 199
cultural sensitivity and, 199
Oral histories, 142–143
Ordinal level measurement, 200–201
Outcome analysis, 264–266

Pain and suffering, of research subjects, 39–40
Panel study, 104
Parallel forms reliability, 204
Parameter, 184–185
Periodicals, 72–73
Pilot testing, 206

Planning-evaluation model, 259–260
Population, defined, 180
Positive correlation, 91–92
Posttraumatic stress disorder (PTSD), 13
Predictive knowledge, 9–10
Predictive validity, 209
Predictor variable, 86–88
Pregnancy, use of DES during, 51
Prescriptive knowledge, 10
Priority issues, in research, 49–56
Probability sampling, 186–190
cluster sample, 189
simple random sample, 186–187
stratified random sample, 187–188
systematic random sample, 187
Problem. *See* Research problem
Process evaluation studies, 264
Professionalization, of social work, 21–22
Program description, in evaluation report, 278
Program evaluation, 257–280
analysis of program impact, 269–270
analysis of program structure, 270–271
cost-benefit analysis, 268–269
described, 258–259
design issues in, 266–268
empowerment, 273–274
ethical issues in, 276–277
formative evaluation, 262–263
needs assessments, 260–262
planning-evaluation model and, 259–260
political context of, 274–276
program implementation and, 262–264
program outcomes and, 264–266
report contents for, 277–279
role of the evaluator in, 271–273
structure evaluation, 270–271
Proportionate stratified sample, 188
Provisional knowledge, 15
Publication, in professional journals, 250–251
Public documents, as sources of literature, 71
Public way of knowing, 15
Purposive sample, 191

Qualitative research, 16–18, 129–150
approaches to knowledge-building, 16–18

Qualitative research (*cont.*)
  compared with quantitative
    research, 16–18
  described, 129
  feminist research and, 144–149
  interviews and, 129–132
  types of, 132–149
  unstructured systematic
    observation, 133–134
Quantitative research, 16–18,
  153–177
  approaches to knowledge-
    building, 16–18
  compared with qualitative
    research, 16–18
  data collection by mail, 171–176
  described, 153–154
  in-person interviews, 165–169
  secondary data analysis,
    154–162
  structured observation
    methods, 162–165
  telephone interviews, 169–171
Quasi-experimental design, 115
Questionnaires. *See* Data collection
  instruments
Quota sample, 192–193

Radio and television, as sources of
  literature, 74
Random assignment, of research
  subjects, 114
Random sampling. *See* Probability
  sampling
Ratio level measurement, 202
Recording errors, 167–168
Reinharz, Shulamit, 144
Rejection level, 241
Relevance, of hypothesis, 95–96
Reliability, 203–206
  correlation coefficient and, 203
  defined, 203
  improving, 206
  methods of estimating, 203–206
  of scales, 222–223
  validity and, 202–212
Replication, 306
Representativeness, 181–182
  defined, 181–182
  mail-out surveys, 171–176
  time of telephone interview
    and, 170
Research design, 101–117
  case studies, 139–141
  characteristics of good, 125–127
  continuum of, 105–106
  for cross-sectional research, 103
  defined, 101
  descriptive, 109–112
  experimental, 112–117

explanatory, 112–117
exploratory, 106–109
for longitudinal research,
  103–104
for program evaluation,
  266–268
purpose of, 102
quasi-experimental, 115
for secondary analyses of data,
  157–158
for single subject research,
  290–305
statistical analysis for, 237
for structured observation,
  162–165
typologies, 102–104
Research interviewing, 165–171
  acquiring complete data in,
    168–169
  advantages of, 166–167
  described, 165–166
  disadvantages of, 167–168
  in-person, 165–169
  procedures in the use of,
    166–169
  telephone, 169–171
*Research on Social Work Practice,* 7
Research problem, 47–56
  defined, 47–48
  identification of, 54–56
  methodology and, 47
  priority issues and, 49–56
  research questions in, 56–60
Research process, steps identified,
  18–20
Research questions, 56–60
  defining, 56–57
  focused, 81–83
  priorities, 57–60
Research reports, 244–246
  literature review section of, 245
  and monographs, 72, 244–246
  of program evaluations,
    277–279
  usual contents of, 245–246
Return rate, on mail-out surveys,
  173–175
Review of literature, 63–80
  in content analysis, 157–159
  in final report, 77–79
  focused research questions and,
    81–83
  importance of, 63–65
  organization of, 76–77
  purposes of, 64
  research design and, 63
  role of the author in, 79–80
  sources of, 66–76
Revised instruments, 223–224
Rival hypotheses, 239–243

Sampling, 179–195
  characteristics of good, 181–184
  defined, 179
  key terms in, 179–186
  nonprobability, 190–193
  probability, 186–190
  proportionate and
    disproportionate, 188
  representativeness and, 181–182
  sample size and, 182
  statistical analysis and, 237
  types of, 186–193
Sampling bias, 184, 239–240, 242
  telephone interviewing, 170
  as threat to internal validity, 120
Sampling error 182–184, 237–243
  defined, 182–184
Sampling frame, defined, 180–181
Scales, 215–222
Schizophrenia, 39
Scientific method, characteristics
  of, 14–16
Secondary data analysis, 154–162
  advantages of, 156–157
  in content analysis, 157–159
  disadvantages of, 157
  in historical research, 159–160
  meta-analysis and, 160–162
  sources of, 154–155
  tasks of, 156
  uses of, 155–156
Self-administered instruments,
  228–230
  advantages of, 228–229
Semantic differential scale, 219–220
Sequencing of items, 226
Siegel, D. H., 7–8
Simple random sample, 186–187
Simpson, Richard, 4
Single system designs. *See* Single
  subject research
Single subject research, 285–308
  advantages of, 305–306
  conditions for use of, 285–286
  described, 285–290
  design alternatives in, 290–305
  disadvantages of, 306–307
  and longitudinal research, 285
  measurement in, 288–290
  and program evaluation, 285
  target for change in, 285–289
  terminology of, 287–289
Snowball sample, 192
Social accounting, 263
*Social Work,* 68
*Social Work Research,* 7
Social work research environm[...]
  20–22
Social workers
  characteristics of, 22

Social workers (*cont.*)
  research utilization by, 3–8
Society for Social Work Research, 7
Software, statistical analysis,
  236–237
Specificity, of hypothesis, 95–96
Split half reliability, 204
Standard reference materials, 66–67
Statistic, 181–182
Statistical analysis, 236–244
  conducting, 236–237
  descriptive, 237–239
  inferential, 240
  selecting statistical tests in,
    242–243
  statistical significance and,
    240–242
  uses of statistics and, 237–243
Statistical regression, 119
Statistical significance, 240–242
Stratified random sample, 187–189
Structured observation, 162–165
  conducting, 164–165
  defined, 162–163
  role of observer in, 163–164
Subhypotheses, 96–97
Summative scale, 216–218
Supervised data collection, 229–230
  group, 229–230
  individual, 230
Survey research, 171–176
  and feminist research, 144–145
Symptom substitution, 293
Syphilis, 30
Systematic random sample, 187

Target behavior, 287–289
  defined, 287
Telephone research interviews,
    169–171
  external validity and, 170–171
  time and, 170
Termination of treatment, in single
    subject designs, 296
Testing, of hypotheses, 239–243
Testing effects, 118
Test-retest reliability, 203
Thurstone scale, 218
Time and motion studies, 263
Traditional beliefs, 11
Training of observers, 165
Treatment carryover, in single
    subject research, 295
Trend study, 103
Triangulation, 276–277
Tuskegee studies, 30

Unit of analysis, 180
  case as, 180
Universe, 180
Unstructured observation, 133–135
  advantages, 134
  disadvantages, 135
Utilization, of research, 3–9

Validity, 206–210
  concurrent, 209
  construct, 210
  content, 208–209

  criterion, 209
  defined, 206–207
  existing instruments and,
    222–223
  external, 122–123
  face, 208–209
  internal, 118–121
  predictive, 209
  reliability and, 202–212
Value, 86
  defined, 86
  frequency of, 86
Variables, 85–89
  associations between, 90–91
  causation and, 89–90
  correlation between, 91–92
  criterion, 86–88
  defined, 85
  demographic, 85–86
  dependent, 86–88
  independent, 86–88
  intervening, 88–89
  measurement of, 198–212
  predictor, 86–88
  selection of, 198
  specifying rules of
    quantification, 198
Vietnam veterans, 13–14
Voluntary participation (of
    research participants), 27–28,
    36–38

Withdrawal, of treatment, 296
Workshops, as sources of
    literature, 73